IN SEARCH OF
BILL CLINTON

ALSO BY JOHN D. GARTNER

The Hypomanic Edge:
The Link Between (A Little) Craziness and
(A Lot) of Success in America

IN SEARCH OF
BILL CLINTON

A Psychological Biography

JOHN D. GARTNER

St. Martin's Press ≈ New York

IN SEARCH OF BILL CLINTON. Copyright © 2008 by John D. Gartner.
All rights reserved. Printed in the United States of America.
For information, address St. Martin's Press,
175 Fifth Avenue, New York, N.Y. 10010.

www.stmartins.com

The photograph of Bill Clinton on page 78 is reprinted by permission of
Getty Images.

The poem "Remembering My Friend Virginia Clinton Kelley" is
reprinted by permission of the author, Rachel Heffernan.

The excerpt from "The Cure at Troy" is reprinted by permission
of the author, Seamus Heaney.

Library of Congress Cataloging-in-Publication Data

Gartner, John D.
   In search of Bill Clinton : a psychological biography /
John D. Gartner.—1st ed.
      p.   cm.
   Includes bibliographical references.
  ISBN-13: 978-0-312-36976-7
  ISBN-10: 0-312-36976-X
   1. Clinton, Bill, 1946–   2. Clinton, Bill, 1946—
Psychology.   3. Presidents—United States—
Biography.   I. Title.
  E886.2.G37 2008
  973.929092—dc22
[B]
                                        2008019612

First Edition: October 2008

10 9 8 7 6 5 4 3 2 1

For Mom,
whose spirit is always with me

CONTENTS

ACKNOWLEDGMENTS

I would like to express gratitude to the people who were kind enough to participate in interviews with me.

In Arkansas, I was delighted to meet Virginia Clinton's feisty friends: Marge Mitchell, Virginia Heath, Nancy Adkins, Berenice Lyon, Dixie Seba, Clover Gibson, Johnnette Taylor, and M. J. Sherer. I was also privileged to interview both the first and last loves of her life, Richard Fenwick and Dick Kelley. Also many thanks to Virginia's co-writer, Jim Morgan.

It was also a pleasure to meet the original friends of Bill who've known him since childhood: Rose Crane, David Leopoulos, Mauria Aspell, Carolyn Staley, Patty Criner, Larry Crane, Phil Jamison, Joe Purvis, and Michael Muldoon. A special thanks to Rose Crane, who was gracious enough to provide me with introductions to many of those friends. I am also grateful to the Arkansas journalists, most of whom have written their own Clinton books, who shared with me the fruits of their many years of Clinton-watching: Ernest Dumas, John Brummett, Meredith Oakley, Paul Greenberg, Jonathan Portis, and Steve Barnes. In Hope, thanks to George Wright, Jr., Jewel Dean Moore, Mary Nell Turner, Jenny Sue McKee, and Elaine Johnson. Many thanks to those in Arkansas who participated in Clinton's political campaigns and gubernatorial administrations: Ron Addington, Marla Crider, Paul Root, Carol Willis, Jim Daugherty, David Folsom, Ann Henry, Ann McCoy, and Mary Anne Salmon.

This book was strengthened immensely by access to two sets of interviews conducted by others. I am most grateful to Charles F. Allen, who generously shared the transcripts of all of his interviews conducted for his book, *The Comeback Kid: The Life and Career of Bill Clinton*. And thanks to David Stricklin of the Butler Center for Arkansas Studies at the

Central Arkansas Library System, who provided me with CDs of their entire collection of interviews from their oral history project on Clinton's Arkansas years.

For my chapter in the economy, I am grateful to those on Clinton's presidential economic team who spoke to me: Leon Panetta, Alice Rivlin, Alan Blinder, and Jeffrey Shafer. Also thanks to Clinton advisers, Paul Begala and James Carville.

For my chapter on the Irish peace process, I was lucky enough to be able to speak to most of the major participants. Almost all of those contacts came through Stella O'Leary, head of Irish American Democrats, as delightful a woman as you'll ever meet. On this side of the Atlantic, I spoke to Tony Lake, Nancy Soderberg, Jane Hull Lute—the National Security Council team who handled Ireland; Niall O'Dowd, Bruce Morrison, Brian O'Dwyer, Trina Vargo, Elizabeth Bagley—people who worked, often secretly, behind the scenes; and George Mitchell, who chaired the peace negotiations that led to the Good Friday agreement, and his assistant, Martha Pope. In Ireland, I spoke with Gerry Adams, Richard McAuley, John Hume, Reg Empey, David Trimble, Albert Reynolds, Dick Spring, and Seamus Heaney (via e-mail). Thanks to Paul Allen and Irish journalists Conor O'Clery and Dan Keenan, who helped paved the way for me in Ireland.

For their insights into the mind of Ken Starr, I thank former OIC attorney Mark Tuohey and my secret inside source whom I cannot name, but refer to as Deep Throat. Also the "masters of disaster," charged with handling the Clinton faux scandals, Mark Fabiani and Chris Lehane. Also thanks to journalists Joe Conason, Gene Lyons, and Sidney Blumenthal, who wrote books about the impeachment.

Traveling through Africa with Bill Clinton was a great opportunity, and I thank the Clinton Foundation for allowing me to accompany them. Clinton's communications director, Ben Yarrow, and, before him, Jay Carson couldn't have been nicer. I'd like to thank the people I interviewed in Africa: Zackie Achmat, Felix Mwanza, Paul Kasonkomona, Farouk Abdullah, and Khamis Mtumwa. In particular, I'd like to thank Kathryn Sutton, the saintly woman in Zanzibar whom I shadowed for two days. I'd also like to thank those experts on Africa and AIDS who spoke to me: Stephen Lewis, Patricia Siplon, Jamie Love, Paul Zeitz, and David Gartner.

I'm grateful to two Clinton biographers who were kind enough to share their insights with me: David Maraniss and John F. Harris, Also thanks to Stanley Renshon and Jerome Levin, two mental health professionals who wrote books about Clinton.

But in particular I owe a profound debt of thanks to Clinton biographer Nigel Hamilton, who was extraordinarily generous enough to review this entire manuscript and teach this first-time biographer the ropes. I don't know how I can ever repay him.

While it is traditional and indeed obligatory to thanks one's editor, my gratitude for the chance to work with Michael Flamini—rising nonfiction star and all-around great guy—knows no bounds. He was unflaggingly enthusiastic, supportive, and creative, somehow always knowing when to leave me alone and when to intervene. Thanks also to his assistant, Vicki Lame. In general, my experience at St Martin's could not have been more positive. From the publisher, Sally Richardson, on down, I found St. Martin's to be a small team of intellectually engaged, dynamic, smart, thoughtful people who publish books the old-fashioned way—reading, thinking and caring about what they help to create.

My shadow support team during this entire project has been my writing group (the Mod Squad, as we call ourselves), which consists of myself, Adam Bellow, and Stephanie Susnjara. Adam, my close friend since high school, has provided ongoing wise guidance since I began my writing career. And Stephanie, whom I adore, went through the entire manuscript three times with a fine-tooth comb. I also want to thank my agent, Betsy Lerner, as always, for her fine nurturing, editing, and selling skills.

It is traditional to thank one's spouse. Every writer knows why. A few kind words cannot begin to acknowledge their long-suffering support. But in my case this is particularly true. As I describe in my introduction, my quest to understand Bill Clinton consumed every moment of my time and every ounce of my strength for two years. Claude was heroic, shouldering virtually all the responsibilities of our household and family, while also reading innumerable drafts. She has been one of the greatest supporters of my writing career.

I also have to acknowledge my four children, Sarah, Hannah, Claire, and André, who have suffered from my neglect over these two years. Now that my journey in search of Clinton is done, and I have returned home, I hope I can make it up to them.

IN SEARCH OF
BILL CLINTON

INTRODUCTION

The Puzzle

Bill Clinton is a psychological puzzle.

When President Clinton's affair with Monica Lewinsky was revealed in January 1998, everyone seemed to be asking the same question: What was he thinking? Biographer David Maraniss dubbed this question the "Clinton Enigma."[1] Not only was the general public dumbfounded, but Clinton had stumped even his closest associates. "I'm still mystified by the Clinton paradox," wrote his former aide George Stephanopoulos. "How could a president so intelligent, so compassionate, and so public-spirited, and so conscious of his place in history, act in such a stupid, selfish, and self-destructive manner?"[2] Former senior White House adviser David Gergen also called Clinton "a mass of contradictions," noting that "he is one of the smartest men ever elected president and he has done some of the dumbest things."[3]

Bill Clinton is even a psychological puzzle to himself. In his autobiography, *My Life,* Clinton describes the moment when he finally had to tell Hillary the truth about his affair with Lewinsky: "I still didn't fully understand why I had done something so wrong and stupid."[4]

Clearly, knowing Bill Clinton well—even being Bill Clinton—is not the same as understanding Bill Clinton.

The idea for this project originated while I was researching my first book, *The Hypomanic Edge,* where I explored the connection between charisma and *hypomanic temperament,* a mildly manic personality that imbues some people with the raw ingredients it takes to be a charismatic leader: immense energy, drive, confidence, visionary creativity, infectious enthusiasm, and a sense of personal destiny. They also have problems with impulse control, frequently in the area of sex. While I was conducting my research for *The Hypomanic Edge,* dozens of people asked me if I thought Bill Clinton fit the profile. It was a question that had occurred to me. If Clinton had this mildly manic temperament, it would explain a great deal about both his strengths and weaknesses, why he is both so gifted and so flawed. This may be the first piece of the puzzle.

Psychiatrists have been aware of this mildly manic character type for almost a hundred years, yet the literature about these people is surprisingly thin: probably because we don't see them in our clinical offices very often, as they rarely feel the need to seek psychiatric help. In fact, we are more likely to see them among our more driven and successful colleagues. These people have been given a dozen names over the history of psychiatry: *manic disposition* (Eugen Bleuler, 1916); *manic temperament* (Emil Kraepelin, 1921); *hypomanic character* (Ernst Kretschmer, 1926); *hyperthymic personality* (Kurt Schneider, 1950); *hyperthymic temperament* (H. S. Akiskal and G. Mallya, 1987); *exuberant* (Kay Jamison, 2004).[5] But the basic behavioral descriptions have been more or less the same. Whether or not the theorist labels them as having a disorder, each notes the same paradox: These people are endowed with special gifts that can make them highly successful and also with unique vulnerabilities that can spell their downfall.

In 1975, Columbia University psychiatrist Ronald Fieve, one of the people credited with the discovery of lithium as a treatment for bipolar disorder, began writing about positive traits associated with what he called the "hypomanic advantage."[6] In 1992, he proposed a new diagnosis, bipolar disorder IIB ("B" stands for beneficial), which he described as "a desirable disorder." The field of psychiatry needs to be "re-educated," he argued, to value this type of person whom we have tended to pathologize. While the patients he described do suffer from periodic depression—hence the bipolar diagnosis—in their hypomanic phase they are the "movers and shakers" who "produce the best of what human beings can contribute to society."[7] In his 2007 book *Bipolar II,* Fieve cited Bill Clinton as a prime example:

"When I think of an exuberant or hypomanic politician, former President Clinton comes quickly to mind, particularly with his magnetic charm and high-spirited personality . . . his garrulous and exuberant political style is definitely the hypomanic type. Not only is the former president quick thinking, verbose, and mildly elated, he is witty, talks fast, and is an ardent debater . . . obviously he is a risk taker and a bit overzealous when it comes to the opposite sex, but here again risk taking and overly zealous behavior are two hypomanic qualities."[8]

Because my field has not been able to agree on what to call these people, I chose the term: *hypomanic temperament.* We see in these people the exact same constellation of traits found in mania, but to a lesser degree. *Hypo,* the Greek prefix for "less than," makes it clear we are talking about traits that are like mania but less extreme. I chose the term *temperament* for two reasons: first, because a temperament is an inborn, biologically based trait that is stable over the life course, and, second, because a temperament is not an illness, but a basic predisposition, which like any other has strengths and weaknesses. Below is a narrative description of the hypomanic temperament synthesized from the literature and my own observations.

HYPOMANIC TEMPERAMENT

The person of hypomanic temperament is filled with a high degree of energy and is very active in both work and other pursuits. They need little sleep, less than six hours. They are restless and impatient. They are quick thinking—thoughts race through their heads, and they jump from idea to idea. They can be distracted, attending to too many things at once. They are creative and unconventional (even if they are conservative), both thinking and living "outside the box." They talk fast, talk a lot, and tend to dominate conversations. They are driven, ambitious, and hard working. They set goals that seem grandiose, yet they appear supremely confident of success. They feel like people of destiny—maybe even destined to change the world in some way. They are gifted evangelists and sales people who win converts to their vision. Their mood is exuberant, sunny, elated, and that mood is infectious, energizing those around them. They are charismatic, persuasive, and attractive. They are charming, witty, gregarious, and good at making people laugh. They like to be the center of attention, want to be the boss, and seek to be the alpha male or female in any group, and thus often come in conflict with authority. They are pushy, meddlesome, and don't take no for an answer. Minor obstacles or delays can easily irritate them and their temper can be unpredictably explosive, but their rages usually pass quickly. They can be suspicious and hostile toward people they feel are impeding their plans or just "don't get it." They are impulsive and urgently want to verbalize and act on an idea or desire as soon as it occurs to them, without first thinking through the realistic consequences. They are risk takers, who seem oblivious to obvious dangers. They have a large libido, are highly sexually active, and can show poor judgment in their sexual behavior. They seek stimulation and excitement. They have an addictive personality and are prone to both chemical and behavioral addictions. They appear to have poor insight into why some of their actions antagonize others or sometimes produce disastrous results.

The relationship between mania and hypomania is more than descriptive; the two groups actually tend to be related—literally, by blood: Hypomanics and people with manic-depressive disorder tend to run in the same family, which suggests there is a true genetic link. Historically, many of the observations psychiatrists have made about people with hypomanic temperament were based on their contacts with the high-achieving, high-energy relatives of their manic-depressive patients. As mental health professionals we see things through the lens of illness, because that's what we study. But we may be looking through the telescope backwards. It is not that hypomanics have a mild form of their relatives' disease, but rather the inverse. The patient is manifesting a pathological expression of a set of genes that, in most cases, are on balance advantageous, which is most likely why they have survived over tens of thousands of years of natural selection. Indeed, relatives of manic patients (who tend to be high in hypomania) have consistently been found to be far above average in income, occupational achievement, and creativity.[9]

Hypomanic temperament should not be confused with the *hypomanic episode* described in the American Psychiatric Association's *Diagnostic and Statistical Manual of Mental Disorders (DSM)*. An episode, as the name implies, represents a dramatic change in a person's normal "premorbid" functioning. According to *DSM-IV,* "the episode is associated with an unequivocal change in functioning that is uncharacteristic of the person when not symptomatic."[10] All of a sudden, a person in a hypomanic episode stops acting like his or her normal self. The person becomes excited, stops sleeping, becomes aggressive, starts spending money, initiates affairs, etc.—and this behavior represents an alarming change. In hypomanic temperament, by contrast, mildly manic traits are stable and fully integrated into the personality. That *is* the person's normal self.

Hypomanic temperament is not a mental illness, and it is not included as a diagnosis in the *DSM-IV*. Because this book is about a real person, Bill Clinton, this is more than an academic point. No doubt, some people will draw the incorrect conclusion that I am making the case that Bill Clinton has a mental disorder. I am not. If I thought that, I would not hesitate to say it, but my research has not led me to that conclusion.

One of the questions I hope to answer in this book, which comprises also part of the Clinton puzzle, is: What makes him so talented as a politician? To understand how Clinton became the dark horse who came from nowhere to win the presidency, one must understand his hypomanic temperament. Clinton has several hypomanic traits that have been integral to his success. The most obvious of these is his charisma. "Can you remember the name of the jockey who rode Secretariat?" Paul Begala, Clinton's former political adviser, asked an auditorium of 150 people at the 2005 Clinton Presidential Conference at Hofstra University. One guy could, but the rest had no idea. "That's because it didn't matter who rode him. He was one of the greatest race horses of all time. Being Clinton's campaign adviser was like riding Secretariat." Secretariat, in fact, was Clinton's nickname, bestowed on him by his 1992 presidential campaign staff.

Another factor is his energy. It is well known that Clinton requires little sleep. He is an inexhaustible campaigner, who runs at full speed for days with only a few catnaps. Like so many others, veteran political reporter Joe Klein recalls being stunned by Clinton's seemingly unlimited capacity for campaigning: "On the night before the New Hampshire primary, well after the last scheduled appearance, I found Clinton going from table to table at a local restaurant, shaking hands, chatting with anyone willing to engage him. He went from restaurant to restaurant through the dinner hour, and then made a tour of the bowling alleys of Manchester—until just past midnight, when there were no more hands to shake, no more places to go except his hotel. He was exhausted and flu-ridden; his face was flushed, his eyes were red and bleary, but he wasn't quite ready to pack it in. 'You want to bowl a game?' he asked me."[11]

Creativity is another important hypomanic asset. Dozens of studies point to greater creativity in mildly manic individuals, in part because their overactive minds generate so many ideas.[12] It's almost impossible to spend much time with Clinton and not notice, as one associate put it, that his "brain is just bursting with ideas that just pour out of him."[13] George Stephanopoulos wrote that Clinton would call him with "fifty ideas a day."[14] One of Clinton's great strengths is his ability to come up with innovative policy ideas that transcend conceptual and political categories.

Finally, Clinton's expansive hypomanic mood makes him sunny, optimistic, and infectiously exuberant. People regularly describe becoming euphoric in his presence, as if he were a drug. This ability to excite those around him is a large part of what makes him so seductive. Stella O'Leary, head of Irish American Democrats, who has spent a lot of time with both Clintons, told me: "He's like the Pied Piper. Everybody is going in the same direction and it's very joyous. It's energizing. It's fun. It's life lived at its peak. Your nerves are just going. This is where you want to be. This is it. It's exciting, and for women it's sexual. You can't resist it."[15]

There is a biological reason for all of this. Neurologically, people with any degree of mania are like cars with Porsche engines but no brakes. The parts of the brain that fuel the drives motivating all human behavior—sex, aggression, hunger, need for affiliation, etc.—are heightened to a fever pitch. This motivational center, called the limbic system, is one of the oldest structures in the brain. It evolved so long ago that the limbic system of a human being is almost identical to that of a lizard. When the brains of actively manic patients are observed on a PET scan (Positron Emission Tomography), a neuroimaging technique that shows which parts of the brain are most active in real time, key parts of the limbic system light up. When these motivational centers are stimulated, people become excited, energized, and ready for action. They are in go-mode, primed to act—not to think rationally about possible consequences. In normal subjects, falling in love, for example, has been shown to excite this part of the brain.[16] These same centers are also stimulated by drugs and alcohol, which, like all degrees of mania, produce feelings of pleasurable excitement, behavioral disinhibition, and diminished judgment.

This brain process helps answer the "What was he thinking?" question. What I call the think-before-you-act part of the brain doesn't work well in hypomanics. The limbic system that drives behavior is normally modulated, regulated, and kept in check by inhibitory connections to the cortex, the most advanced part of the brain that controls higher-level thinking. New research shows that in manics, as well as in other people with impulse control problems, layers of cortex immediately surrounding the limbic system are defective, or at least seem to under fire.[17] Thus, like a burnt-out circuit breaker, they cannot regulate the surges of powerful energy produced by a hyperexcited limbic system. Therefore, it is not simply a defect in "character"—the charge repeatedly made against Bill Clinton—but a defect in wiring, if you will, that allows hypomanics to blithely act out impulses, oblivious to their probable disastrous consequences.

Though everyone has focused on Clinton's sex drive, his problems with impulse control have multiple manifestations, as is often the case for most hypomanics. For example, Clinton was constantly battling weight problems because he could not bring his compulsive eating under control. As Maraniss wrote in his Clinton biography, *First in His Class*, "He was a young man of oversized appetites. Any aide who spent time with him could tell stories of his inhaling apples in a few massive bites, swallowing them core and all. Hot dogs went down so fast they barely touched his teeth. The mansion cook could not bake chocolate chip cookies fast enough. Plates of enchiladas and nachos disappeared in seconds."[18]

Hypomanics are also *impulsive talkers*. They get in trouble for speaking off the top of their head, so much so that one could almost say they suffer from foot-in-mouth disease. This weakness on Clinton's part was on dramatic display in Hillary's 2008 race for the Democratic presidential nomination. Clinton's reputation as an astute politician, not to mention his wife's presidential ambitions, was badly damaged by Clinton's off-the-cuff remarks.

Clinton also has trouble containing his aggressive impulses. What few among the general public knew, but no one in the White House could avoid knowing, was how uncontrolled his temper really was. David Gergen called him "Mount Vesuvius," stating that Clinton had the worst temper of any man he had ever met in public life by "a magnitude of at least two."[19] When Bill Clinton was a boy, none of his friends knew of his stepfather Roger Clinton's physical abuse. As is so often the case, it was a family secret. And within Clinton's inner circle, his temper has been like a family secret, too, at least until the 2008 primary battle when it was on display, often captured by concealed video recorders. "Shame on you," Clinton would tell reporters, chastising them for the tone of their election coverage while waving a finger in their face when he didn't realize he was on camera. While Clinton was chastising them for the tone of their election coverage, he only made it worse when these "purple fits" became the story, and the game became to catch Clinton getting mad. Up until then Clinton had managed to keep his anger management problem under the radar. What he wasn't prepared for was that the radar has gotten stronger since he last ran for office; today anyone with a cell phone can put video on YouTube.

Sex, hunger, and aggression are basic biological drives, and in Clinton they are *all* in overdrive. In an earlier era we called these drives *appetites*, and that was a very descriptive term. This palpably insatiable hunger was integral to his rise. Arkansas senator David Pryor said, "The first time I met him—I knew that he was hungry. You could sense it. It was like meeting a jaguar that was ready to pounce."[20] But Clinton's oversized appetites have also been the source of his falls. In short, Clinton's success and his excess have a common origin in this biologically based excess of drive. As biographer John Harris noted, "Clinton's appetites in nearly all respects—for people, ideas, food, women—could be excessive, but this is what ultimately set him apart. . . . voluminous appetites got him in trouble. Voluminous appetites carried him out of trouble."[21]

When I conducted the research for this book, I interviewed many people who knew Clinton well. In virtually every case, after I described the traits of the hypomanic temperament, the interviewees were taken aback: "That's Clinton," they would say. A number of people asked me if this profile was *based* on Clinton. In not a single case, did anyone disagree or even express doubts about the description fitting Clinton.

"You could paste his picture over that definition in the dictionary," said Arkansas reporter Meredith Oakley.

I started this book with a self-flattering conceit: With my expertise in hypomania, I would easily be able to solve the Clinton puzzle that has baffled so many writers. But my conceit was wrong. While I had discovered *a* hidden factor that helped explain Bill Clinton, it was only one missing piece of the puzzle. Exploring Bill Clinton's mind was like an extended archeological dig, revealing strata upon strata.

To begin with, while it is well known that Clinton is gifted, he is far more gifted than most realize. While *genius* is a loaded word, Clinton either is one or borders on it. Of the nearly one hundred people I spoke to, virtually all declared Bill Clinton to be the smartest person they had ever met in their entire lives—and some of them were pretty smart themselves. "Most Americans realize this was a very smart man," said Alan Blinder, a Princeton economist who served on his economic team. "They don't realize quite *how* smart he was, because he was a good enough politician to hide it."[22] Clinton has an almost photographic memory. If he meets someone once for a few minutes, when he runs into them again two years later in a totally different setting, he'll not only remember their name, he'll remember the names of their pets. And he reads *everything*—gets it, remembers it, and integrates it with everything else he's read and heard. He's not just a policy wonk—he's a policy wunderkind. Policy experts in many fields have declared without exaggeration that Clinton knows more about their specialty than they do. David Osborne, author of *Laboratories of Democracy,* a book about innovative state governments, said: "You call him up and ask, 'Who's doing interesting things in housing?' And he can tell you what *everyone* is doing—every last housing experiment in every state."[23]

But that's not all. Not only is he off the IQ chart. He's off several charts. Try this brief thought experiment: Think of the smartest person you know. Now, think of the warmest, most empathic person you know. Odds are you didn't think of the same person. That's because these are two completely independent traits that have no statistical relationship to one another. The odds of the same person being the highest on *both* traits are minuscule. If Clinton were one out of a thousand on both traits, the combined probability would be the product of those two numbers, or one out of a million. When you additionally consider that Clinton is on the extreme end of the bell-shaped curve on other core inborn traits, such as extraversion, intellectual curiosity, and of course, hypomanic energy, it may seem that Clinton won the genetic lottery in a big way. He simply has more God-given talent than any politician we've seen in a long time.

Psychoanalytic interpretations also account for several pieces of the Clinton puzzle. For example, from the time he was born, Clinton has been torn between two women who jealously competed for his affections, and he has been unconsciously replicating this family drama ever since. His grandmother, Edith, who essentially raised him for the first four years of his life, was aggressive, smart, ambitious, rigid, suspicious, and fiercely protective—a personality much like that of Hillary. While most boys marry their mother, I argue that Clinton married his grandmother, who was his de facto mother in his earliest years.

Here lies one of the secrets to understanding the Clinton marriage. Edith was not a warm people person—just the opposite. She was a powerfully intimidating presence, but nonetheless a reassuring one for Bill, whom she guided and protected. One of the things I learned in my research was just how important Hillary has been to Bill. She structures his life, as his grandmother once did, and she has also been his protector, fighting his enemies with the ferocity of a mother lion guarding her cubs.

In Arkansas, Hillary became famous for accosting Bill's political rivals at public events, loudly challenging their statements about her husband, prompting at least one, sitting governor Frank White, to literally run out the back door when he saw her coming. (She "kicked the dog shit out of him," remarked Paul Fray, former Clinton campaign co-manager.) In some ways Hillary's failed campaign for the 2008 nomination reminded me of a standard plot from the sitcoms of the 1970s—the one where the husband and wife switch roles for a week. Predictably, each fails miserably at trying to do what the other one does. One reason the vaunted Clinton machine sputtered in this primary battle was that Hillary was trying to play Bill's role—the charismatic politician—which is not her forte. And Bill was trying to play Hillary's role—the loyal attack dog—which is not his. To make matters worse, Bill's aggressive stance was seen as unbecoming for a former president. The public backlash from Bill's remarks—calling Obama's opposition to the Iraq war a "fairy tale," for example—was incredibly damaging to his wife's campaign. But this was mild treatment compared to what Hillary used to do to his rivals. Bill must have felt he owed it to Hillary to be her attack dog after she has done the same for him throughout his career. For almost thirty years she was his Edith, and now it was his turn to be hers.

In contrast to Clinton's grandmother, his mother, Virginia, was a more exuberant free spirit. In his earliest years, when Clinton resided with his grandmother, he could only visit his mother sporadically, much like an affair. Virginia resembles, both in appearance and personality, many of the women he has had affairs with, including Monica Lewinsky. Just as young Bill deeply loved and needed both women who competed for his affections, grown-up Bill has always simultaneously needed a relationship with both types of women, each of whom plays a foundation role in his psyche, the Edith-like Hillary and his Virginia-like lovers. This simple insight sheds light on Clinton's relationship with Hillary, helping to explain both why he is drawn to her and why, despite the fact that he genuinely loves and depends on her, he still feels the need for other women.

A word on my method: Mental health professionals have been writing psychologically informed biographies, usually called psychobiographies, ever since Freud. But none to my knowledge have ventured outside their office or the library into the real world to interview people who knew their biographical subject. For journalists, this is the standard method of research, of course, but we psychologists are not trained as journalists. While it was not my intention to create a new genre, it was clear to me that I would need to employ the methods of an investigative journalist to have any hope of credibly solving the Clinton enigma. I began to call my approach *psycho-journalism,* to distinguish it from both conventional journalism and traditional psycho-biography.

Traditionally, psychological biographies are both reductive and overly deterministic. Boiling down the life of an eminent individual to a simple psychological formula always seems to make the subject somehow smaller. But as I got closer to Clinton, something more complex happened: He got both larger and smaller.

The Clinton paradox is that even as he has come to represent in some people's eyes the essence of carnality, deceit, and selfishness—the lowest aspects of human nature—he is also a larger-than-life embodiment of our highest impulses: a humanitarian, who saves lives by the hundreds of thousands, and a peacemaker, who has healed intractable conflicts around the world.

To explore these aspects of Clinton, I took two international trips. I traveled to Ireland, interviewing most of the major players in the Irish peace process. What emerged was a portrait of a man who has served as the world's family therapist, making inspired interventions to heal ancient hatreds. Today the Irish still love Clinton: I found it hard to buy myself a pint of Guinness in Ireland, so many people wanted to buy me a drink when they heard I was writing a book about Bill Clinton. He is one of the most popular people on earth—even as his status in the United States has waxed and waned—in large part because of his peacemaking efforts (just as George Bush is widely despised internationally for waging the Iraq war).

And I traveled to Africa. Each summer Clinton visits Africa to review the work of his foundation. In 2007 I was able attach myself to his entourage. Clinton is saving close to a million lives by bringing cheap AIDS drugs to poor countries, solving a public-health crisis that has stymied the world for decades. Watching thousands of Africans respond to him as if he were a prophet was a powerful experience. He positively glows with euphoria as he walks into the crowds, extending his long arms into the sea of people, while dozens jostle to touch him at once, desperate to lay a hand on his finger, his wrist, or even just the hem of his sleeve.

And a few months later, after I returned from my Africa journey, I was watching Clinton on TV, looking like neither a humanitarian nor a great political talent, as he burst into tirade after tirade in his efforts to help his wife's dying campaign. Such is the Clinton puzzle. Who is the real Bill Clinton? The adulterer or the family man? The genius or the person who does incomprehensibly stupid things? The humanitarian overflowing with compassion or the self-centered narcissist who explodes with rage? They are all him, of course. And understanding him in all his complexity became my mission.

Oddly, being uncredentialed as a journalist had its advantages. Some of the people I talked to, especially in Arkansas, had very negative views of the press. Many had been interviewed before and felt their words had been "twisted" to portray a Clinton they did not recognize. Being a professor from Johns Hopkins with an earnest demeanor, and a lot of persistence, made it easier to win access to subjects for interviews.

My method differed from that of a conventional reporter in several respects. For example, my clinical experience affected the way I approached interviewing my subjects. Whenever possible, I tried to conduct my interviews in person, typically over a long meal at a nice restaurant. My aim was to form a *relationship* with my interviewees, win their trust, and provide a space where they would feel comfortable opening up. The number of people I interviewed for this biography, between seventy and eighty, is in the normal range, but the length of the interviews—typically between one and two hours—was not. The average transcript was forty pages long.

As a result, I became accustomed to being routinely surprised by what people revealed to me once we got rolling. Friends of the Clinton family, many now in their eighties, told me things about Bill Clinton's background that have never before been revealed, at least not publicly. While it was never my intent to write a sensationalistic book, in the course of my research I unearthed information about Clinton's family that many may regard that way.

For example, Clinton's mother, Virginia, who also had a hypomanic temperament, was hypersexual from a young age, and engaged in numerous affairs over most of her life. She modeled an adulterous lifestyle that young Bill, hypersexual by temperament to begin with, couldn't help internalizing. This is an important factor in understanding Clinton's sexual behavior: like mother, like son.

I also learned that the long-standing rumors that Bill Clinton may be illegitimate are perhaps more than rumors. Indeed, I believe that it is possible that I may have found the identity of his true biological father.

In revealing these findings, it is not my purpose to embarrass former president Clinton, invade his privacy, or expose the memory of his mother to opprobrium. It is a clinical imperative that impels me to explore these hidden facets of his life—a public life that came to involve us all in 1998, when the president's relationship with Monica Lewinsky led to the impeachment of a serving president for the first time since the nineteenth century. For good or ill, it brought the White House, the U.S. government, and the Congress almost to a standstill for many excruciating—and excruciatingly embarrassing—months. Learning the true psychodynamics behind what some historians dubbed "the scandal of the century" promises also, I hope, to give us a better understanding of what lay behind that seminal saga.

Many people have asked me, bottom line, is this a "pro-Clinton book" or an "anti-Clinton book"? I have always said my goal is to understand him, not judge him. But that doesn't fully answer the question. I think the reader will sense that I like Bill Clinton, and in several respects, admire him. I had that basic feeling going into the project, and the more I learned about him, the more that basic intuition was reinforced. Some of that sympathetic posture is the perspective of a psychotherapist. In our work, having a basic regard for someone, empathizing with them, and even liking them does not preclude you from understanding them. In fact, we believe that it helps. It's not that I gloss over his flaws—far from it. But my perspective is admittedly a forgiving one, and I often portray his foibles in comedic terms rather than with condemning tones. Almost thirty years of practicing psychotherapy, not to mention many years as a patient in psychoanalysis, have taught me that only he who is without neurosis should cast the first stone.

Has Clinton, the great seducer, seduced me, too? In part, yes. I am not immune to his charm, as becomes particularly clear in the final chapter, where I follow him through Africa. But, ultimately, I think my regard for Clinton is based in large part on reasoned judgment. It's hard for me to see how anyone who has carefully studied Bill Clinton's life, warts and all, could deny that he is an extraordinarily talented person who has earnestly striven to do good since he was a young child. Indeed, as we shall see, he has accomplished much good: fixing Arkansas's educational system, helping to mend the U.S. economy, making peace all over the world, and, most recently, saving hundreds of thousands of lives in Africa. Who among Clinton's critics has accomplished more?

I know from experience that hypomanics elicit extreme reactions. Certainly that has been true with Clinton. Magnetic charisma can make the hypomanic seem larger than life, and their stupid mistakes can make them seem lower than dirt. But neither view portrays them as the whole people they really are. My most earnest desire was to delve more deeply into the truth of who Bill Clinton is, because despite all that has been said and written about him, I didn't think his story had been fully told.

Finally, a personal note is in order. This story is not about me, but I am a character in the narrative. I cannot take myself out of the plot the way most journalists would. Psychotherapists study people in a very specific and unusual way. Through countless hours of supervision as a method for better understanding them, we are trained to examine our own subjective reactions to our patients, a process we call "analyzing countertransference." We monitor ourselves both for evidence of distortions stemming from our own biases and unresolved neurotic conflicts and for valid insights our intuition may be producing. Normally, this process of self-analysis is undertaken in private: through clinical supervision, consultation with colleagues, or personal introspection. In the interest of deepening our understanding of Clinton, I'm going to take the risk of exposing these personal reactions both to Clinton and to the people I interviewed, and describe how I was able to interpret them, performing my analysis of countertransference in a very public way on the page.

I can't take myself out of the plot of this book for yet another reason: As I conducted my research, two narratives became inextricably intertwined: Bill Clinton's story, and the story of my quest to get that story. For two years, during almost every waking moment, I dedicated my considerable energies toward solving the Clinton puzzle. Along the way I met some remarkable people, had some colorful experiences, and faced some extraordinary issues. I don't know how I could fully share my conclusions with you, the reader, without including you in the process whereby I reached them.

This, then, is an account of my journey as a roving psychologist, as I traveled from Arkansas to Africa in search of Bill Clinton.

PART I
Origins

1

Like Mother, Like Son

· VIRGINIA ·

Clinton is not as enigmatic as he might appear. Much of his behavior can be accounted for by the simplest and most commonsense psychological explanation of all: He takes after his mother.

As a psychologist, I knew I could never comprehend the man without understanding his parents. While Bill Clinton's every move has been overreported, overexposed, and overanalyzed, Clinton biographers have, for the most part, accepted Virginia's version of her life at face value, relying on her memoir, *Leading with My Heart.* But my clinical instincts told me there was more to Virginia's story than meets the eye. What I had not expected was how much more I would discover when I traveled to Hot Springs, where I interviewed her oldest friends as well as the first and last men she ever loved. By the end I had unearthed a startling portrait of an amazing woman that shed a new light on the psychology of her son. Friends and associates, most now in their eighties, provided me with straight answers about Virginia, answers that often contradicted the official version of events presented by Virginia in her memoir.

Virginia was an unforgettable character who always left a strong impression. Part of the impression was visual. In high school she began wearing the signature heavy makeup that would become her trademark. "She stood out, with that makeup, she really did. She piled it on," said

Jenny Sue McKee, who attended high school with her. Indeed, virtually everyone I spoke to about Virginia brought up her makeup.

From midlife on, Virginia sported a white stripe down the center of her black hair, creating an appearance that reminded many of a skunk. She achieved this effect by coloring her hair black, then leaving a swath undyed. She liked the look, and in this, as in so many things, she didn't give a hoot what anybody else thought. She dressed in idiosyncratic ways that made her stand out: sporting white cowboy boots to formal black-tie events; donning a white Mexican wedding dress to a funeral; and at election time, covering herself from head to toe—literally—in campaign buttons.

But a far more powerful impression was made by the force of her personality. She was intensely gregarious. She "never met a stranger," her friends Marge Mitchell and Nancy Adkins told me, and she always managed to be the center of attention in any room. "She'd mix with anyone. She loved people. If she walked in that door right now, she'd hug and kiss me, and probably you too," said McKee. And she was funny, "a cutup," according to McKee. In their yearbook Virginia wrote, "I'd like to take life seriously, but things are just too funny." Virginia was a tireless extravert who commanded attention. And as we will see in her son, her endless need to be the center of attention had a compulsive, driven quality: "Truth is I like bright colors and I like people to notice me. I think Bill and Roger and I are all alike in that way. When we walk into a room, we want to win that room over. Some would even say we *need* to win that room over. . . . If there are one hundred people in a room and ninety-nine of them love us and one doesn't, we'll spend all night trying to figure out why that one hasn't been enlightened."[1] Indeed, Bill Clinton would forever view anyone who didn't like him simply as someone who had yet to see the light. It has been said that in Bill Clinton's world there are two types of people: "constituents and potential constituents."[2] Virginia was oblivious to the normal social boundaries that might prevent her from commanding attention. For example, when she was a student nurse in New Orleans and would go to clubs to hear live music, she got into the habit of jumping onto the stage with the performers. "When we had time off we would go to the French Quarter and hear Dixieland Jazz or big band music," she wrote, "and I would embarrass my friends by getting up and singing with whoever was up there. I wasn't obnoxious or anything, I was just convinced I had more talent than most of the singers we heard, and didn't want to deprive anyone of the chance to hear me."[3]

Virginia had extraordinary energy, drive, optimism, and self-confidence that made people feel good when they were with her. In short, she had that hypomanic charisma. "She was bigger than life," said Bill's childhood friend Larry Crane. But in addition to having hypomania's assets, she also manifested its excesses and liabilities.

Virginia needed continuous stimulation and excitement. She chain-smoked, gambled, drank, and partied, all while running a very successful and demanding practice as a nurse anaesthesiologist, which required her to be on call twenty-four hours a day for seventeen years. She seemed to have an endless capacity to burn the candle at both ends throughout her life. As she wrote in her memoir, "For someone working the hours I was working, nightlife was a strain. On the other hand, how could you resist?"[4]

"She laughed hard, drank hard, played hard, and worked hard," said Larry Crane. "And she loved a party."

Virginia describes herself as "flirtatious," and Clinton biographers briefly allude to rumors of her having had affairs but pursue it no further. However, to understand how Bill Clinton became who he is, it's important to know that these were more than rumors. Extramarital sex was a lifestyle for Virginia; perhaps we could even say an addiction.

Joe Purvis's mother was one of Virginia's best friends in high school, and Joe had been friends with Bill Clinton since their mothers walked down the streets of Hope, together pushing their boys in strollers. "There are things I probably shouldn't tell you, and I won't," Joe Purvis told me, "but Virginia was exuberant in her love of life, and people, and good times . . . and she loved guys. There was always a guy in Virginia's life."

Like Bill, Virginia had a long string of adulterous affairs that till now have been undisclosed. Her liaisons, including her five marriages (she had four husbands, but married Roger Clinton twice), were often impulsive, and usually showed poor judgment. The extent of her promiscuity was one of the most surprising findings in my research. And, of course, when confronted about her sexual liaisons—she lied. As we shall see, young Bill Clinton was not shielded from this. Just the opposite. He was inculcated into the Kabuki dance of adultery, jealousy, and lying from an early age, and it became an unconscious paradigm that was burned into his psyche. "If Bill has been shown to have a roving eye, he comes by it naturally," Joe Purvis told me.

These traits expressed by Virginia—energy, drive, impulsivity, optimism, infectious exuberance, creativity, and charisma—are all signs of hypomania. Hypomanics are highly gregarious, active, and need little sleep. They often seek out pleasure and excitement in such areas as sex, gambling, and substance abuse. They behave impulsively, often showing poor judgment about the probable consequences of their behavior. And when things blow up in their face, they rarely take personal responsibility. They are often unconventional mavericks and creative visionaries who unapologetically do things their own way, and think the world should follow their lead, not the other way around. If they have a self-esteem problem, it's that theirs is outrageously high.

In the social hierarchy of Hope, Virginia's family, the Cassidys, occupied the bottom rung, just one step above African-Americans. In those days, people like them were called "common," what today we might derogatorily call "white trash." But brimming with the unquenchable innate confidence of a hypomanic, Virginia wrote, "I've never felt inferior to anybody. . . . I like myself—did even as a girl."[5] When one girl told Virginia that her parents had forbidden her to play with her because Virginia's family was "not good enough," it didn't even faze her. "That's all right, I have lots of friends," Virginia retorted.[6] Virginia's inborn high self-esteem was captured in a photo that appeared in the local paper, the *Hope Star,* which featured half a dozen high school girls in bathing suits positioned around a diving platform. "I was standing at the very top. I had a nice figure, but the thing that people comment on is my facial expression: the camera had caught a look of supreme self-confidence that makes me look older than my years. As one friend said, 'This was before people talked about attitude, but you had it even then.'"[7]

Like most hypomanics, Virginia had a powerful, positive exuberant force inside of her that she used to overcome all obstacles, both internal and external. "I compensated by calling attention to my cheerfulness, my flamboyance, my optimism, my upbeat outspokenness. I kept the darker feelings inside, deep down and out of sight."[8]

Yet, there is one extraordinary trait that Virginia passed on to her son that has nothing at all to do with hypomania. All the people I spoke with described her as the most loving and caring person they had ever encountered. This was not mere sentimental praise for the dead. Over and over people who knew her for decades emphasized to me how her capacity for love was a phenomenon unprecedented in their experience. Many employed spiritual language to explain this exceptional gift. As we shall see in Chapter 3, Bill Clinton's ability to feel and communicate love was an irreducible part of what made him the most charismatic political figure in a generation.

Virginia died soon after finishing her memoir. Bill Clinton read the manuscript with Jim Morgan, who co-authored Virginia's as-told-to memoir, at his side in a cabin in Arkansas. When Clinton finished the book, he looked off into space for a moment, and said: "Mom lived a large, messy, sprawling life."[9] But if she had lived a smaller, neater, and more contained one, she never would have produced someone as remarkable as Bill Clinton. As Virginia's old high school boyfriend, Richard Fenwick, said: "Some people around here just can't get it through their heads. No matter what Virginia did, no matter who she ran around with, from her being a president of the United States emerged."

· THE FAMILY DRAMA ·

It was the same nightmare, night after night. Except it was no dream. As young Virginia lay in bed, seeking the refuge of sleep, the madness would begin. Her mother would scream at her father, curse him, beat him, hurl things at him.

"I remember lying awake in the dark in that little house on Foster Avenue, listening to my mother shrieking at my father in their bedroom next door," Virginia recalled in her memoir. "Just pacing the floor and screaming. Sometimes this would go on all night . . . These fits went on for years."[10] Her mother, Edith Cassidy, accused her father of cheating on her. While Virginia was too young to understand the source of her mother's "nightly screaming fits," she understood that her beloved father was being accused of doing something bad with another woman. Her father, Eldridge Cassidy, would deny it emphatically, repeatedly pleading with his wife to be reasonable, begging her to calm down and consider the terrified young child in the next room. For three generations in Bill Clinton's family, the plot line would be much the same: accusations of adultery and emphatic denials.

Virginia's parents, Edith Grisham and Eldridge Cassidy, grew up next door to each other in the southwest corner of Arkansas, in the hamlet of Bodcaw, population one hundred. Actually, they grew up outside

Bodcaw, in an area called Ebenezer Community that consisted of only three families, two of whom were the Grishams and the Cassidys. These families barely eked out livings, raising cotton on their hardscrabble farms. The real price of cotton had been dropping steadily since the mid-1800s, which reduced the subsistence farmers of Arkansas to an existence well below the poverty line. When Edith and Eldridge married in 1922, their horizons seemed pretty limited. They crossed a little dirt road in front of her parents' house and moved a hundred yards away into a four-room tin-roofed shack.

It was Edith's drive that got them out of Bodcaw. After Virginia's birth, in 1923, Edith insisted they move to the big city of Hope, seat of Hempstead County, with a population of around five thousand. "So it's no wonder that my mother wanted to move from the monotonous country to the aptly named Hope," wrote Virginia. "In Hope, at least, there were possibilities."[11]

Though she never graduated from high school, Edith dreamed of becoming a nurse, and enrolled in a correspondence course taught through the Chicago School of Nursing. "For something like eighteen months she received her lessons and pored over them at the kitchen table and then shipped them back as quickly as she could. Her energy was amazing, because while she was doing this, she was also keeping house, and fixing meals and taking care of me," wrote Virginia.[12] Edith received a practical-nursing degree in the mail. That was sufficient for her to get good-paying work, and more important in the Depression years, steady work, at the first rung of the professional ladder. By all accounts she was an excellent and hardworking nurse.

Virginia recalled: "I inherited some of my mother's willfulness—which could be good or bad depending on how I used it—as well as her energy and ambition." The force of Edith's personality had a dark side: She was aggressive, suspicious, and controlling, while in comparison Eldridge was relatively amiable and passive. "Eldridge was a nice guy who was just hen-pecked," said Joe Purvis. "Edith was stronger than cat food. She was a control freak. She was the one in charge." Purvis remembered that when Edith came to pick up Bill from kindergarten, he was impressed by her nurse's cape and uniform, but also noticed that she had a "stern demeanor" that scared him. Virginia's cousin Dale, according to one friend of the family, thought Edith was just "plain mean."

From her father Virginia inherited the sunny optimism and sociability that we would later associate with Bill Clinton. She wrote, "I had also inherited my father's outgoing personality and his love for people."[13] In later life Eldridge ran a small grocery store. In small towns the grocery was the local hangout, where people gathered and talked. So it was the ideal environment for the extraverted Eldridge. "My father loved to be with people. He had an infectious smile, which lit up the room." He was "irrepressibly friendly."[14] Virginia's friend Virginia Heath recalled that "Eldridge was well liked. He had a wonderful personality and was real kind and nice to everyone."[15]

Eldridge's store was one of the few places where both blacks and whites shopped. Eldridge was an unusual white man in Depression-era Arkansas. Genuinely unprejudiced, he treated his black customers as friends. Playing with black children in his grandfather's store is one of Bill Clinton's earliest memories. "Bill could not understand why children with whom he played every day should not be able to attend school with him," wrote William Coleman III, Clinton's African-American Yale Law School roommate. Coleman found Clinton's racial attitudes unique among whites. "Dealing with these issues at an early age caused him to reject racism with a personal ardor that, frankly, I have found rare in people who are not themselves victims of racism."[16] At Yale the blacks segregated themselves, as happened at many universities in those days, but Clinton appeared oblivious to the color line. One day "a tall, robust, friendly fellow with a southern accent and a cherubic face unceremoniously violated the unspoken taboo by plopping himself down at the 'black table.'"[17] Clinton became a regular member at the table, the only white student at Yale to do so.

Everyone remembers Eldridge sold illegal whiskey that he kept hidden under the apples. Hempstead was a dry county (and still is), but the police typically tolerated one designated bootlegger, and in Hope it was Eldridge. Ironically, the man who supplied his whiskey would become Virginia's second husband, Roger Clinton.

"Eldridge drank a lot," Virginia's high school friend Jenny Sue McKee told me. One biographer respectfully describes him as suffering from "a moderate drinking problem."[18] Eldridge introduced Virginia to drinking early in life, offering her belts of whiskey beginning at age twelve. Virginia became a drinker, and all the men she liked were drinkers, too. "I knew all her husbands. They were all real nice, but they all drank," said McKee. In 1957, Virginia's father died at age fifty-six, in part due to liver-related complications suggestive of alcoholism.

There is a strong link between substance abuse and even the mildest forms of mania. While hypomanics are naturally high, they often artificially seek to maintain or even enhance their preferred mood state. As mentioned earlier, drugs, alchohol, and hypomania have a similar neurological mode of action: They stimulate the same pleasure center in the brain, a small limbic structure the size of a pea called the nucleus accumbens, which is fueled by the neurotransmitter dopamine. Virginia used alcohol excessively (incidents with alcohol are mentioned twenty-six times in her memoir), and she was a chain-smoker, as well. There was "never a moment when there wasn't a cigarette in my mouth, my hand, or an ashtray nearby."[19] Virginia smoked unfiltered Pall Malls, five packs a day. Indeed, vulnerability to addictions runs through Bill Clinton's family tree. His grandmother, Edith, became addicted to painkillers late in life and his half brother, Roger, was both an alcoholic and a cocaine addict.

In addition to chemical substances, Virginia would use behaviors such as gambling, sexual acting out, and unending social activity to maintain her upbeat mood. Evidence suggests that these behaviors also stimulate the limbic system and cause the release of dopamine in the nucleus accumbens. Hypomanics are *addictive personalities*. They may be workaholics, sexaholics, shopaholics—typically they are not limited to one compulsive behavior—but underneath there is a common cause: their underlying hypomanic temperament.

The Clinton family, including Bill, participated in family therapy as part of Roger's drug treatment, which makes Bill Clinton the first president to have participated in psychotherapy (or at least the first to publicly admit it). One of the insights he obtained from these sessions was, "I think we're all addicted to something," as he told his friend Carolyn Staley. "Some people are addicted to drugs, some to power, some to food, some to sex. We're all addicted to something."[20]

On the other hand, it seems doubtful that Virginia herself gained much insight into her own addictive personality from her brush with psychotherapy. Her close friend Nancy Adkins said: "I went with Virginia to all of Roger's court-mandated drug education classes. After we got home, she poured us each a tall glass of whiskey." Adkins asked: "Virginia, do you think we ought to be doing this? We just got out of a drug education class."

"Why not? We're not the ones with the drug problem," replied Virginia.

The combination of her mother's ambition and energy and her father's optimism, gregariousness, and a weakness for substances equipped Virginia with all the elements that compose a hypomanic temperament. This biological underpinning goes a long way toward explaining why Virginia Cassidy would become a serial adulterer, but in addition, layered upon this neurological foundation were psychological issues, rooted in her experiences with her dysfunctional family.

One of Freud's most enduring insights was his discovery of the "repetition compulsion." Put simply, there is a powerful *unconscious* drive to re-create in one's adult relationships the relationships you experienced as a child. In my twenty years of practicing psychotherapy, there is no single idea that I have found to be more useful or universal. Time and again, the origins of the most inexplicable, destructive relational patterns can be found there. It is as if, when we are born, our minds are like wet plaster, and the structure of the relationships we encounter forms an impression that hardens into a mold. We're just not sexually attracted to potential romantic partners who don't fit our mold. What feels right to us, powerfully and compellingly so, are the comfortable and familiar relational patterns of the past. We re-create our childhood paradigm using three basic techniques: We pick partners who are inclined to play their assigned roles; we provoke them to behave in these familiar old ways; and, finally, we project our past family figures onto them, distorting our perceptions to convince ourselves that they are behaving like figures from our childhood even when they are not. And, amazingly, we engineer all of this outside of our own awareness.

Paradoxically, it is the traumatic relationship patterns from the past that we are most compulsively driven to repeat. The theory has it that re-creating the traumatic situation allows us to feel a sense of mastery over it. It's not being done to us. We're doing it, which allows us to feel more in control. The irony is that when we are unconsciously driven to repeat destructive patterns, we are *out* of control by most objective standards.

To understand the pattern Virginia was repeating, consider her mother's nightly screaming fits, which she experienced over and over again. Usually, when we think of traumatic events, we think of hurricanes, war, or rape. But psychologists believe that it is the stone in your shoe that makes you lame; repetitive experiences do more damage than a one-time catastrophic event. These screaming fits were so traumatic because they went on night after night. Secondly, these events were caused by malevolent human intent, as opposed to bad luck (e.g., natural disaster, illness, accident), making them much more traumatic. This relational pattern—fights over accusations of adultery that are repeatedly denied—was seared into Virginia's unconscious, and she was programmed to replicate it. Virginia unconsciously re-created her parents' tragic drama in her own adult relationships.

If Eldridge were inclined to be unfaithful, his job gave him ample opportunity. Before opening his grocery store, he delivered ice to the kitchens of Hope's women. The gregarious Eldridge used to like to "stop off and have coffee with various customers—usually the prettiest ones," recalled a boy who assisted him on one of his routes.[21] But the unanimous consensus among the people I spoke to was that Eldridge was not unfaithful. "I never heard of Eldridge going with any women," Virginia Heath said. "Oh Lord, he'd be the last guy to be unfaithful," said Joe Purvis. However, whether or not Eldridge actually cheated, young Virginia repeatedly witnessed her enraged mother accusing him of infidelity, which he denied over and over again. This laid down a pattern Virginia would feel a compulsive need to repeat, a blueprint she would follow the rest of her life. "Roger would keep me awake all night with his tantrums and his accusations of infidelity and his jealousy about everything under the sun," wrote Virginia.

Ironically, the rumors around town were that Edith, rather than Eldridge, was sleeping around. "Her relatives would later talk about relationships they thought she had with a few doctors," wrote Maraniss. Those relatives were deceased when I conducted my interviews, but I spoke to Peggy Lloyd, archival manager at the Southwest Arkansas Regional Archives, whose aunt had worked in the same hospital with both Edith and Virginia. Lloyd said her aunt disliked both mother and daughter because, she said, "they were both man crazy." Jenny Sue McKee told me, "It was *Mrs.* Cassidy who had the affairs. . . . Virginia took after her in that." Thus, Virginia's identification with her mother was another important contributor to her adult sexual behavior.

I had difficulty finding many people left alive who remembered Edith Cassidy. But one woman in Hope, Jewel Dean Moore, had quite a story to tell about Edith Cassidy's jealous rages, which supports Virginia's claim that her mother suffered from pathological jealousy, bordering on paranoia.

Today, Mrs. Moore is ninety-one years old and blind. Yet still spry, she makes lunch for her two grown sons every day. Seventy years ago, Jewel was a twenty-one-year-old newlywed, working as a cashier in a grocery store that was jointly owned by Eldridge Cassidy and his cousin Calvin. "It's still all very fresh in my memory. I've forgotten a lot of things, but some things you don't forget," Jewel told me. Before she began work at the grocery store, the Cassidys' neighbors warned Jewel about Edith. "I don't think you want to work there," they said. "She's already run off two or three girls."

Everything seemed to be going fine, until one day Edith offered Jewel a ride home. Once they were alone in the car together, Edith "proceeded to tell me that she did not want me to come to work no more. That was to be my last day.

"'I won't have Eldridge being nicer to anyone than he is to Virginia and me,'" said Edith.

Jewel wasn't sure what Edith meant by that but gathered that she was jealous, imagining some kind of relationship or mutual attraction with Eldridge. The thought had never crossed her mind. Eldridge had been a perfect gentleman toward her.

Jewel appealed to Calvin. He laughed and told her to come back to work. But Edith refused to be ignored. She came into the store one Sunday morning when Calvin was not there and, standing in the middle of the store amid the customers, she began shouting in a booming voice: "Jewel Dean! I've warned you and I've warned Eldridge: If you continue to work, you'll take the consequences!"

Edith stepped up her campaign of intimidation. First she sent Jewel a threatening letter. Then Edith began coming into the store and glaring at her. "She would sit behind the counter and stare at me for two or three hours." Edith's stare could be quite intimidating. According to Virginia, "I've never seen anyone burn with intensity the way she did. Those eyes could bore in on you and disintegrate you with their heat."[22]

"It got so bad that when I saw her coming I started having a chill," said Jewel.

When the staring campaign failed, Edith got rougher. She began positioning herself behind the counter. And each time Jewel would pass "she would knock up against me, saying, 'You little bitch,' and things like that under her breath." The neighbors across the street warned her that one night Edith "got up on a drinking spree, and she was out in the yard screaming. She was going to shoot and kill Eldridge, and she was going to kill me."

The neighbors warned, "You want to watch out for her. She could be dangerous." Jewel's dad lent her his pistol, and after that she came to work every day with a concealed weapon.

"I went to Calvin and said: 'I can't come to work anymore.' I was on the verge of a breakdown.

"He said, 'All right, don't come into work tomorrow. Tonight I'm gonna talk with Eldridge. Either he's gonna buy me out, or I'm gonna buy him out.'" Eldridge had no money, so Calvin bought him out. He came to Jewel's home and assured her parents that she could come back to work, and to further reassure them, he told them he had obtained a restraining order against Edith, forbidding her to enter the store. This was a serious commercial setback for Eldridge. The Ward 4 grocery he had co-owned with Calvin was a very successful operation, with several full-time employees and located in a good section of town. After Calvin bought him out, Eldridge ended up renting a much smaller store with a dirt floor in a poor African-American neighborhood, and that is the store everyone now remembers.

A second psychodynamic layer in Virginia's psyche to affect her adult sexual relationships was oedipal. Freud believed that every girl, at a deep unconscious level, wants to sleep with her father and kill her mother, the chief rival for her father's romantic affections—just as every boy supposedly wants to sleep with his mother and kill his father. According to Freud, almost every conceivable mental problem is rooted in these types of conflicts. This sweeping view has been debunked. Indeed, if you want to pick a single factor that accounts for mental illness, you're better off looking at genes rather than Greek myths. But while it may now seem laughable to think that oedipal conflicts explain everything, it doesn't mean that they explain nothing. While I hesitate to invoke the Oedipus complex, since the entire discipline of psychobiography has fallen into disrepute largely because so many psychoanalysts reduced the actions of their famous subjects to this simple formula, there is good reason to emphasize oedipal dynamics here. While these dynamics affect every family to some degree, there is reason to believe that in Virginia Cassidy's family they were of primary importance, since they fit what we know about both her development and her adult behavior. For example, all of Virginia's sexual encounters I learned about involved a love triangle. Almost without exception, Virginia became involved with married men. This pattern is too consistent to be a matter of mere chance. If she were indiscriminately promiscuous, why not have sex with single men? At a deep unconscious level, there had to be a psychic reason why she was compulsively, systematically, and exclusively attracted to married men.

While oedipal feelings are normal and universal, there are reasons why they became so intensified in Virginia. Even in a normal family, she would have been a "daddy's girl," and there is nothing wrong with that. Neighbor Jenny Sue McKee told me, "Her daddy idolized her. So she was closer to her daddy than she was her mother." Virginia's memories of her father are all warm ones. For example, though he had to leave for work to pick up his ice at 3:00 A.M., he always made sure to stop by the house to give a kiss to his little "Ginger"—a pet name for Virginia only he used. "That was the highlight of my morning," she wrote.[23]

At the opposite pole, Virginia had an exceptionally cold and hostile relationship with her mother, whom she describes as someone with "a vindictive, manipulative mind," who would "stop at nothing" to hurt people she thought had betrayed her.[24] Considering her mother's nightly screaming fits, it's not hard to understand Virginia's feelings. While she lay listening to her mother shrieking, Virginia heard her father begging his wife to calm down for their daughter's sake: "Please, please, the baby," he pleaded. "Please, the baby has to go to school tomorrow. Please."[25]

While her father was trying to protect Virginia from her mother's aggressive tirades, Virginia was lying in the dark wishing she could protect her father. The fact that she couldn't drove her into a hateful rage: "It hurt me very much to lie there listening, hearing my sweet daddy pleading with her to calm down. . . . She would keep shrieking and sometimes she would lunge at him and try to hurt him physically. He protected himself, but he never took the offensive. I thought at the time, *Why don't you stand up to her, maybe strike her once? Maybe, just maybe, that might teach her a lesson.* But he didn't. [Emphasis in the original.]"[26]

We can't blame Virginia for wishing physical violence on her mother. Her mother's actions toward her father were among "the cruelest acts I've ever witnessed."[27] She probably wouldn't have minded striking Edith herself, if she could have. Likely, Virginia harbored the classical oedipal fantasy: If Edith were conveniently killed, she and her father could live in peace happily ever after. Which, under the circumstances, wasn't an entirely unreasonable idea.

Freud said that the intensity of oedipal feelings is naturally attenuated by the loving feelings every child feels toward their same-sex parent, the one that they are supposedly competing with. So, for example, while a three-year-old girl might tell her mother, "You can't love Daddy. Daddy is mine," there are other times when the emotional pendulum swings the other way, and she wants Dad out of the picture so she can have Mommy all to herself. Freud called this the "negative Oedipus complex," and it offsets or counterbalances aggressive and competitive feelings toward the same-sex parent. The problem here is that Virginia had virtually no positive feelings for her mother that could offset her aggressive ones. In her memoir Virginia has virtually nothing good to say about her mother. Virginia Heath, her friend for almost fifty years, recalled, "Virginia never did speak real good of her mother. She and Virginia didn't get along."

According to Freud, parents have oedipal feelings as well. And it seems likely that in this family the oedipal triangle was not just a matter of Virginia's fantasies, but an accurate description of the dysfunctional family dynamics. Though not overtly incestuous, there was a romanticized connection between Virginia and her father that, at the very least, bordered on the inappropriate, and Edith was jealous of their bond, all of which is illustrated by this story that Virginia recounts: "At four thirty in the morning, I felt somebody shaking my arm. '*Baby*,' a man's voice whispered. '*Baby*,' I rolled over and squinted into the face of my father, who was smiling. 'Come, go with me,' he said. . . . Daddy would wake me early and want me to go have coffee with him at the little all-night café down the street. But of course this would make mother mad. 'You let her sleep,' she would tell him. . . . Between us there were no secrets, and these predawn hours were when we talked the most."[28] Clearly, all three members of this family were deeply involved in this oedipal drama to an unhealthy degree. As Heath put it: "There was jealousy there. He was crazy about Virginia. And Virginia was partial to him. And Edith didn't like it." Bill Clinton agreed: "Mammaw [Edith] had been hard on her [Virginia]. Perhaps because she was jealous that Papaw loved his only child so much."[29]

Maybe Freud was wrong. Maybe every girl doesn't want to marry her father and kill her mother, but this one did.

If we braid these psychic strands together, Virginia's adulterous adult behavior was driven by no less than at least four psychological components. First, on a psychodynamic level, Virginia had an unconscious attraction to love triangles, an oedipal desire to steal another woman's husband, who in most cases also happened to be an older man. Second, she was modeling her mother's infidelity. Third, she had a compulsion to reenact the nightly traumatic family ritual over infidelity. And, finally, at a biological level, her hypomanic temperament heightened all her drives, including her sex drive, to a pitch that made her prone to act on them.

The resulting combination was a real femme fatale—a woman whose sexual behavior would be described as out of control by most people's standards.

· A HOT ROCK ·

Richard Fenwick, Virginia's high school boyfriend, lives in the small Arkansas town of Camden, just north of the Louisiana border. Though he is eighty-five years old, Fenwick plays golf every day. He has a ruddy face with an impish grin, a shock of thick white wavy hair, and an offbeat, sly sense of humor. "I bet you didn't expect to meet a character like me," he chuckled.

Fenwick and Virginia met in sixth grade. "We both came from the wrong side of the tracks—the poor side of town. We were poor, real poor. We were so poor that my mother made me eat my cereal with a fork, so my brother could drink the milk. Now, that's poor. And that's a true story. My children don't believe it, but it's true."[30] Fenwick, Virginia, and their other friends banded together to survive their Depression childhood. "We grouped together and helped one another in our troubles."

Fenwick recalled that despite her carefree demeanor, Virginia was no underachiever. Like Edith, Virginia was ambitious and focused. "She knew from the very beginning that she wanted to be a nurse, and she knew that she would do it."

Jenny Sue McKee recalled, "She was smart in school. She didn't play around. She made good grades." She was a member of the National Honor Society, along with the science club, music club, library club, and press club. And she showed traits of leadership, being both a member of the student council and freshman class secretary.

But the drive that was most intense in Virginia was her sex drive. She says that she "developed early" and "discovered boys early, too."[31] In her high school yearbook, she "wills" to a friend "my magnetic attraction for boys," to which the editors of the yearbook added, "(Help us, please, if she turns it on full force)."[32] She also developed a reputation for being "loose." "Hop-along Cassidy" was what one of her boyfriends nick-named her, because he thought that Virginia Cassidy would hop into bed with just about anyone who came along.[33]

Fenwick described how their relationship evolved: "By ninth grade we got old enough to call it a date. For fifteen cents we had a Coke and a Lucky Strike cigarette, and that was a date." But if they could borrow his brother's car, they "had a little more time alone." As Virginia mentions slyly in her memoir, the object of having a car "wasn't necessarily trans-portation."

Fenwick said, "If you want to put it plainly, she was one hot baby. If you unzipped your zipper, she'd beat you to the floor. She just loved it. She was crazy about it, the whole thing. It was real. It was physical. It was there. If there was a way to do it, we got it done. We're talking about quite a gal. She was a hot rock. She was ready. Some women are just like that. I guess Bill Clinton inherited some of that."

Though Fenwick became her steady high school boyfriend, Virginia would never allow herself to be fully tied to one boy. She wanted to play the field and refused to be contained by Fenwick's jealousy, or anyone else's. Virginia wrote, "There was a song out when I was young called 'Don't Fence Me In.' I liked that song and I liked the ideas it conveyed. I dated several boys during my first couple of years in high school; I wasn't jealous of them, and if any of them got jealous because I was going out with others, I crossed him off my list."[34]

Fenwick had to accept that "I was not the only cock in the walk. She had other dates." But he wasn't happy about it. Conflict about fidelity made their relationship "kind of a love-hate thing." But he knew better than to try to control her. "She was a freewheeler. If she made up her mind she wanted to do something, she'd do it. She didn't ask about whether you liked it or not."

When she was still a high school student, Virginia began her habit of dating older married men. According to McKee, she dated a number of local businessmen: "For some reason, she particularly liked car dealers." McKee thought that if some people in town looked down on Virginia, it wasn't because she was poor, as she claimed, but "because of how boy crazy she was, who she dated. She didn't care whether they were married or not." At one point, Virginia began dating McKee's youngest brother. When McKee's father saw them together in Texarkana, he read his son the riot act: "'I'm gonna tell you right now, I don't want you goin' with that girl. I'm not gonna have it,'" he said. "I don't think he had to say why," said McKee. "It was Virginia's reputation for running around and all."

After Fenwick graduated from high school and before he left for the service in World War II, Virginia wanted to get married. Virginia wrote, "The house on Hervey Street [where she grew up] had a front porch with a swing, and Richard and I would sit out there for hours on end, talking and swinging, ruminating about our future . . . Most people in town expected us to get married someday, and I guess we did too."[35] Virginia proposed, but Richard said no.

"We knew—or I did—we'd never get along as man and wife," Fenwick told me. When I asked him why, he cited several reasons: "First of all, I was leaving for the war and felt like I was never coming back. And I remember telling Virginia, 'That's stupid. I'm getting ready to go overseas and get killed.' I knew I was going to the Pacific Rim till the end of the war—if I lived." Then there was the practical problem that they had no money. "I guess we would have made it OK in the bedroom, but we couldn't afford a bed." But the last reason he declined her proposal was probably the most important: Fenwick just didn't believe that Virginia was capable of remaining faithful to him for that length of time. He reasoned that if she was unfaithful while he was living in Hope, he could only assume that more of the same would go on when he was halfway around the world for an extended length of time. "If I'm in New Guinea, Japan, or the Philippines, and she's back here in nursing school . . . well, you know, dah, de, dah, dah, dah—a lot of things would have happened that I would not have been real pleased with. . . . There already was a lot of that going on."

Though they weren't married, the couple parted with some ill-defined understanding. "Before we parted, Richard gave me a ring," she later wrote. "It wasn't an engagement ring exactly—more like an engaged-to-be-engaged ring. Richard says now that he must have gotten it from a Cracker Jack box, because we sure didn't have the money to buy fine jewelry. But it didn't matter. I loved it. The ring was the thing, its circle tying the future to the past. We kissed for the last time on my front porch swing, two kids about to discover that there are no guarantees in this old world."[36]

Though they stopped dating when Fenwick left for the war, for the rest of their lives they remained "close, real close," he said. One of the first things people mention about Virginia was her fierce loyalty. "If she was your friend, you had one, in every way, for life," said Fenwick. "A lot of times in life, you have a lot of acquaintances, but not many friends. A friend is a person who is going in the door when everyone else is going out. . . . We had an understanding, whatever the other one needed, we'd do it, no questions asked. If she said she needed twelve hot bricks in the morning, I'd find them, and bring them to her. And she would do the same for me."

At a fundraiser during the time Clinton was governor of Arkansas, Virginia surprised Fenwick, he recalled, by hugging him from behind. "She looked at my wife and said, 'I still love this old son of a bitch, and I always will.'"

· LOVE AT FIRST SIGHT ·

"I want you to know something: There *is* such a thing as love at first sight,"[37] wrote Virginia, recalling the moment she set eyes on Bill Blythe. They met in the emergency room of Tri-State Hospital in Shreveport, Louisiana. It was a hot July night in 1943, and Virginia was working as a student nurse in the emergency room when Blythe brought in a woman complaining of severe pain in her side. Blythe was holding her hand and soothing her when Virginia walked into the room to collect a medical history.

"When I stepped into that room I was stunned. It's been more than fifty years since that night, but I remember it as if it were yesterday. I looked at that tall, handsome man, holding that woman's hand, and he turned and his eyes met mine. He smiled, and the only way I can describe it is that he had a glow about him. . . . And he was being so nice to her, so considerate. She was obviously in terrible pain, and he would squeeze her hand and lightly rub her brow and lean over and talk to her and smile. And all I could think was, *I've got to know if they are married or not.*"[38]

If one looks at this incident with a clinical eye, part of what attracted Virginia to Blythe was the fact that he *was* there with another woman, one with whom he was obviously romantically involved. Virginia's pattern—an unconscious replication of her oedipal triangle—was that she was only attracted to men who were attached to other women. Second, as someone with a hypomanic temperament, she was more prone than most to impulsively dive headfirst into a liaison with someone she knew nothing about.

Obviously attracted to one another, they both lied about their current attachments. Blythe lied by saying the woman whose hand he had been stroking was "just a friend." Relieved, Virginia asked no further questions. Blythe noticed that she was wearing Richard Fenwick's pre-engagement ring and asked, " 'What does that mean?'

"And just like that I said, 'Nothing.' After four years of going with sweet, wonderful Richard, I told this total stranger that my ring didn't mean a thing."[39]

As soon as the hospital staff wheeled his friend into surgery to remove her appendix, Blythe took Virginia on a date. She had to be back in her dorm half an hour after her shift ended.

" 'Well,' he said, 'that's time enough for a Coke.'

"I never talked and drank as fast in my life," wrote Virginia. "We literally had fifteen, twenty minutes. And I remember we kissed that night, which was something you didn't do in those days—kiss on the first dates. But I knew the moment I laid eyes on Bill Blythe that all rules were out the window. The next day he called me, and the next night we saw each other again—and every day and night after that. . . . What we had was the textbook definition of a 'whirlwind romance.' It was wartime and you had to talk fast. . . . We talked fast, played fast, fell in love fast."[40] The operative word here is "fast." The speed with which events unfolded had as much to do with the fast-revving engine inside of Virginia as it did with the external circumstances related to the war.

Virginia impulsively entered into a union with a man she hardly knew, and much of what she thought she knew was completely false. She thought he had never been married, but he had been married—four times. For Blythe, his union with Virginia would be the last of five marriages; for Virginia it would be the first of five. She thought he had no children, but he had two, one of whom was illegitimate, and it is possible that both were (there is some confusion on this point). For that matter, Blythe was illegitimate himself. Virginia certainly didn't know that Blythe, who was only twenty-five-years old, was still legally married to his fourth wife when he married her, making him a bigamist. Blythe even lied to Virginia about why he was in Shreveport (though why he thought this necessary is unclear). He told her that he was passing through town on a sales trip, and that he was on his way back to his hometown of Sherman, Texas, to be inducted into the military. In fact, Blythe's military records show that he had already entered the service when she met him, and had been in Shreveport for several months waiting for his orders.

They drove to Texarkana to be married by a justice of the peace on September 3, 1943. When they got back to Shreveport, Bill got in his car and headed to Sherman, Texas, to ship off to Europe. "I had known this man two months," she wrote, "and now, suddenly we were married."[41]

Two years later, in December 1945, Bill Blythe returned from Italy. He and Virginia met for an exciting reunion in Shreveport. Blythe got a sales job in Chicago, and went there to look for a house, while Virginia waited for him in Hope. On May 17, 1946, Blythe called Virginia with good news. The house they had wanted was theirs. He was coming back to Hope to reclaim his now pregnant bride and start their life as a family. He was so excited that he threw a case of bourbon in the back of his car that rainy night, and decided to drive straight through from Chicago to Hope without stopping. He never made it. He had a blowout, lost control of his car, and was killed. The car was found turned over off the road, but he was not inside. He had had enough strength to pull himself from the wreck, but then he collapsed in a drainage ditch and drowned in a shallow pool of water.

Several drivers that night recalled "being passed by a dark-colored Buick going at a high rate of speed."[42] It's more than a metaphor to say that in every aspect Blythe and Virginia's relationship had moved way too fast.

· A TALE OF TWO MOTHERS ·

Three months later Bill was born. Virginia, a young mother with no husband and no money, did what so many single mothers have done before and since: She turned to her own family for help. Virginia wanted to start her career and needed child care, but she couldn't afford to pay for it. Edith Cassidy, who was only forty-three, certainly had the energy to help raise a child. It was the only logical choice. But once Edith agreed to help, she took over entirely. "Mother was totally involved in showing me how mothering was done."[43] As often happens when an adult child moves home, Virginia and her mother regressed to their old roles. She wrote, "I felt like a lowly student nurse again, running around practically taking notes while . . . my mother was playing God."[44] Edith took charge of caring for infant Bill—feeding, changing, and putting him to bed. Neighbor Jenny Sue McKee told me, "When he was real little, Edith cared for him. I mean, she did more than Virginia ever did."

From a psychoanalytic perspective, the most important thing you can know about Bill Clinton's early years is that he was torn between the love of two women, each of whom adored him and resented the other. From the moment of his birth his place at the vertex of a love triangle became a permanent part of the structure of his life. During his first four years, Bill would live with and be raised by his grandmother Edith. When Virginia demanded four-year-old Bill back, Edith and Virginia almost ended up in court fighting for custody. For the rest of his childhood, Bill would live with Virginia—and make frequent visits to Edith and Eldridge's home in Hope. "They were competing for him his entire life," Rose Crane, his lifetime friend who grew up next door, told me.[45]

While these two women would vie for his affections, young Bill continued to love them both, deeply, fiercely, and passionately. Though his love for each seemed like a betrayal of the other, it was inconceivable to him that he could ever give up either one of them. He just wished they could get along, and understand that he needed them both.

The connection between Bill's later infidelities and his early experience of being torn between the loves of two women has been made by a number of astute observers. David Maraniss implied as much on the first page of his biography: "It is central to the understanding of the man he would become that he began life in Hope with no father and, in essence, two mothers who competed for his love and attention."[46] However, the press howled when Hillary Clinton made a similar observation. Discussing possible ways in which his background might have contributed to his "weakness" for infidelity, she was quoted in *Talk* magazine as saying: "He was so young, barely four, when he was scarred by abuse. There was a terrible conflict between his mother and grandmother. A psychologist once told me that for a boy, being in the middle of a conflict between two women is the worst situation. There is always the desire to please each one."[47] The irony about the embarrassing public drubbing that Hillary took over this comment was that she was absolutely right. Hillary was not suggesting that this was an excuse for Clinton's infidelity, which was how the press spun it, but an explanation, which is not the same thing. "I don't believe anybody could fairly read that article and think that she was making excuses for me," Bill Clinton said in her defense. "I have not made any excuses for what was inexcusable and neither has she, believe me."[48]

In his autobiography, Bill Clinton clearly recalls that he was caught in the crossfire between his mother and grandmother, but focuses on the bright side: "[Grandma] was also full of anger and disappointment and obsessions she only dimly understood. She took it out in raging tirades against my grandfather and my mother both before and after I was born, though I was shielded from most of them." His mother and grandparents "loved me very much; sadly much better than they were able to love each other or, in my grandmother's case, love my mother. Of course, I was blissfully unaware of this at the time. I just knew that I was loved. For all their own demons, my grandparents and mother always made me feel I was the most important person in the world to them. Most children will make it if they have one person who feels that way about them. I had three."[49]

Like Virginia, Bill inherited a biological constitution that would intensify his drives, reduce his impulse control, and impair his judgment when he was tempted to act on those impulses. This hypomanic temperament alone would heighten his general vulnerability to sexual acting out. But layered on top of that was a very specific set of childhood relationships, which he would internalize and repeat in his adult life, that pushed him down the path of infidelity. He was torn between two women since birth, and the powerful unconscious force of the repetition compulsion would keep him stuck in that position as an adult. Though the women would change, the fundamental structure of his relationships remained constant. But even more specifically, he would remain stuck between two very distinct types of women—one resembled his grandmother, and the other his mother.

From the very beginning Edith and Virginia were opposites in their roles, personalities, and values. Clinton remembered his grandmother as "bright, intense, and aggressive."[50] Edith had a hard edge when it came to relations with people. She didn't trust them, and for the most part she didn't get along with them. The notable exception, of course, was young Bill, whom she doted on. In her parenting style Edith was a rigid, controlling taskmaster who both imposed structure and provided a sense of stability: "She had Bill on an unrelenting schedule—he ate his breakfast at the same exact hour every day, had his bowel movement on schedule— napped, played, ate, burped, slept, in an unwavering cycle,"[51] wrote Virginia, who imagined that Bill would naturally bristle at such limits— after all, she had. Virginia theorized that Clinton's lifelong habit of tardiness was a reaction to his grandmother's overly rigid schedule.

Edith, who was tough, driven, and ambitious, pushed little Bill to excel: "She had begun to focus her ambition on him. . . . I can still see them sitting at that kitchen table by the window on Hervey Street, Bill age three or four and Mother in her late forties by then, her dark eyes as intense as could be while she drilled him with homemade flash cards. Actually they were playing cards that she would arrange in the crossbars of the window, and she would quiz Bill on the numbers, one through ten. He loved learning even then, but of course he didn't dare not learn, if that's what his Mammaw wanted him to do. You didn't cross her."[52]

Virginia's personality was the diametric opposite of Edith's. She was a sunny extravert who adored people, and a fun-loving, physically attractive, free spirit who imposed no limits and obeyed none. She wrote that she was "not one for rules," and in the case of Bill, she "imposed very few rules on him."[53] While Edith did the work of caring for him, Virginia's role was to specialize in play. In this respect she was more like an older sibling than a mother. "Most mothers are happy for their babies to sleep, but I remember wanting so much for him to wake up and *play* with me. [Emphasis in the original.]" She even complained to the pediatrician that Bill slept too much, and wondered if she should wake him—but he told her no. The doctor, who had probably never heard this presenting complaint before, pointed out that most mothers, exhausted by the work of caring for an infant, are usually grateful when their babies sleep, so they can rest themselves. But Edith took care of most of the work—leaving young Virginia bored, and wanting someone to play with. "Reluctantly," wrote Virginia, she took the doctor's advice.[54]

The most important event in Bill Clinton's childhood took place when he was eighteen months old: Virginia left him for two years in her mother's care, and moved to New Orleans. There she trained at Charity Hospital to achieve her specialization as a nurse anaesthetist. It's hard to fault Virginia for this decision. The training was crucial to her career: It allowed her to establish a private practice in anaesthesiology that, against all odds, held its own in competition with Hope's M.D. anaesthesiologists until the mid-eighties—an amazing testimony to her energy, moxie, and skill. The practice became so successful that she was able to earn an upper-middle-class income and take on employees, an astounding feat for a woman in rural Arkansas during this era. To have become a professional and an entrepreneur in the 1940s makes her a legitimate feminist pioneer. In addition to the economic benefits, she was a wonderful role model for Bill, who has always respected the competence of strong women. When she left for New Orleans, Virginia had no doubt that she was doing it as much for young Bill as for herself. But looking back, we can also see that this was a traumatic loss for her son, one that would have profound and permanent effects on his development. He desperately missed his mother, and over the next two years their contact would be fleeting and precious—much like an affair.

Psychotherapists often ask patients to recall their earliest memory. Early memories are not random shards of data. Instead, they are fraught with deep feeling and developmental significance, and are remembered for a reason. Early memories are emblematic, which is to say, they are symbols that stand for more than just the specific event recalled. Indeed, they represent many events from the past that had a similar theme, most of which are no longer remembered but still exert force on the psyche. Bill Clinton's earliest memory is found on the first page of his massive autobiography—where he recalls that only once during the two years Virginia was away were he and his grandparents able to visit Virginia in New Orleans. When the time came for them to return to Hope, they said good-bye to Virginia on the train platform. "I'll never forget what happened. . . . As we pulled away from the station, Mother knelt by the side of the railroad tracks and cried as she waved good-bye. I can see her there still, crying on her knees, as if it were yesterday."[55]

In her memoir, Virginia recalls that same scene: "When Mother took Bill from my arms and boarded the train north, I literally dropped to my knees by the tracks, I was aching so."[56]

This was more than the recollection of one painful moment in Clinton's childhood. His mother's absence was an open wound during his early years. From Bill's crib in his grandparents' home he could hear the train that passed right by his house. Elaine Johnson, vice chairman of the Clinton Birthplace Foundation that maintains the home as a museum, toured me through the house. When we got to Bill's bedroom she said, "Bill once told me that a freight-train whistle is one of the loneliest sounds in the world." It was a train that took Virginia away, and every time he heard that whistle blow he must have thought of his mom. He longed for her. Bill would wait for the phone to ring, and when it did, Clinton was "always hoping it was Mother calling from New Orleans."[57]

The Cassidys could not afford to visit Virginia, or to pay for her to make visits home. In fact, they did not pay for their one trip to New Orleans that Bill and Virginia remembered so well. It was paid for by the man Virginia began dating before she left Hope—Roger Clinton. Virginia Heath, who began socializing with Virginia and Roger during this time, told me that Roger frequently flew Virginia back to Hope on weekends. Virginia would stay with Roger, and sometimes she would steal young Bill for brief visits with her there. On occasion Bill would spend the night with her at Roger's house. Thus, in his early years, when Bill did have contact with his mother, they were stolen moments. He could only rendezvous with his longed-for sexy young mother in a love nest across town.

One excerpt from his autobiography reveals the slightly erotic connection he felt toward his mother, her bright makeup, and especially her long hair. Ever since the time Freud first proposed that children have erotic feelings, and toward their own parents no less, the notion has raised objections. Freud never meant that young children have visions of intercourse. Rather, they experience feelings of attraction, longing, and desire that are inchoate, and will later form the basis for adult sexual feelings.

Beauty is in the eye of the beholder, of course, but to young Bill Clinton there was no doubt that his mother was gorgeous. "From the time she came back home from New Orleans," Bill Clinton wrote, "when I could get up early enough, I loved sitting on the floor of the bathroom and watching her put makeup on that beautiful face. . . . Until I was eleven or twelve, she had long dark wavy hair. It was really thick and beautiful, and I liked watching her brush it until it was just so. I'll never forget the day she came home from the beauty shop with short hair, all her beautiful waves gone. It was not long after my first dog, Susie, had to be put to sleep at age nine, and it hurt almost as badly. Mother said it was more in style and more appropriate for a woman in her mid-thirties. I didn't buy it, and I never stopped missing her long hair."[58] This passage shows how the normal erotic feelings of childhood, an attraction to his mother's hair, became combined with poignant feelings of loss and desperate desire. After years of separation, young Bill was so sensitive to losing any part of Virginia that his deep feelings of abandonment were triggered by something comparatively minor—a haircut. He never stopped missing her long hair and, unconsciously, never stopped seeking to find it over and over in new women.

In many respects the women Bill Clinton had affairs with resembled Virginia. The press commented extensively on the physical similarities between Virginia and Bill's lovers—too much makeup, slightly plump, big hair. Between Monica Lewinsky and Virginia, they are particularly striking. Furthermore, the similarities in personality between Virginia and Clinton's lovers are as striking as their physical ones. Like Virginia, these women were warmer, younger, more exciting, and less straitlaced than the woman he lived with. And Bill could only have them in a rendezvous in a love nest across town.

Though young Bill Clinton had a desperate longing for his mother, he *relied* on his grandmother. She was his primary caretaker—his rock. For him, Edith became the archetype of the woman you can really count on—a woman who is smart, ambitious, aggressive, rigid, and controlling, and who has a hard edge with people. One who is education-oriented and will push you to achieve your potential. One who won't leave you, no matter what. Because she raised him during the first four formative years of his life, when push came to shove, Bill must have felt that it was the tough cookie you could depend on in the long term.

As will become clearer, Hillary Clinton resembles Edith Cassidy in personality in many respects. At an unconscious level this is precisely what attracted Bill to her in the first place. And despite what cynics might say, there is no question that Bill loves Hillary deeply, and needs her as desperately as he once did Edith. In short, Bill married his grandmother.

If young Bill had one powerful wish, one that any child in his position would have felt, it was to be able to simultaneously have *both* Edith and Virginia, and for them to get along with each other. He loved them both, and their conflict presented him with an impossible dilemma. He could never choose between them.

He needed both women.

· TORN BETWEEN TWO WOMEN ·

Marla Crider had a romantic relationship with Bill Clinton in 1974, when he was a twenty-seven-year-old congressional candidate and she was a twenty-year-old college student working on his campaign. When Marla became involved with Bill, he was not yet married to Hillary, Crider hastened to tell me, though she knew they were seriously considering marriage. Both Bill and Hillary had just recently graduated from Yale Law School. Hillary was in Washington working for the Watergate committee while Bill was in Arkansas running for Congress. What Crider told me about the relationships among the three of them illustrates how Clinton's childhood love triangle manifested in adulthood.

Crider was conflicted about talking to me. Her relationship with Clinton had been written about before, and in her opinion past writers had gotten the story wrong. She was also concerned that I might have a political agenda, but when I explained that I was a psychologist trying to understand Bill Clinton, she was intrigued. "I have been hoping someone would do that for a long time," she said. One of the writers who had previously interviewed Crider was Jerry Oppenheimer, who wrote *State of a Union,* a bestseller about the Clinton marriage. When Crider read the book, she felt shocked and betrayed to discover that it opened with a scene from her relationship with Clinton, a scene she thought had been distorted.

This is how the book opens: Bill asked Marla to retrieve something from his desk at home where, consciously or unconsciously, he had left a letter from Hillary in plain sight on the desk. Of course, Marla could not resist reading it: "I still do not understand why you do the things you do to hurt me," it read. "I know all your little girls are around there, if that's what it is, you will outgrow this. They will not be with you when you need them. They are not the ones who can help you achieve your goals. If this is about your feelings for Marla, this too shall pass. Let me remind you, it always does. Remember what we talked about. Remember the goals we've set for ourselves. You keep trying to stray away from the plan we've put together."[59] Oppenheimer portrays Crider as being disturbed by this alien and "chilling" bond that she could not understand, based on an "intellectual blueprint," as if "mere feeling did not matter." Oppenheimer's perspective was that Bill and Hillary elevated a cynically ambitious political alliance over true love.

Yet this was absolutely not the way Crider perceived it. "That was the spin Oppenheimer wanted to put on it. Frankly, my impression was that this was more personal. You know people can have plans for their marriages, have plans for their lives together."

Oppenheimer is not alone. One poll found that 53 percent of the American public perceived the Clinton marriage to be "a professional arrangement" rather than a "real marriage."[60] But Marla read the letter as an expression of a loving relationship between two people who had talked about their future. As we shall see over the course of this book, Oppenheimer did get it wrong, as have many people. While their relationship has been "the most dissected relationship in American life," its true dynamics remain "difficult to gauge from the outside," according to *The New York Times*.[61] These dynamics can be much better understood when you consider how well they follow Bill's psychological blueprint.

Bill and Hillary love each other, and they always have, as Marla could plainly see. Everyone I have interviewed has attested to it. "Even in offstage moments, Bill and Hillary would be physically affectionate, holding hands, or he'd drape a hand over her shoulder," said one press aide.[62] Another friend commented, "This kind of chemistry can't be faked."[63] I think that is true. It would be virtually impossible to fake it, and totally impossible to successfully fool everyone who knows them well. Clinton biographer and *Washington Post* reporter John F. Harris, who spent years as a professional Clinton watcher, came to the same conclusion: "Even the cynics in the Clinton fold almost invariably arrived in the end at the same noncynical answer: She loved him, and felt loved by him in return. Over the course of a decade covering the Clintons, one found very few people who worked or socialized closely with them who did not in the end believe this."[64]

What is less clear to many people is why. One night when they were together, Marla asked him what it was about Hillary that made him love her. His answer might seem strange if we did not know his family history: "She challenges me every moment of the day. She makes me a better person. She gets me started, kicks my butt, and makes me do the things I've got to do."[65] An odd description, to be sure. It almost sounds like a parent getting a lazy child ready for school. But it's a very apt description of the role Edith played in Bill's life. Edith was the taskmaster—drilling him on numbers, keeping him on time, controlling his diet—but Bill always knew it was for his own good. She was tough, but she was making him a better person. He felt safe relying on a person like that.

Veteran Clinton campaigner Carol Willis, who began with Clinton during the 1974 campaign, said: "This woman's as tough as nails. They don't come tougher, male or female. She is tough. No matter how tough you think she is, you've underestimated her." Willis meant this in a positive way, but not everyone experienced her toughness that way. Descriptions of her by veterans of the 1974 campaign portray her in an unflattering light that has shades of Edith Cassidy written all over them.

When Hillary left Washington and came to Arkansas to join the campaign, she jumped in at the eleventh hour to join a team that had built up an incredible esprit de corps, energized by the phenomenally charismatic Bill Clinton. The campaign was unfolding brilliantly. Though he ultimately lost a close race against what all regarded as an unbeatable incumbent, the campaign launched him in Arkansas politics, and ultimately set him up for a successful run for governor. But Hillary saw the campaign as undisciplined, and she aggressively took complete control in a very dismissive way—much as Edith had taken over Clinton's child care when he was an infant. Like Edith, "who just didn't know how to get along with people," she appeared to be tone-deaf to the feelings of the staff, who uniformly found her abrasive. Like Edith, she was a controlling, angry martinet. "There were few people she tolerated in that office. She was very dictatorial. She literally came in and just turned everything around, changed everything. . . . She would get furious if there was any frivolity. *Furious*. It was like—'Have you forgotten what our goal is?' . . . It was almost like she was angry the whole time," said Crider.[66] Nor was this just Marla's reaction. Ron Addington, the campaign co-manager, told me that when Hillary arrived in August, her attitude was "you guys don't know what the hell you're doing—I'm gonna straighten this place out.

"She was boss and there was no getting around that," said Addington.[67]

Bottom line, did Hillary's drill-sergeant tactics help or hurt the campaign? It depends on who you talk to. Campaign co-manager Paul Fray said, "None of those kids really liked her. She would come in, want to run the show, tell everybody what they were supposed to be doing."[68] Fray and others have argued that her effect was to suck the energy and enthusiasm out of the campaign. Many staffers just quit. Addington told me that "Hillary lost us that election." On the other hand, some argue that while she may have been bossy, she knew what she was doing. Diane Blair, who became lifetime friends with Hillary, recalled that her takeover of the campaign had the effect of "markedly improving the professionalism and effectiveness of our ragtag volunteer efforts."[69]

Understanding how Hillary fits the Edith mold helps explain one of the other mysteries about the Clinton marriage: Hillary's physical appearance. Though in recent years she has evolved into a very stylish, nice-looking woman, this has been the result of a major makeover. When she and Bill got together, she was unquestionably homely. She dressed plainly, in shapeless garments known coincidentally as "granny dresses," wore no makeup, kept her thick hair long and unstyled, and was always seen wearing the thickest, largest owl-eyed glasses imaginable. Arkansas journalist Gene Lyons called it the "early 70's lumberjack look." It was at this time that the unfounded rumor that Hillary was a lesbian began. Jim Daugherty, a native Arkansan who worked in Bill's first campaign, recalled that Hillary looked like a "hippie" with "very frizzy hair, and frankly," he said, "she was not an attractive person."[70] Bill's mother and all those who knew him were blatantly shocked, and Hillary's looks would be openly discussed as a political liability for some time. Hillary's unattractiveness was not just in the eyes of traditional Southerners. Her friends at Yale Law School noted it as well. Hillary was "deliberately unattractive," commented another classmate.[71] Her lifelong friend Lanny Davis teased her: "Lurking somewhere beneath that headband, and those glasses, and that dress is a beautiful woman."[72]

For years, people have wondered, why is someone as magnetically attractive as Bill Clinton married to a plain Jane who seems to have all the sex appeal of a librarian? From that people drew the cynical conclusions about her being a professional partner in power, not an object of romantic affection, because it seemed almost self-evident that he couldn't be attracted to her. However, the fact that Hillary was not attractive may actually have been, paradoxically, part of her attraction for Bill. As Clinton acknowledges, the Edith he knew growing up was not particularly attractive, though, he hastened to add, "she had obviously been pretty once."[73] During the time young Bill knew Edith, "she was not attractive at all, in any way," according to McKee, in large part because she was severely overweight. While psychoanalysts would argue that most boys marry their mothers, Bill was marrying his grandmother. Widely regarded as one of the sexiest men alive, he did not choose Hillary despite her plain looks, but in part because of them.

If Hillary was Edith in Bill's psychic world, Marla more closely resembled the warm, sunny, sexy Virginia, not only in temperament, but in physical appearance. She was not simply more attractive than Hillary, "she was definitely his type," said Paul Fray. "Dark hair, round face, she fit the mold; there've been others too, like that. They all look a little bit like his mother."[74] Oppenheimer wrote that years later, when Fray and his wife, Mary Lee, saw Monica Lewinsky for the first time, "They turned to each other at once: 'Marla,' they both said instantly."[75]

Not only was Hillary in a love triangle with Marla, who served as a psychic stand-in for Virginia, she was also in competition with the original Virginia herself. Just as Virginia had once hated Edith, she instinctively disliked this Edith substitute. When Hillary made her first trip to Arkansas, meeting Virginia for the first time, Virginia took an immense, immediate dislike to her future daughter-in-law.

"Virginia loathed Hillary," said Mary Lee Fray.[76] Much of her reaction had to do with Hillary's physical appearance. Virginia recalled being shocked by how "different" Hillary looked: "No makeup. Coke bottle glasses. Brown hair with no apparent style. . . . Roger and I were polite, I guess our expressions gave us away."[77] Bill went on and on about how wonderful, and pretty, and smart Hillary was, but Virginia could not believe that her son had brought home "a hippieish female who cared not a whit about makeup!"[78] Hillary's indifference to the traditional standards of beauty had a willfully defiant quality. Before they went to meet Virginia for the first time they stopped off at the Frays' house. Mary Lee recalled, "She had a scarf on. No makeup. . . . If I was on the way to meet my future mother-in-law, I would have at least combed my hair."[79] The importance of makeup as a defining difference is an important one. Virginia had been famous for her heavy makeup since high school. She even opens her memoir with a lengthy scene in which she applies her makeup, step by step, before Bill's first inaugural. Her other great vanity was her hair, which she brushed for hours. For Hillary, rejecting even the pretense of effort at makeup and the grooming of hair was a symbol of the new feminist rejection of the traditional female role.

Culture clash: That's how the immediate visceral antipathy Virginia felt toward Hillary has been explained. That's how Bill explained it: "There was almost a kind of cultural tension between Mother and Hillary," Bill said.[80] And Virginia agreed. "I was from Hope. She was from Chicago. I grew up in the war years, she in the anti-war years. Rural vs. city. South vs. North, makeup vs. natural look."[81]

I think there was a deeper reason Virginia had an instant dislike of Hillary, beyond regional differences and the culture wars of the 1970s—a far more personal reason buried in Virginia's unconscious, and more intimately connected to her life story. As we have pointed out, Hillary shared many personality traits with Edith, Virginia's mother. She was smart, aggressive, hardedged—a veritable re-embodiment of the woman Virginia had hated all her life. Virginia's violently allergic reaction to Hillary was caused, we are led to believe, by the fact that Hillary confronted Virginia with something so unfamiliar—the seventies look. But in fact Hillary was presenting her with something all too familiar: a smart, tough, bossy woman competing with her for Bill's affection. For the first part of her life, Edith had been her rival for her father's love, while for the rest of her life Virginia had to compete with Edith for her son's love. In a backhanded way, Virginia admitted to feeling competitive with Hillary from that very first encounter: "I might have resented her being a lot smarter than I am. I've told you that I've never been jealous in my life, and I'm not going to admit to it here."[82] But, of course, she was.

Bill was furious with his mother and Roger. "Bill shot us a withering look. 'Come here you two,' he said, and you could tell he meant *right now*. It was like he was our father and we were two bad children. He got us into the kitchen, and he told us in no uncertain terms, 'Look, I want you to know that I've had it up to *here* with beauty queens. I have to have someone I can talk with. Do you understand that?' His eyes bored through us like my mother's used to do."[83] Though she is talking about Bill, it is psychologically relevant that Virginia's association is to her mother's burning eyes.

Psychoanalysts have long used Freud's technique of free association.

The psychological assumption behind the technique is that even associations that appear random are not, but reflect deeper psychic connections. It is not just because Bill is mad that Virginia remembers her mother's eyes. It was not that unusual for Bill and Virginia to get mad at each other, but nowhere else does she invoke the most physically powerful remembrance of her mother's intimidating presence. The first encounter with Hillary activated these powerful, frightening early memories. Like in a horror movie, where the monster the heroes thought they had defeated keeps returning, there was the horrifying feeling that Edith was back.

There are debates about whether Hillary and Virginia ever overcame their rivalry. While most people will say that both women grew to love and respect each other, under their breath they will also tell you that both women learned to fake it in large measure for family harmony. If Virginia's antipathy was merely an initial culture shock, as it has been presented, then presumably over the years she would have had time to acclimate to Hillary's strange customs and appearance. But clearly there was something deeper and more intractable at work.

Gail Sheehy tells a revealing story. When she was working on a magazine article about Hillary during the first presidential campaign, she flew to Arkansas to interview Virginia. When Sheehy phoned Virginia from her Hot Springs hotel to confirm their interview time, Virginia decided she had better things to do than talk about her daughter-in-law:

" 'I've decided I don't have time for the interview,' she said. 'The ponies are running today.' "

Sheehy, who had flown all the way from New York for this interview, understandably pleaded with Virginia to reconsider.

" 'But I've come such a long way, and your son *is* running for president.' "

" 'Yeah, but your article is only about Hillary anyway.' "[84]

Bill, of course, desperately sought harmony between his wife and mother, as any man would. But in Bill's case there was an extra burden of unfinished psychic business at work. All his life the rift between Edith and Virginia had been a source of enduring pain. And he had always nurtured the deep wish that the two women he loved could just get along. Understanding that background also helps explain a peculiar wrinkle in another triangle, the one involving Hillary and Marla.

Crider had another area in which she wanted to set the record straight, one that has great relevance to this discussion: "I read in one book that Bill told an aide, when Hillary came in the front door, to sneak me out the backdoor. That absolutely never happened. In fact, oddly enough, it was just the opposite." Bill seemed to *want* to bring Hillary and Marla together—not the swiftest move, one would think, for a man trying to conduct two sexual relationships simultaneously. For example, when Hillary needed to be picked up at the airport, Bill sent Marla. "Let me tell you, Bill Clinton thrived on me and Hillary being in the same room. Knowing what we knew about each other and all—he wasn't uncomfortable with that a bit. There was no putting me out the backdoor, because he truly did need that."

What was the need? Perhaps it was an egocentric thrill, but more important, it was a manifestation of his deepest childhood wish: Bill Clinton wanted Hillary and Marla to get along, just as he had always hoped Edith and Virginia might. He wanted them to be one big happy family, even though the idea was completely unrealistic, to say the least. But the fantasies of childhood don't bow easily to reality.

One day Hillary asked Marla, in a cutting way, in front of the campaign staff, if she knew where Bill's socks were, saying, "I figured that you would know." Crider's take on Bill's reaction to this is very illuminating. "He was going, 'All right, you cut it out, you two. Hillary, good gosh, we're trying to take care of business here.' He was very involved and very animated about it, but he didn't get upset. It was more like—OK, you two stop that now. Almost like a parent would scold two kids." Bill reacted as if this was an immature squabble among family members, because to him Marla and Hillary represented his mother and grandmother, who did squabble immaturely.

In the interest of peace, Marla offered to leave the campaign several times. Bill consistently refused, saying he needed her, though it was obvious that her presence was becoming increasingly disruptive. Marla did not have the feeling that he just wanted to keep her around for sex. The poignant urgency with which he begged her to stay seemed like an undeniably genuine emotional response. Hillary and Bill finally had a knock-down-drag-out fight over Marla in front of Paul Fray, which ended with Hillary jumping out of their car and walking home. Hillary had finally insisted that he get rid of Marla, and Bill had flatly refused. Fray called Marla to say that "the final confrontation has finally taken place," and he believed that Marla "had won." Everyone in the campaign knew of the rivalry, and they were rooting for Marla. But Crider herself finally decided it was time for her to go. The situation was untenable. Things simply could not keep going on as they were. "He would never, ever cut that tie. I had to do it. He would never cut the tie."

We think of a womanizer as a predator who deceives, uses, and then discards women. But this is simply not Bill Clinton's modus operandi. His need for continued closeness with his ex-lovers seems to be unquestionably genuine. He and Marla are still friends.

I raised this idea with Rose Crane, the woman who grew up next door to Clinton. She smiled at me slyly. "Bill Clinton never says good-bye."

After losing his mother once, when she moved to New Orleans, Clinton never wanted to say good-bye to her again. Nor has he ever wanted to say good-bye to the women who who represented Virginia for him.

Crider told me that many years later a mutual friend mentioned to Hillary that she was planning to visit Marla. Hillary said something that astounded her: "There will always be special women that Bill loved, that will be important to him, that will hold a special place in his heart."

All serial adulterers are not alike. Bill Clinton is not the remorseless cad so many have tried to portray. If he were, Hillary probably would have left him long ago. Clinton has a deep emotional need for two women that he cannot explain and does not understand. Hillary was right. And who would know better than she?

Clinton has lived his whole life in the same place where he was born: torn between two women.

· RELIVING HISTORY ·

"Those who cannot learn from history are doomed to repeat it," wrote philosopher George Santayana. Though Santayana was not a psychotherapist, a pithier summary of psychotherapeutic wisdom would be hard to find. Human nature is such that repeating old relational patterns is our default option. To break the mold takes disciplined self-awareness garnered over time, as takes place in any successful psychotherapy. Virginia never took part in such a process, and even her closest friends will readily admit that self-reflection was not her strength. As a result, she re-created the destructive family drama of accusations and denials of adultery that had terrorized her as a young child—complete with all-night screaming fits by her spouse, Roger Clinton. By acting out these old patterns, she also passed them on to the next generation.

To the reader of Virginia's memoir, it's abundantly clear that Roger Clinton was a terrible choice, and that Virginia should have been able to see that before marrying him. Almost every conceivable red flag was flying conspicuously, warning her that Roger Clinton was trouble. But he was exciting trouble.

Roger opened a Buick dealership in Hope, but a large part of his allure was that he came from Hot Springs, where they would eventually move. Nicknamed "Dude," he was Hot Springs personified, a "lot more dashing, in a dangerous sort of way, than most of the men in Hope," wrote Virginia. "He dressed fit to kill, with sharp creased trousers and a fine tailored sports coat and two-tone shoes. . . . His hair was dark and curly, and his eyes twinkled when he talked because he was always about to say something funny. He was the life of the party and he partied a lot. . . . When he was playing host, you've never seen such strutting in all your life. But the thing was, he made you feel like strutting too."[85]

From the beginning, Virginia and Roger's relationship centered on wild partying. About this aspect of her life, Virginia is pretty forthcoming: "We were heavy, heavy partiers in those days." Virginia describes what they did for fun: "Most of the things Roger liked doing were illegal in Hope—I'm talking about drinking and gambling."[86] When friends came over to Roger's, he would turn the coffee table upside down and use it as an improvised craps table. He and his friends would drink and throw dice all night long. Sometimes the fun turned dark, escalating into fistfights.

Roger's Buick dealership in Hope didn't work out. Either he ran it into the ground or, as rumor had it, he lost it in a game of craps. In either case, the couple left for the much more compatible fast-moving Hot Springs.

Virginia Clinton could not have lived the life she did in any place other than Hot Springs, Arkansas. The Hot Springs of her era was unlike any other city in America. It was simultaneously both the Las Vegas of the South and the classic small Southern town, seamlessly blending the perils of vice with the virtues of neighborliness. It was a place where everybody knew your name and no one cared what you did for fun. This small resort town of twenty thousand people, with its natural beauty and healing waters, also had another attraction—illegal gambling and finely appointed houses of prostitution. Hot Springs was, quite literally, a steamy town. The hot springs for which the town is named still trickle down into the town center, releasing constant vapor into the air. Elegant casinos like the Southern Club and the Vapors operated in that same town center, right on Central Avenue, with the hearty approval of the thoroughly corrupt local government. Like Las Vegas, these clubs boasted world-class entertainment. All the big acts stopped there. Also like Vegas, Hot Springs had a reputation for being mobbed up, but even its gangsters were neighborly. Shoot-outs and murders were unheard-of. Al Capone vacationed there, and is said to have declared Hot Springs off limits to violence—even gangsters have to relax.

"All the gangsters I knew were real gentlemen, as nice as they could be," Virginia's friend Nancy Adkins told me. Vice was the main engine of the local economy, and an integral part of the otherwise proper Southern culture. It was a perfect fit for Virginia, who wrote, "I'm not one for rules, and the only rule in Hot Springs was to enjoy yourself—a rule I could handle. . . . Hot Springs let me be me with a vengeance."[87] This unique cultural context that helped form Bill Clinton was both a special time and a special place. The Hot Springs he grew up in doesn't exist anymore. Old-timers will tell you, as Virginia's friend Nancy Adkins put it, "the Puritans ruined this town." In the late sixties reforming governor Winthrop Rockefeller shut down illegal gambling in Hot Springs. The Southern Club is now a wax museum. And the three gigantic gold balls that stood stacked one upon another in front of the Vapors are now painted black. The building is home to the Tower of Faith Ministry, a storefront church.

Roger's older brother, Raymond Clinton, was the successful one in the family, and one of the "boss dogs" in town. He gave Roger a job running the parts department in his dealership, and he rented a nice house to Roger and Virginia (Roger told Virginia he had bought it, which she later learned was a lie). The house was a former casino, and Bill's friends all remember playing in the former gaming room. Raymond was part of the action in Hot Springs. He operated the Belvedere Club. "The club offered the full menu of wink-wink 'illegal' pleasures," reported Gail Sheehy, "liquor, crap tables, waitresses who could be persuaded to get familiar with the paying customers."[88] To help Virginia get started in her nursing practice, Raymond procured for her the job of being the nurse for the local prostitutes. According to Paul Fray, "He let her be the nurse for the girls in the cat-houses. She was the one who did the checking on the ladies."[89] Virginia said she was always glad to hear that one of "Maxine's girls" was admitted to the hospital for surgery, because "Mr. president of the bank might not pay me on time, but Maxine's girls would."[90]

Roger's best friend, Gabe Crawford, was married to Roger's niece, also named Virginia. The Crawfords and the Clintons became close friends, and partied together. A former Miss Hot Springs, Virginia Crawford (now Virginia Heath) is a platinum blonde who "likes bright colors." The day we met she was wearing a fluorescent orange suede vest, lined with matching orange fur. For almost fifty years Heath was close friends with Virginia, from 1947 up until the time of her death.

Heath remembers their early years as one big drunken party: "We used to go out, and drink, and cut up, and dance, and play the slots. We'd go to the Southern Club on weekends. We'd get half loaded and do a snake dance around the tables, you know, like a conga line, go get steaks, have some drinks, go upstairs and gamble. Well, we'd run around town and just do silly stuff. Heh, heh." (Heath had an almost indescribable giggle that punctuated her most provocative comments.)

In her memoir Virginia Clinton recalled one particular story: "Virginia Heath insists on reminding me of the times when we would visit them and I would climb up on the counter, obviously under the influence of something like Roger's moonshine, and sing this absurd song I made up—'I'm the Hempstead County idiot,' it went. Which I obviously was."[91]

As you might expect, there was a lot of drunk driving in those days. In fact, reckless driving under the influence of alcohol was considered to be fun. "At that time you could have a bottle rolling around in the back. The police wouldn't bother you. When you think about what we used to do, it makes your hair stand on end," said Heath. Virginia Clinton recalled one incident she witnessed in which a drunken Roger and a drinking buddy were playing a game to see how close they could get to the back of an eighteen-wheel truck at high speed without having an accident. The front hood of their car almost disappeared under the truck's cab. When Virginia, who was following in another car, caught up with them, she screamed at them at first, but then ended up dissolving into laughter with them over the prank. "Back then—especially in Hot Springs—getting drunk and crazy was considered cute, and though I hate to admit it, for a time, I thought it was too."[92]

In its heyday Hot Springs boasted all the big acts. Virginia claimed to have never missed a show, and with her hypomanic extroversion, she was never content to be a mere spectator. She continued her habit of jumping onstage: "I particularly remember a night . . . when the performer was Georgia Gibbs, later to become famous for her song 'Tweedle Dee.' I knew all the words to the song she was singing and I couldn't contain myself. So I simply excused myself from the table, and I guess Roger thought I was going somewhere to powder my nose. Next thing he knew, I was standing onstage and singing along with 'Her Nibs,' Miss Georgia Gibbs. Roger had to have an extra drink to settle his nerves."[93]

It was clear from the get-go that Roger Clinton ran around with other women. Virginia recounts one incident that took place before they decided to marry. A friend told Virginia that Roger was entertaining a stewardess at his house. "As I say, I'm not a jealous person, but I sure as heck don't like somebody making a Hempstead County idiot out of me. I must have been home alone with Bill, who was probably three at the time, because I decided to take him with me while I went over to Roger's to investigate. So I packed up the future president of the United States and we drove across town to pursue my own domestic policy." When she got to the apartment, it was pretty obvious that Roger had been "entertaining": "There was expensive and extremely sexy lingerie all over the apartment—lacy bras draped over chairs, silk stocking on the floor, garter belts and filmy little slips cascading off the edge of the bed." The first thing she did was rip up the woman's return trip ticket and flush it down the toilet, but she wanted "a public humiliation." "With Bill in tow, I walked around the apartment thinking, *What's the worst thing I can do to him?* . . . So I took it all [the lingerie] and hung it outside on the clothesline. There was no way anybody who drove by could miss it. . . . Everybody in town saw that Roger Clinton was *seriously* in the doghouse."[94]

It's impossible not to wonder: Why did she bring her young son on this errand? For all she knew, she might have found Roger and the stewardess *in flagrante* when she entered the house with Bill. Though it's hard to know exactly how he processed this dramatic scene, it could not have failed to make a strong impression on this brilliant, sensitive child. It's frankly disturbing that Virginia relays the story in so cavalier a tone, as if it's just another funny anecdote. As psychoanalyst Stanley Renshon wrote in his character study of Clinton, *High Hopes,* "Missing from her thinking when she recounted this incident in her biography, as well as when it actually happened, is an appreciation of its effect on her son."[95]

Virginia would later write that her life was "like a country song," a genre that frequently centers around sexual betrayal, and she was indeed teaching Bill the music that accompanies the dance of adultery. At an un-conscious level she was inducting young Bill into the culture of infidelity.

As one is struggling to absorb this scene in Virginia's memoir, the very next sentence after the lingerie-on-the-line story is, literally, "Mother knew it was coming . . . but she still wasn't ready when I told her I was marrying Roger."[96] In one breath she was hanging another woman's lin-gerie on his clothesline. In the next, with no transition or explanation, she's marrying the man, as if that were the most natural sequence in the world.

I asked Virginia's co-author, Jim Morgan, about this. Was there any awareness on her part that bringing young Bill on this errand was poten-tially harmful to him? Was there any awareness that for her to marry Roger immediately after this incident boggles the mind? Did she have any insight at all, at least in retrospect, that this whole relationship had re-flected poor judgment—that it was a bad choice? Virginia spends a lot of time in her book bemoaning all the trouble she's seen and the hardships she's had to overcome. But, as the reader can see, most of that trouble was self-induced. (Indeed, after the physical abuse became unendurable, she divorced Roger Clinton, only to immediately remarry him!) Did she have some concept of her role in her own difficulties? The answer to all of these questions was a simple no. "She wasn't one to reflect a lot on her life. Not one to look back and regret any of her choices," Morgan said. I asked these same questions repeatedly when interviewing people who knew her most of her life, and the answer was always the same. "She was a very, very bright woman, but not very introspective," said Rose Crane. "I never saw her doubt or second-guess herself. She wasn't the type to ask 'where did I go wrong?' She just handled whatever life dealt her."

To put this in context, hypomanics are often blind to the fact that they have not just been dealt bad cards, but chosen them. Typically, they are oblivious to the role their own acting out and bad judgment have played in their suffering, and that of others. Even with the benefit of hindsight, they just don't get it. In fact, much the opposite; rather than feeling repentant, they often feel victimized. As we shall see, Bill Clinton was frequently criticized for the same attitude. This massive denial of responsibility is so unbelievable, and yet such a consistent trait among hypomanics, that I have speculated that there may be a neurological ba-sis for it—like color blindness. I mentioned earlier that the layer of cortex that modulates impulses—what I call the think-before-you-act part of their brain—is impaired. I think this deficit continues retroactively: For the most part they don't think about it after they act, either.

In addition to this biological explanation, there is a psychological one. The reenactment of the repetition compulsion is almost always unconscious. Virginia was re-creating the dynamics of infidelity and jealousy she had witnessed in her own family of origin. And so, what seems like outrageously poor judgment to us just felt natural to her.

She was reliving history.

Edith and Roger Clinton "hated each other" from the beginning, and their relationship never improved. "Mother remained amazingly immune to Roger's charms, and I still couldn't understand it." Her disapproval of him wasn't always passive. Roger had given Virginia a white leather jacket. "The coat had a fringe, and when I would do the shimmy, the whole thing would shake. I loved that coat." One night, she was looking everywhere for it. "Mother knew I was looking for it but she hadn't uttered a word. Finally, I said, 'Mother, do you know where my white leather jacket is?' A sinister look of satisfaction came over her face.

" 'I burned it,' she said."[97]

Once Virginia and Roger decided to get married, Virginia announced that she wanted her son back. Edith consulted a lawyer about fighting for custody of Bill, and only dropped the case when her lawyer told her she could not win. So, at age four, Bill came to live with Roger and Virginia.

Because she despised Roger, Edith boycotted Virginia and Roger's wedding. In fact, the only people who attended the ceremony on June 19, 1950, were Virginia Heath and her husband, Gabe.

"Ya, we stood up with them," Heath told me.

She couldn't remember why there were no other guests. They were married in a small brick house across the street from the Oaklawn racetrack. It wasn't a chapel. "That's just where the preacher happened to live." What Heath remembers about the ceremony is this: "We were all half loaded, Roger especially," Heath told me, giggling.

Predictably, Roger did not change his cheating ways. He would sometimes be absent for days at a time, offering outrageously implausible explanations. "For much of the time that I was married to him, I had no idea of Roger's whereabouts," she wrote. "He would go off on what were supposed to be one-day business trips, and it might be several days before he came home. When he did he'd be packing the lamest excuses you've ever heard in your life. Actually, in hindsight, some of them were pretty funny." Once, for example, Roger had gone to Memphis. When he re-appeared three days later he claimed that the Mississippi River bridge linking Tennessee and Arkansas had burned, and it had taken days to make it passable. "This was a *concrete* bridge, mind you. I beg your par-don? I may have been born at night, but it wasn't *last* night." Another time he said he was driving home and came upon a bunch of country workers moving a cemetery from one side of the highway to the other. " 'Well, it would have been *sacrilege* to cross,' Roger said—he related this with impressive piety—so he stopped and waited for them to finish, which took two or three days. Roger told these stories so often I think he began to believe that they were actually true."[98]

The night Roger Clinton's father lay dying his family was frantically trying to locate him. Finally, in exasperation, his brother Raymond looked at Virginia and said, " 'Well, *you* must know where to look.' "

" 'I do not,' " Virginia told him, " 'I never rolled one wheel looking for Roger Clinton.' "

After his father died "they finally found Roger many hours too late, sound asleep out at the house of a lady friend on Lake Hamilton."[99]

Virginia had no doubt that Roger was womanizing, but she wasn't jealous, and she offers this explanation: "Number one, I was always re-lieved that I was going to get some quiet time. Let carousing dogs carouse, you know. And number two, it's not in my nature to chase off looking for some man."[100]

But the most important reason Virginia wasn't jealous is left unstated: By looking the other way, Virginia was able to justify her own dalliances.

In her memoir Virginia portrays Roger as being pathologically jealous, like her mother. She claims that as he descended into alcoholism, Roger became paranoid, irrationally accusing her of infidelity with escalating frequency, intensity, and violence.

"That's a lie," Heath said. "Roger had plenty of good reason to be jealous." And she proceeded to tell me about some of Virginia's affairs.

To discuss Virginia's history of infidelity during the time she was with Roger, you need to go back to the beginning of their relationship, be-cause she began by committing adultery *with* Roger. She wrote that she did not know Roger was still married when they met. "I knew he had been married, but we never really talked about his wife. I assumed that they were divorced."[101] She claims to have learned the truth decades later. "It turns out that Roger was still married—to his second wife—when he and I met, which is why his family may not have looked too favorably on me at first. . . . It's truly amazing to me what you can go down to the courthouse and find out about people—court records show that in July and September of 1951, Ina Mae filed against him for overdue child support. . . . And I didn't know a thing about it."[102] I recall thinking, when reading that passage, that the story seemed fishy to me. How could she be oblivious to his marital status when his wife, Ina Mae, lived right in Hot Springs?

Sure enough, Heath told me, "That's a lie. There are a lot of things in Virginia's book that aren't true. Virginia knew Roger was married when she met him. Sure she knew. She separated them." And she apparently did so with a threat of force. "Ina Mae came down there [to Roger's house in Hope]. And Virginia was hiding behind the door. She had a chain in her hand, and she was going to whip her with the chain—but Roger took it away from her."

Heath further claimed that Virginia's third and fourth husbands were also married when she became romantically involved with them, as well, and "she separated them from their wives too." Though in her memoir, Virginia claims that both husbands three and four, Jeff Dwire and Dick Kelley, were divorced when she began dating them.

According to Heath, when the Clintons still lived in Hope, Virginia had an affair with her cousin Dale's husband, despite the fact that Dale was one of Virginia's closest lifelong friends. Dale's husband had a friend and business partner, and "she told me she went with him, too."

"Was he also married?" I asked.

"Yah, that don't make no difference."

Jenny Sue McKee confirmed that Virginia had affairs, with both Dale's husband ("he was a snake in the grass") and his friend. I asked if Dale knew. McKee said, "She was suspicious, but she never did know." Dale was also reputed to be pretty "wild," herself marrying five times, which is one of the reasons she and Virginia were such kindred spirits.

When Bill was in second grade, Virginia and Roger moved to Hot Springs, and a large part of Virginia's life began to revolve around the Oaklawn racetrack. Virginia estimated that she spent "a third of her life" at the Hot Springs track, and the joke around town was "God help the patient who gets sick after the bugle blows." Conveniently, Oaklawn allowed Virginia to indulge many of her appetites. The racing crowd was a close-knit community that provided ample opportunity for social intercourse for the frenetically extraverted Virginia. It was a place where people drank, smoked, and gambled. And finally, it provided fertile opportunity for extramarital affairs. Heath remembers one racetrack lover in particular: "There was this horse trainer at the cheap track—good-looking fella—she called him Adonis—I can't think of his name."

Consistent with Virginia's pattern, the Adonis was married. Apparently Virginia was quite serious about him, and hoped he would leave his wife for her, despite indications to the contrary. "This man had a wife that had a lot of money," said Heath. "We tried to tell her that, but she wouldn't listen to us. I think she finally learned the hard way. I took her to meet him one day at his motel. They smooched around the car for a while. He would always call her when he got into town—it was off and on for a long time."

Virginia even went after Heath's husband, Gabe. One night, Heath left the two of them alone at the house, but had to return unexpectedly after she had a minor car accident. "The lights were out. The doors were locked, and they didn't come down for five or ten minutes, even though I was banging on the door." When Heath mentioned this to Roger, "he whipped her that night." But nothing was ever said about the incident again and, amazingly, they continued their friendship as before.

Clinton biographers mention that there were lots of rumors about Virginia dating married doctors. Virginia tried to diffuse these rumors in her memoir, calling it harmless flirting: "I'm friendly. I'm outgoing, and I like men. Always have, always will. Men like me, too. Back then there wasn't an open war between the sexes, and there was a lot of flirting back and forth between the doctors—most of whom were men—and the nurses, who were virtually all women. It didn't mean anything."[103] Heath confirmed my suspicions that Virginia Clinton was soft-pedaling the truth: "Virginia was a big liar. No one would believe that of her, but I knew all her tricks. She could lie better than anybody. . . . Of course she went out with lots of doctors. *Lots* of married doctors. Everyone knew that." Heath remembers discussing Virginia's affairs with doctors with Virginia's best friend, Marge Mitchell: "Marge said how everyone in town knew about the doctors she went with. It was all over. It wasn't gossip. It was true."

Heath dropped another bombshell: "Uncle Roger told me that little Roger [Virginia's second son, born during her marriage to Roger Clinton] wasn't his. Roger senior said he knew because he had been sterile for years. Ina Mae said it couldn't be Roger's, because he couldn't have children. And he told me who the daddy was. I just never have told anyone his name. He's a doctor here in town." Whether Roger Jr. is aware of these claims is not known.

Though Virginia claimed that Roger's jealous rages were unfounded, she does admit to intentionally provoking his jealousy, out of spite: "He took to following me occasionally. I would be driving home from work and see him in my rearview mirror, back in traffic, but definitely watching every move I made. Sometimes, out of sheer meanness, I would lead him on a wild-goose chase."[104] But the consequences were not always so funny. Virginia's provocations could trigger the all-night rages that transformed their home into a madhouse. "I'm sure I drove him to anger on many nights when we were out," she wrote. "I won't try to pretend that I'm oblivious to the power of female sex appeal, and I certainly recognize a handsome man when I see one. I won't even deny that I was often put out with Roger and didn't mind seeing him suffer a little. But even though Roger liked to dance and was a good dancer, he usually left me sitting at the table while he went to the back room to throw dice with the boys. Then he would emerge drunk to find me dancing with someone else. . . . On nights like that our house was just bedlam from the time we got home until dawn's early light, by which time Roger would usually have yelled himself to sleep."[105]

The net result of her infidelities and her taunting was that Virginia replicated the dynamics of her parents' marriage. The parallel is not entirely lost, even on Virginia: "As Roger's life got more and more out of control, he began to terrorize me in earnest, making the same kind of wild accusations my mother had tortured my father with."[106] But throughout it all, Virginia is entirely unaware that it was she who had forced her sons to repeatedly experience the most traumatic events of her own young life. Over and over Bill and Roger had to lie in their beds, unable to block out the sound that came through the thin walls of their small home: accusing, screaming, hitting.

During the impeachment fiasco, millions of Americans simply couldn't comprehend how Bill Clinton could have committed adultery—and then looked them in the face and lied about it. Is it so incomprehensible? Not when you consider that night after night young Bill Clinton heard his mother proclaim over and over again: I did not have sex with that man.

· THE BIRTHDAY CLUB ·

In 1981, Virginia's career came to a sudden halt. It is a testimony to her entrepreneurial spirit that she had managed to stay afloat as long as she had. Though she was only a nurse, she had maintained a private practice in anaesthesiology, directly competing with M.D. anaesthesiologists for over thirty years—an incredible accomplishment. It was inevitable that the medical establishment would ultimately prevail. When Virginia and the hospital were named in a malpractice suit, after a seventeen-year-old girl died under Virginia's care (whether she made an error or not was never determined), the hospital established a policy of requiring that M.D. anaesthesiologists be used for all surgeries.

It's also a testimony to the power of Virginia's denial that she never believed this day would come. Even on the day the board of the hospital met to discuss her lawsuit, she was confident that they would back her 100 percent and continue to use her services. "We tried to warn her, but she wouldn't listen," her friend Marge Mitchell, who is also a nurse, told me. "Times had changed." Virginia's feeling of invincibility was irrational—but also very typical for a hypomanic.

The ending of her thirty-three-year career "nearly crushed me," wrote Virginia. "It was more than work. . . . It was my life. . . . I was as low as I ever remembered being."[107] In my experience, interviewing and reading biographies of hypomanic entrepreneurs for my book *The Hypomanic Edge*, the failure of a business is a point at which they are most vulnerable to becoming depressed, unless they can immediately hurl themselves into a newer and even bigger undertaking. The inevitable sense of failure, disappointment, and betrayal is bad enough, but an accompanying period of involuntary inactivity is intolerable to a hard-charging hypomanic. Having all that energy with no place for it to go is like being a caged tiger. They often develop what we call an "agitated depression," as they repetitively ruminate about their downfall, which is what happened to Virginia. She reports that she had difficulty concentrating, in part because she found herself "obsessing" about how she had been mistreated. Over and over the phrase "put out to pasture" intruded into her thoughts. She gave up performing basic tasks, like cooking. "Here I was facing this void. . . . I felt empty inside."[108]

Fortunately, Virginia married Dick Kelley, on January 17, 1982. According to Bill, Kelley was the most stable man his mother ever married. Her friends all called him a "gentleman." Kelley more or less took care of Virginia during her depression. Kelley was a sweet man to have put up with her, admitted Virginia. Semiretired, Kelley worked on Mondays. The rest of the week he was home taking care of the house (now that Virginia was no longer shopping or cooking) and contentedly "buzzing around chopping off tree limbs." Virginia was withdrawn. "When I go inside, she goes outside; when I go outside, she goes inside," Kelley complained to a friend. Virginia wanted to reenergize herself with frantic action—as she had done so many times before—but the spark plug wasn't firing. The old hypomanic engine was revving, but she couldn't get the car in gear—instead she was just obsessively grinding her gears. "On those days when Dick was gone, I would think about rolling up my sleeves and plunging into . . . cleaning out drawers." The problem was she couldn't motivate herself, even to clean a drawer. Her coping strategy was to blame Kelley: "Cleaning out drawers is a woman's thing. Then he would come back Monday night and for the rest of the week I would think, *Oh I can't clean out that drawer with Dick around*. It was an excuse but it worked. I didn't clean out the drawer and I was angry at Dick about it."

She had met Kelley at the Oaklawn racetrack, where they both had boxes. Virginia's only condition for getting married was that she be allowed to maintain her separate box with her friends. She still needed her independence.

I went to Oaklawn on a race day to see if I could speak to Kelley; I had been told that he almost never misses a race. Both physically and psychologically, Oaklawn has always occupied a central place in Hot Springs. The opening of the season is a long anticipated citywide event, and every race day has the feeling of a sporting event, a casino, and a church social all rolled into one. The box seating area is an impressive space. A gigantic sheet of glass, several stories high, is all that separates spectators from the track. When the horses round the bend, thundering toward the finish line, the ground rumbles as the hoofbeats grow stronger, and the crowd shouts louder and louder. As the horses pass, seconds before the climax, everyone is screaming. And then groans of anguish, shouts of joy, the buzz of conversation. It's all over till the next race, twenty minutes later. The boxes are divided only by a simple metal rail, as they ascend in stepwise fashion, like bleachers, from the glass at track level. This architectural form fits perfectly the social function of this space. Between races people mill about, visit, and talk, often about the bets they made: who won, who lost, and particularly which pick or combination of picks just missed. They ask after one another's families, behaving like a community of people who have known one another forever. As far back as anyone living can remember, Virginia was there.

"*Everybody* knew Virginia," Eric Jackson, manager of the track, told me. "She was always here. Always said hello to everyone."[109] Virginia became the belle of this ball.

Dick Kelley still attends races, though he is so ill it sometimes takes several security guards to help him to his box. His box is in the most coveted position, right up against the glass—as close as you can get to the race without being a jockey. He was frail and spoke slowly the day we met: "She was a very exciting woman. A very intelligent woman. She loved people. *Loved* people. She had a lot of friends." Kelley also emphasized the amount of energy that went into her career. "She worked hard. She had to get up at five every morning to be at the hospital. And she had to take care of her boys. She loved her sons. Loved those boys." His memories of their time together are very positive. "She was a great gal. We had a lot of fun. She hadn't ever been anywhere, but together we traveled around the world. We went to Hawaii, Paris, New Orleans, San Francisco, Las Vegas. We probably went to every racetrack there is. The Kentucky Derby, you name it. . . . We had a good life."

Then, in the spring of 1984, Virginia was hit by a second blow—her son Roger was arrested for dealing cocaine. He was imprisoned for all of 1985. Psychologically the roof caved in for Virginia. Looking back on that year, Virginia wrote, "I was probably clinically depressed for all of 1985." She doesn't elaborate on her symptoms, except to mention that she gained fifteen pounds. Weight gain is a very common neurovegetative sign of major depression, or as Virginia put it: "Depression is hell on a diet."[110]

However, despite the fact that she was clinically depressed, "I never once thought of going to a psychiatrist. Instead my friends and I started the Birthday Club."

Virginia and a group of her oldest and closest friends began to meet every Friday at a local restaurant to "hoot, and laugh, and have a couple of drinks to wash our cares away. . . . The Birthday Club is more than a bunch of rowdy old ladies who like to drink at noon; it's a life support system."[111]

Virginia had been dead for twelve years when I visited Hot Springs, and a number of the Birthday Club's original members had also died. But those in the Birthday Club who are still alive continue to meet once a month at Fisherman's Wharf. The oldest member, Clover Gibson, was just a few weeks from her hundredth birthday when I visited. Membership is frozen at twelve women, and a new member can only join when an old one dies or quits. Many of the Birthday Club members were women whom Virginia had met at Oaklawn.

When I entered the back room of Fisherman's Wharf, Berenice Lyon, age ninety, whom I had spoken to over the phone to arrange the visit, hugged me tight, like an old friend.

"When did you get in? Why didn't you call me to let me know if there was anything you needed? Do you need anything? You come right here and sit with me."

The women asked me to say a few words about why I was there. I explained that I was a psychologist writing a biography of Clinton, and I believed that past biographers had neglected the role played by Virginia. Before all the people who knew Virginia passed on, I wanted to record their recollections. Clearly, they were touched. In short order, these women who had just met me were treating me like family.

The day I came happened to be Marge Mitchell's birthday, and on that basis she insisted that I sit next to her. She interjected, "It's my birthday; you bring that handsome young man over here next to me."

"Oh, since when do you need a birthday to give orders?" one of her friends quipped.

Clearly, I was the guest of honor, but instead of making me feel comfortable, their kindness was making me anxious. After my conversations with her high school boyfriend, Richard Fenwick, and her friend Virginia Heath, I knew I would be revealing things about Virginia that would look pretty scandalous in most people's eyes. But now these older women, who were treating me so graciously, regarded her as their patron saint. They'd kept the flame of their faith in her alive, and I was about to desecrate the memory of their beloved Virginia. I felt like a Judas.

The nicer they were, the worse I felt. I looked around the room and saw only warm smiles. A feeling of panic lodged in my chest, as if a metal band surrounded it, making it difficult to breathe. They all wanted to talk to me, touch me, take my picture, ask me questions, laugh at my jokes, and tell me their stories. They asked how long I was staying. When was I coming back? Would I bring my family next time? Did I have pictures? Marge Mitchell announced that "tomorrow you're going to be my guest at the races, and after that some friends are taking me out for my birthday, and you're coming! I don't want to hear no argument about that."

"Doesn't he just look like a young Bill Clinton?" Marge Mitchell declared.

"He does. He really does!" Nancy Adkins agreed enthusiastically.

"Come on now! Get our picture," Marge demanded, and the flash went off.

Woman after woman talked about how loving Virginia was. One woman remembered how Virginia had faithfully visited the woman's mother when she was a patient in the hospital. She always knew Virginia had come for a visit because of the bright red lipstick print she found on her mother's forehead. They spoke of her charisma, how when she sauntered into a room, she filled it with energy and immediately became its focus. She was exuberant and fun loving. Her infectious, positive energy made everyone around her feel good. She was colorful—her clothes, her famous makeup, and her personality. She was a "character," an "original," always very much herself—a fully genuine person. "The only fake thing about her were her eyelashes" was one line from a poem Rachel Heffernan wrote in tribute to Virginia after her death.*

---

* Heffernan later mailed me the poem:
  Remembering My Friend Virginia Clinton Kelley

I liked the way Virginia lit up a room when she walked in.
I liked the genuine way she had of making you feel special.
I liked her unique love of people from all walks of life.
I liked the way she never changed, even though she had the honor of being the president's mother.
I liked the fact that the only thing false about her were her eyelashes.
I liked her ability to cope with adverse situations.
I liked her laughter, it was contagious.
I liked her hands. They were always reaching out to shake with a stranger, or hug a friend.

Berenice Lyon said: "Let me tell you about Virginia, she was a very, very caring person. I've lived a long time, and I've just never known anyone who cared so much about people. I worked for a group of doctors for thirty years, and I never saw anyone who cared about her patients as much as she did. She radiated something. . . . It just flowed out of her. When you were with her, you just felt good. She didn't exactly live by the book. And she didn't give a hootenanny what anyone thought about it either! But, I want to ask you something: How many people do you know who *care,* really care about other people? Stop and think: How many?"[112]

This exceptional combination of charisma and a capacity to feel and communicate love is a trait that Bill Clinton became famous for. It was an essential ingredient in what made him "the most talented politician in a generation."[113]

And in this way, too, he takes after his mother.

· A CONVERSATION WITH BILL'S "SECOND MOTHER" ·

After the Birthday Club, I drove with Marge Mitchell to her house for an interview. Marge Mitchell might as well have been Bill Clinton's second mother. She and Virginia saw each other or spoke every day for fifty years. Marge and Virginia called each other "sister," because they felt as close as sisters, and neither had ever had a biological sibling. They met at Oaklawn, where Marge worked as the track nurse at the time.

Marge is a spirited, short, thin, blond woman, with tan skin weathered from a lifetime of sun, and a piercing gravelly voice, from a lifetime of smoking. Every room in her home, where we met, has a beautiful view of Lake Hamilton, whose waters practically lap up to the deck that wraps around the back of her house. The house itself is crowded with tchotchkes, and every wall is covered with pictures of Bill Clinton. There are pictures of him at every age, playing his saxophone, spitting watermelon

---

I liked her heart. It was as big as the world.
I liked her stamina. She kept on keeping on, no matter what came her way.
I liked her joy of living, and live she did with so much zest.
I liked her way of sharing her good times.
I liked "Virginia Clinton Kelley." I think she knew this.

seeds, standing in the sun, beaming. It struck me how radiant he was in all of them. Whatever that magical aura is that he has, he has clearly always had it.

Marge said that she always thought of herself as Bill's second mother. She used to drive Bill wherever he needed to go when Virginia was working, which was often. Bill and his gang of friends spent many hours at Marge's house, his home away from home. The door was never locked, and she made the atmosphere as inviting as possible. Marge liked having young people around. There was a pool table in the basement, a piano Bill loved to play, and a powerboat at his disposal. After Bill went away to college, he always returned to hang out at the Mitchells' house with his girlfriends. Marge said these girls still keep in touch with her. Bill was particularly close to her late husband, a judge, who served as a role model for him. Overall, the Mitchells' home was both a safe and a welcoming place for Bill. "Me and my husband never argued," Marge said. "He told me once that only lawyers get paid to argue, so why fool with it? And so we didn't. It was a very peaceful house. Even the physical atmosphere, by the water here, is peaceful. And I think that's one of the things Bill liked about it." Compared to the hellacious fighting at his own home, the Mitchells' lakeside retreat must have been a welcome refuge.

"I'm a believer in the ministry of presence. Do you know what I mean by that? Virginia was present. She was always there, really *there* with you. Anything you needed, she would be there. Virginia and I could have been sisters. When it comes to people we don't care what you got, or what you don't got. If someone's in need, we want to be there. It's not that we're saints. I sure ain't no saint. But it's just people you meet every day in life that need some help from you, and you gotta help 'em. Most of the time when you've helped somebody, you've helped yourself a lot more."

She meandered, for over an hour, about any number of topics. She was clearly someone who could talk and talk. But I felt helpless to interrupt her and direct the interview because I didn't feel comfortable asking about what was really on my mind: Virginia's sex life. Finally, I could stand it no longer. I had to broach the topic that was driving me to distraction. "I've heard rumors that Virginia was involved with a number of men," I said, nervous about how she might react.

"She probably was," Marge replied matter-of-factly. "But I think if two people are twenty-one, that's their business. As far as any marriages she broke up, no, I don't think so. Yah, she was a flirt. She was very friendly. She was a toucher. She was a hugger. But she never really broke up anyone's marriage."

Relieved and encouraged, I pressed further:

"I spoke with Virginia Heath. And she said that Virginia had affairs with doctors while she was married to Roger."

"One doctor, at least, that's probably true." Marge nodded. "But it didn't break up a marriage. Maybe that's not the right gauge. But I knew those people, and I never heard there was a real problem. That couple never got a divorce. They stayed together. . . . Sister was in a bad marriage then."

I gently challenged the notion that Virginia had never broken up a marriage:

"Well, Virginia Heath says that she *did* break up Roger's marriage to Ina Mae. In her memoir, Virginia says she didn't know that he was still married, but Virginia Heath says she knew Roger was married when she met him, and Virginia separated him from his wife."

Marge waved her hand dismissively: "Well, everyone knew that."

"Everyone knew that?" I asked.

"Well, sure. She set her goals on him. That's an open book."

I mentioned that Virginia Heath had also claimed that Virginia separated her third husband, Jeff Dwire, from his wife.

"I think so. She spent an awful lot of time in that beauty shop. [Dwire and his wife owned and ran a salon together.] I mean, she went every week, and had an opportunity."

While I had felt like Judas, betraying all these believers, when Marge spoke, the constriction in my chest vanished. I could breathe. It was OK. Marge knew about Virginia's sexual behavior, and she wasn't defensive or feigning ignorance about it. It just wasn't that important to her, not compared to what she felt *really* mattered. The facts were the same, but now suddenly the picture looked completely different, as if the foreground and background were suddenly reversed. Up till that point I had been thinking with gathering force: "She's a nice lady but . . . oh my God, she really slept around!" Now that "truth" seemed turned on its head. You could just as easily say: "OK, so she had a lot of affairs . . . but what an amazing person to have touched those around her so profoundly." The truth was so subjective, depending on how one interpreted it.

"Would it be fair and accurate to say that you knew about the affairs but you accepted them, as part of her? That what mattered most to you was her friendship, her 'presence,' her love?"

Marge smiled, pleased that I really got it. Thinking out loud, I said, "Maybe it's hard for people to understand, with both Virginia and Bill, that infidelity can coexist with a profound capacity for love."

"Bill Clinton was a pro at affairs. Ain't nobody gonna deny that. That's part of him," Marge said.

Then she grabbed a picture off the table next to us.

"But, look at this picture," she said. Taken in the White House, the photo shows Bill Clinton hugging Marge from behind, looking into the camera with a big beaming smile.

"I've known Bill Clinton almost all his life. And he has always been the most loving person. You see here, he's hugging me so tight, nearly broke my neck, and you can see the love he has in his eyes. If he thought I needed something, there isn't anywhere he would be other than Hot Springs. He would never be too busy. That's true for me, for the whole bunch you met today, even for some baby he don't even know. He is for real. Bill Clinton is for real. He is the most real person. Look at his eyes. Can you feel the love? That's real. Can you feel it?"

"Yes, I can feel it," I said. And I could. His blue eyes seemed to reach through the picture and touch me. It was a kinesthetic sensation I had never felt before.

As I stood on her doorstep ready to leave, Marge grabbed my hand. "You have a chance to tell the world who Bill Clinton really is. You don't know the favor you're doing the world. And I admire you."

Then she tightened her grip—and looked at me more intently.

"It's a very important mission, and I think you are the one who will write it like it is. Make sure you get it *right*. And you tell 'em. Tell 'em who Bill Clinton is."

I squeezed her hand back

"I promise you, Marge," I said, hoping to reassure her, "I'll do my very best to get it right."[114]

2

Searching for Bill Clinton's Father

Clinton never knew his father. Because Bill Blythe was killed before he was born, there was no father-son relationship to influence his psychic development. The major thing his father contributed to his personality was his genes.

So to better understand Clinton's genetic endowment, I began to research Bill Blythe and his family. But as I pursued my research, I came across an unexpected obstacle: No one was certain who Bill Clinton's biological father really was. According to Virginia, Clinton's father was her deceased husband, William Blythe. But since the day Bill Clinton was born, people have had their doubts. I soon realized that before I could speculate about the genes he had inherited, I had to try to figure out whom he had inherited them from. My search for Bill Clinton's father became a strange piece of detective work.

Virginia wrote, "Bill came home in November, 1945." After Blythe was discharged from the army, he made a brief stop at his parents' home in Texas and then met Virginia in Shreveport, where they had first met. This was partly for sentimental reasons and partly for practical ones. "After all, I was living at home in the room next door to my parents', and Bill and I had a lot of catching up to do."[1] Bill Blythe was eager to get started with his new life, Virginia wrote. And "he was going to start working on becoming a father immediately."[2]

Almost exactly nine months later, on August 19, 1946, Bill Clinton was born.

There is, however, an awkward discrepancy in this story. Bill Blythe was *not* discharged in November, as Virginia claimed. According to army records unearthed by David Maraniss, which he discussed in his book *First in His Class,* Blythe was discharged on December 7, *eight* months before Bill Clinton was born.

Nine months before Bill Clinton was born, Bill Blythe was in Italy.

Maraniss was not the first to notice this discrepancy. "For years afterward, there were whispers in Hope about who little Billy's father was, rumors spawned by Virginia's flirtatious nature as a young nurse and by inevitable temptations of people to count backwards nine months from the birth date to see who was where doing what."

Joe Purvis has been a lifelong friend of Clinton's, literally. Their mothers pushed their baby carriages together down the streets of Hope. "I've heard rumors about who Billy's father is for a long time," Purvis told me. "I asked my daddy one time. He just smiled and said: 'Gosh, we just don't know.' But I could tell he knew a lot he wasn't saying."

Along with Maraniss, the other biographer who has pursued the paternity issue is Nigel Hamilton, author of *Bill Clinton: An American Journey.* He asked scores of Clinton friends and relatives about the issue and found that "when questioned on tape half a century later, most relatives and friends of Virginia's simply shrugged or went silent, wishing to speak no ill of the dead." However, he added, when speaking off-the-record or not for attribution, "Not a single one in confidence believed Bill Blythe had been the child's father."[3]

In an interview in January 1992, Maraniss confronted Virginia with his discovery that War Department records showed Blythe did not return until December. Virginia explained it away by saying that she had suffered a dangerous fall, and her doctor had insisted on inducing labor a month early. "I think she was defensive about it," he told me.

But if Virginia's story is true, why didn't she relay that same version of the events when she dictated her memoir to Jim Morgan in 1993? Why lie, saying he came home in November? It is also revealing that Virginia makes no mention in her memoir of this dramatic fall that supposedly led to the urgent need for a c-section? I asked Jim Morgan, Virginia's co-author, if Virginia had ever mentioned anything to him about a fall or needing to be induced early when she told him the story of Bill's birth. She hadn't.

Indeed, I could find no one who recalled such a fall. The doctor who delivered Bill Clinton is dead, but I spoke to the nurse who was in the delivery room at the time, Wilma Rowe Booker, now ninety years old.

"I was the first person to spank Bill Clinton's butt, ha, ha," she cackled. "But I wasn't the last."

She reports that Bill was indeed delivered by cesarean section, but has no recollection as to why. She recalls no discussion of any fall or any sort of accident that required them to operate. However, that proves little, because she was not familiar with the details of Virginia's case or care. "They just pulled me off the floor and said go to the OR."

Richard Fenwick held Bill Clinton in the hospital the day he was born. "Five or six of us were at the Diamond Cafe by old Highway 67, and somebody said, 'Virginia had that baby.'" Richard and his buddies piled into the car and rushed to the hospital. Happily, they passed the young infant around.

"Did she mention having an accident before Bill was born?" I asked.

"An accident?"

"She didn't say anything about having had a fall, or needing to induce the baby early because of a fall?"

"That's not ringing any bells. I believe that she would have told me if she had fallen."[4]

What we know about the pregnancy and delivery does not suggest that the baby was anything but full term. For example, Virginia clearly recalled that she had morning sickness, sometime "before Christmas 1945." Since we know that Blythe stopped home in Sherman, Texas, before meeting Virginia, the second week in December is the earliest they could have met in Shreveport. Even if she conceived at the very first opportunity, which is unlikely in itself, it would be highly unusual (though not impossible) for her to experience morning sickness less than two weeks later. Most cases of morning sickness occur between four and six weeks of pregnancy.

The known details of the birth also suggest full-term delivery. The obvious first question is: What did the baby weigh? Unfortunately, different biographers report different birth weights. Maraniss reported six pounds eight ounces. Biographer Nigel Hamilton reported seven and a half pounds. And Hillary Clinton biographer Gail Sheehy reported that Virginia said he was eight and a half pounds. All of these figures are based on recollections or what Virginia recorded in her baby book. For some reason, no one has been able to obtain the actual birth certificate. But anyway, none of these are low birth weights, which would be a clear indicator of premature birth.

Wilma Rowe Booker didn't remember the birth weight, but did recall that "he was a big, pink, healthy-looking full-term baby." She told me, quite emphatically: "There is absolutely no way he was premature. I was a nurse forty years. I know what a premature baby looks like. He wasn't small, wrinkled, or lethargic. He never needed an incubator."[5]

Fenwick also recalled no discussion of Bill being premature. "He wasn't premature. He wasn't early, except maybe by an hour or two."

What does Bill Clinton know or believe? We don't really know. In his autobiography Clinton affirms the Blythe story, of course, but there are hints that he may have his doubts about whether Blythe was really his father. One person who did speak on-the-record to Hamilton was a close Clinton friend, Jim Blair. "In my own opinion, Blythe is not the father," he said. Blair recalled an incident in which a Louisiana man "insisted that his dad had been out with Virginia about nine months before Bill Clinton was born and that Bill Clinton was a dead ringer for his brother." Rumors like this had swirled for years, but what is significant here is that Blair discussed the rumor with Clinton. Blair claims that Clinton said that he believed the story "might be true."[6] In other words, Clinton is unsure of his paternity. He just doesn't know.

One hint that Clinton might not believe that Blythe was his father is the way he has related to his alleged half siblings or, more to the point, not related to them. Clinton being Clinton, we would expect him to reach out and embrace them—if he was confident that they were the children of his biological father. Not only has he not made any effort to get to know his supposed half siblings, it appears as if he has been avoiding them.

On Father's Day 1993, *The Washington Post* broke the story that Bill Clinton had a half brother, Leon Ritzenthaler, the retired owner of a janitorial services company living in northern California. On the second page of *My Life,* Clinton describes what happened: "In the article he [Leon] said that he had written me during the '92 campaign, but he had received no reply. I don't remember hearing about his letter, and considering all the other bullets we were dodging then, it's possible that my staff kept it from me. Or maybe the letter was just misplaced in the mountain of mail we were receiving."[7] Obviously, after the *Washington Post* article, Clinton had to meet his long-lost brother. He did meet him, but only once, and then only when he happened to be in northern California on a campaign stop. "Since then we've corresponded in holiday seasons," Clinton wrote, which suggests that Ritzenthaler is merely one of thousands of people on Clinton's Christmas card list. Clearly Clinton has kept contact to a bare minimum.

In the case of his possible half sister, the contact has been less than minimal, and Clinton can offer no explanation as to why. "Somewhere around this time, I also received information confirming news stories about a daughter, Sharon Pettijohn, born Sharon Lee Blythe in Kansas City in 1941, to a woman my father later divorced. She sent copies of her birth certificate, her parents' marriage license, a photo of my father, and a letter to her mother from my father asking about 'our baby,' to Betsey Wright, my former chief of staff in the governor's office. I'm sorry to say, for whatever reason, I've never met her."[8]

And all this from a man who claims, I'm sure sincerely, to have hungered all his life for even the smallest scrap of information about his real father. If he thought Blythe was his real father, wouldn't he want to learn all he could about him from his other two children?

Another tantalizing clue, revealed in Carl Bernstein's 2007 biography of Hillary Clinton, is that nine boxes of Clinton's papers were taken home and later hidden in a vault by Betsey Wright. These files have never been made public. "There were a number of things I thought too sensitive to be left in those general files," said Wright. What was in these ultrasensitive documents? Wright listed several things, but the first one she mentioned was "my working files on Clinton's father."[9]

On balance the preponderance of the evidence seems to suggest that Bill Blythe is likely not Bill Clinton's father, and Clinton at least suspects as much.

But then, who is? "I'm kind of surprised that no one has tried to solve this mystery," Joe Purvis said. "Who's his daddy?"

I did try to solve it.

At the time I wrestled with whether this was the right thing to do. I was seeking to neither embarrass Clinton nor invade his privacy. And functioning in my new role as psychologist–investigative journalist, a profession which essentially never existed before, I had no precedent or principles to guide me as to where the ethical boundaries might lie. I had vowed to devote myself to solving the mystery of Bill Clinton's psyche, and here was 50 percent of his DNA unaccounted for. The more we learn in the field of genetics, the more of behavior we discover is genetic. In the end I elected to seek the answer and let the chips fall where they may.

David Maraniss told me that he had heard of a reputed father living in Louisiana. One of the man's sons contacted Maraniss and told him that his father claimed "he had fooled around with 'Hop-Along Cassidy' when she was a nurse, in Shreveport, and believed that he was Bill Clinton's father." Maraniss scheduled an interview with the Louisiana man, but before they could meet the alleged father passed away. Maraniss dropped the investigation. Something about the whole thing felt wrong to him from the start. "The guy seemed a little squirrelly." Maraniss couldn't recall his name thirteen years later when we spoke.

While there have been a plethora of rumors about who Clinton's father might be, within Hope itself, among the people who were actually there when he was born, "there was this presumption that it was this doctor in town," Maraniss said, though he couldn't honestly recall his name either.

All of this was mere speculation, until I spoke with a journalist who covered the Clinton family for many years. He did not wish to be identified. Over a decade ago he, too, heard the same rumor about a doctor from Hope, and an old friend of Clinton's told the reporter the reputed father's name. The doctor still lived in Hope, and rumor had it that he too had a son who looked just like Clinton. Without making mention of the paternity issue, the reporter called this doctor to schedule an interview. He said only that he was doing research on Clinton's family during their years in Hope. The doctor sounded "real nervous and jumpy." Unlike the squirrely man from Louisiana, who seemed to be seeking publicity, the doctor from Hope seemed eager to avoid it. The doctor agreed to the interview, but only with anxious reluctance. The reporter drove several hours to Hope to meet him, and the doctor knew that he was traveling a long distance, but when the reporter arrived at the appointed meeting spot, the doctor no-showed without explanation or apology. "I thought that spoke volumes," the reporter said. It certainly sounded like the behavior of someone who might be hiding something. Like Maraniss, this reporter could not recall the man's name, which I found somewhat maddening.

However, I discovered that there were not many doctors in Hope at the tail end of World War II. Drawing on both the records of the Arkansas Medical Society and the recollection of people who lived in Hope at the time, I was able to identify only six doctors. Because the military had taken most of the young doctors, all but two of the doctors in town at that time were elderly.

When presented with the list, my reporter quickly recognized the name of Dr. George Wright as the man he had tried to interview. Maraniss, too, confirmed by e-mail that George Wright was the name he had been trying to remember. Wright was one of the two doctors in town who were not senior citizens.

Virginia had told Virginia Heath that she had an affair with a doctor in Hope. I asked her if George Wright was the doctor Virginia had talked about. She said it sounded familiar, but she couldn't be sure. The name George sounded right, though. There was only one doctor named George in Hope.

Dr. Wright is now deceased. And thus, the trail quite literally appeared to go dead. What could I do to take the inquiry any further? I decided to go to Hope, Arkansas. When I arrived the first place I headed for was the tiny local public library, where I had been told I could find a complete collection of Hope High School yearbooks. I came bearing a portable scanner, hunting for photos of the Wright brothers, to see for myself if, as rumor had it, they bore a resemblance to young man Clinton. The yearbooks are housed in a small room entitled "genealogy research center," and it is maintained by an auxiliary of elderly women interested in the history of Hope. Thumbing through the yearbooks, I was not at first overly impressed by a strong resemblance. Half brothers often don't look that much alike. But then I saw a picture of Dr. Wright's oldest son, Larry Wright, as a sophomore, that sent a chill through me. Though I couldn't articulate precisely what features made the likeness so uncanny, the boy who shook President Kennedy's hand seemed to be staring straight at me.

"You look like you found something," said a woman sitting at the next table, who appeared to be in her eighties. She was there with a friend, and I figured that she was one of the volunteers who informally maintained this room. When I explained what I was doing, she said: "I know who Bill Clinton's father is, but I'm not naming any names."

"Really? Does it begin with a W?" I asked, showing her the yearbook picture of Larry Wright.

Larry Wright and Bill Clinton, head to head (from their yearbook photos).

"As a matter of fact, it does. Dr. George Wright was Bill Clinton's father. Everyone in town knew that."

"Everyone knew? I heard that there were lots of different rumors about a variety of suspected fathers."

"Oh, no. There were not lots of different rumors. There was one rumor, and it was no rumor. Everyone in Hope knew it was Dr. Wright."

"How did you know it was Dr. Wright?"

"I had personal knowledge."

"*Personal knowledge?*" I asked, trying to imagine what that could possibly be.

"One of Dr. Wright's best friends told me that Wright said to him: 'I'm Billy Blythe's father.'"

The woman did not wish to give her name. "I still live a few blocks from all these people," she said. But I found others in Hope who confirmed that Dr. Wright being Clinton's father was an open secret in this town of a few thousand.

The only thing left to do was to interview George Wright Jr., one of Dr. Wright's sons, who was still living in Hope. I was anxious about the meeting. What did he already know or suspect? How would he react?

I met with George Wright Jr. in his home in Hope. I had told him over the phone that I was researching a book about Clinton, without mentioning the paternity question. Wright and Clinton, who are the same age, were kindergarten classmates, and he had been interviewed before by past biographers on that basis, so he wasn't surprised to hear from another author. Wright was a tanned, tall, handsome man with piercing blue eyes and salt-and-pepper hair. On one hand, I could see why people might say that he bears a resemblance to Bill Clinton, but on the other, it wasn't a striking one.

"I can tell you how Bill and I became friends. It's because of our parents. Our families were friends. His mother and my father and my mother were in the medical field. When my dad moved here he set up practice, almost immediately, in May of forty-six. Virginia helped Dad set up his office, and worked for him, right off the bat." I had never seen mention of this close personal and professional relationship between Virginia and Dr. Wright, so I was intrigued to learn of this.

When I finally broached the topic that had brought me there, much to my relief George Wright was not perturbed. He waved his hand dismissively and said, "I've been hearing that rumor for years and years. People ask me that all the time. I've heard that, and heard that. People always say, 'You two look alike.' We're both about the same height with blue eyes.

"The thing is, it's just not possible, because my father didn't move to Hope until the spring of forty-six." Dr. Wright bought their family home and started his practice on April 8—the date sticks out because it was also the day George Jr. was born—which would suggest that Dr. Wright met Virginia too late for him to have fathered Bill Clinton, who was born four months later in August.

However, as he and I talked, it became clear that it was far from impossible. Dr. Wright was discharged from the air force and returned from England in the summer of 1945, a year before Clinton was born. And while Dr. Wright only moved to Hope in April 1946, it would be logical to assume that he had made at least one trip to Hope before relocating there. I pointed this out to George Wright, who said, "I never really thought about that, but I guess you don't just drive into town with a moving truck, not without checking the place out first."

In fact, now that he thought about it, Wright had a vague memory of having heard the story of how his father had met with members of the medical community to see if Hope had a need for a general practitioner before moving to town. As mentioned earlier, it was a pretty small circle, about half a dozen doctors who had privileges at the Julia Chester Hospital, where Virginia worked.

Though it is speculation, one imagines that a doctor visiting Hope on a mission to meet and greet the local medical community would have found the exuberantly gregarious and flirtatious young Virginia hard to miss. That Virginia helped him set up his office—"right off the bat"—almost as soon as he arrived, at least suggests the possibility that they had formed some kind of relationship before he actually moved there.

One of my aims was to learn as much about Dr. Wright as I could. If he indeed was Clinton's father, here I would find half the genes that helped produce this remarkable person. Like Clinton, Dr. Wright was an intellectually gifted self-made man. His father abandoned the family when he was just fourteen, leaving him, his mother, and his four siblings to fend for themselves. "He was poor, dirt poor." Through his intelligence and hard work, he graduated from high school at age sixteen. For four long years he worked in his brother-in-law's cotton field to earn the money for college, where he completed all the requirements for medical school in an amazing two and a half years. He was accepted into Louisiana State University medical school, but after he was accepted the dean wrote him a letter, informing him regretfully that while he had completed all his premed requirements and been admitted, it was a university rule that students must have completed at least three years of college. He would have to finish one more semester before beginning medical school. "He hitchhiked from Shreveport to New Orleans to see this dean of the medical school, and explained to him that he didn't have enough money for another semester—and they let him into LSU." At his fiftieth medical school reunion one of his classmates recalled that George Wright was "the poorest person I ever met in medical school."

Like Bill Clinton, Dr. Wright was a workaholic: "He was married to medicine. The only meal we ever saw him was breakfast." And like Clinton, Wright typically functioned on little sleep. "Your body doesn't need as much sleep as you think it does" was one of his mottos. But it is unclear whether, like Bill Clinton, he truly had a diminished need for sleep or had simply learned to adapt to the requirements of covering the medical needs of a whole town.

Like Clinton, he could be intermittently explosive, especially when he was tired: "He had a Scotch-Irish temper."

And like Bill Clinton he was very intelligent. "He was bright, a real bright guy." Though he was only a general practitioner in a small town, he had a considerable reputation in southwest Arkansas, especially for his knowledge of cardiology (specialists were a rarity in rural Arkansas in the 1940s). Several other people in Hope had emphasized to me how smart Dr. Wright was, and how bright his children are. George Wright Jr., who admits that school was never his thing, possibly due to an undiagnosed learning disability, is the least academically inclined of the siblings. He sells cars for a living. But both of his brothers are professionals. His brother Randy, an attorney, has served as the district area prosecutor (a job similar to Bill's former position as state attorney general) and may soon become a judge. Their brother Larry, a doctor, is medical director for an elder care center in northwest Arkansas, and a national expert on gerontology.

Bill Clinton's astounding intelligence had made me suspect that a rumor about his father being a doctor made sense, at least genetically, since intelligence is largely inheritable. Clinton's IQ is off the map, higher really than we can measure. The theory that Bill got his intelligence from Virginia had always seemed inadequate to me. She was, according to everyone who knew her, very smart indeed. But as bright as Virginia was, no one ever accused her of being an intellectual. Her son Roger said that she had "street smarts," an assessment Virginia herself thought was accurate. "She'd been around. You couldn't run a con game on her, just couldn't do it," Carol Willis told me. But she was not a reader with an interest in ideas. Could Bill Blythe have supplied those genes? It seems unlikely. There is simply no evidence that Bill Blythe—drifter, bigamist, and high school dropout—was in any way gifted. Blythe's other son was in the janitorial services business.

Bill Clinton has been a voracious reader from a very early age. "I was reading little books when I was three,"[10] Clinton said. Several people in Hope confirmed that Bill Clinton not only read by the age of three, but read prolifically. "Everybody knew he was going to be something. He was so smart. He was reading books at three and four. While a lot of kids were out in the yard playing in the sand, Bill was reading," recalled Jenny Sue McKee. "He started reading the newspaper in first grade," said Virginia.[11] Lifetime friend Patty Criner said Clinton "reads nonstop" and has "since he was a kid." It was a joke among his friends: "Hey, want to go over to Bill's house and watch him read?" As an adult he is always reading at least three books at any one time, and with what is often described as a photographic memory, he seems to retain virtually everything he reads. Hillary Clinton has said that there is "hardly ever" a moment when Bill is not reading: "If he could get away with it he'd read when he drove. He'd read all the time."[12]

In fact, research comparing identical and fraternal twins seems to suggest that roughly 50 percent of reading ability is inherited. Assuming that there are reading genes (the actual genes have yet to be isolated), Clinton could have inherited them from Dr. Wright, who was also an inveterate reader. "I always saw him reading—always keeping up with what was happening in medicine," said George Wright Jr., "I don't think he ever watched TV." Like Clinton, Dr. Wright was always reading more than one thing at a time. Wright recalled that his father always had a huge stack of books and journals on the table next to his chair that he was actively reading at any one time. He also had a large, overstuffed library in his office. He remembers his father sitting in that chair, wearing his reading glasses with an intent look of concentration, reading for hours, not looking up, even when he and his brothers wrought total mayhem throughout the house. "I used to tease him that the wrinkle in between his eyebrows was from the intense look of concentration he wore on his face when he was reading."

Wright remembered that Virginia and Roger Clinton were frequent guests in their home. While his parents socialized with the Clintons, he and Bill would run off and play. But when Bill turned seven, Virginia and Roger Clinton moved to Hot Springs. It would have been easy to lose touch at that point, as so often happens to young friends when people move. However, Dr. Wright established a new annual tradition. Every summer he rented a house on Lake Hamilton in Hot Springs during his annual two-week vacation. Every summer, young Bill would spend a large part of the Wrights' vacation living with them on the lake. If Bill Clinton was his biological child, Dr. Wright had cleverly found a way to have annual visitation with his son without anyone being the wiser.

Wright admitted he'd always wondered if there might be anything to the rumors. "If you had any information that helped zero in on this, I'd be interested."

When I shared with him what I knew. Wright was taken aback. "Is that so? We'll I'll be. . . . I think we both need another beer!"

Wright disappeared for a moment, heading back to his garage, where he keeps his beer refrigerated. I stared across the table at his beer can. I had rehearsed this moment in my head many times, when imagining the day I would meet George Wright Jr. Ultimately, only a DNA test would solve this mystery. And for that I would need either a piece of him, or something which he had recently touched and conveniently deposited some saliva into—something like the beer can now inches away from my hand. I hesitated. It was wrong, I knew, from about half a dozen vantage points . . . and yet, the *answer* was right in front of me . . . but should I really cross this line? While I struggled with temptation, the window of opportunity closed. George Wright reemerged, holding two beers.

"Here you go. You know, you've just given me more information than I've gotten in my whole life about this. Wow. I've always wanted to say to Bill: Hey, all this crap about us being half brothers, is there anything to that?"

I explained that there was a way to know for sure. It would involve a DNA test. A sample of his DNA could be cross-referenced with Clinton's DNA, which I imagined might be available from the infamous blue Gap dress through the Freedom of Information Act.

"I wouldn't do anything like that, I mean, not behind Bill's back. But if he were willing . . . That would be interesting. I would like to find out. I would like to do that DNA deal. It would just be nice to know."

3

One in a Quadrillion

· HITTING THE GENETIC JACKPOT ·

Even the most virulent Clinton critics would not deny that Clinton is extraordinarily gifted. Before we even consider the effect of Bill Clinton's childhood on the formation of his personality and career, we need to examine his genetic endowment. Like Secretariat, to whom he has been compared, Clinton was simply born with more God-given political talent than any of his contemporaries. Statistically, Clinton is a freak of nature.

In his profile of Clinton for *GQ*, George Saunders speculated: "My guess is that if you rated a million people on the basis of aptitude and verbal skills, and powers of persuasion and retention and simple physical energy, Clinton would come out near the top in all categories."[1] I think Saunders is right in his intuition that Clinton wasn't just born off the chart. He was born off multiple charts.

There are probably more, but I will discuss five of those traits. Two, mentioned by Saunders, are *intelligence* and *energy* (one component of hypomanic temperament). In addition, Clinton is a statistical outlier on three core inborn dimensions of personality that we will discuss shortly: *intellectual curiosity, empathy,* and *extraversion.*

There is an impressive body of research pointing to intellectual curiosity, empathy, and extraversion as foundational dimensions of personality. For a hundred years academic personality psychologists have been trying to identify and name the basic axes on which to map the human personality. In recent years the "five factor" theory, developed by Paul Costa and Robert McCrae at the National Institutes of Health, has won a surprisingly unanimous degree of acceptance in the field. In searching to solve this old problem they turned to an improbable source: the dictionary. Where past personality psychologists had started with abstract theories about human nature, and then looked for data to validate it, Costa and McCrae built from the ground up. They reasoned that because we are social creatures, collectively we have made many nuanced observations about personality traits that have become part of the language: Using a complex statistical technique called "factor analysis," Costa and McCrae were able to boil down the eighteen thousand traits found in the dictionary to five basic megafactors. I will argue that Clinton is extraordinary on three of them.*

Research using the five-factor model has shown that these basic building blocks of personality are largely innate, and family environment has surprisingly little impact. "It turns out that you get virtually identical results with identical twins reared apart and identical twins reared together," said McCrae. And, in turn, adopted children, who share the same family environment with their adopted siblings, but no genes, show no correlation in their personalities with their adopted siblings. "They are as similar to one another as any two people picked at random." In essence, then, these measures of personality are measures of temperament, genetically based, inborn, fundamental predispositions. So if Clinton is exceptional, it is because he was born that way.

On three of the five dimensions of personality uncovered by Costa and McCrae, all data converge to put Bill Clinton off the charts. From my questioning of people who knew him at every stage of his life, it is clear that he had these tendencies since he was a toddler, and manifested them throughout his life. When we add to these three personality variables his astoundingly superior intelligence and his enormous hypomanic energy, we have our own five-factor model to explain Bill Clinton.

---

* The other two, which I will not discuss here, are *neuroticism* and *conscientiousness*.

That Clinton is an outlier on so many traits is one clue as to why he is such a rare specimen. The odds of two independent events both taking place are equal to the odds of the first event multiplied by the odds of the second. For example, while the odds of flipping a coin and getting heads are 50 percent, the odds of flipping two coins and getting heads both times are 25 percent (½ multiplied by ½). Even if we estimate conservatively, and say Clinton is only one out of a thousand on each of these five dimensions, the odds of one person being that extreme on five independent traits is one thousandth to the fifth power, or one out of a quadrillion.

· A MIND THAT WON'T QUIT ·

Intellectual curiosity is a large component of a core personality dimension that Costa and McCrae have labeled "openness to experience." By any measure Clinton is extreme on this trait: "He is insatiably curious about everything," said Hillary.[2]

His omnivorous curiosity leads Clinton to read everything. Betsey Wright, who served for a decade as his chief of staff when he was governor, noted: "It is truly one of the things that distinguishes him from most active politicians, that *he never stops reading*. Most politicians don't have the time for it, and furthermore, convince themselves that they pretty much know what they need to know. And he never knew enough! He never read enough! He always had three or four books going—*always*!"[3] One of the frequent comments one hears about Bill Clinton is that there is no topic he doesn't know something about. William Coleman, one of Clinton's law school roommates, noticed that Clinton never seemed to sleep, but instead, each night read through a rather eclectic selection of books. "I would go to bed, get up at six, and find him on the same couch reading a completely different book—a murder mystery, Schopenhauer, a Thomas Wolfe novel, or a book on foreign policy."[4]

Add to this the fact that since he was a child, Clinton has had the gift of being able to speed-read. "I knew he was a fast reader in high school," high school friend Phil Jamison told me, "because a few minutes after the last bell rang, I'd mention the night's reading. And he'd say, 'I did that already.'" Marge Mitchell, Virginia's close friend, also remembers his skills as a young speed-reader: After she handed him an article about something "he just glanced at the page, and I said, 'You didn't read it.' And he said, 'Ask me anything you want about it.' Damned if he didn't know everything about it, point by point." Thus, his innate curiosity combined with his speed-reading ability, superior memory, and general intelligence allow him to read, understand, and retain enormous amounts of material on a wide variety of topics.

In this way, Clinton resembles Theodore Roosevelt, who also evidenced extremes in brilliance, hypomanic energy, and intellectual curiosity. TR complained that he had a "reading disease" because he was incapable of reading less than a book a day, even when he was president. He often stayed up most of the night reading. He also wrote prolifically and on a wildly diverse set of topics—thirty-eight volumes of history, natural science, and biography. Roosevelt was described as "the most vigorous brain in a responsible position in all the world" by H. G. Wells—a description that could well apply to Clinton.[5] Indeed, as we shall see, Clinton and Roosevelt have a lot in common.

Clinton has a hypomanic intensity that interacts with his natural curiosity, driving Clinton to extract information with the same insatiable hunger that characterizes the way he gratifies his other drives. Phyllis Anderson, who worked as his secretary for ten years when he was governor, remembers him rapidly gobbling apples in big chunks, core and all, while discussing policy with his senior advisers. For many years that moment stuck in her mind. "It became a metaphor for the way Bill Clinton gobbled up, digested, and stored in memory so much information on so many topics."[6]

Clinton's intelligence, greed for information, and turbocharged brain have made him the master of multitasking. Recent research has shown that most people are extremely limited in their abilities to multitask. René Marois, a neuroscientist and director of the Human Information Processing Laboratory at Vanderbilt University who has conducted research on the topic, concluded that it is "a core limitation." Humans have an "inability to concentrate on two things at once."[7] For normal humans that is probably true, but Clinton is not normal. "With his extreme intelligence, he has the ability to conduct a conversation over the telephone, play solitaire, watch TV, and have a newspaper open in front of him at the same time, and somehow be involved in all of them," said Arkansas journalist Gene Lyons. Hillary has always been amazed by this uncanny ability: "He'll be watching some obscure basketball game, and he'll be reading, and talking on the phone, all at the same time, and knowing exactly what is going on in each situation. I mean, if you stopped him and said, 'What's the score?' he'd tell you. If you stopped him and said, 'What did the person you were talking to just say?' he'd repeat it verbatim. And if you stopped him and said, 'What did you just read?' he'd say what he read. So, he is really blessed with an incredible power of concentration which he can focus on more than one thing at a time."[8]

Roosevelt also had this extraordinary multitasking facility. He would, for example, double dictate, narrating a biography of Cromwell to one assistant (with masses of dates and other technical information recited from memory) while dictating official correspondence to another. And he would often do this while simultaneously carrying on a third activity. One reporter who joined Roosevelt for breakfast was amazed to see him read a stack of newspapers "at a speed that would have excited the jealousy of the most rapid exchange editor." Even more remarkable, doing this in no way took him out of the flow of conversation. And like Clinton, somehow Roosevelt missed nothing in either realm. "Had anyone supposed that his inspection of the papers was superficial, he would have been sadly mistaken. Roosevelt saw everything."[9]

In terms of the five-factor theory, open individuals are also "prepared to entertain new ethical, social, and political ideas," explained McCrae. They are curious about the *values* of others, as well as their ideas. Georgetown, where Clinton went to college, is a Jesuit university. Though Clinton was a Southern Baptist (a rarity at Georgetown in those days), he was more curious about Catholic theology than most Catholics. Elizabeth Bagley, a former member of the Clinton administration, told me this story, which had been told to her by one of Clinton's old professors, Father Otto Hentz: "He would always come late. He'd always sit on the windowsill and never take notes. One day he came up at the end of the class and said to me, 'Father, do you want to go out for a beer? I have some questions about what you talked about today.'"

Annoyed, Hentz was thinking: "'Yes, well you're always late and you never took a note. I mean, how could you remember anything about what I said?'" But he agreed to the beer. When they spoke over drinks, Clinton asked him detailed questions in which he quoted at length, verbatim, what Hentz had said in lectures throughout the year. Hentz was dumbfounded. "He remembered everything." They talked and talked, and went on for hours. Clinton was asking so many deep, complex questions, and he seemed so passionate about Catholic theology, that Hentz finally said to him:

" 'You know, Bill, did you ever think of becoming a Jesuit?'

" 'Well, don't you have to be Catholic first, Father?' " Clinton replied.

"He was just a seeker, with incredible intellectual curiosity," Bagley told me.

When you combine all this with Clinton's enormous empathy, which we will discuss in the next section, you get someone who is driven to learn everything there is to know about policies that can improve people's lives—a policy wonk. Clinton is someone who religiously attends Renaissance weekends, where policy makers discuss creative ideas and initiatives. He is always looking for novel solutions to old problems, especially ones that transcend conventional dichotomies and established ideological boundaries.

Clinton is a ravenous sponge in search of new policy ideas, soaking up knowledge wherever he can find it. Bob Nash, Clinton's senior executive assistant for economic development when he was governor, attended the National Governors Association meetings with Clinton. "When the formal meetings were over, the staff members would all go to the bar and talk about what was going on in their states, new programs and such. Most governors would go off to these highfalutin parties and things, and go where other governors were. Bill Clinton would be at the bar with staff members from seven or eight different states, picking their brains, listening to them about new things that they were doing in their states. He'd sit there for an hour with us, and the other staff members would say, 'God, I wished I worked with a governor like that.' "[10]

Clinton reads everything related to public policy, and even more remarkable, remembers it all. Journalist Joe Klein wrote in *The Natural* that Clinton "seemed to know everything there was to know about domestic social policy. . . . Oh, could he talk policy! He seemed to know more about the school choice experiment in East Harlem than the governor of New York did; he knew all about the competitive bidding for sanitation contracts in Phoenix, the public housing manager in Omaha who'd come up with a great after-school program for kids in the projects, the terrific for-profit welfare-to-work program in New York."[11]

More than just having a great fund of knowledge, Clinton has a genius for integrating different ideas and points of view and seeing how the pieces can fit together. Clinton's synthetic abilities produce creative solutions outside the box of the usual choices.

Arkansas columnist John Brummett, who has been a Clinton observer for decades, calls Clinton a "third option guy": "Clinton is a synthesizer of policy and political philosophies. . . . When presented with two alternatives, he will almost always insist that he can cook up a third alternative that's a mix of the two, and better."[12] Clinton's third-way political orientation became trivialized in many people's minds as "triangulation," a political tactic (masterminded by political consultant Dick Morris) of staking out middle-of-the-road positions that could appeal to both the left and right. But more than a gimmick, this is really how Clinton thinks. When I spoke to Morris, he insisted "that's really how Clinton's mind works. I was just helping Clinton to be Clinton."

The downside to being perpetually open to new ways of looking at things is that it can be paralyzing: There is always another side to any question. Arkansas journalist Bob Steele believes that Clinton's "biggest weakness" is that he is "indecisive," a sentiment strongly echoed by many of those who have worked with Clinton. "He will not make a decision until he has studied it from every angle known to man."[13] And once he makes a decision, he may soon after change his mind, because he never stops seeking more opinions and information that can put the matter in yet another new light. No decision is ever final "until it is irreversible," said John Brummett. When Clinton was governor he vetoed a bill, one that he previously had been in favor of. Because it was after hours on Friday, he had the veto slipped under the door of the legislative clerk's office. But after talking to more people, he changed his mind yet again, and had an assistant pull the vetoed bill back under the door with a coat hanger so he could "unveto" it. Many have accused Clinton of going back and forth on various issues because, they say, he wants to please everyone (which is true) and has no convictions (which is not true). At least in part this problem is due to the fact that, since his mind is always open, no issue is ever closed.

Clinton's capacity for synthesis and novel third-way options is one manifestation of his creativity. In the introduction of this book I mentioned the evidence linking mild mania to creativity. Hypomanics can be idea-generating machines. French psychiatrist Jean-Pierre Falret, one of the first to study mildly manic states, wrote in 1854: "The profusion of ideas is prodigious."[14] In addition to rapidly generating ideas, hypomanics often jump from topic to topic across relatively loose chains of association. The result can be simultaneously disorienting and impressive. While their flight of ideas can sound like a loose chain of free association, this also allows them to make intellectual connections between things most people would never think to combine, and this is believed to be one of the sources of their creativity. The first time George Stephanopoulos met Clinton, this is what took him aback: "For the next half hour, I joined him on the first of countless stream-of-consciousness tours across the political landscape of his mind, from the party rules for picking superdelegates, to the turnout of black precincts on Super Tuesday, from how the credit crunch was bankrupting small businesses in New Hampshire, to how microenterprise loans could help farmers in the Mississippi Delta— and he swooped from issue to issue without losing his thread. . . . I was blown away."[15]

Hypomanics also evidence "pressured speech," a tendency to speak quickly, at length, to the point that it can be difficult to interrupt them. Their minds are whirring, and it's hard for them not to articulate what is bursting out of their brains. Their flight of ideas yearns to take wing. So, not only do hypomanics have a lot of ideas, they also have a compulsive need to verbally express them. Clinton loves to talk, and because his interests are so wide-ranging, no topic is outside his purview. Ann McCoy, who worked with him as an administrative assistant, in both Arkansas and the White House, said, "He would talk, and talk, and talk. He knows something about everything. He was just interested in every subject and he wanted to talk about it."[16] Once again, Clinton resembles Theodore Roosevelt, about whom John Hay once said that guests at a four-hour dinner with the president were only required to supply four minutes of conversation because TR would take care of the rest.

Consider the profile of Clinton's postpresidential life by David Remnick in *The New Yorker*. In this article we see many aspects of Clinton's mind on display, including his wide-ranging curiosity, memory, and intellect, along with his hypomanic energy, flight of ideas, and pressured speech. Remnick, who describes Clinton as "manic," narrates the story of an exhausting trip with Clinton that involved multiple stops around the country and the world. After attending the World Cup in Germany, they boarded Clinton's plane for Africa. Staff members had to be brought in in shifts to keep Clinton busy playing hearts, but eventually it was time for bed. By 2:30 A.M., the lights had been dimmed and people were starting to fall asleep. But just as they were drifting into sleep, "a familiar voice beckoned from the doorway: 'Hey! How you doing, guys?'

"Clinton sat down on the arm of the seat and eased his way into a near-soliloquy that lasted two hours. First, he talked about lightbulbs—their history, their physical properties, their contribution to greenhouse gases, the latest developments in bulb technology. He talked about alternative fuels, ethanol research, the politics of ethanol, the value of tar sands, and the near inevitability of hundred-dollar-a-barrel oil. He talked about the relative virtues of hybrid vehicles and electric cars and whether Detroit had conspired to kill their development. He pronounced oil depletion an opportunity: 'But we need to make fixing climate change as politically sexy as putting a man on the moon.' And as the 'conversation' veered into politics, Clinton talked about one of his recent favorite books, a study by Harold Holzer of Lincoln's speech of 1860 at Cooper Union, which launched his campaign for the Republican nomination." The reader gets the idea, but Remnick continues on for another full half page following Clinton's chain of associations in this "conversation," which he put in quotes. After over two hours, Clinton would have continued on but, "at around four-thirty, with Chad still in the distance, Jay Carson [his aide] finally managed, with a series of coughs, stifled yawns and expressive chin-lift gestures, to cue Clinton to call it a night. 'Well, O.K., you guys,' Clinton said. 'Good talking to you. We're going to have a *great* time in Africa.' "[17]

Clinton was just born this way. And this trait would have manifested itself no matter what environment he was raised in. No one modeled this behavior for Clinton. In fact, just the opposite: Everyone around him thought it was downright peculiar. Beginning when he was a child, Clinton simply could not stop his brain from expressing his stream of ideas out loud. At home, Virginia noted, "From the time he was a little boy, his mind has been in perpetual motion. He was thinking of this, figuring out that, analyzing the other." And "sometimes the little niceties"—such as "not talking with his mouth full—take a backseat to whatever brilliant idea his mind has seized on."[18]

In school, he wrote, "I talked too much. It was a constant problem in grade school."[19] His second-grade teacher complained that he answered virtually every question before other children had had a chance to raise their hands. In sixth grade, he was similarly admonished. Though his academic grades put him first in the class, he graduated third, because of his low grade in deportment for talking too much. His teacher said, "Billy, you're either going to grow up to be governor or get into a lot of trouble. It all depends on whether you learn when to talk and when to keep quiet." Clinton noted that it "turns out she was right on both counts."[20]

Given Clinton's combination of intellectual gifts and proclivities, he certainly had the potential to become a noted intellectual or academic. What made him a politician instead were his concern for people and his need for constant contact with them. The president of Rhodes House at Oxford told Virginia: "You know the only thing that keeps your son from being one of the greatest intellectuals of all time? . . . His love and understanding of people."[21]

· A HEART AS BIG AS ALASKA ·

At a staff retreat at Camp David in 1994, where the facilitator asked each participant to "describe their best qualities," Clinton said, "I have a good heart. I really do." Indeed, "he has a heart as big as Alaska," wrote John Brummett.[22] A big heart is one way to describe what Costa and Mc-Crae have called "agreeableness." Agreeable people are: "sympathetic, kind, warm, helpful, considerate, cooperative, trustful, pleasant, and generous."[23] In situations where there is interpersonal conflict, they will seek peaceful solutions rather than respond with hostility, and they are quick to forgive. When people around them are hurt or in need, it troubles them, and they want to help. The agreeable person "is fundamentally altruistic. He or she is sympathetic to others and eager to help them."[24]

Agreeable people are empathic. When I asked Paul Begala what made Clinton such a talented politician, he quickly said: "Empathy. He's more able to authentically walk a mile in your shoes than anybody else I've known." When people want to lampoon Clinton, they will sometimes quote his famous line, "I feel your pain." But Begala was with Clinton the day he said those words: "It wasn't phony." In his somewhat cynical book about Clinton, *Because He Could,* Dick Morris, the former Clinton adviser turned professional Clinton critic (he works as a commentator on Fox News and now advises Republicans exclusively), gave Clinton his due on this point. In a chapter entitled "Running on Empathy," Morris wrote: "Clinton's uncanny capacity for empathy is the key to understanding him. . . . He truly felt people's pain, and it catalyzed him to action."[25]

Clinton has manifested these traits since he was a toddler, Virginia said. One of the special things she noted about Bill right away was that "he was just so kind, and caring."[26]

"I've seen him care about people, and reach out to them, since I was eight years old," said his childhood friend David Leopoulos.

In fact, Clinton feels others' pain to the point that he not infrequently openly weeps for them, and his teary response is so infectious that it can trigger tears in others. This creates the opportunity for powerful political theater, all the more powerful because it is genuinely felt. Leopoulos was with Clinton in New Hampshire, and recalled how Clinton's empathy routinely triggered an epidemic of tears. "He had to hear everyone's story. Some of the people were crying, and had terribly sad stories. Clinton started crying, too, and then we were all crying." Stephanopoulos recalled one such encounter during the New Hampshire primary: "When Mary Annie Davis confessed tearfully that she had to choose each month between buying food or medicine, he knelt down, took her hand, and comforted her with a hug. Even the hardest bitten reporters in the room were wiping tears from their eyes."[27]

You almost can't talk to anyone in Arkansas about Bill Clinton without being told in the first five minutes how caring he is. Though he knows tens of thousands of people, he never fails to comfort any one of them when they have had a tragedy or loss in the family. "Somehow he's always the first phone call. I don't know how he does that," marveled Leopoulos. Personal assistant Ann McCoy said, "In the area of personal caring about other people, no matter how busy he was, or what his schedule entailed, if a friend died, if he heard of an illness, or a tragedy of a friend, or someone he cared about, he immediately would turn his attention to that. And he'd make a phone call, or he'd make arrangements to be there."

Morris has argued that Clinton's uncanny empathy is a dual-edged sword, the key to understanding "both his strengths and his weaknesses."[28]

For example, Robert Rubin, who first served Clinton as head of the National Economic Council, and subsequently as secretary of the Treasury, noticed that Clinton's "unusual skill as a listener," which allowed him to "relate to someone else's point of view in a way that made that person feel not just heard but understood," often led to misunderstanding. "Clinton listened so sympathetically that people who were unaccustomed to him often took it as duplicitous when he later came out against their position. . . . Sitting in White House meetings over the years, I would say to myself or the person next to me, 'That person is going to think Clinton is leaning toward his position. But he's going to get a big surprise, because Clinton doesn't agree at all—that's just how he listens.' "[29]

A related problem, noted Morris, is that because Clinton empathizes with everyone's point of view, he has difficulty making decisions. Because he sympathizes with people holding divergent views, and doesn't want to make anybody mad, the result can be a paralyzing state of "passivity" that causes him to "procrastinate, delay, and avoid decisions."[30]

There is another drawback to being such a nice guy. Machiavelli once said that if a prince had to choose between being loved and feared, he is better off being feared. Or as Lyndon Johnson put it more crudely, "If you have their balls in your pocket, their hearts and minds will follow." Scratch away the thin veneer of civilization and the psychology of human leadership is not that different from that of our closest cousins, the chimpanzees. The alpha male rules because the other males fear he will physically hurt them if they challenge him. But Bill Clinton is clueless about winning through intimidation. He's incurable in his faith that we can all be brought together by mutual love and understanding, and he invariably tries to seduce his enemies rather than scare them—and he sometimes seems to give away the store in an effort to avoid conflict and find common ground. As a result, he gives the appearance of someone "who can be rolled."[31] Or, as Clinton put it, "I've always had a desire to avoid conflict, which has led my political enemies to underestimate me."[32] In politics it can be as important to punish your enemies as it is to reward your friends. It's a limitation to be all carrot and no stick.

Clinton's fundamental agreeableness comes in direct conflict at times with his hypomanic temper. After he impulsively explodes, he immediately feels bad and wants to heal the breach between himself and the person he has just attacked. The contradictory combination of a temper and empathic warmth sometimes leads to humorous situations. Ernie

Dumas, an Arkansas journalist, told me that one day he got this call from Clinton:

"'This is Bill Clinton. This goddamn motherfucking editorial you wrote this morning is the biggest piece of shit I've ever read.' He was raging.

"'What? What, what are you talking about, Governor?'

"'This goddamn editorial is just . . .'

"'What editorial are you talking about? There are three editorials here. Which one are you talking about?'

"'Well, that one in the middle there, about our education supplement.'

"'Governor, I didn't write that.'

"'Well, who did write it?'

"'Jim Powell wrote that.'

"'That is not my position on the issue at all, it's incorrect.'

"'Hold on, Jim is in the next office, let me go get him.'

"'No, no, don't do that, just forget about it.'

"'Well, if something is wrong, he will want to know about it.'

"'No, no, no, don't do that. I'm a little upset, but just forget about it.'"

After he yelled at Dumas, Clinton's anger had dissipated, and now he wanted to repair any rift it might have caused. "He didn't want me to hang up feeling badly about it," Dumas said. "He went on talking about another thirty or forty minutes on other things, so that after a while it was more or less forgotten about. Things like that always happened." Indeed, two other journalists told me similar stories.

There is also some value to inspiring a certain amount of fear in the people who work for you. When Clinton began as president, one White House veteran gave him a sage piece of advice: "Your own staff won't take you seriously until you fire someone." Clinton demurred, "I'm not very good at that." He wasn't, and it hurt him. His administration was plagued by leaks to the press. Had he made an example of even one staffer, they might have stopped, or at least slowed. In a fit of rage Clinton sometimes demanded that someone be fired. Because he didn't have the heart to fire them himself, he'd tell a staffer to do it, but then unfire them the next day. In one case a junior staffer made the unforgivable mistake, in Clinton's mind, of excluding local crowds from an invitation-only national event in Macon, Georgia. Clinton exploded. "I want him dead, dead," he said in a blind fury. "I want him killed. I want him horsewhipped." Three days later, when he was calmer, Clinton had commuted the unfortunate staffer's death sentence, saying merely, "I want to know who did this, and I want him fired." But when the culprit was found, Clinton just said, "Damn it, I hope he gets a real talking to."[33]

Despite its very real drawbacks, empathy has been Bill Clinton's secret political weapon. "He is the most popular person on the planet earth right now," James Carville said in the spring of 2007. "Why? Why, when he goes to India, do they have hundreds of thousands of people? Was his India policy really any different from that of George Bush? I doubt it. When people look at him, they say, 'This guy cared about us.'"

· PEOPLE, PEOPLE, AND MORE PEOPLE ·

The distinction between extraverts and introverts is one of the oldest in psychology. First made popular by Carl Jung in 1911, it has been the subject of thousands of studies. Most people think of extraverts as gregarious, which they are, but the trait is broader than that. "In addition to liking people and preferring large groups and gatherings, extraverts are also assertive, active, and talkative. They like excitement and stimulation and tend to be cheerful in disposition. They are upbeat, energetic, and optimistic. Salespeople represent the prototypic extraverts in our culture."[34] These traits overlap in some respects with hypomania, and perhaps with good reason. Studies show that extraverts, like hypomanics, evidence greater use of dopamine, the neurotransmitter that fuels the pleasure center in the brain that helps motivate behavior.

Because he combines empathy and extraversion, Clinton both cares for people *and* craves contact with them. The result is that he has been a crowd-pleaser ever since anyone can remember. Next-door neighbor Jenny Sue McKee said, "I used to see him riding his tricycle, wearing his cowboy outfit, waving at every person and car that passed like he was the mayor of Hope."

When Clinton was governor of Arkansas he attended five to six community events a day. He couldn't bear to miss a single human gathering and virtually never refused an invitation, which drove the people in his scheduling office nuts trying to juggle his time. Clinton never lost his

enthusiasm for this endless panoply of local events.* "Isn't this a wonderful way to spend our lives?!" Clinton asked one assistant after a particularly grueling road trip that got them back to Little Rock at 1:00
A.M.[35] Clinton never met a crowd he didn't like.

Even in politics, perhaps the most extraverted of professions, Clinton
is in a class by himself. Veteran political reporter Joe Klein described
being astounded by his "driving need for contact with people, people,
and more people." There is an insatiable quality to his unending need
for human connection. "There was a physical, almost carnal quality to
his public appearances. He embraced audiences and was aroused by
them in turn."[36] Paul Begala recalled campaigning with Clinton in a border town in Texas. The mostly poor and working-class Mexican-American
audience loved him. "He's right on the rope line, shaking hands, and
they pull him in. Like a vortex they were sucking him in, so that he literally left the ground. The Secret Service agent had to grab him by the back
of the belt and drag him back to earth. They literally wanted to devour
him, they wanted to own him. Later we were on the plane and I said, 'My
God, that's got to be a little scary.'

"He blinked his eyes and said, 'Are you crazy? That is great!' He loved
it, every facet of it."

What is perhaps most interesting is the way these traits interact. For
example, Clinton's extremes of both empathy and extraversion interact

---

* Kay Goss, his day-to-day liaison to local officials when Clinton was governor,
wrote a partial list of the types of events she attended with Bill Clinton, presented
here despite its length, or perhaps because of it, because it is so illustrative: "industry
recruitment, county fairs, pie suppers, local rodeos, pork, beef and chicken bar-
b-ques, chicken fries, catfish fries, auctions, homecomings, open houses, sports
events, reunions, weddings, funerals of leaders, church functions, local fund raisers,
coon suppers, goat bar-b-ques, poultry festivals, rice festivals, tomato festivals,
brick festivals, Christmas lighting ceremonies, lodge meetings, kindergarten, ele-
mentary school, high school or college graduations, seminars, workshops, rallies, fire
department demonstrations, committee meetings, classes, classroom visits, water festivals, ground breaking ceremonies, ribbon cutting dedications, plant openings, birthday celebrations, political party functions, interest group conventions and events,
town hall meetings, press briefings, airport arrivals, cultural events, plays, ballets, disaster scenes, book signings, baseball, basketball, football, little league games, holiday
celebrations, teas, coffees, hospital tours, labor meetings, chamber of commerce ban-
quets, peach festivals, water festivals, horse races, dog races, parades, toad contests,
eating contests, wine festivals, and many more."

in such a way that he craves not only contact, but *warm,* intimate contact. While many extraverts love public adulation and attention, Clinton really wants to personally touch every member of the crowd. I was told over and over that no matter how briefly Clinton interacts with you, for that moment you feel like you are the only person in the world to him. He seems to be able to "crawl into your soul," even in the most momentary of contacts. When most politicians work a rope line, as they shake your hand they break eye contact to find the next person. Begala demonstrated for me how Clinton does it. Clinton looks you in the eye the whole time he is shaking your hand. As he is moving toward the next person in line, he feels blindly for them with his other hand, so he never breaks eye contact with the person whose hand he is shaking until he actually turns away. "It's a small mechanical thing, but it had a huge effect. Clinton wants to pour everything into you, even if it's for five seconds on a rope line."

Because Clinton has both a photographic memory and an immense interest in people, he remembers virtually every person he has ever met. It is uncanny how he can meet someone once, for only a few moments, and then see them years later in a different setting and greet them warmly by name, as if they were old friends. He even remembers extraordinary details about them. "He'll meet you once, and two years later ask you, 'How is your dog Blimpie doing?'" Marge Mitchell told me.

Paul Begala's favorite story of this ilk occurred when he accompanied Clinton on a state visit to South America. "Clinton always makes a point of meeting the common people who serve us at these events. So we were walking through the kitchen when Clinton stops in front of a dishwasher and says, 'Miguel! Why aren't you in Peru?' He met the guy for three seconds in the kitchen at another event years ago in another country, and he remembered him." The advantages of this trait for a politician are obvious; everyone likes to be remembered. While most politicians have aides at their side to remind them of who they are meeting, so they can pretend to remember them, Clinton really does remember them.

As a result of the three-way interaction of his openness, extraversion, and agreeableness, Clinton is insatiably curious, not just about policies and ideas, but also about people. He is ravenous to hear people's *personal* stories. No matter how many people he's talked to, each new person interests him. "It's what I like about politics," he has said. "You learn something. You hear another life story. It's like being able to peel another layer off an unlimited onion every day."[37] Begala said that Clinton "always believed blindly that everyone he meets knows something that he doesn't know, that he needs to know, and he wants to draw it out of him. That is a winning thing that makes people like you."

Clinton's insatiable appetite for personal stories is one of the reasons he is frequently late. According to people who have worked for him, he will not cut short a conversation with anybody for virtually any reason. He is so deeply engaged in hearing the story of the person he is talking to that he is oblivious to requirements of time and space. His appointment secretaries in both the governor's mansion and the White House told me frankly that this drove them insane, but they were powerless to do anything about it. "We would try to stop him from talking to people and move him on," said Mary Anne Salmon, Clinton's gubernatorial appointments secretary. "He would totally ignore us, because he wanted so much to engage with that person. That is the reason that he was late to just about everything scheduled, because he sincerely wanted to finish conversations. It was important to him. He wasn't just being late. He was talking to people about things that concerned those people."

His endless hunger for personal stories came into play in a big way during what some have regarded as the defining moment of the presidential debate with George Bush.

"The campaign reached its climax in the second presidential debate on October 15, 1992, in Richmond, Virginia—a town meeting that included spontaneous questions from the audience," wrote Joe Klein. "Toward the end of the debate, an African-American woman asked a confusing question: 'How has the national debt personally affected each of your lives? And if it hasn't, how can you honestly find a cure for the economic problems of the common people if you have no experience in what's ailing them?'

"Bush: 'I'm sure it has. I love my grandchildren. I'm not sure I get . . . help me with the question.'"

"Q: 'Well, I've had friends who've been laid off from their jobs.'

"Moderator: 'I think she means the recession . . . rather than the deficit.'

"Bush: 'Well, listen, you ought to be in the White House for a day and hear what I hear . . . I was in the Lomax AME Church. It's a black church just outside Washington, D.C. And I read the bulletin about teenage pregnancies, about the difficulties people are having making ends meet . . .'

"After more such struggle, it was Clinton's turn—and he did something quite extraordinary. He took three steps toward the woman and asked her, 'Tell me how it's affected you again?'

"The woman was speechless. Clinton helped her along, describing some of the terrible economic stories he'd heard as governor of Arkansas. But the words weren't as important as the body language: The three steps he had taken toward the woman spoke volumes about his empathy, his concern, his desire to respond to the needs of the public. Bush, by contrast, was caught gazing at his wristwatch—hoping desperately that this awkward moment would soon be done.

"And indeed it was: The presidential campaign was, in effect, over."[38]

Paul Begala knew the election was over the day the Bush campaign agreed to the town hall meeting format: "We knew that Clinton would win that town hall debate in a rout because of his empathy. We knew what we had with Clinton. Bush was tethered to his little chair. Clinton would sit on the edge of the stool, with one foot on the ground and the other knee bent, poised. He looked like a sprinter on the blocks. And as soon as someone asked something he would sprint out, come right up to them and engage them. I couldn't believe that Bush agreed to do it. But when he agreed to a town hall format, we thought: 'Oh my God, this guy's toast.'"

4

The Boy Who Walked
to Church Alone

· THE SEEKER ·

Early every Sunday morning, eight-year-old Bill Clinton got himself up, bathed, put on a jacket and tie, picked up his large Bible, and walked a mile down the hill to Park Place Baptist Church. "When I was a kid I walked alone a mile or so to my church every Sunday. It wasn't something my parents did, but I somehow felt the need."[1]

But Clinton never defines *what* that need was.

Whatever it was, the need must have been strong. Reverend Dexter Blevins remembered, "He was there every time the door opened."[2]

What drove Bill Clinton to church at eight? What was he seeking? I would suggest that if you can crack that code, you will have unlocked one of the keys to who Bill Clinton really is.

"How many kids would go to church alone on Sunday if they didn't have to?" asked longtime childhood friend Patty Criner. The scene in her family on Sunday morning was quite different: "My mother had to drag three kids brutally into the car to take us to church." And when they came to the corner, "every single Sunday, here comes Bill Clinton walking down the street." His neighborhood friends remember watching Bill from their car windows, passing him as he made his way down the hill. "He looked so small carrying that big Bible," another friend recalled. None of them attended Park Place Baptist, a plain redbrick box next to a barbecue joint. So in that way, too, it was a solitary journey. "I don't know a single friend of his that went to that church," said Criner.

While Clinton's friends were being driven to church by an external force, Clinton was being driven by an internal one. "It was something that was within him. Something that he had to do," said David Leopoulos.

The religious influence did not come from his parents. They were entirely unchurched. Sunday mornings they typically could be found sleeping off a hangover after a night of clubbing, not singing hymns. When Clinton was ten he asked to receive baptism by immersion. The pastor felt obliged to visit the Clinton home to ask his parents' permission. It was easily granted. But Virginia and Roger were so indifferent to church that neither thought to attend Bill's baptism. Carolyn Staley, a pastor's daughter, recalled that when "he made a personal decision to become a Christian," signified by the public ritual of baptism, "none of his family was there."[3]

There was, however, a Christian influence in Bill's family: his African-American housekeeper. Virginia recalled: "Mrs. Walters was a Christian woman. Maybe the most Christian person I've ever known. But she was the kind who *lived* her Christianity, not the more common kind who spends so much time bending your ear about how godly he or she is. . . . Mrs. Walters taught Bill the Golden Rule and other lessons about how to live and get along and how to treat people in this world. She would eventually work for us for eleven years, and after that her daughter Maye would take over and work for me for thirty years. Both had a tremendous influence on my children's lives."[4]

Many people told me that there is no place Clinton feels more comfortable than an African-American church. Mike Gauldin, who served as Clinton's press secretary for six years when he was governor, said, "I've seen him a lot of places, and I don't think I've ever seen him more at home than at black churches."[5] During his first campaign Clinton would visit five or six African-American churches a day with Carol Willis, who is both African-American and the son of a preacher. He recalled how elated the services made Clinton. "He was rocking and rolling and shaking his bacon," Willis laughed, shaking his head at the memory. "He never wanted to leave."

Of course, Clinton never wants to leave any public gathering, but Willis noticed that church services had a uniquely calming effect on him. "When he'd hit the church house you'd see a whole different person. The church always seemed to be a soothing thing for him. It seemed to relax him, to ease him out," said Willis. "His spirituality was for real, man. You can't fake that. Spirituality has sustained him through a lot of his trials and tribulations. He often talked about it."

Growing up in the Bible Belt, with his inborn temperament, young Clinton was naturally drawn to church. Clinton, the empathic extravert, would have been hard-pressed to find a social environment better suited to his naturally warm people-seeking instincts. Church meant fellowship. And the Christian worldview, which stresses caring, altruism, and peacemaking, naturally resonated with his instinctive personal values. He also loved the music. Clinton sang in a church choir almost throughout his entire life. "He loved the people and the music at church," one high school friend told me.

A shared mood of mild elation is often induced by singing songs of worship, which must have appealed to Bill Clinton's hypomanic side. Hypomanics naturally seek out experiences that put them in an expansive mood, and thus they have a natural affinity for euphoric religious experience, as I wrote about in *The Hypomanic Edge*. People of this temperament are particularly drawn to *ecstatic* worship. Though Clinton attended a traditional white Southern Baptist church, he seemed perpetually drawn to both Pentecostal and black churches, where worship is more rapturous, intense, and uninhibited. As a kid he would often find his way to the Pentecostal Gospel Sing at Redfield between Little Rock and Pine Bluff. "Those who know the president will say that he worships most easily amid gospel music and in Pentecostal services," wrote one reporter, "explaining that he loves the raw unbridled honesty of Pentecostal worship, during which people pray and move their hands and speak in tongues."[6]

Though Bill Clinton's temperament alone would explain his attraction to church, it appealed to the young boy for another reason: as a way of coping with his chaotic family environment. He craved structure, values, and normalcy, especially in a culture where "normal" families went to church.[7] At the most basic level, he craved peace. Church must have been a safe haven—a sanctuary in the true sense of the word.

Virginia understood that Bill was seeking a different path than the lifestyle she and Roger had adopted. These choices were Bill's reactions against the behaviors she and Roger modeled, a truth that she managed to both know and deny at the same time.

"Bill's reaction to Hot Springs's excesses have also probably helped shape him. He is simply not a gambler, nor is he a drinker. He's always been a religious person, but he's like Mrs. Walters. He lives his Christianity, he doesn't talk about it. He never gave any overt indication that he didn't approve of my gambling, or of our social drinking; he just simply moved quietly in the other direction." Virginia would never quite take the extra step of admitting that her own behavior was the primary "Hot Springs excess" her son was reacting against. Bill was "probably repelled by much of what he saw in Hot Springs," wrote Virginia, careful to deny that her son might have found some aspects of her own behavior repellent.[8]

Clinton turned to church in part to cope with the pain of living in his family. He needed to create a better world in which to live: "The violence and dysfunction in our home made me a loner, which is contrary to the way people see me, because I'm gregarious, happy, all that. . . . I had to construct a whole life inside my own mind."[9] Clinton turned to Christianity. The most important function church provided was a chance to write a new narrative about his life, one that more closely fit his inner sense of who he really was. While Virginia would admit that the plot of her life closely resembled a bad country music song, Clinton had a different tune in mind as he joyfully sang hymns in church.

Clinton was seeking role models to help him forge a new identity. In church, the other adult men, and especially the pastor, provided them. But most of all, young Bill Clinton looked to Christ and other biblical heroes: "I was very influenced as a child by the biblical stories."[10] For example, he wrote, "My favorite movies during this time were Biblical epics: *The Robe, Demetrius and the Gladiators, Samson and Delilah, Ben Hur,* and especially *The Ten Commandments,* the first movie I recall paying more than a dime to see. I saw *The Ten Commandments* when my Mother and Daddy were on a brief trip to Las Vegas. I took a sack lunch and sat through the whole thing twice for the price of one ticket."[11] The symbolism couldn't be more apt. While his parents left him, to party in Las Vegas, Clinton sat alone in a dark movie theater fantasizing about the life of Moses.

Clinton read the Bible cover to cover many times. Patty Criner recalled that when he was governor he had fifteen Bibles, including the large one she remembered him carrying to church as a child. One day Criner pulled a few of them off the shelf. "In every one of them there were handwritten notes, page after page after page." Other staffers told me that Clinton had filled up all the space in the margins of his Bibles with lengthy notes scrawled in red, blue, and green ink. Carol Willis described him as "a biblical scholar. . . . He can do what most preachers can do: quote you chapter and verse." Paul Begala described Clinton as having a "deep facility for Scripture," noting that he often brought up specific passages from the Bible in their conversations. Few voters ever knew about Clinton's religiosity, however, because he always felt it should be private, and most important, not exploited for political gain. "I spent months flying around with him," said Begala, "and we would talk about religion more than anything else. He's a very spiritual person."

In my study of charismatic leaders, who almost invariably have a mildly manic temperament, I have found that by adolescence they all experience a deep feeling of destiny. A persistent intuition, more powerful than external reality, tells them they have an important role to play in changing the world. I think that Bill Clinton had that unusual feeling. Even more unusual, throughout his development, others who knew him well had the same sense that he was destined to accomplish great things. Though Bill was just one of the gang, his closest friends sensed that he was different. Carolyn Staley felt that he was "called" to some important work, and was being "uniquely prepared" for some large service to humanity.[12] Leopoulos said, "We knew there was a sense of destiny."

Typically, the young hypomanic identifies with some larger-than-life historic figure who represents the idealized self whom they feel they are becoming. While all adolescents have heroes, hypomanics are markedly different in the intensity and duration of these identifications. They feel an intimate connection to these icons, who in essence they claim as spiritual ancestors, and they internalize these heroes as lifelong guides to their actions—their personal North Stars. Thus, while most boys have posters of sports stars on their walls in grade school, few bring those posters to college. They have moved on to more realistic dreams. Hypomanics don't move on. To them this grandiose identity is more real than real, and they devote their lives to actualizing it.

Clinton found his ultimate role model not in the Bible or history, but in contemporary society. Begala recalled that when the picture of young Clinton shaking hands with Kennedy was being widely circulated and everyone believed that Clinton had identified most with Kennedy in his youth, Clinton told Begala, "That's all true, but my real hero was Martin Luther King."

Roger Clinton Jr. recalled, "My brother had the whole 'I Have a Dream' speech memorized." Bill would repeatedly deliver the speech in their living room verbatim to the somewhat mystified young Roger. When he was delivering King's oratory, Clinton was internalizing King as a role model. King was a minister called by God to change the world by addressing injustice and healing the breach between blacks and whites. According to Begala, one scripture quotation that Clinton repeated over and over again, like a mantra, was a passage from Isaiah: "And he shall be called healer of the breach." "That's how he most profoundly sees himself," said Begala, "a healer of the breach."

I believe that by the time Clinton was an adolescent, he felt called by God to change the world (or at least Arkansas), and that for him, politics was a religious calling. Clinton told Carolyn Staley that he felt "called" to enter politics, and that for him it was a form of "ministry."[13] "Ministries come in different shapes," said Carol Willis. "I think his was 'I'm going to be a good politician. I'm going to make things good for people.'" This view has been a stable part of Clinton's self-concept throughout his life. During the 1992 presidential election campaign, Clinton said in an interview, "My faith has taught me to see this as a ministry."

The summer after Bill Clinton graduated from high school, he ran into his tenth-grade history teacher, Paul Root. He went up excitedly to Root: "Let's go drink some coffee," he said, "I want to talk to you." They conversed for an hour, with Clinton doing most of the talking, in a feverish tone. "He was talking about changing the world!" said Root.[14]

The next summer, when he returned from his first year at Georgetown, the people of Hot Springs were surprised to see that his hair had gotten longer, and he now wore rope sandals. One day their family friend Toni Karber saw "the most amazing sight. . . . There came Bill sauntering down the street with the sun setting behind him, and the long hair and the sunset produced a halo effect. Then they saw the sandals, and that did it. 'Look,' Toni said to her friend, 'Bill looks just like Jesus.'" Virginia said this encouraged Clinton to keep the beard and long hair. The Jesus look reflected something about who he aspired to be. People "would come along and say he looked like Jesus—well, he thought that was wonderful!"[15]

· PEACEMAKER ·

On July 13, 2006, I spent an evening having dinner in Little Rock with Bill Clinton's closest childhood friends, David Leopoulos, Rose Crane, Mauria Aspell, and Carolyn Staley. They jokingly called themselves the "hearts club," after the card game they played together all the time when they were young. They still play hearts when they get together, and Clinton is known for playing the game obsessively late into the night with whomever he can find. Like Bill, they were all now just turning sixty.

None of Clinton's close friends had any idea that Roger Clinton was an alcoholic who terrorized his family at night. "We were in and out of his house all the time, every day. None of us suspected," David Leopoulos told me. Leopoulos first learned of the abuse from a magazine article during the 1992 presidential campaign. "I just felt sick when I read about it," he said with evident pain in his voice. "I wish I could have gone through it with him." Leopoulos recalled that there were times when Bill would stare off into space, almost in a trance; you couldn't get his attention for several minutes. "Now I wonder if he was replaying traumatic scenes from the night before in his head."

When Roger came home drunk and belligerent, Virginia would abruptly usher the hearts club out of the Clinton home. "I never understood it," said Crane. "Virginia would just suddenly, out of the blue, say, 'Now it's time for you children to go home now.' I was afraid I had done something wrong. But she would say, 'Honey, you didn't do anything. But you go on home now, and we'll come back tomorrow.'" Only Rose's younger brother, Larry Crane, recalled suspecting that the real reason they were being summarily dismissed had something to do with Roger's drinking. "I remember Roger being a real asshole, saying things about 'those damned kids.'" But the rest of Bill's friends said that they have only positive memories of Roger Clinton. He was always nice to them.

Virtually all of the attempts to understand Bill Clinton psychologically have centered on the impact of his growing up in a home with an abusive, alcoholic stepfather. And indeed, most of Clinton's publicly discussed attempts to understand himself therapeutically have been framed in the language of the Adult Children of Alcoholics (ACOA) movement. In 1984, Roger Jr. was caught selling cocaine, and sent to court-mandated counseling. At that time Bill and Virginia participated in the family therapy sessions that were part of Roger's recovery program. The therapy "forced me to begin a serious process of reexamining my life," said Clinton. "In counseling I learned that he [Roger Jr.] and I were archetypes of children of alcoholics, and that I basically was required to grow up before my time."[16]

A "parentified child" is what psychologists term children called upon to function as adults prematurely, and Clinton is, in many ways, a textbook case. "I felt like I never got to complete my childhood," he said.[17] This premature maturity was apparent to others as well. "I always thought he seemed older than everyone else," Staley told me. "He was born an adult," added Rose Crane. Of course, if a child is gifted, as Bill so obviously was, then he is more able to take over adult responsibilities. "From the beginning Bill was a special child—smart, sensitive, mature beyond his years," wrote Virginia.[18] Given his giftedness, it was almost inevitable that he would step in to compensate for the inadequacies of his parents. In ACOA language Bill Clinton embodied the archetype of the hero, the child who strives to save his dysfunctional family.

The most striking manifestation of Bill's being a parentified child was that he essentially became a parent at age ten, when his half brother was born. He virtually adopted Roger Jr. as his son. "I was the father" to Roger, said Clinton.[19] Virginia and Roger Jr. each confirmed this independently in their own memoirs. "Bill was father, brother, and son in this family. He took care of Roger and me," wrote Virginia.[20] Roger Jr. wrote: "I don't recall much about my abusive father before I was five years old. Bill was really more of an important figure to me. He was almost obsessive about wanting me near him and was my best friend, my guardian, my father, and my role model."[21]

In the morning Virginia was usually gone when the kids awoke; she had to be at the hospital by 5:00 A.M. for surgery. It was Bill's job to get Roger Jr. and himself ready for school. "Bill would get himself up, get little Roger up, and get them out the door to school," said Staley. And Bill would take care of little Roger after school as well. He simply took Roger with him everywhere he went. "Roger would go with Bill and me to lots of places we went. It was fatherly love, brotherly love. The message was: 'I'm going to take you under my wing. I'm not going to leave you home alone. You're my little brother,'" said Staley.[22] It's a remarkable older sibling who never finds his younger brother to be a pest or a burden, who never says, "Get lost; let me play with my friends." Virginia found it amazing that Bill took on the role of father without being asked, while never seeming to resent it: "Bill never once complained about having his little brother around. That to me was the most amazing thing."[23] He even brought little Roger on dates. "When Bill started dating, he'd often take me with him," wrote Roger Jr. "This was never as awkward as it sounds. He'd tell the young woman I was going along and that was it."[24] Because Virginia had a full-time housekeeper, she swears that she never needed Bill to take care of little Roger, and never pressured him to do so. "I worked unusually hard to make sure that Bill was never responsible for his brother." In her opinion, that wouldn't have been fair. "He did it on his own. He just took responsibility."

The childhood experience of being young Roger's protector helped to shape a permanent sense of responsibility for those weaker than himself. "Part of his charisma is an instinctual feeling for vulnerability," said Begala. "I've seen this a hundred times. He'll go right past the multimillionaire contributor, and focus in on the one person who's grieving, or hurting, or angry. He has this incredible radar. It's really impressive. And I think people are drawn to that." Clinton gives disproportionate attention to the people least likely to be noticed. Whenever Clinton would attend any kind of dinner for example, Clinton would always go back into the kitchen to shake hands with the cooks and waiters and dishwashers. James Carville said, "He always pays the most attention to the most vulnerable person in the room. If there's somebody in a wheelchair, or an old person, he'll go strike out for that person first. And in that one act he just elevates the room."

The inverse of this is that Clinton becomes enraged when any member of his staff treats people of lesser prestige or power badly. It triggers the rage he must have felt watching his stepfather beating up on his mother and brother. "The unforgivable crime in Clinton Land was always to be rude to little people," Carville told me. "You could tell Clinton to kiss off, and he'd just tell you something back. If you didn't show a senator enough respect, somebody would call you and say, 'Hey, you've got to be careful.' But if you told the cleaning lady to kiss off, then you were done. That was the unforgivable sin."

The heroic child feels responsible for maintaining peace, order, and stability in their family, and Clinton recognized that he was a peacekeeping force of one in the conflict zone that was the Clinton home: "The manifest tensions between them abated a little just because I was kind of the force for peace."[25] Clinton would be the first to agree that there is a downside to his tendency to avoid conflict: efforts to try to appease, mollify, and please everyone. "In an alcoholic family . . . I learned some good skills about how to keep people together and try to work things out. On the negative side, if you grow up in an environment that causes you to want to avoid trouble, you tend to keep peace at any cost. A leader can't do that."[26]

On the other hand, the peacekeeping role Clinton learned quickly generalized to other relationships in ways that had positive impacts. These inclinations were evident by age five. Joe Purvis, who attended kindergarten with Bill in Hope, told me that Bill "was always at the center when fights broke out. He was always the peacemaker. He healed the hard feelings. He just had a way of offering conciliatory words and bringing people together." In grade school, too, "Bill was a peacemaker stopping playground fights."[27] Leopoulos recalled being harassed by a group of local "hoods" at the bus stop. "You know the type, from *American Graffiti*—a pack of Camels in the sleeve of their white T-shirts— they liked to bully smaller kids. . . . These guys walked up to us. They started making threatening comments to me, and I was terrified." Clinton, seeing what was happening, intervened without even having to threaten violence. "Bill just stepped right in front of me and said, 'What's wrong, guys?' He was very peaceful, and somehow it defused. The guys just walked away." Clinton gives new meaning to the term "disarming personality." Michael Muldoon recalled that he and his girlfriend broke up for a week, during which time Clinton took her on a hayride. Word got out that Muldoon was mad, and ready to do something about it. "I think he got the idea that I was going to whip his tail. I was a redneck tough guy. But he didn't seem worried. He just had the kind of personality where it was impossible to get mad at him, and I think he knew it. It was impossible not to like him. If I had even tried to start anything, he would have talked me out of it. I don't think he ever did anything to make anyone mad at him during all of high school and junior high school."

The fact that Bill was very tall for his age also didn't hurt. "He didn't have to fight because he was bigger than everyone else," said Larry Crane. Bill remembers only once hitting another boy. He was so guilt ridden that he called the boy's house to make sure he was OK.

· OEDIPAL VICTOR ·

When Virginia wrote, "Bill was father, brother, and son in this family. He took care of Roger and me,"[28] she is almost saying, without openly acknowledging it, that Bill played the role of husband as well. All boys go through a phase of wanting to replace their father as their mother's love object. In normal development the young boy must come to terms with the reality that this is not going to happen: He must surrender his grandiose fantasy of replacing his father, and instead find his true place in the social and moral order. An "oedipal victor" is a child who, if he is male, doesn't just fantasize about besting and replacing his father, but actually achieves this goal in some measure in reality. The oedipal victor forever carries a sense of grandiosity, entitlement, and indestructibility. In his own private mythology he is a hero of epic proportions, and that will forever shape his self-concept. As Freud noted, "A man who has been the indisputable favorite of his mother keeps for life the feeling of a conqueror, that confidence of success that often leads to real success."[29] And Bill was indeed Virginia's favorite. The wall outside the living room was dedicated to Bill's medals, awards, and pictures. Carolyn Staley and David Leopoulos used to refer to it as "the shrine." "We used to joke that there ought to be candles around the pictures."[30]

Just as there had been a thinly disguised, erotic, oedipal component in Virginia's relationship with her own father, she now created a similarly inappropriate cross-generational bond with her oldest son. "Bill then took the place of his mother's husband. Virginia shifted her needy affections to her boy," wrote Gail Sheehy in her biography of Hillary Clinton, *Hillary's Choice*. Psychologist Jerome Levin, who wrote *The Clinton Syndrome* about Clinton's sexual addiction, said, "I think his mother was very seductive with him."

Carolyn Staley recalled that Virginia's standard opening line when she came home was "You know, nobody has told me all day how cute I am."

All the children, especially Bill, would then say, "You are adorable, Virginia, you are just so cute."

Virginia would smile and say, "Thank you, I needed somebody to tell me I'm cute."[31]

As Sheehy noted, "Thus did Bill learn how to flatter women and make them purr."[32] Indeed, his peers noted that he would often compliment their mothers' appearances in ways that felt vaguely inappropriate. As one high school friend, Kathy McClanahan, recalled, "If your mother had shorts on that she'd worn for forty years, he'd say, 'Oh, I love your outfit,'" which made McClanahan want to "slap him" and say "give it a rest."[33] Bill had been trained to flirt, and this no doubt contributed to his compulsive need to behave seductively with every woman he met.

Bill remembered watching Elvis's debut on *The Ed Sullivan Show* with Virginia, who fell in love immediately with the singer. "If I hadn't had children and a job, I'd have spent the rest of my days traveling from Elvis concert to Elvis concert," she wrote.[34] It's probably no coincidence that Bill emulated Elvis, the man who had so enthralled his mother. One of Clinton's favorite pastimes, according to his childhood friend Patty Criner, was to "cruise around Hot Springs doing impersonations of Elvis."[35] Criner recalled that "he would roll down his windows and turn on the radio, singing Elvis Presley's 'Blue Suede Shoes' at the top of his lungs, driving down Central Avenue."[36] Thus, in a displaced way, Bill could be his mother's erotic ideal. "He looks remarkably like the young Elvis Presley," wrote Virginia, about a picture of young Bill on the band bus.[37] He inhabited the Elvis persona so well that Clinton's 1992 campaign staff nicknamed him Elvis.

Predictably, this kind of inappropriate attention from his mother produced intense ambivalence in young Clinton. On one hand, it was exciting and gratifying; on the other, it was overstimulating and repellent when it became too overtly incestuous. When Virginia sought out Bill to replace her husband Roger as her Saturday night date, it was too much for young Bill to handle. "Bill now had to be her date for nightclub hopping with her rowdy drinking crowd, . . . an experience that seems to have simultaneously intrigued and repelled the boy."[38] "It was fascinating," Clinton told Sheehy, but "I didn't like to be around dark smoky places where people were drinking too much. I had a real negative association with alcoholism. I think subconsciously I was afraid it would happen to me."[39] He became positively allergic to the club scene. Although the big national musical acts stopped at the Hot Springs clubs, and Clinton was an avid musician with a thirst for new aesthetic experiences, he couldn't handle being Virginia's date in this boozy, libidinally overheated atmosphere. Leopoulos told me, "He didn't like going to the nightclubs. His mom wanted him to come to see all the stars. He'd just say, 'I don't feel comfortable there.'" But it was not a simple matter of Clinton rejecting his mother's vices. As Sheehy wrote, he was both "intrigued and repelled" by participating with Virginia in her racy lifestyle, and it was almost impossible to fully resolve this ambivalence. Dick Morris told me he thought there were two Bill Clintons: "Saturday night Bill," who as an adult enjoyed illicit sex (the only real vice he picked up from his mother's fast Hot Springs lifestyle), and "Sunday morning Bill," the clean-cut, church-going idealist. Both sets of feelings were real, and both were part of him, but because of the unresolved internal conflict between them, Clinton could not fully integrate them into one consistent identity.

Bill fulfilled another spousal function that often falls to parentified children: He served as Virginia's confidant. In a normal marriage, adults share their problems primarily with their husband or wife. In a family with an oedipal victor, the child is the parent's preferred sounding board.

Virginia developed what David Leopoulos called an "interesting ritual" that he and the other members of the hearts club dubbed "kitchen court." Coming back from work, Virginia "would drive up the back of the house at breakneck speed, wave to us, and go in the back door. No matter what we were doing, we would stop, go into the house, and then it would start. Virginia would toss her purse with a shoulder-length strap onto the kitchen counter and most always say, 'I just can't believe it.'"

"Bill would say, 'What can't you believe?' "

A detailed discussion of whatever was bothering Virginia would ensue. We can be sure Virginia was not turning to her husband, Roger, for advice and support in these matters. As Leopoulos noted, "she probably didn't or couldn't have that dialogue with her husband."

Paradoxically, the inappropriately adult role that Clinton played in his family may provide our first clue in explaining some of the well-known chinks in Clinton's conscientiousness. Along with adult responsibilities, Clinton had adult freedoms. On one hand, that he readily volunteered for such extraordinary levels of adult responsibility displays an extraordinary level of conscientiousness. But on the other, there was no one above Bill in the family hierarchy with the moral authority to provide discipline. Clinton's friends were amazed that he was allowed to do whatever he wanted. As Virginia noted, Bill's friend Carolyn Staley "marveled at how loosely our household was run." In truth, Virginia set no limits at all on young Bill, in part because she was still rebelling against her own mother, and by extension, her mother's firm discipline of Bill. While

Virginia described her mother as a "strict disciplinarian," she consciously went in the opposite direction, stating that she "imposed very few rules on" Bill.[40] That Clinton grew up virtually without parental limits has no doubt affected the part of his character that feels he is entitled to make his own rules for his conduct. In most respects Bill's personal rules were far more stringent than any that a normal parent would have imposed on him, but that doesn't change the underlying circumstance that while Clinton was growing up he had authority over himself.

To pick one small but important concrete example: As an adult, Clinton has always been famous for being egregiously late. As a child, he came and went where and when he chose, without ever having to ask permission, explain his whereabouts, account for his time, or meet a curfew. Virginia was particularly proud that she set no restrictions on him concerning time: "I never put a curfew on either of my boys."[41] She saw no reason why they should rush "to meet some arbitrary hour of the clock."[42] Clinton would become infamous for his lateness. In Virginia's mind, the root of Bill Clinton's tardiness was her mother's rigid punctuality during the first four years of his life when he lived with Edith. "This period probably explains his inability to follow a schedule. After being bound to my mother's strict regimen for so long, I don't doubt the man sometimes feels a need to dawdle."[43] It never occurred to her that her own lack of limits about punctuality might have had more to do with it. Thus, Clinton is highly moral in big things, in taking responsibility for the whole world in fact, but feels resentful when people who seem to be missing the big picture nickel-and-dime him about abiding by petty mundane requirements like meeting "some arbitrary hour of the clock."

Another problem oedipal victors face is that at some level these children cannot deny the obvious reality that they are, in fact, not adults. Thus, they perpetually struggle to keep at bay the fear that they are faking it. The oedipal victor must cope with the constant insecurity that they are just fooling themselves and everyone else. Clinton's need for constant affirmation is frequently commented on by observers. Compulsively, Clinton seeks feedback telling him that he is truly the hero he believes himself to be. Paradoxically, this odd combination of confidence and insecurity has probably served him well in politics. If he never felt like a hero, he might not have felt called to higher office. However, if he were really completely confident about that identity, he wouldn't have been compulsively driven to prove it, handshake after handshake, in a permanent campaign.

· THE THREE STAGES OF ROGER ·

Stage 1. Repeating Abuse

Looking for Punishment. Those who have pointed to Clinton's abusive background as a source of his troubles, including Clinton himself, have focused exclusively on the coping skills it forced him to learn, such as peacekeeping. Surprisingly, the more traditional psychodynamic view—that someone with his background would be unconsciously driven to *repeat* the abusive relationship—has not been widely discussed. As we have seen, because of the repetition compulsion, Clinton always needed both an Edith and a Virginia in his life.

But he also *always needed a Roger.*

We don't know if Bill was physically abused by Roger. We do know that young Bill had to watch helplessly as Roger beat his mother and his brother, which in many ways could be even more traumatic. Along with the rest of the family, he lived under Roger's reign of terror, anxiously waiting for the next attack, ready to flee at short notice. Roger Jr. wrote in his memoir, "Many evenings my mother would sneak Bill and me out of the house and take us to the nearby Capri motel."[44]

A central force that drives the repetition compulsion is the powerful attachment children form to those who care for them. Bill was very attached to Roger, who had been a part of his life since he was a toddler. We first experience love in the context of those early intimate relationships, and always associate love with that very specific context. Re-creating those relationships feels familiar, feels right, feels like coming home.

Soon after his mother divorced Roger Clinton, teenage Bill had his last name legally changed to Clinton. Though everyone called him Bill Clinton up until then, his legal name was Bill Blythe. Why on earth would Bill change his name to Clinton immediately after his mother had divorced Roger? Clinton has said he did it for his little brother, so that they would both have the same last name. While this is plausible, I think there is a deeper psychological motive that explains the peculiar timing of the name change. After his mother severed the connection with Roger, Bill felt a psychic need to restore it. The problem is that, throughout his adult life he has continued to attempt to restore that connection with Roger, through surrogate abusive older male figures, and this is one of the secret causes of many of his crises.

Betsey Wright, his longtime Arkansas chief of staff, knows Clinton better than most. She told Gail Sheehy that Clinton often seems to have a compulsive need for a "punisher" in his life. "He's looking for the cat-o'-nine tails," she said, and "there's a multitude of people who do that for him."[45] However, because his need for punishment is unconscious, Clinton doesn't feel any responsibility for provoking these attacks. In his mind, they just keep happening to him.

A "funny" story that Clinton tells so often it has become his "signature," according to Sheehy, is this: "You know the story about the guy who falls off the mountain? He's falling down the canyon to certain death. Then he sees this little twig coming out of the mountain and he grabs for it—his last chance. He's holding on for dear life, and the roots start pulling out of the mountain. He looks down at the drop hundreds of feet below and cries out, 'God, why me?' This thunderous voice comes out of the heavens and says, 'Son, there's just some people you don't like.' "[46]

The God in the story is a father figure persecuting the man for no discernible cause, and indeed the pattern Clinton keeps repeating is one of being randomly attacked for no rational reason. Roger's unprovoked, unpredictable alcoholic rages were not brought about by anything Clinton had done. In that respect they were like thunderstorms—a metaphor many would use for Clinton's own attacks of rage. And yet it would not be accurate to say the aggression was not personal. In this story, as in Clinton's childhood, a father figure is intentionally hurting his son but doesn't know why he's doing it.

The son is being victimized. Consistently, both Clinton's allies and enemies would criticize him for casting himself as a victim: "Most of all, aides recoiled at the candidate's bouts of self-pity and flailing anger," wrote John F. Harris in *The Survivor,* his account of the Clinton presidency.[47] And yet, this is precisely the experience Clinton is re-creating, because he was a victim of Roger's abuse. Over the course of this book, we will identify key moments in Clinton's career, impeachment being only the most notable example, where Clinton's unconscious desire for punishment was an invisible guiding hand pushing him toward self-destructive behavior that invited abuse.

Identification with the Aggressor. In abused children, there is almost always a part of them that "identifies with the aggressor," as Anna Freud wrote in *The Ego and the Mechanisms of Defense.* The child not only internalizes his or her role as the abused child, but also the role of the abusive adult. It was inevitable that Clinton would internalize Roger somewhere in his psyche. And so, just as Bill Clinton was unconsciously driven to repeat the experience of being abused, he was also on occasion unconsciously driven to abuse others. Because Clinton is generally an exceptionally warm and generous person, these eruptions of aggression always seem like anomalies, even to the people he has screamed at. And yet, they are part of a consistent pattern. This is Clinton's hidden shadow.

Among his staff, Clinton was famous for his rages. Dick Morris wrote that "his is a primitive anger manifested by red-faced screaming, a wildly pointing accusatory finger, and utterly self-righteous tirades."[48] What is interesting is that these rages have an irrational and unpredictable quality, as did Roger's. And those he rages at often feel like bewildered, helpless children, as young Bill must have felt. "For those on the receiving end, it is a frightening and unforgettable encounter," wrote Morris.[49] Even David Gergen, a large, confident man who is not easily intimidated, even by presidents, found the experience overwhelming. Once on Air Force One Clinton "erupted so violently that I wished I had a parachute."[50]

In one incident Morris claims that Clinton "tackled me and knelt over my prone body, ready to punch me, before Hillary pulled him off, shrieking at him to control himself."[51] This is the only reported incident I've found of Clinton being physically violent. Nonetheless, something Hillary said to Morris immediately following this event is revealing of a deep pattern: "He only does that to people he loves!" she said.[52]

More specifically, Morris pointed out that his aggression was typically directed at close aides—people who were dependent on him. This, too, is a reenactment of Roger Clinton's pattern. Roger took his rage out on his dependents—his family. Clinton, too, would pick on "people who were close to him, even symbiotic with him. People who wouldn't fight back, who wouldn't talk about it. People he had some control over."[53]

Though most of Clinton's flaws were well known, his anger was like a family secret. "Aides who leaked everything else would never dare speak out of school about his rages."[54] This, too, re-creates one of the distinguishing aspects of his childhood pattern—its secrecy. As I mentioned, I spoke to Clinton's closest childhood friends, who hung out at Clinton's house almost every day but still had no idea about Roger's alcoholic outbursts of fury.

In light of this it is not insignificant that the aide who took the brunt of Clinton's rage was the most boyish looking of them all, George Stephanopoulos. Gergen confirms that Clinton "would usually blow at least once in the morning and straight into the face of George Stephanopoulos." This pattern began early in their relationship. Stephanopoulos reported that during the 1992 campaign, each day he "braced for the morning outburst. . . . If the yelling got real bad, I would disconnect the speaker phone by picking up the receiver. No reason for the rest of the campaign to hear the candidate melt down. . . . While he talked I'd pretend to slap myself on the face."[55] Through some unspoken agreement, Stephanopoulos became the whipping boy. "Clinton's anger was a more impersonal force; like a tornado. The tantrum would form in an instant and exhaust itself in a violent rush. Whoever happened to be in the way would have to deal with it; more often than not that person was me. . . . My job was to absorb the anger . . . ," wrote Stephanopoulos.[56] Gergen speculated that "perhaps he [Clinton] felt that George was the son he never had and could trust him to take it."[57] Gergen may have put his finger on something deeper than he realizes here, because in Clinton's unconscious psychic world Stephanopoulos was indeed playing the role of "son." Stephanopoulos was a stand-in for the earnest, well-meaning young Bill Clinton, who had had to absorb random undeserved outbursts of anger from his stepfather.

Abusers often go through cycles of remorse, repentance, and repetition, as Clinton seemed to do with Morris. "He was very apologetic and promised it would never happen again. But it did."[58] No doubt, Roger had made similar promises in moments of repentance, only to break them again.

Morris sent Clinton a note saying that he couldn't handle being around that kind of anger, because his own father had had a terrible temper. Morris's note seems to have had the effect of a good interpretation in psychotherapy. It made Clinton conscious of what he was doing unconsciously—repeating the role of his abusive stepfather—and, no doubt, Clinton was horrified. Only then did he stop, and this time it was finally over. Clinton never yelled at Morris again.

Stage 2. The Punching Bag Strikes Back

In Bill's inner psychodrama, being abused is the first part of the script. But the young hero always triumphs in the end; he is battered but never defeated. Because Clinton never did have the chance to understand and work through his Roger issues, he was unconsciously compelled to play out the dark psychodrama of his childhood, repeatedly seeking out and provoking situations where Clinton-the-hero would be brutalized and left for dead, and then miraculously rise again.

The 1994 Republican congressional victory would be one of Clinton's great electoral spankings, but to everyone's surprise, he bounced back stronger than before the loss of Congress.

"Do you know who I am?" he asked Newt Gingrich. "I'm the big rubber doll you had as a kid, and every time you hit it it bounces back. . . . That's me—the harder you hit me, the faster I come back up."[59]

This is an extraordinarily revealing metaphor. That it relates to a child's toy suggests how old a self-representation it is. The rubber doll metaphor conveys two essential elements of Clinton's style. The first is that his face is meant for punching. The doll is a punching bag, after all, and one that repetitively puts its face right back in front of the fist that struck it—coming back for more punishment. Second, and this in some ways encompasses Clinton's entire career, the rubber doll is indomitable: You can abuse it—but you cannot defeat it. It will keep bouncing back until you tire of striking it. Clinton has a masochistic need to actively put his face in front of an angry man's fist, but also the hypomanic confidence to believe, without doubt, that it is his face and not the fist that will ultimately prevail. Clinton often bragged that even as a kid "I had a high pain threshold." As an example he cited a car accident in high school: "My jaw hit the steering wheel real hard, and it was the steering wheel that broke, not my jaw."[60]

Young Clinton's strategy of perpetually bouncing back, enduring and transcending Roger's abuse through his indomitable optimism, cheerful friendliness, and goodness wasn't working: At age thirteen, Clinton had what he called a "major spiritual crisis." Despite young Bill's prayers and good works, despite his best efforts at peacemaking, the breach in the Clinton household was not healing. It was getting worse, as Roger's drinking escalated, and he descended into madder outbursts of increasing violence. One night, when he was fourteen, young man Clinton would have to take matters into his own hands. The big rubber punching bag didn't just bounce back; it fought back.

"I'll never forget that scene as long as I live," wrote Virginia.

"One night Daddy closed the door to his bedroom, started screaming at Mother, then began to hit her," recalled Clinton. ". . . I grabbed a golf club out of my bag and threw open their door. Mother was on the floor and Daddy was standing over her, beating on her. I told him to stop and said if he didn't I was going to beat the hell out of him with the golf club."

Roger slumped in his chair. "He just caved, sitting down in a chair next to the bed." Clinton, the parentified child, switched quickly from angry avenger to limit-setting parent. As Virginia recalled: "Bill said, 'Daddy, stand up.'

"And of course Roger couldn't. He mumbled and snarled and slurred and stumbled, but his legs wouldn't lift him.

" 'You must stand up to hear what I have to say to you,' Bill told him. 'Daddy, I want you on your feet.'

"Roger, reeling, looked at Bill, and Bill caught him by the arms. 'If you can't stand up, I'll help you.' Bill lifted Roger from his seat and held him up as Roger wobbled, scowling. And I'll never forget how straight Bill looked him in the eye. 'Hear me,' he said to Roger. 'Never . . . *ever* . . . touch my mother again.' "[61]

"We didn't have any more trouble for a good while," Bill recalled proudly.[62]

Two things are striking about this story. The first is Bill's total physical dominance. "By that time I was bigger and stronger than he was sober, much less drunk."[63] The other, perhaps more subtle, aspect is how completely Bill and Roger had reversed roles. Bill sounds like he is the father putting a child in a time-out. He towers over Roger Clinton, physically, psychologically, and developmentally. In this oedipal struggle, there was no contest.

The final violent confrontation between Bill and Roger took place when Bill was sixteen. The event has central importance in the mind of

Roger Clinton Jr., who begins his memoir, *Growing Up Clinton,* with a description of the scene. When he was six, Roger Jr. was lying on his bed listening to his parents argue when he heard "a soft thud" and ventured out of his room to investigate:

"My father was bending my mother backwards over the washing machine, grasping her throat in one hand and a pair of scissors in the other. Shocked by what I was seeing, I stood helpless and frozen, unable to even scream. Finally I pulled myself away and ran out the front door to the house next door."

He was looking for Bill.

" 'Bubba, come quick!' I screamed, 'Daddy's killing Dado [Virginia].'

"We ran back to the house, rushing through the open garage door. My brother opened the door that led to the utility room and the kitchen, wrenched my mother from my father's grasp, and shoved her back next to me. My father stood there, his eyes raging, the scissors still clutched in his hand."[64]

Bill pulled little Roger behind him with one hand, and Virginia behind him with the other. Then he turned to face Roger. He was seething.

" 'You're not going to hurt them anymore,' " he said to his stepfather. " 'You're not going to hit mother, and you're not going to hit Roger anymore. We're not going to take it anymore. If you hit them, you're going to have to go through me.' "[65]

"This time it *was* over," wrote Virginia.[66] Roger never hit them again.

After that violent scene, Clinton understandably had a confused set of emotional reactions. "I suppose I was proud of myself for standing up for Mother; but afterward I was sad about it too. . . . I wish I had someone to talk to about this, but I didn't, so I had to figure it out for myself."[67] One cannot help but feel for Clinton, how bewildering and painful this must have been. One cannot help wishing that he could have gotten the help he needed with his Roger issues, both for his sake and ours. It might have spared us all his unconscious compulsion to reenact his family drama on the world's largest stage.

No doubt Roger Sr. was surprised to see such a show of force. During his political life Clinton's friends and adversaries would also be taken by surprise when Clinton-the-appeaser would switch gears and become Clinton-the-avenger. "Both Clinton's adversaries and his own team underestimated the president's strength," wrote John F. Harris. "The strong side of Clinton's character was easy to miss because he so often put his accommodating side on display."[68] Two important political examples, both from mid-1995, serve as excellent illustrations.

The election of 1994 that gave the Republicans the majority in the House of Representatives for the first time in forty years was widely seen as a repudiation of Clinton's leadership. It was a punishing beating, and after the election Clinton seemed much like a whipped dog. "The people who toiled for Bill Clinton were long accustomed to outbursts and anger. What greeted them now was more frightening. Much of the time Clinton was literally absent from the West Wing. . . . Even when he was physically present he was emotionally gone. . . . He simply checked out."[69] When Terry McAuliffe, Clinton's close friend and chief fundraiser, came to visit him in the White House two days after Christmas—almost two months after the election—he was "shocked" at how "depressed" Clinton's mood seemed. "The President looked as down in the dumps as I'd ever seen him."[70]

Clinton seemed to crawl, more than bounce, back. Following the advice of Dick Morris, a semisecret adviser who normally worked exclusively for Republicans, Clinton's survival strategy was to lurch rightward toward the political center—triangulating—in what looked like pandering to the new conservative zeitgeist. As it turned out, taking back the middle ground would prove to be a winning political strategy, isolating his opponents on the far right, and one that was also truly in keeping with Clinton's long-standing belief in third-way politics that stressed accomplishing progressive aims through conservative means. But at the time, the midcourse correction made it appear to many that Clinton had no inner values he would fight for. He appeared weak.

In the showdown between Clinton and Gingrich over the budget, Gingrich and the congressional Republicans proposed what Democrats believed were draconian budget cuts aimed disproportionately at programs for the poor and elderly, like Medicaid and Medicare. It also altered the tax code to regressively shift the tax burden from the rich to the poor, with capital gains tax cuts for the wealthy stock-owning class and a drastic reduction in the Earned Income Tax Credit for the working poor. "Gingrich was supremely confident" that Clinton would cave and cut a deal, agreeing to the bulk of what they demanded in order to avoid a government shutdown.[71] "I know that Gingrich was telling people up on the Hill that it was just a matter of time before Clinton would cave and go his way," said Leon Panetta, who served as Clinton's chief of staff at the time. Panetta

felt obliged to remind the Republican leadership, "Look, this is a negotia-
tion, this isn't a surrender."[72] But the Republicans were so certain that
Clinton would fold that they "had not devised a strategy for the alternative," wrote Harris.[73] A good deal of that attitude could be attributed
to Gingrich's own hypomanic hubris. With "presumption and zeal that
bordered on the messianic," Gingrich proclaimed he was leading a "revolution." "I am a transformational figure," he grandiosely declared.[74] Gingrich
would later admit: "People feeling confident in their own strength often
fail to take proper measure of their opponents."[75]

But it wasn't just the president's opponents who underestimated him.
The congressional Democrats and Clinton's own staff believed pretty
much the same thing. Against the strenuous advice of almost his entire
staff, and to the horror of the Democratic congressional leadership, Clinton had been readily agreeing to one Republican demand after another.
Said Panetta, "A lot of us were nervous that the president had probably
gone too far in his offering," and they had no idea how much further he
might go. Stephanopoulos wrote that they joked about disconnecting
Clinton's phones, "to keep him from calling Newt and trading away the
store."[76]

Clinton had agreed to the Republican's overarching goal of balancing
the budget but in fact held firm on not cutting programs for education
and the environment, and for Medicaid and Medicare. The proposed big
cuts in Medicaid and Medicare ignited Clinton's secret hot button—they
targeted the weakest and most vulnerable.

In May 1995, the Republicans sent a delegation to the White House to
negotiate what they believed would be Clinton's surrender. To their understandable surprise, they met a different Bill Clinton that day, the one
who stands up to bullies to protect women and children. "Let me tell you
there are a lot of older women who are going to do pretty darn bad under
your budget," Clinton told them.[77] Just as he once told Roger Clinton that
if he wanted to beat Virginia or little Roger, "you're going to have to go
through me," he now told the assembled Republicans: "If you want to
pass your budget, you're going to have to put someone else in this chair."[78]
He turned to Bob Dole, who would be his rival in the 1996 election: "I
don't care what happens. I don't care if I go to five percent in the polls.
I'm not going to sign your budget."

None of Clinton's own people could believe it. "Clinton's defiant stand had surprised and elated his own team."[79] Vice President Al Gore said: "Mr. President, you should say that to the American people. It's very moving to hear that you are willing to lose this election for what you believe in. Just one little thing: When you said you don't care if your popularity goes down to five percent, I think it would sound a little better if you said, 'I don't care if my popularity goes down to zero.' " Clinton put his arm around Gore. "No, that's not right, Al. If I go down to four percent, I'm caving."[80] The room erupted in laughter.

Panetta, who admitted to me that he was as pleasantly surprised by Clinton's defiant stand as anybody, thought it was a defining moment in his presidency. "Clinton had made a very important decision for a guy whose whole life had been devoted to winning the presidency. And now he was occupying an office that he loved, that he had wanted. He was, I think, someone who really believed the office was meant for him. To make the decision that he might have to do something that would cost him that office was a very important Rubicon for Bill Clinton."

With no federal budget in place, all "nonessential" federal workers were sent home, and most federal government services ceased. The country was not happy, and they blamed the Republican Congress; it was a political disaster for Gingrich's revolution. Clinton's poll numbers shot up, while Gingrich's plummeted. Clinton's defiant stance sounded almost Churchillian. Of the Republican budget, Clinton said: "I will fight it today, I will fight it next week, and next month. I will fight it until we get a budget that is fair to all Americans."[81] Even Clinton was enjoying the new Clinton. As one aide said of the new defiance, "He likes standing up. Once you get used to it, it's fun."[82] Clinton's goal line stand on the budget began to shift the momentum from Gingrich back to Clinton, a process that would bring Clinton back from "being nearly irrelevant" after the 1994 electoral debacle to "nearing invincibility" heading into the 1996 presidential reelection campaign.[83]

At the same time the newly assertive Clinton was facing down another bully, Slobodan Milošević, the leader of the Serbians, who had entered into a campaign of ethnic cleansing in his expansionist drive to take over Bosnia. For three years NATO and UN forces had pursued a policy of "muddling through," trying to contain the violence and open channels for diplomatic negotiations. It wasn't working. The Serbs were escalating their atrocities.

In July 1995, the Serbs attacked Srebrenica, which ironically had been the UN's first designated safe area for Muslims to find sanctuary under UN peacekeepers' protection. The Dutch UN forces in Srebrenica repeatedly called for air strikes against the Serbs. Typical of the confusion and lack of will for combat that had characterized the UN and NATO responses up until then, the requests were refused.

The Serbs invaded the town, and went on a terror spree. Twenty-three thousand women and children were rounded up and expelled. Many of the women were raped. On July 14, between four and five thousand men were loaded into trucks and driven into the countryside, where they were interrogated and forced to dig pits.

One survivor described what happened next: "During our first day, the Serbs killed approximately five hundred people. They would just line them up and shoot them into the pits. The approximately one hundred guys whom they had interrogated and who dug the mass graves then had to fill them in. At the end of the day, they were ordered to dig a pit for themselves and line up in front of it. . . . They were shot into the mass grave. . . . At dawn . . . a bulldozer arrived and dug up a pit . . . and buried about four hundred men alive."[84] In all, eight thousand people disappeared, all presumed dead.

To the Clinton foreign policy team, it seemed as if they had no viable options. National security adviser Tony Lake likened it to being in a "vise." The UN presence had become a hindrance since they couldn't fight and seemed only to offer the Serbs opportunities to take hostages. According to a "dual key" agreement, both the UN and all the NATO allies had to approve all military strikes, which made decisions to use force slow, cumbersome, and minimal to nonexistent. And it would defy NATO rules for the United States to act alone. The Congress was against military action, preferring instead to lift the arms embargo on the Muslims and let them defend themselves. Polls showed that only 3 percent of the American electorate saw Bosnia as a "major foreign policy issue for the United States."[85] Eighty percent of the American people were against involving American troops in combat.

Nonetheless, despite the extreme political risk, Clinton unilaterally began a major bombing campaign against the Serbs, in order to force them to stop their aggression and come to the bargaining table.

"I'm risking my presidency,"[86] Clinton told Lake, who has described Clinton's new policy with regard to all our allies as "Tell, don't ask."

Nancy Soderberg, staff director for the National Security Council, wrote that Lake "made it clear to our allies that they had no veto over our approach; we would act with or without them."[87]

They chose to join us.

Operation Deliberate Force was the largest NATO mission in history up until that point, involving thousands of bombing raids. Clinton said to his team that they must "roll every die" to stop the genocide.

Lucky for Clinton, and the world, he rolled and won. The Serbs declared a cease-fire and agreed to negotiate what would become the Dayton peace accord.

Tony Lake wrote that Clinton's more muscular stance was more than just a shift in policy; he, too, felt that he was meeting a *new* Clinton in mid-1995.

We can almost see Clinton going through the stages of his relationship with Roger in his approach to Bosnia.

First he endures it—muddling through. For the previous two years, wrote Lake, the president would "visibly wince" whenever the subject of Bosnia came up, which it did almost every day.[88]

Then Clinton became episodically enraged. There were also "occasional explosions of anger for good reason, but for no good purpose."[89] On one foreign trip, Clinton even exploded at Lake. Shaken, Lake told presidential aide Bruce Lindsey, "If he ever does that again, I'll quit."[90]

Finally, as he did with Roger, Clinton took control and fought back.

"By 1995, all meetings with him were more crisp and presidential," wrote Lake. "On Bosnia, he was clearly in command of the subject, of his government, and of himself."[91] When I spoke to Tony Lake, he said he really believed Bosnia was Clinton's finest hour, and that if he deserved a Nobel Peace Prize, which Lake thought he did, it was for Bosnia even more than for Ireland or the Middle East. By taking the risk to act alone, to meet genocidal force with force against the wishes of the American people, the Congress, and the allies—Clinton single-handedly turned the entire catastrophe around.

If Milošević wanted to slaughter civilians, he was going to have to go through Clinton.

It is worth noting the metaphor Clinton used in his July 18 memo, four days after the slaughter of the innocents in Srebrenica, in which he announced a new, more robust policy of air strikes: "The United States can't be a punching bag in the world anymore."[92]

Stage 3. Forgiveness

In the spring of 1967, during Clinton's junior year of college, Roger's throat cancer, which he had contracted in 1965, worsened dramatically. Over the next year, as Roger was dying, Clinton initiated a process of reconciliation with his stepfather. Bill drove from Georgetown to Hot Springs over many weekends to be with him. Roger was hospitalized several times over the course of the year at Duke Medical Center in Durham, North Carolina. Though Virginia rarely came, Bill visited Roger every time he was at Duke. "Though Duke was too far away for me to go regularly, Bill didn't miss an opportunity to come down from Washington, D.C., whenever Roger was in Durham," wrote Virginia.[93] During one period in the spring of his junior year, Roger was in Duke for six weeks. Despite the fact that Clinton was in the middle of his semester and working on Capitol Hill as an aide to Senator William Fulbright, he visited his stepfather every weekend, leaving every Friday afternoon to make the six-hour drive through the Virginia hills. These visits provided a series of private moments for the two to make their final peace. "As sad as those weekends were, they were a healing time for both Bill and Roger," wrote Virginia. Clinton himself wrote, "On those long, languid weekends, we came to terms with each other, and he accepted the fact that I loved him and forgave him."[94]

Frequently, Bill would take Roger out of the hospital for a drive, and they would drive around for hours. While Virginia was unaware of any "true confessions" by Roger, or "demands" made by Bill—no big talk that cleared the air—in their own silent ways, both men were searching for reconciliation. Bill felt he finally achieved it on Easter Sunday when he took Roger to services at the Duke chapel. "I will never forget it," Bill told his mother. "We went over to Chapel Hill and saw all the dogwoods, the redbud trees. It was just stunningly beautiful. It was one of the most beautiful days I can remember in my entire life. And it was a wonderful experience we had, just the two of us."[95]

In between visits Bill wrote Roger a series of encouraging letters, including this one reproduced in his mother's memoir. Still deeply religious, he encouraged Roger to get spiritual help: "Mother told me you all went to church Sunday. If both of you would just make up your mind to do that every Sunday, no matter what, it would sure help. I believe, Daddy, that none of us can ever have peace, unless they can face life with God, knowing that good always outweighs bad, and death doesn't end a man's life. You ought to look everywhere for help, Daddy. You ought to write me more."[96]

In this same letter Bill finally laid out the truth of his feelings, both good and bad, as he was trying to make his peace with Roger: "I think I ought to close this letter now and wait for your answer but there are a couple of things I ought to say first. 1) I don't think you ever realized how much we all love you and need you. 2) I don't think you have ever realized either how we have all been hurt . . . but still really have *not* turned against you."[97]

In 1987, I wrote a paper entitled "The Capacity to Forgive," arguing that forgiveness can be a road to higher levels of psychological maturity.[98] Otto Kernberg, who served as medical director and resident guru at New York Hospital–Cornell Medical Center, where I completed my postdoctoral training, has argued that people with immature personality structures fixated at more primitive stages of development see themselves and the world in black-and-white terms. Mature personalities, by contrast, are capable of maintaining more realistic images of self and others that integrate both good and bad aspects. True forgiveness means acknowledging your anger at someone who has hurt you without demonizing them. Without minimizing the gravity of the offense, you are able to recall your positive memories of the offender, and still have empathy for them, as you struggle to integrate your conflicting feelings into one realistic image of who they are.

Young Bill Clinton showed this capacity to an advanced degree at an early age in his attitude toward Roger. "Bill had as much reason as anyone to hate him, to hold a grudge, but he didn't. He loved and forgave him," wrote Virginia. "In fact, Bill was instrumental in making me put aside my own anger at Roger. . . . He's told me time and again, whenever I fall back on my black-white view of the world, 'Mother, there are two sides to every story.'"[99] Bill wrote: "I never stopped loving Roger Clinton, never stopped pulling for him to change, never stopped enjoying being with him when he was sober and engaged. . . . Like most alcoholics and drug addicts I've known, Roger Clinton was fundamentally a good person. He loved mother and me and little Roger. . . . He was generous to family and friends. He was smart and funny. . . . The really disturbing thing about living with an alcoholic is that it isn't always bad. Weeks, sometimes even whole months, would pass while we'd enjoy being a family, blessed with the quiet joys of an ordinary life. I'm grateful I haven't forgotten those times."[100] Virginia agreed, "He loved Roger very much . . . loved him with all his faults."

In this Bill was a stark contrast to little Roger, who was never able to forgive his father or see him in any way but all bad: "I always thought of my dad as a cruel, mean, frightening man. Growing up, I never thought he really cared about my mother, my brother or me. . . . I rarely saw any other side of him. . . . If he ever loved me, I wasn't aware of it."[101] Roger would become a drug addict and alcoholic. During court-mandated drug treatment, it came out in his family therapy sessions that he had always hated his father. "In the course of those sessions, Roger admitted how much he hated his father, and Virginia and Bill learned for the first time how profoundly Roger had been affected by his father's alcoholism and violence," wrote Hillary.[102]

According to Kernberg's view, another manifestation of this same maturity is the ability to accurately recognize both the good and bad in oneself. Evidence that young Clinton had this capacity is found in this part of an autobiographical essay he wrote in eleventh grade: "I am a person motivated and influenced by so many diverse forces I sometimes question the sanity of my existence. I am a living paradox—deeply religious, yet not as convinced of my exact beliefs as I ought to be; wanting responsibility yet shirking it; loving the truth but often times giving way to falsity. . . . I detest selfishness, but I see it in the mirror every day. . . . I view those, some of whom are very dear to me, who have never learned how to live. I desire and struggle to be different from them, but often am almost an exact likeness." His teacher gave him a hundred for a "beautiful and honest" attempt to go "way down inside." Bill Clinton at age sixteen was readily able to acknowledge his complexities and contradictions, to see both good and bad in himself, and to live with it even as he struggled with it.

As an adult Clinton continued to maintain awareness of both his dark and light sides. When Clinton was governor in 1982, he once told an undergraduate politics class that "the political giants were usually a combination of darkness (insecurity, battles with depression, family disorder) and of light (sense of history, a desire to serve the public). In the great leaders the light overcame the darkness."[103]

Bill's capacity to forgive those who have hurt him generalized far beyond his stepfather. His capacity to have empathy for his enemies is one of the traits that dumbfound those who know him best. Clinton virtually embodies the Christian dictum to love your enemies through his empathy for those who have most viciously attacked him. Rose Crane recalled, "Me with my mean, sharp tongue, I'd say something critical about one of his political enemies who had pulled some dirty trick on him, and he would say: 'You have to understand, it's not their fault, they're just having problems.' "

Judy Gaddy, who worked on Clinton's gubernatorial staff, chided Clinton for being so forgiving of his political enemies. Clinton responded, "Don't be upset with them. They're a product of their upbringing. He's a product of his environment."[104] Leon Panetta agreed, saying that "Clinton by nature is someone who doesn't retain animosity; he is not someone who is vindictive. About someone who is very harsh with him, he'll say, 'Well, this is why he had to do it, so I understand.' He has a tremendous amount of empathy in that way."

"Clinton would often talk about how much he admired Mandela and how much he tried to emulate him in not carrying hate," wrote Terry McAuliffe. But even McAuliffe was shocked by how Mandela-like Clinton could be. On August 1, 1999, they were off to an Army-Navy football game, and McAuliffe brought up, with great satisfaction, the recent news that Linda Tripp had been indicted for her illegal tape recordings of Monica Lewinsky, recordings that both betrayed her friendship with Lewinsky and paved the road to Clinton's impeachment. He was taken aback by Clinton's response: "You know, Mac, I've got to tell you, I really feel sorry for that woman. . . . She's really had a rough life. She had a really, really bad marriage and she got divorced. . . . It wasn't her fault, Mac. I hope it's behind her."[105]

Clinton seems to be saying of those who have tried to destroy him, as Christ did while hanging on the cross, "Forgive them, Father, for they know not what they do." To be able to say that, and truly mean it, suggests to me that Clinton has reached an elevated level of moral and spiritual development. That this can coexist with his deficiencies in other areas may seem contradictory, but people *are* contradictory.

Many looked to Bill Clinton's abusive home life to find the roots of his skills as a peacemaker. However, from their analyses, one gets the impression that all there was to the story was that Clinton learned to distract and mollify his volatile stepfather with his sunny demeanor, producing peace at any price. Bill Clinton would never have become one of the most effective peacemakers in history simply by being an appeasing charmer. The deeper roots of his peacemaking abilities are here, in his final search for reconciliation with Roger Clinton.

The eight-year-old boy who walked a mile to church every Sunday would eventually travel the world with his gospel of reconciliation.

PART II

Arkansas Politics

5

Three Pairs of Shoes

· THE ONLY TRACK ·

In 1956 Bill Clinton's family bought their first television set. "Strange as it was for a kid of ten years old, what really dominated my TV viewing that summer were the Republican and Democratic conventions. I sat on the floor right in front of the TV and watched them both, transfixed. . . . When Adlai Stevenson, the nominee in 1952, accepted his party's call to run again, he said he had prayed 'this cup would pass from me.' I admired Stevenson's intelligence and eloquence, but even then I couldn't understand why anyone wouldn't want the chance to be president."[1]

In 1982, more than twenty-five years later, a student in a politics and literature class at the University of Arkansas asked him: "Why, considering all your other choices, do you do politics?" Their teacher, Clinton friend Diane Blair, recalled that "Clinton paused, clearly thinking up some elaborate and eloquent answer, and then he simply shrugged and grinned: 'It's the only track I ever wanted to run on.' "[2]

When did Bill Clinton begin running for president? Perhaps the question should be rephrased: When did he realize that he was born to run? People have been predicting Clinton would be president since he was in second grade, the only president in American history to be nominated for the office by his peers and mentors before he was even old enough to vote. As Bill Clinton moved through his education and began his political career, the sense of inevitability grew in intensity until, as Arkansas journalist Meredith Oakley told me, "It just became conventional wisdom here in Arkansas that he would be president." How did they know? A Secretariat emerges once in a generation. The most common response I got in all my interviews was "I can't explain it. I just knew."

Bill Clinton attended Boys State in 1963 when he was sixteen. Sponsored by the American Legion, Boys State is an educational program aimed at introducing promising high school students to government service through participation in mock elections. Only four boys at the Arkansas Boys State convention would be elected by their peers to go on to the national convocation, Boys Nation, in Washington, D.C. Clinton was determined to be one of those four.

When Clinton got to Boys State he saw some of his old friends from Hope. Joe Purvis, who had known Clinton since they were both babies, was delighted to see him again, but he didn't think Clinton had a chance in hell of winning the election. For starters, Clinton was pudgy, not usually a good thing for someone who wants to be popular in high school. And visually he couldn't have made a worst first impression. "I remember thinking he was wearing the ugliest shorts I ever saw in my life," Purvis said. "'Are you color blind?'" he asked Clinton, who had no idea what Purvis was talking about. "He looked at me like I was crazy, like, I've got a shirt and pair of pants on, what's the problem? They were so ugly, they looked like something you'd put on a sofa. They had little stripes—like, red and gray—not khaki or blue like normal shorts. I wondered if someone had made them for him. They must have. They don't allow people to sell things like that off the rack. Thank God someone's picking his clothes now." Like his mother, Clinton had the innate self-confidence of the hypomanic. He may have been a little porky, and his clothes may have been very dorky—but he felt like a winner.

Typically, the boys who won the elections were star athletes. For example, the boy reputed to have the governor's spot all sewn up was Mack McLarty, a wealthy, amiable, handsome high school football quarterback from Hope. Bill's lack of athletic ability was another handicap in his bid to become a leader among boys. McLarty, who had also attended kindergarten with Bill, and would later serve as his White House chief of staff, recalled that Clinton liked to play sports, but "he was perhaps not as coordinated as he would like to remember." George Wright, who also played football for Hope, said, "When Bill was fifteen or sixteen, he was big and clumsy. Not an athlete."

But Clinton had a plan. Clinton told his Hot Springs high school classmate Phil Jamison that if he could personally meet every one of the hundreds of boys there, they would like him, and he would win. He wasted no time. "Clinton was thoroughly familiar with the camp culture before he arrived and had plotted his senate race while other boys were still finding their way around. . . . He formed a campaign team that canvassed the cabins at night and posted himself outside the cafeteria at six-thirty each morning, working the breakfast crowd like a factory gate."[3] Ron Cecil, another friend from Hot Springs, was "amazed by his friend's political savvy and the urgency with which he shook the hands of strangers."[4]

Joe Purvis quickly changed his mind about his old friend having no chance to win. Even as a boy, Clinton displayed a campaign technique that would become his signature, Purvis recalled. "He was a phenomenal campaigner. He just outworked people. He was shaking your hand with one hand and holding your shoulder or arm with the other. And he's fixing his gaze on you while he's talking to you. He could spend a few seconds with you and it felt like a few minutes."

Bill won election to Boys Nation in Washington. There he got to eat lunch with venerable and irascible Arkansas senator William Fulbright. It was a useful introduction. When he was in college, Bill would work for Fulbright and gain his first exposure to national politics.

But the big prize was the chance to meet Kennedy. One hundred "senators" rode in two buses to the White House. Daniel J. O'Connor, who was in charge of the boys, instructed them on proper etiquette in the White House. Stay in line. Don't wander off. Don't crowd around the president. One boy stood out in his memory: "Clinton was curious about what lay in store for the boys that morning. His own intentions were clear. He asked O'Connor whether he could have his picture taken with President Kennedy. 'Sure,' O'Connor said. 'But I'm not sure what the Secret Service regulations are. We'll have to see when we get there.' Clinton pressed the issue. It sure would be great, he said, if he could get his picture taken with the president. The boy from Arkansas, O'Connor recalled, 'certainly seemed bound and determined.' "[5]

He certainly was. Clinton recalled that "Kennedy walked down the steps and began shaking hands. I was in the front, and being bigger and a bigger supporter of the President's than most of the others, I made sure I'd get to shake his hand even if he shook only two or three."[6] Bill also made sure a friend had a camera at the ready.

Virginia said: "I'd never seen him get so excited about something. When he came back from Washington, holding this picture of himself with Jack Kennedy and the expression on his face . . . I knew right then that politics was the answer for him."[7] Patty Criner remembered, "Shaking hands with John Kennedy . . . that touched him. He knew that he could do something through politics that would influence people at home."[8] Michael Muldoon said, "That handshake did something to him. I think that from that moment on he aspired to be president. The handshake changed him, and stayed with him forever."

At sixteen, Bill decided firmly on a career in elected politics. "I decided I wanted to be in public life as an elected official. . . . I knew I could be great in public service."[9] When Clinton ran for president in 1992, the picture was widely circulated as "the beginning of my presidential aspirations." Clinton does not admit daring to dream that high at sixteen, yet "I probably felt as Abraham Lincoln did as a young man, 'I will study and get ready and perhaps my chance will come.'" He had high hopes. "I thought at the time I wanted to be senator," still no small aspiration.[10]

A few months later, President Kennedy was assassinated. Phil Jamison remembers the look on Bill Clinton's face: "He was motionless. Not even a twitch on his face. Yet you could feel the anger building up inside him."[11] The tragedy of Kennedy's assassination could only have intensified Clinton's sense of identification with him.

Freud believed that the death of a beloved figure hastens a process of internalization and identification with the "lost love object." Most anyone who has lost a parent has experienced this phenomenon. After their death you review your relationship with the departed and find connections with them you had not acknowledged before. Clinton did not have a personal relationship with Kennedy, but he was a cherished role model, and he had laid hands on young Bill Clinton. The handshake was a "benediction" of sorts.[12] Psychologically, in Bill's mind, there was the feeling that a torch had been passed. The day before his inauguration there was one thing Clinton made sure to do: He went to Arlington Cemetery and placed a white rose on JFK's grave.

Even before Clinton graduated from college, there were people who seriously believed that he would be president. Bill's high school principal, Johnnie Mae Mackey, predicted it. Paul Root, Clinton's history teacher, said that Ms. Mackey had had that premonition about a student only twice in her career ("The other guy was unemployed when I last inquired," Root added wryly).

There's a Southern expression for something that is certain: "You can write it down." David Leopoulos told me he did just that in 1964, the year they all graduated. He wrote something on the back of an envelope and gave it to a friend of his with an interest in politics who ran a local bookstore, saying, "I have two predictions here. And when they come true, I want you to call me." The first one was: "Bill Clinton will be governor of Arkansas." The second was: "Bill Clinton will be president of the United States." "And he did call me both times."

Clinton dated a woman named Denise Hyland in college. When she was traveling in France during summer vacation, she told some Texans she met, "Remember the name—Bill Clinton—because someday he will be president."[13]

Carolyn Staley had had a strong premonition that he would be president since they were both fifteen: "I've always known, since we were in high school. I have known deep down in my heart that he would make a run for the presidency. It was an unspoken thing. . . . Even the cards I sent him in high school and college, many, many times alluded to the presidency."[14] Staley remembers taking a tour of the White House when she was in college and fantasizing about how it might be redecorated under a Clinton presidency. "When Bill's here, we're not going to have all this French furniture. It's going to be filled with the world's finest American antiques," she declared to herself. "And when I walked through statuary hall, I thought, 'See that niche right there, there's going to be a bust of Bill Clinton.' I just really believed that."

· A FORCE OF NATURE ·

By the time Clinton left for his freshman year at Georgetown, he had already decided that he would be returning to Arkansas to run for public office. After garnering as much knowledge, contacts, and credentials as he could in the larger world, he would come back and put them to work for his community back home. When Bill Clinton returned to Arkansas in 1973, he had been to Georgetown, Oxford, and Yale. Having completed his prestigious academic odyssey, he was ready to run for office.

Bill took a job as a law professor at the University of Arkansas at Fayetteville. During his job interview "he charmed us all right out of our mortarboards," said the dean. They had just one concern: Clinton wasn't planning to use his position at the university as a "springboard" for a political career, was he? He assured them he wasn't—but, of course, he was.

Students loved him. He was charming, thought provoking, and an easy grader. One thing that made Clinton stand out was the concern he showed for African-American students, many of whom were in serious danger of flunking out because their prior education had not prepared them adequately for law school. "Sink or swim" was the school's basic posture. "Dive in and rescue" was Clinton's approach. Clinton organized review sessions for African-American law students after school in the student lounge and at his home. Carol Willis, one of those students, said: "Bill Clinton was a different kind of professor: a man that reached out to black law students to try to help them." Though it may be something of an exaggeration, Willis says that there is a whole generation of black lawyers in Arkansas who owe their careers to Clinton.

On virtually the day he stepped on campus, Clinton began his first campaign. He sought a congressional seat long occupied by a secure Republican incumbent, John Paul Hammerschmidt. The famous symbol of the 1974 campaign, which is now on display in the Clinton Presidential Library, is a pair of worn black shoes with large round holes in the soles. Giving new meaning to the phrase "working the shoe leather," Clinton pounded the pavement, meeting voters, until he literally wore right through the soles of his shoes. In fact, one person who worked closely with him during the campaign told me, he wore out *three* pairs of shoes. How many miles must one walk to wear holes in three pairs of shoes in nine months? Those shoes are concrete physical evidence of the almost inhuman level of physical energy generated inside this intensely hypomanic man. Clinton's energy is one of his greatest political assets, but paradoxically, it is also one of his greatest areas of vulnerability, as we shall see.

For Clinton, running for office was more than a metaphor. The *Arkansas Democrat* reported, "Clinton runs—literally, physically runs—from place to place as he strives to meet as many of the district's eligible voters as possible."[15] Bill Clinton's electoral strategy when he ran for senator with Boys State had been simple: If he could personally meet every boy there, they would like him, and he would win. Clinton applied that same strategy to his run for Congress: He endeavored to make personal contact with every voter in his district. Clinton estimated that he met a hundred thousand voters in nine months, one pie social at a time. One law student who drove him, Jim Daugherty, recalled that Clinton never passed a voter he wasn't determined to meet. "There'd be many a day when we'd be driving along—late for an appointment somewhere—and he'd say, 'Jim, stop here. Stop here. Pull over.' And he'd jump out of the car and run out to some guy standing out in a field working on a fence and shake his hand and introduce himself. He wanted to meet everybody." Because he still believed that "if anyone ever got a chance to meet him, they'd like him," said Daugherty.

Clinton was a "relentless, tireless and dogged" campaigner said longtime Arkansas politician David Pryor. "I used to be pretty good in politics, in having the energy to go from town to town, but Bill Clinton could cover two times the towns that I would. And when we'd come off the road late at night, I'd go to bed by eleven or twelve, and he'd work the bowling alleys and all-night cafés till 2:00 A.M. He had an insatiable desire and tremendous energy."[16]

"He's a force of nature," said Patty Criner. "That's what Hillary calls him." In this way Clinton very much resembles our most hypomanic president, Theodore Roosevelt, who was described by one journalist as "an irresistible force." Roosevelt was described by a contemporary as having a "superabundance of animal life" beyond what was "ever condensed into a human being."[17] One British observer said that the two most impressive natural phenomena in America were TR and Niagara Falls. Like Clinton, he was a tireless campaigner, in a class by himself. When he won the governorship of New York, in a surprise, narrow, come-from-behind victory, he had made as many as nineteen speeches a day on his whistle-stop train tour of upstate New York. When Roosevelt ran for vice president, McKinley, the man at the top of the ticket, campaigned from home, while Roosevelt made 673 speeches in 24 states, covering 21,000 miles, speaking 20,000 words a day to a total of three million people.[18] What one reporter said of Roosevelt's campaign style would apply in equal measure to our dark horse, Bill Clinton: "He ain't runnin', he's gallopin'."[19]

I think it is more than a metaphor to say that hypomanics are a force of nature. Like electromagnetic energy, their power has two aspects.

Their seemingly limitless capacity for physical and mental activity is the most visible manifestation of their force, but just as electricity has a magnetic component, hypomanic energy generates an interpersonal magnetism we call charisma. "Clinton exuded an animal magnetism that drew both men and women," wrote David Gergen."[20] In similar fashion, Roosevelt had a force field that "surrounded him as a kind of nimbus, imperceptible but irresistibly drawing to him everyone who came into its presence."[21] Like magnetic energy, it can polarize people, repelling some with the same force that attracts others. More than any politician in recent memory, Clinton aroused powerful feelings of both love and hate, while in his day Roosevelt was "the most despised and at the same time the most loved man in the country."[22]

Studies show that people naturally become infected by hypomanic enthusiasm. "Nothing, it would seem, is quite so wildly contagious as exuberance," wrote Johns Hopkins psychologist Kay Jamison in her book *Exuberance*.[23] Senator Pryor saw this in Clinton: "He has tremendous energy and it's contagious."[24] Clinton's 1974 campaign co-manager Ron Addington said, "His energy just rubbed off on people." As one *New York Times* reporter wrote, Roosevelt's energy had a similar effect on the mood of those around him: "You don't smile with Mr. Roosevelt; you shout with laughter with him, and then you shout again."[25]

Exuberant moods and behaviors "act on the same reward centers in the brain as food, sex, and addictive drugs," wrote Jamison.[26] Thus, when the exuberant leader is able to induce a euphoric state in his followers, he is actually having the same effect on their brain chemistry as a drug. People literally get *high* on Clinton. As Maraniss wrote, "People who fell into his orbit found it exhilarating. Life around him, they said, seemed more vital, closer to the edge, less routine, more physically and intellectually challenging."[27] People who worked for Clinton during his 1974 run for Congress still regard it thirty years later as a peak experience. "Just mention the 1974 campaign to anyone who was a part of it, and a smile will come across their face," said Ann Henry.

The sense of esprit de corps charismatic leaders induce is a central part of their appeal. "Exuberance draws people together," wrote Jamison. It "pumps life into social bonds and helps create new ones."[28] As Ann Henry, who worked in the campaign, told me, "We were joined together for a cause, and it created bonds among each other that are still present." Lifetime friendships were forged in the white heat of Clinton's energy.

When people are pumped up they work harder. Studies show that people who work for charismatic leaders work longer hours and feel more confident about taking risks. "It was contagious, the energy level, and the excitement, and the enthusiasm. People were willing to work long hours for him because it was catching," said David Folsom. "Clinton makes you work twenty-four hours a day," Carol Willis told me. "It wasn't just me doing it, it was everybody. The guy inspired you to do that because he did it himself."

The ultimate statement about Clinton's charisma is that it was an article of faith among those working for him in 1974 that they were working for a future president of the United States. "This is not unique to me. I'm sure others have told you. After being around him two or three weeks, you just said to yourself, 'This guy is going to be president,' " David Folsom told me. "I've never felt that way before or since about anyone else." "Most of us knew from day one, instinctively knew, that this guy was going to be president," said Carol Willis. "We started the drive to the White House in 1974. Say whatever you want; he was just destined to become president." Marla Crider told me, "We didn't have any doubts. We all knew he was going to be president. We were changing the world."

· THE PEGASUS COMPLEX ·

Paul Costa, one of the originators of the five-factor model, told me that there are some people who, like Icarus, a figure of Greek myth, "endeavor to fly above the normal boundaries of time and space." Though Costa did not relate this idea directly to Clinton (he is forbidden, as a federal employee, from making psychological statements about political figures), the idea came up during our general discussion of Clinton. The problem for those with an Icarus complex is that "none of us can escape gravity forever. Eventually the wax wings melt, and you fall."

Somewhat tongue in cheek, we might say that Clinton has a Pegasus complex, not only to extend our horse metaphor, but because the wings on which Clinton rose were integral to his biology, more like the wings of Pegasus than the artificial wax invention of Icarus. But, like Icarus, Clinton flies until he crashes. Hypomanics don't just wear out their shoes. They wear out themselves, and everyone around them, too. Because they are powerhouses of energy, it's easy to forget that they have limits to their endurance. Inevitably, when they push past those limits, as they almost always do, there is a cost.

"Most of the personal and political mistakes I made in my life were because I tried to do too much and was exhausted," wrote Clinton.[29]

It is somewhat amazing to contemplate how much of the Clinton puzzle is explained by this one simple factor: fatigue. It is during the 1974 campaign that we first see breakdowns in Clinton's judgment and conscientiousness, and it is directly related to his level of physical exhaustion.

· DIMINISHED NEED FOR SLEEP ·

His 1974 campaign co-manager, Ron Addington, found dealing with Clinton's fatigue to be maddening: "The second he finished being a public person he would just crash. He would just fall asleep sitting in the chair. He was so exhausted that he couldn't have a rational conversation. We couldn't discuss a decision. He'd just pass out." When Clinton returned from a road trip, Addington just took one look at him and knew he hadn't slept in days. "I would see him with those big bags under his eyes, and I would know he was coming off a marathon of four or five days without sleep."

One of the *DSM-IV* (the fourth edition of the *Diagnostic and Statistical Manual*) diagnostic criteria for both mania and hypomania is a "diminished need for sleep." For Clinton, who has a mildly manic temperament, this is not an aberrant state, but rather his *normal* state. Bill "doesn't need a lot of sleep. . . . He's up late at night, every night. . . . He's been blessed with a wonderful constitution and great stamina," said Hillary.[30] "He just doesn't sleep. He just doesn't believe in it," said Carol Willis. "If the phone rings at three in the morning, either someone is dead, or it's Bill Clinton," Willis said with a chuckle.

Hypomanics have the unique ability to feel rested after a small amount of sleep. Clinton has mastered the power nap. He can grab small snatches of sleep virtually anywhere, any time, at will, and then feel refreshed and ready to go. "If he has a minute off, he has an incredible ability to catnap, which is part of what keeps him fueled up," said Hillary.[31] It was during the 1974 campaign that he began to lean heavily on his ability to survive a brutal schedule with these naps. "He could take a ten-minute nap in the vehicle, and it was as if he had eight hours of sleep," said David Folsom, one of his law school student drivers from the 1974 campaign. He continued the same pattern as governor: "Well, he didn't sleep but a maximum of five hours a night. He could take a power nap quicker than anyone I ever saw, and he would be completely renewed when he woke up from that, and ready to go again," said a woman on his gubernatorial staff. And Clinton continued relying on power naps as president. Ann McCoy, who worked with him as an administrative assistant in the White House, told me that "he had a room at the White House, a small office right off of the Oval Office, with a comfortable chair, where he would occasionally take a power nap." One day she asked him: "How do you go to sleep so quick like that?" He said, "I just imagine a big hole in the back of my head, and I just focus on that."

That Clinton can fall asleep anywhere at the drop of a hat is not just testimony to his talent at power napping. It's also a sign that he's so sleep deprived, he's essentially one stop from passing out at any given moment. And indeed, Clinton is known for falling asleep at inappropriate times, when he does not intend to. For example, during the 1974 campaign, Clinton was supposed to have a meeting with J. Bill Becker, the head of the state AFL-CIO. They planned to drive together from Fort Smith to Hot Springs, and talk on the way. Addington recalled, "Becker was a real important guy, and a real busy one." Clinton was supposed to meet Becker at nine, but didn't show up until midnight. "Becker was pissed." And then, to add insult to injury, "ten minutes after Clinton got in the car, he fell asleep, when they were supposed to be having this real important private meeting."

Passing out at unexpected and potentially embarrassing moments became a way of life for Clinton. "All of our friends are very tolerant," said Hillary. "They know if they invite Bill over for dinner, if they get him there, and get him fed and relaxed, he's likely to fall asleep in the middle of the conversation in the living room. I've seen him fall asleep while the rest of us carry on our conversation, wake up, contribute to the conversation, and fall back to sleep." Several people told me similar funny stories. An amazing testimony to Clinton's mental abilities is that even when he sleeps through half a discussion, he can concentrate better than most people do fully awake. Hillary recalled a legal continuing-education seminar she took with Bill: "We were in the seminar, and the fellow was showing us a problem on the screen. It was a pretty hard problem, and Bill was asleep. . . . The fellow was asking about the answer to this problem.

None of us were really catching on. Bill woke up, answered the problem, and fell back asleep."[32]

The problem is that Clinton "makes big mistakes when he is tired. He makes big mistakes by blowing off the handle. He says things he wishes he didn't say," said Carol Willis.[33] "When he's tired, he becomes erratic, and he makes little dumb, stupid kid errors," Willis told me. "Most of them are harmless errors, but if you make them on the bigger stage, they get magnified."

· INABILITY TO TOLERATE DOWNTIME ·

Hypomanics can't tolerate rest. Though they need less sleep than average, they still manage to get much less sleep than they need, because their motors are always revving and they don't know how to turn the engine off. Like most hypomanics, Clinton can't tolerate downtime, and whenever his staff tried to impose it on him, he rebelled.

Judy Gaddy, who worked with him in the governor's office, recalled: "One time he was having terrible allergies, and we were trying to get him to rest, and he wouldn't rest." Gaddy put her foot down: "I want you to stay at the mansion. You can't come here. We don't want you here," she insisted. "Well, he came here fifteen times, and I said, 'Governor, get back in your house.'" Meekly, Clinton obeyed. The problem was that even when his body was at rest, his mind was still in motion. Although he was banished from the office, Clinton generated scores of new ideas, which he then wanted to implement immediately. Gaddy learned that "the bad part about giving him free time is that he just sits there and dreams up other things." The recovering Clinton called her dozens of times with new ideas. Gaddy finally gave up and brought him back to work, realizing that "we need to keep this boy busy, because if we don't, he's going to drive us all crazy."[34]

Even a few minutes of inactivity could drive Clinton to distraction. When she was in charge of the governor's schedule, Mary Anne Salmon got "tired of people fussing that he was always late." So one day she built thirty extra minutes into his schedule, "unannounced to him," with the result that, for once, instead of being late, Clinton arrived early to an event. It meant that for a few moments he had nothing to do, and it made him furious. "He was just irate. It was a waste of his time. After that I never tried to build time in his schedule."

Clinton couldn't tolerate brief moments of inactivity in the White House either, recalled Ann McCoy. "He did not like to have any sort of lag time where he did not have anything to do. In fact, he would get angry. 'Why are we here five minutes early?'" One example stood out in her mind. "I will never forget when we had Arafat and Rabin in September of 1993. It was an incredible thing. We had five thousand people on the lawn. We had press everywhere.

"Clinton said impatiently, 'When are we going down? Why are we not going down? We have everything set up on the back lawn.'

"'Because we cannot go on until eleven o'clock. It's live TV, so we can't go.'"

"He looked at his watch and said, 'But that's ten minutes. What am I going to do for ten minutes?'

"'Well, why don't you show Arafat and Rabin around the White House?'

"He just looked at me: 'But seriously,' he said, 'what are we going to do for ten minutes?'

Clinton himself has long recognized the problem posed by his exhaustion. The root problem is that he cannot tolerate the solution: rest. One day during the 1992 campaign, Clinton told Begala, "'Every important mistake I've made in my life I made when I was tired. You guys got to give me a break.'" Begala agreed, and built some free time into his schedule: "So then we'd give him a down day, and you know what he would say? 'Why aren't we out there? That Ross Perot is in three different states today. George Bush is out shaking a thousand hands! I can't tolerate it!'"

Even though intellectually Clinton understood that his relentless pace was deleterious and wanted to modulate it, he couldn't.

Indeed, Clinton requires someone to *force* him to get rest. Leon Panetta, who took over as chief of staff in the summer of 1994, feels that one of the most important interventions that he made was scheduling a two-hour blackout period in the afternoon when Clinton could have no meetings. Panetta didn't ask Clinton's permission to do this; he imposed the ban on him—which was exactly what Clinton required, because he cannot impose such limits on himself.

· WEARING OTHERS OUT ·

Hypomanics physically wear out the people who work with them; it is simply impossible for a normal person to keep pace. A lot of people have come and gone from the Clinton camp out of sheer exhaustion, Addington believes. "He could just suck all the working energy out of you. He sucked all the work out of most people in the first round."

Case in point, Addington lined up a cadre of law students to drive Clinton to campaign events. The need for drivers became apparent the first time Addington was in a car with Bill Clinton driving—it was the most terrifying drive Addington ever took in his life. Clinton was behind the wheel, talking, gesticulating, driving too fast, and paying little attention to the road: "He was just a horrible driver. He would get behind people, and be tailgating, and driving so fast down hills, as fast as that car could go. He didn't pay any attention. And we just said, 'Shoot, you are not going to drive.' "

The young men who drove Clinton had to work in shifts to keep up with him. Like the classic character from a western movie who is galloping a long distance in a hurry, Clinton always needed fresh horses. (Once again we see a parallel with Theodore Roosevelt, though in Roosevelt's case the need for fresh horses was more than a metaphor: During his North Dakota cowboy phase, he rode up to forty hours straight, requiring as many as five horses in succession.) In 2006 I was able to speak to David Folsom and Jim Daugherty, two former law school roommates who had shared the Clinton driving responsibilities thirty-two years earlier. "I was twenty-seven, and I couldn't keep up with him," said Folsom. "We had to work in shifts. One day I picked him up at 4:00 A.M. at his home. We made a swing through the entire district, and by the time I dropped him back at his house, it was 6:00 A.M. the following day. We had been on the road for twenty-six hours. I let him out at his house, and he said, 'Tell Jim Daugherty to pick me up at eight o'clock.'

"I said, 'Eight P.M.?'

"He said, 'No, eight A.M.'

"We had been on the road for twenty-six hours. He was back on the road two hours later, and it probably took me two or three days to recover."

Jim Daugherty confirmed his former roommate's account: "I was twenty-three. Back then I had a lot of energy, but he wore my ass out, excuse my French. He would get up at the crack of dawn, and it was a twenty-hour day. I've never been involved with anyone who had that kind of get up and go." Daugherty would be trying to catch his fourth and fifth wind to keep pace with the man he was driving. "I don't know that he ever lost his first wind."

During his 1992 presidential campaign, the press had to cover him in shifts as well. Even then it was like running a triathlon. Rose Crane remembered that after the campaign was over the press people on Clinton's bus had T-shirts printed up reading: "I survived Camp Hell." She recalled one stop in New Hampshire in particular; scheduled for forty-five minutes, Clinton turned the event into a four-hour empathy-athon. "We were there so long that Peter Jennings and his crew were literally laying down on these benches out in the mall, just exhausted." Jennings groaned, pleading that he couldn't get up.

I asked Paul Begala how he had the stamina to ride in the campaign saddle with Clinton. He broke into a boyish grin: "I refused to learn how to play hearts. That was my defense." Clinton would be playing hearts on the plane at 3:00 in the morning, when they landed, and even though his first meeting was at 10:00 A.M., Clinton would say: "Who wants to go to the hotel and play cards?"

"Sorry, Governor, I don't know how" was always Begala's reply.

Clinton would pick off two or three other staff members, and they would play until 6:00 A.M., without Begala.

"I went and got some sleep."

· DROPPING THINGS ·

Before 1974, there are no reports of Clinton suffering from exhaustion. Until he entered his first political race, he always seemed to defy gravity. His capacities seemed so infinitely elastic, he could always take on more without breaking a sweat. None of his high school friends remembered him being harried, overtaxed, or frenetic, even though he was engaged in dozens of activities. "He was busy, but we all were, and I don't think any of us really noticed how much he was doing," one friend told me. "When I was a kid, I thought I was busier than anybody else I knew," wrote Clinton, "but there still seemed to be worlds of time to just be with people."[35] "When you step back and see all the things he had going after class, it makes you ask: How did he ever practice, how did he ever study?" said Phil Jamison. "But we never thought about it then. He wasn't apparent as somebody who was running around with his tail on fire. He made it look easy."

One of Clinton's law school roommates, William Coleman, feared that Clinton was going to flunk out of Yale. Though purportedly a full-time student, he was also working full-time on the campaign of U.S. Senate candidate Joseph Duffey. Clinton was in charge of the Third Congressional District in New Haven (though Duffey lost the election, he won Clinton's district). It was November, and Bill "had attended few classes and paid even less attention to the mountain of case law they were supposed to have read." It wasn't that Clinton didn't take the time to read; Clinton read literally all night. Coleman would see him reading on the couch in the living room when he went to bed at night, and he would still be lying on the couch reading, surrounded by a stack of diverse books, when Coleman woke up in the morning. But none of those books were law books. Clinton didn't appear at all anxious about the pit he seemed to be digging for himself. "What I perceived to be a crisis made me anxious for Bill. He, on the other hand, was serene and confident, even nonchalant."[36] Then Coleman found out why. "Magically, before examinations, he borrowed some good notes, mine among them, disappeared for three weeks, and performed quite well."[37] Clinton could juggle it all without dropping the ball.

In 1974, for the first time, Clinton started dropping balls. His electoral effort was so all-consuming that he exceeded his own seemingly infinite capacities. For example, he became conspicuously deficient in his professorial duties. "Colleagues chortled at the sight of Clinton in a frenzy because he had waited until the last minute to prepare the exam. Students were answering the first question while Clinton was still writing the next."[38] He was also perpetually late in grading exams. Two law students met each other on the fairway at the local golf course over summer vacation. One shouted to the other: "I finally got my grade in Clinton's class . . . from the fall semester!"[39] And then there was the time that he simply lost the exam blue books for an entire class.

"Boy, that was a fiasco with him doing those classes," Ron Addington said, shaking his head. Addington recalled standing over Clinton, who was lying down in a hotel room at one in the morning with a stack of blue books by his bed the day the grades were due. Addington had to "wake him up and force him to grade them."

"I just got to sleep fifteen minutes, just let me sleep fifteen minutes," begged Clinton.

"He would sleep and I would just wake him up, again. 'You have got to grade some more papers.' He would grade another blue book and go back to sleep."

Other minor details of daily life went by the boards, as well. One night, at one thirty in the morning, Addington got a call from Clinton, who said: "'I haven't got any electricity. And I don't have any water either. How am I going to get up and teach my class?'

"Come to find out, the electricity had been turned off because he didn't pay his electric bill. Same way with his credit cards. God, he just had all these canceled credit cards and stuff because he didn't pay his bills. I literally had to get his mail and get a campaign volunteer to be his bill payer."

Clinton became sloppy even on the most basic level: personal hygiene. People say he smelled. "I remember arguing with him: 'Deodorant is not optional!'" Marla Crider told me. His clothes were often disheveled, mismatched, and dripping with sweat. Staffers made regular runs to K-mart to keep him in clean clothes. "He would wear the same old suits, and we had to go and get some more suits for him, because he would just wear them out. They were so nasty by the end of the day," said Addington. While never a fashion plate, Clinton had not been known before for breakdowns in personal hygiene. No one in high school remembered him being sweaty, smelly, or scruffy.

Clinton had reached the limits of what even he could juggle. After 1974 he began dropping things, sometimes literally. For example, when he was governor, Clinton took a trip to Washington, D.C., to give testimony in the Senate about issues that affected Arkansas. Carol Rasco, Clinton's human services aide, remembered that Clinton came down to the lobby of the hotel wearing "the worst-looking tie . . . I'd ever seen in my life. It was dirty and frayed." Rasco told Clinton: "You can't wear that tie." He just "hadn't really looked at it," absorbed, as he always was, in a dozen more pressing matters. They bought him a new tie in the hotel gift shop. As they left the hotel Clinton's mind continued to whir, oblivious to his immediate surroundings. "We almost got killed in the middle of the street," said Rasco, because "he's taking his old tie off, putting on the new one, trying to tie as he walks, and gesticulating, dropping stuff. And we're having to pick it up," while cars were whizzing by.[40]

It's not hard to understand why Clinton was dropping stuff, why he lost exam booklets, forgot to pay his electric bill, even neglected to change his clothes. He was wearing out himself, his clothes, and his drivers barreling down the only track he had ever wanted to run on, with fierce, all-consuming intensity. In 1974 the moment he had been training for all his life had arrived. He heard the bell and burst out of the starting gate, scattering everything in his path.

And once he started running, he never stopped. Even the real Secretariat got to rest when a race was done. His trainer would help him cool off, give him a rubdown and some fresh hay. But Clinton was his own trainer, and his philosophy was summarized in his favorite scripture, one that Begala said he quoted more often than any other, Galatians 6:9: "Let us not become weary in doing good." Clinton used this passage in his 1990 gubernatorial inauguration, and then again in his first presidential inauguration. In this passage we see a perfect confluence of Clinton's biology and ideology. It was a passage he quoted to inspire himself, pump himself up, and keep himself going full bore, as he believed Galatians commanded him. Clinton became a practitioner of the "permanent campaign" almost twenty years before the phrase entered the lexicon. The end of one campaign was the first day of the next, and Clinton did not stop his relentless pace, but kept the momentum going.

Clinton lost the 1974 election narrowly. However, though he lost, Clinton's charismatic campaign had become the focus of statewide attention, and he had become a rising star. In 1976, at age thirty, he would become attorney general—the youngest in the nation. In 1978 he would gallop into the governor's mansion, becoming the youngest governor the nation had seen in forty years. In this, too, Clinton's career resembled that of Theodore Roosevelt, who "rose like a rocket" in politics. At age forty-two Roosevelt became the youngest president in American history. Kennedy, at forty-three, was second. And Clinton, at forty-six, would be the third youngest. Clinton, the political prodigy, had come "further, faster in the political world than any member of his generation," wrote Maraniss.[41]

But even Pegasus has to come down to earth sometime. If he will not land voluntarily, he will crash, because even "the greatest that ever was" can't defeat gravity forever.

6

The Education
of Governor Clinton

Clinton set three records during his years in Arkansas. Together they tell the tale of his rise, fall, and resurrection. At thirty-two, he became the youngest governor in America. At thirty-four, he lost his reelection bid, after only a single two-year term, and became the youngest *ex*-governor in American history. At thirty-six, he recaptured the governor's mansion, and the "Comeback Kid" then became the longest-running governor in Arkansas history. Bill Clinton learned, and he improved. But this is not only the story of his personal evolution. It is about the coming together of Bill and Hillary as a political team.

· THE CHILDREN'S CRUSADE ·

In 1979, when he became governor at thirty-two, Bill Clinton looked ten years younger. With his boyish face and longish hair, he looked like he belonged in a college dorm, not the governor's mansion. His three chiefs of staff—known as the "bearded troika"—were all in their early thirties, wore jeans, and, as the nickname implies, sported beards. These "hippies," as some old Arkansans saw them, stormed the capital with an urgent sense of mission. "We were all so young and idealistic, and so caught up in all the power, that we thought we could change the world.

We got carried away," first-term press secretary Julie Baldridge later conceded.[1] It was dubbed the "children's crusade."

"He was young, charming, intelligent, and pretty cocky in his first term," said Mary Anne Salmon, who worked in the governor's office for many years. In his first term Clinton's ambitious agenda and youthful zeal had the unmistakable scent of self-important overconfidence, an impression that was magnified by the exuberance of his young followers. Indeed, Baldridge admitted that their attitude was: "We're here, we've been elected, we know what we're doing, just get out of the way."[2] As a result, according to Mark Johnson, director of the North Little Rock Development Program, "the public perception of his whole first administration was a bunch of thirty-year-old bearded liberals who were going to tell these dumb Arkies how to do things."[3]

Since he was a boy, Clinton had felt called to save his state, and now that his destined moment had arrived, he threw himself at the task with total abandon. Clinton's optimistic plans for Arkansas had been bottled up inside him under pressure like a briskly shaken bottle of soda pop, and they now exploded out of him. One staffer called it a "pent-up progressive agenda." Combining grandiosity with impatience in typical hypomanic fashion, Clinton assumed he had a "mandate to transform the state, [and] he wanted to do it all in two years," wrote Maraniss.[4] "They were going to change the world overnight," said Arkansas columnist Ernie Dumas.

Clinton became a whirling dervish to accomplish this overnight transformation, and he inspired his staff to work harder than they had ever imagined they could. "Working for Governor Clinton is nonstop activity," wrote Carol Willis.[5] "If you're working for him, you're working around the clock, twenty-four/seven," said Baldridge, who recalled being so pumped up that she "went around all the time thinking: What next? What next? What next?"[6]

The sheer quantity of Clinton's proposals reflects his frantic pace. Clinton had made fifty-three specific promises during the campaign, and he actually assigned someone to keep track of them to make sure he accomplished them all. Baldridge recalled that the very first day the legislature was in session, Clinton submitted an overwhelming raft of proposed bills.* "We had a 150-bill gubernatorial legislative package ready to go

---

* In this respect, Clinton once again bears a striking resemblance to Theodore Roosevelt, who, at twenty-four, was the youngest member of the New York House of

on the first day of the legislative session, and actually passed it out when they were sworn in and seated. It was a very ambitious time."[7] Legislators joked that Clinton's legislative package was so huge that they had to "strain their backs lifting it."[8]

Arkansas columnist Ernie Dumas told me that there was something "chaotic" about Clinton's administration because "he had hundreds of ideas." As fast as his young aides could generate memos about their new policy proposals, Clinton would respond with suggestions and orders to move ahead. If he was leaving to make a speech, he'd walk out the door with "a stack of memos two feet tall" from his staff, filled with new ideas. In the back of the car, he'd be writing his speech, going through the memos, and dictating responses. When they stopped at a gas station, an aide traveling with Clinton would call the office: "You do this, you do this, and you do this."[9] "Within thirty minutes or an hour, we'd have a response to our questions," said Baldridge. "You never had to wait. Lord knows, I've learned in years since, how much more slowly most of the world moves."[10]

Hypomanics are idea-generating machines, but not all their ideas will necessarily be good ones. For example, Clinton spent a small fortune taking out full-page ads in *The Wall Street Journal* advertising Arkansas as a good place to do business. He was ridiculed for this largesse, which failed to generate even a single response. Then there was the wood-chopping project that sounded good on paper. In an effort to kill two birds with one stone, unemployed men were taught a trade—wood chopping—and in the process they would chop firewood to help poor people heat their homes. However, after spending thousands of dollars, it produced little in the way of job training or wood and became a symbol of grandiose-sounding Clinton projects that were just hot air. "$62,000 Spent by Job Program; Only Three Cords of Lumber Cut," read the headline.[11]

When Clinton was defeated after two years as governor, the conventional wisdom was that he had lost because of "Cubans and car tags." The "Cubans" was a reference to Cuban refugees that President Carter

---

Representatives. The "cyclone assemblyman" submitted as many as twenty progressive bills a day to the legislature, entering the House chamber each day "as if ejected by a catapult." President Benjamin Harrison, who appointed the crusading Roosevelt to head the Civil Service Commission, complained that young Roosevelt "wanted to put an end to all evil in the world between sunrise and sunset," as Kay R. Jamison noted in *Exuberance: The Passion for Life.*

had housed in Arkansas at Fort Chafee, much to Clinton's chagrin. The Cuban detainees rioted, and though Clinton could not be fairly accused of any real mismanagement, film footage of the riots, which his opponent, Frank White, made liberal use of in his campaign commercials, gave a visceral feeling of a state under threat and out of control.

The car-tag issue seemed relatively innocuous at the time it was enacted. In an effort to raise money for road construction, Clinton had hiked the fees for car registration. The increase was a mere thirty or forty dollars per car, but it enraged a large number of people. Unfortunately, the fee was computed by weight. The logic was that those who damaged the roads the most with heavy vehicles should pay a proportionate amount of the cost to repair them. Originally, the measure was aimed at the trucking industry, but being the powerful lobby that they were, they successfully pressured the administration to exempt them. As a result, the poorest people with the oldest cars had the biggest increase. Many didn't find out about it until after waiting in line for two hours at the Department of Motor Vehicles. And if they didn't have the extra forty dollars with them that day, they had to come back again when they did. Every month one-twelfth of the population reregistered their cars, which meant every month a new group of people were freshly outraged, keeping the issue alive all year. But while Cubans and car tags were the visible sources of discontent, these comparatively minor issues would never have been enough to topple a popular governor with a strong base of support. The more fundamental problem was that the attitude of the children's crusade had just offended too many people.

Most people were unaware that Clinton had accomplished quite a bit in two years, launching a set of initiatives that was extraordinary in both breadth and depth. "Virtually every area of public policy was covered: economic development, education, energy, environmental policy, health and human services, improvements in the infrastructure, taxation and tax incentives. . . . Clinton's first-term legislative achievements were many," wrote Arkansas journalist Meredith Oakley in *On the Make,* her book about Clinton's Arkansas years.[12] Patty Criner, who served as press secretary during the first term, told me, "I wrote out a list of our legislative achievements; it was twenty pages long."[13]

The irony was not lost on Clinton, who said that "at the moment of my greatest achievements in the legislature, I also made errors which would be responsible for my defeat." His basic problem, Clinton acknowledged, was "trying to do too much too soon."[14] This sort of over-reaching is a typical hypomanic problem. For example, among hypomanic entrepreneurs, expanding too quickly and outrunning cash flow—trying to do too much too soon—is one of the most common causes of bank-ruptcy in what would otherwise be a successful business.

In retrospect, Baldridge saw how naive she and her fellow crusaders had been in failing to anticipate the inevitable backlash produced by their attempts to transform Arkansas overnight. "Just taking human nature into consideration, and realizing that people don't like to move quickly, they don't like to feel pushed, looking back it's predictable that we stepped on some toes, and caused some people some consternation and anger."[15]

Indeed, it was predictable that the good old boys who ran Arkansas before Clinton showed up to change everything would feel inclined to punish this boy who had "gotten too big for his britches." At some level in his mind, Clinton must have known he was cruising for a bruising. Unconsciously, he was reenacting his Roger issues, almost as if he were asking to be taken behind the woodshed for a beating. In not so subtle ways, he provoked the powerful elite. For example, he "showed up late for virtually every public appearance and kept powerful businessmen waiting in his gubernatorial reception room," wrote John Brummett.[16] When someone so young keeps powerful older men waiting, especially in the South, where respect for elders is essential to good manners, "they have a tendency to get insulted," said Baldridge.[17] These men did not take kindly to what they saw as a sign of disrespect from this whippersnapper, even if he was governor. They'd seen lots of governors before, and yet none of Clinton's predecessors had wasted their time with such indifference.

And Clinton provoked them not only with his style, but also with the substance of his proposals. The first Clinton gubernatorial administra-tion blithely took on virtually all of the state's biggest special interests simultaneously with its high-minded reforms. Rudy Moore, one of Clin-ton's three chiefs of staff, recalled: "We alienated the utilities because of some regulatory issues. We had alienated the timber industry over clear-cutting issues. We had alienated the poultry and the trucking in-dustry over the licensing issues. So, all of a sudden, there were all these strong interest groups that were mad at Bill Clinton and the administra-tion."[18] Those were just the top three. Clinton also enraged the banking industry and the Arkansas Medical Society. Furthermore, there was a tone of bravado in these provocations. Clinton's team "seemed to amuse themselves taking on every entrenched interest in a state where entrenched interests were inordinately strong," wrote Brummett.[19] It was like waving a red flag in front of a bull.

Two years later, when announcing his candidacy for the 1982 governor's race, Clinton would assure voters that he had learned his lesson by saying: "When I was a boy growing up, my daddy never had to whip me twice for the same thing."[20] This striking phrase is pregnant with meaning. One of Freud's original insights was that people often reveal things about themselves, things that they may not be conscious of, in the words that they choose. Clinicians are trained to listen for these telltale phrases, and when the patient's words strike the clinician's ear as odd or unusual, he or she must look to the patient's past to see what idiosyncratic personal meaning they might have. Probably no candidate in history has ever declared their intent to run for office by invoking a childhood memory of being beaten by their father. However, when we consider the unconscious script of the Roger psychodrama, this peculiar phrase doesn't seem peculiar at all. At some level Clinton felt a compulsion to be whipped, and then to bounce back, and finally to be reconciled with his tormentors. In this respect Clinton's entire poltical career in Arkansas can be understood as a renactment of the three stages of Roger.

Indeed, according to script, the rubber doll would bounce back.

· HILLARY TAKES CHARGE ·

It was "catastrophic" when Clinton lost his reelection bid in 1980. Suddenly he was someone "with a great future behind him."[21] He couldn't face the press for weeks after the defeat. He was "deeply depressed," said Meredith Oakley, who remembered him as utterly deflated, both physically and emotionally. Virtually everyone I spoke to used the word "depressed" to describe Clinton's state of mind in the months immediately following the election.

After he left the governor's mansion, Clinton took a job in a private law firm. When Oakley visited him there she was struck by how incongruous he looked: a larger-than-life figure stuck in a small private office. Hillary, desperate to pull Clinton out of his funk, called Dick Morris, a political consultant they had used before. She brought him back to

Arkansas to begin plotting Bill's comeback. Morris, too, couldn't believe how "out of place" Clinton looked, "a big man cramped in a little office," now reduced to wandering the hallway searching for a secretary to do his typing. Morris thought that Clinton was so down that it seemed "futile to talk him out of his depression."[22]

Clinton would get his motor going again. The problem was that Clinton's motor has two speeds, off and hyperdrive. What he lacked was the ability to regulate that motor. John Brummett observed that Clinton was like an overheated engine with a broken regulator. "The Governor needs a governor," he wrote. For those not familiar with the anatomy of engines, a governor is a mechanical device responsible for regulating speed. Brummett's insight is a profound one, because at the most basic level, the hypomanic's difficulties are mechanical. In the hypomanic brain, the neurologically based mechanism responsible for regulating speed functions marginally at best, leaving their tachometer chronically in the red zone. Perhaps for that reason it is not coincidental that Leon Panetta, too, likened Clinton to a combustion engine when we spoke: "All these points are flashing and there are a lot of little explosions going on. And if you contain that energy and make it work, that car is going to be remarkable in terms of its performance. But if you can't contain it, it is only a matter of time before that engine blows up."

In my studies I have found that behind every successful hypomanic stands a more levelheaded, controlled partner—a spouse, an assistant, a colleague—who serves as an external governor. For Bill, that person is Hillary. Hypomanics require external structure to compensate for the underperforming inhibitory structures in their brains, much as an amputee requires a prosthetic limb to walk. This image of a prosthesis is more than a metaphor. In the case of someone missing a leg, it's obvious that they have a physical disability. When that disability is inside the brain, it is less visible, but no less real.

During Clinton's childhood, this regulatory function had been performed by his grandmother Edith. Though Hillary may not have known it, unconsciously Bill had been expecting her to be his Edith. Before they wed, Clinton explained to Marla Crider that one of the reasons he loved Hillary, as I stated earlier, was that "she challenges me every moment of the day. She makes me a better person. She gets me started, kicks my butt, and makes me do the things I've got to do."[23] In a sense, Clinton put Hillary in a position where she *had* to be his Edith, whether she wanted to or not, if they were to realize their shared life goals. After Clinton's defeat it was obvious to Hillary that if they were to have a political future, her intervention was required.

This was not the marriage Hillary had been expecting. "This might sound naive now," admitted Hillary, "but I really felt that being a public official was a job like any other. He would do his job, and I would do mine, and we would have our private life together. . . . A person who marries a doctor isn't expected to stand by his side while he performs surgery."[24] Though Hillary and Bill discussed politics on a daily basis, her involvement had been behind the scenes, and one step removed. Several people confirmed that Hillary was not very involved in either the first Clinton gubernatorial administration or the failed 1980 reelection campaign. Instead, she was focused on building her law career during that time. However, "Bill's defeat changed the rules," wrote biographer Nigel Hamilton.[25] When Hillary saw that Bill had gone down in flames, she had to intervene. "Hillary realized that she would have to step in and develop discipline," Leon Panetta told me. "In 1978, they were a two-career couple," wrote Dick Morris. "In 1981, Hillary became the manager of their joint political career."[26] It was a specialization of functions that fit their abilities. While "no one would ever accuse Bill Clinton of being a manager," a member of his Arkansas staff told me, Hillary was a born manager.

"As I always tell people, if you want a hug, go to Bill. If you want something done, go to Hillary," said Ann McCoy, who worked for the Clintons in both Arkansas and Washington.

Ironically, the change most Arkansans saw in Hillary was not one that revealed her increasingly assertive executive role in the marriage, but rather one which suggested that she was becoming a more traditional wife. Up until the 1982 comeback campaign, Hillary had maintained her maiden name, Rodham. In the early 1980s, this new feminist trend was simply unheard-of in Arkansas, and there was no doubt in anyone's mind that it had hurt Bill politically. A variety of friends and supporters had quietly tried to persuade Hillary to take Bill's name. It is interesting to note that the only person who never brought the issue up was Bill. He was gallantly fixed in his loyal support of her right to keep her maiden name, and proudly refused to consider the political calculus of it. When a reporter asked him if Hillary's having kept the name Rodham had hurt him, he said, "I hope not." But exit polls showed that it had. In the end it was the pragmatic Hillary who made the decision. "I came to realize how my personal choices could impact my husband's political future," she wrote. "I learned the hard way that some voters in Arkansas were seriously offended that I kept my maiden name. . . . I was an oddity because of my dress, my Northern ways, and the use of my maiden name."[27]

And so Hillary changed both her name and her appearance. As one legislator put it, Hillary had to "change her name and shave her legs."[28] The "natural look" had been a shock to the Arkansas system, recalled Ann McCoy. Hillary looked like a "hippie" with her "curly hair and big glasses," and needed to "doll herself up a bit" to look more like a Southern woman. She cut her hair, colored it blond, and began wearing contacts, makeup, and colored hair bands that matched her new fashionable clothes. "It was an important gesture, and it was well received," said Meredith Oakley. "She helped him mend a lot of fences just by coming off as a little bit more traditional."

But Hillary's name change revealed a true change that was more than cosmetic. "They were suddenly Bill and Hillary Clinton, and not Bill Clinton and Hillary Rodham, in more ways than just name only. Suddenly, they were a political team," said Oakley.

In 1982, Hillary took a leave of absence from her law practice, packed up Chelsea, and hit the campaign trail. "The 1982 campaign was a family endeavor. We loaded Chelsea, diaper bag and all, into a big car. . . . With Chelsea on my hip or holding my hand, I walked up and down streets meeting voters."[29]And she met a lot of them. Hillary was "not only active in the campaign but had a public appearance schedule almost as full as her husband's," wrote Oakley.[30] Oakley had met Hillary on many occasions, but she recalled the day in 1982 when she first heard Hillary speaking on the campaign trail: "My God, I was blown away when I heard her speak. She was very effective. She was articulate, amusing, and made good contact with a massive audience at some political fish fry. I wondered—why hadn't she done this before?" Up until then, Hillary had been unpopular for the most part, even among stalwart Democrats.

Hillary continued working behind the scenes as Bill's closest adviser, as she had always done, but she was now supervising him more intensively. Bill would call her about "twenty times a day," according to Gail Sheehy, and "It wasn't a ritualistic 'I miss you' nighty-night type of call; it was more like checking in with the dispatcher and getting fresh orders: 'Bill, you need to call so-and-so *today*.' "[31]

One of the things Hillary kept a close eye on was Clinton's level of exhaustion. She knew bad things could happen when Bill got tired, as he's prone to do. Late one night on the campaign trail, Clinton was playing hearts with John Brummett. Clinton called for another hand, and Hillary sharply called out from the back of the plane: "Bill, no. You need to get some rest. The last thing you're going to do is play cards."

"Aw, honey, just one hand," Bill chuckled.

"We played one highly uncomfortable hand," recalled Brummett. "We couldn't wait to get through it. He cowered a bit when she laid down the law."[32]

Like Edith, when Hillary said it was time for bed, you didn't want to argue with her—it was time for bed.

Hillary also took up Edith's role as Bill's protector. She would show up unexpectedly at events where their opponent, Governor Frank White, was speaking and loudly challenge White's statements about her husband, in essence heckling him. At one event, White practically ran for the exit when he saw Hillary in the audience while Hillary shouted questions at him as he beat a hasty retreat. "She was yelling at me as I left. . . . I didn't stay to hear it but she was screaming. You couldn't win, confronting the former governor's wife. She was a woman and this was the South. You'd look like a bully. But that was Hillary's style—ambushing campaign opponents of her husband."[33]

While Hillary's attack might have offended White's views of Southern womanhood, fleeing out the backdoor to escape a female's tongue-lashing was not exactly the image of Southern manhood, either. Hillary inflicted real damage. "Hillary beat Frank White when Clinton ran against him in '82," said Paul Fray, his campaign co-manager from the 1974 campaign. "She gets up there on that stump and she could kick the dog shit out of you. Frank is still reelin' from it, I don't mind tellin' you."[34]

Hillary would make a similar intervention in a famous scene during the 1990 primary against Democratic challenger Tom McRae. McRae was giving a press conference, and Hillary "just happened to be wandering through the capital," said Dumas. The planned surprise attack was made to look spontaneous. "She walks over and just destroys his life in about two minutes. She humiliated him. Hillary just wanders up to the edge of the crowd there and steps forward into the limelight:

" 'Get off it, Tom!'

"All the cameras turn and focus on her. And poor old Tom, he don't know what to say. He just stammers and flounders and that was the end of his campaign. Nobody ever paid attention to him again. It was all over."

Protecting Bill with the ferocity of a mother lion was very much part of being an Edith. It was a role Hillary would play again and again, even when she had to defend him against charges of adultery that wounded her deeply. If you messed with Bill, you were going to have to deal with Hillary.

· THE GOVERNOR NEEDS A GOVERNESS ·

"Today is Easter," a legislator said on the day of his second inauguration. "He is risen."[35] The Comeback Kid became the first person in Arkansas history ever to regain the governorship after being turned out of office. Rising from the ashes of the 1980 debacle, Clinton not only reclaimed the governorship, but went on to establish a highly successful ten-year reign in Arkansas. This turnaround was all the more remarkable because it required Clinton to fundamentally alter his way of doing business. He had to learn from his mistakes and compensate for his weaknesses in an entirely new way.

Almost none of the staffers from the first administration were invited back, which understandably caused some bitterness. From the moment Clinton began his comeback campaign, his staff was built with an entirely new prototype in mind—the diametric opposite of the children's crusade. Clinton didn't need young, high-spirited staffers to throw gasoline on the fire of his exuberance. He needed mature adults who would channel, temper, contain, and structure his impetuous enthusiasm. "He realized that he needed some older folks on his staff," said Paul Root, Clinton's old tenth-grade history teacher, who worked for Clinton as an education expert during his second administration.[36]

High energy and enthusiasm combined with poor impulse control and judgment are traits we associate with youth, and for that reason, hypomanics often seem like overgrown children. "You must always remember," said one British diplomat about Theodore Roosevelt, "the President is about six."[37] Clinton was often characterized as a child by Arkansas political observers. Cartoonist George Fisher regularly depicted Clinton as a baby in a carriage. "Draw me ugly, but get me out of that baby buggy," Clinton demanded.[38] Fisher obliged by putting the boy governor on a tricycle for the next several years.

Hillary concluded that Bill needed a "tough as nails manager," according to Dick Morris, and she recruited her friend Betsey Wright, another Edith type, to come to Arkansas to help aid Bill's political comeback.[39] After he won, Wright would serve as his chief of staff. "I have always thought it was Betsey Wright who cobbled Bill Clinton back together," said Bobby Roberts, one of Clinton's longtime senior staffers, "with the help of Hillary."[40]

In Clinton's childhood there had been one person who had effectively managed him, his grandmother Edith Cassidy. The governor did not need a governor so much as a governess. Wright acknowledged that she was essentially Clinton's "nanny," though chronologically she was only three years his senior. It was an "oxymoron," said Wright, to speak of "Bill Clinton's adult life." Thus, "the role I gave myself was his Disciplinarian, Nag, and Confronter of Behavior."[41]

To be an Edith, you must bring order to Clinton's chaos, and Wright's first task was to organize his records. Clinton had built up an amazing contact network, but all the essential information about his political supporters was found in handwritten notes on thousands of loose slips of paper and three-by-five index cards that he kept in shoe boxes. Wright put all this data into a computer. "The dedicated computer room in the campaign headquarters near the Capitol ran around the clock, churning out Glad-to-Meet-You letters, fundraising solicitations, special letters for black supporters, for first-time supporters, for teachers, for the elderly. Letters to friends of Bill went out in an endless stream. No other politician in Arkansas had anything comparable. The computer became the extension of Clinton's tireless personality," wrote Maraniss.[42] "Whenever Clinton came back from a trip, he would walk into her office, and Betsey would simply hold her hand out," Arkansas journalist Steve Barnes told me. "She had trained him to empty his pockets into her hand. There would be airline napkins with names written on them, a school program with names underlined. They would put that into the data bank."

But more than just organizing his records, Wright took control of organizing his entire life. Like Grandma Cassidy, she kept strict control over his schedule. "She almost seemed to wake him up and tell him when to go to bed at night. She tried to schedule his every meal and every meeting," wrote Dick Morris.[43] Indeed, there was no aspect of Bill Clinton's life she did not try to manage. Calling her a "martinet," Dumas said that Betsey was "an extremely controlling woman" who "endeavored to control every aspect of Bill Clinton's behavior." In an earlier interview Dumas said, "Everything Bill does, she examines! She runs his life, and then Hillary runs the rest of it."[44] Wright micromanaged every aspect of Clinton's office with an iron fist. No one saw Clinton unless they went through her. "She monitored every piece of paper that flowed in and out of that office, and the activities of all the staff," Dumas said. Some people even called her "Governor Wright." Her other nicknames were "the witch," "the bitch," "the iron maiden," and perhaps most revealing of all: "mother superior." "She didn't let him make any independent decisions if she could help it," said aide Bobby Roberts.[45] In particular, she endeavored to strictly monitor and limit the commitments he made because "left to his own devices, he'd have personal obligations pending to a number of people approximating the population of the United States."[46]

Like Edith, Wright wasn't afraid to be harsh with anyone, including Clinton. "You have to absolutely crush his skull to get his attention, because his mind is on so many things at once," said Wright. "You had to shake him and say, 'You stop, pay attention to this, this is what's important now, guy.' "[47] Wright was so parental she even enforced table manners ("Watching him eat reminds you of how a kid eats," said one Arkansas journalist).[48] "Once when he was noisily chomping on an ice cube, his mouth impolitely open, and he reached into his cup to get another ice cube, Wright swatted it out of his hand," wrote Maraniss.[49]

Edith was more than a disciplinarian, of course. She was fiercely devoted to Bill, as only a mother or grandmother can be. And in this respect as well, Betsey was the perfect Edith. She "would have died for him," according to John R. Starr, editor of the *Arkansas Democrat*.[50] Dumas recalled that "in all those years she devoted herself to Bill Clinton, eighteen hours a day. She was up before daylight, and worked night and day."[51]

In one respect it is ironic that Betsey Wright was the central force of stability in Clinton's life, because she herself is widely regarded as emotionally unstable. "Betsey is just crazy," Dumas told me. Dumas is a longtime friend who "loves Betsey," but he acknowledges that he is "one of the few people who can tolerate her extreme personality."

Most people I interviewed didn't go as far as Dumas in saying that

Wright is "crazy," but they used phrases like "unstable," "overly emotional," and "often tearful," and that she has "mood swings." By her own
admission, when Wright left Clinton in 1989, she was "burnt out and in
a state of deep depression."[52] (I spoke to Wright by phone a half dozen
times over several months seeking an interview. She always seemed overwhelmed: "I just can't deal with thinking about my relationship with Bill
Clinton right now; try me again in a few weeks.") But at the same time,
every person I spoke to in Arkansas unanimously agreed that Betsey
Wright did a terrific job. It seems counterintuitive that an aggressive
yeller who is prone to mood swings would prove to be the optimal choice
for Clinton's chief of staff, until we recall that this was precisely Edith's
personality. Then it makes perfect sense: Clinton was more receptive to
taking direction from someone who reminded him of his grandmother.

"Say what you will, it worked," John Brummett wrote of the Wright-
Clinton collaboration. Wright "had been effective in Arkansas disciplin-
ing Clinton, keeping him from making too many commitments or errors
of judgment, even if it required a screaming match." Brummett argues
that the key to Clinton's problems during his early presidency was that
"his inner circle contained no overwrought screamers willing to get in
his face or treat him as someone who needed handling."[53] The same
thought occurred to Dick Morris: "During his disorganized first two
years as president, I often thought how he needed Betsey back. Had she
been in the White House in 1993 and '94 she would have taken the
president to boot camp all over again and restored his forces."[54] In fact,
Clinton's administration did become more focused when he hired Leon
Panetta to replace "Mack the Nice" McLarty as chief of staff. Panetta
took more of a drill sergeant stance with Clinton, as Betsey had once
done. When it came to being Clinton's chief of staff, Panetta told me,
"I've often said my army experience was probably a lot more important
than my political experience."[55]

· IT TAKES A VILLAGE OF EDITHS ·

While Betsey was the Edith-in-chief, Clinton had other women on staff
who served *in loco parentis*. "Clinton benefited from challenging, obsessive, protective, and parentlike staffers who used varying complementary
styles to keep him in check," wrote Brummett. "We were all mothers and

we sometimes just treated him like a child," said one staffer, and, indeed, parentlike staffers were exactly what Clinton required. For example, Clinton needed a parental figure to tell him when enough was enough when it came to his appetite for speaking engagements. Clinton, the super-extravert, always had at least three events a day and often as many as five or six, said Mary Anne Salmon, his scheduling director. Clinton's guiding principle seemed to be that his capacities, not to mention the boundaries of space and time, were infinitely elastic. Clinton accepted virtually every speaking invitation he was offered, often double and even triple booking himself, leaving his staff the unpleasant job of expressing his regrets and making excuses. "He can't say no, so that became our job," said Salmon.[56] Not only did they have to learn to say no politely to the disappointed people who wanted Clinton to speak, they had to say no to Clinton. "You almost had to put the reins on him and say 'Whoa!' " said Judy Gaddy, who took over the scheduling department from Salmon. Gaddy called it "the worst job in state government," because Clinton "wants to cram thirty hours' worth of work into every twenty-four hour space. And he's just sure there's a way to do it."[57]

In a similar fashion, Clinton's staff was perpetually trying to set limits on one of his other great appetites: food. Clinton, who was like an "accordion" in the way he would rapidly expand and contract and expand again, was famous for gorging himself on junk food. Arkansas journalist Bob Lancaster used to run into him at the movies, where he was amazed to see Clinton routinely order "triple-buttered popcorn." "I had never seen that before. I asked him one time, 'How does that work?' " Clinton showed him. "They would fill the popcorn bag about a third of the way, and then they would just load it down with butter, and add a third more popcorn, and then load it down with butter, and pour on the top third, and load it down with butter, so he had triple-buttered popcorn."[58] The press would make jokes like "Is the forklift with the governor's lunch here yet?"[59] The den mothers on his staff were constantly trying to impose controls to contain his eating. Steve Barnes recalled one breakfast meeting at the governor's office with platters of goodies. "Clinton kept munching away at these cupcakes," he said. "He picked up another one, and some woman on his staff ran over there and snatched it out of his hand in full view of everybody, and he gave her this scowl. Well, he sulked the rest of that meeting. He just looked at her with this baleful expression, and just sulked like a child for the rest of the meeting."

· THE CRUSADE FOR CHILDREN ·

One day while he was in junior high school Bill Clinton read a newspaper article about Arkansas being one of the poorest and least-educated states in the nation. Virginia said she would never forget that moment. He "saw the same old thing we read all the time—that Arkansas's here on the bottom." Bill was mad. He couldn't accept that. He needed to understand why. "He turned around and said to me, 'Let's say Maine was on the top. Mother, aren't the kids in Arkansas born with the same brain that they have in Maine?' And then he asked me the same question about black and white people."[60] There must be a way to fix these problems, Clinton thought, and he vowed to himself that he would do it. When they were in law school Bill told Hillary, "I promised myself a long time ago, if the people of Arkansas will let me, I'll break my back to help my state. That's my life. That's the way it has to be for me."[61] Now he was in position to make good on his childhood promise.

In his first term he had tried everything he could to help Arkansas, and it had been a disaster. Clinton learned that when you grandiosely try to change everything, you risk accomplishing nothing. "If you do a lot of things, and you talk about a lot of different things while you're doing it, the perception may be that you haven't done anything," he wrote.[62] Now he would try the exact opposite strategy. He would focus on just *one* thing, one thing that could change everything.

If the kids from Arkansas had the same brains as the kids from Maine, and if blacks had the same brains as whites—what explained the difference in their achievements? It came down to one word: "education." Education reform became his all but exclusive focus.

There was another big change as well. From the outset, the education reform campaign was a joint effort with Hillary. Hillary's newly active involvement in Bill's career and Bill's newfound discovery of a focus could not be coincidental. "He wants to do it all," said *Newsweek* political correspondent Eleanor Clift, "and he has a hard time harnessing everything into a single achievable goal. That's where Hillary comes in."[63] Clinton is like the sun—radiant, warm, burning with almost infinite energy, and shining everywhere. Hillary is more like a magnifying glass, focused and detail-oriented. When the sun's rays pass through a magnifying glass, you have a concentrated beam of light that can burn through wood. "Their skills complemented each other," said Mary Anne

Salmon. "Her focus helped him to focus, rather than going off in all directions."[64]

Bill and Hillary did not choose the education issue at random. It was "part of their core beliefs," said Charles Allen, who coauthored the Clinton biography *The Comeback Kid*. Bill had always felt a sense of mission about education's ability to actualize human potential. Indeed, he felt his own rise had been largely due to education. Hillary, who had studied child development at Yale, also well understood the enormous impact of education, especially for children who would otherwise be disadvantaged. Many I spoke to believed that a shared passion for education, ideas, and learning was a large part of what attracted Bill and Hillary to each other in the first place. They met at Yale Law School as fellow students, and intellectual discussions "were part of their attraction from day one," said Allen.[65] "The thing they have in common is a tremendous interest in the world and information, in just wanting to know all they can about any and everything," said Paul Root, adding, "I think that's what has held them together all these years."[66]

Finally, education was a political winner. Everybody wants their children to have a better life. The Clintons had a new children's crusade, but this one was *for* children, not by them. Though no first lady of Arkansas had ever played such an active role in government, the issue was also just right for a governor's wife. "*They* were raising a child in Arkansas, and it was her future too that they were trying to secure. In this they were one with all Arkansans," said Meredith Oakley. "It was a very good issue for them."

The education campaign was superbly planned and systematically executed, showing a new Clinton discipline. "That campaign from beginning to end was brilliant," said Roy Reed, a professor of journalism at the University of Arkansas who covered Clinton for *The New York Times*. "You can write a textbook on how to do a political piece of work and use that as an illustration."[67]

The first discipline was rhetorical: Clinton had to stay on message. Left to his own devices, Clinton can wander all over the intellectual map. Not here. Just as the mantra of his 1992 presidential run would be "It's the economy, stupid," the mantra of his 1983 gubernatorial administration could have been: It's education, stupid. "It's not that we ignored other issues, but we didn't *talk* about them," explained Betsey Wright.[68] Clinton always wants to talk about many issues at one time, but as Leon Panetta pointed out, "The bully pulpit doesn't work, very frankly, if you are dealing with five or six issues at once." Thus, it was a great act of self-discipline for Clinton to talk about only one thing, education, for almost an entire year.

The tone was set in the very first words he spoke as governor. In his January 11, 1983, inaugural speech Clinton announced that "over the long run, education is the key to our economic revival and our perennial quest for prosperity."[69] He declared it to be "more important to me than anything I have ever done in politics."[70]

The timing was right for Clinton's message. A highly publicized national report by the National Commission on Excellence in Education, "A Nation at Risk," warned of a "rising tide of mediocrity" in the nation's schools. In the 1980s there was great concern about America's diminishing competiveness in the global marketplace, especially in comparison to Japan, where students were studying harder and getting better test scores. With increasing frequency, failures in the U.S. education system were seen as the root cause of America's economic decline. If America was at risk, then Arkansas was practically in intensive care. Traditionally at the bottom of the heap in most statistics, Arkansas was ranked forty-ninth in education, just behind Mississippi, as it was on many measures of wealth and achievement (which prompted the darkly humorous quip, "Thank God for Mississippi"). More than half of Arkansas's schools didn't have art, music, chemistry, physics, computer science, or foreign languages. It seemed to Clinton that Arkansas had an "inferiority complex" and a sense of resignation, as if "God meant for us to be last, God meant for us to be poor."[71]

While it's hard to imagine now, the idea that economic prosperity and education were linked was novel to most Arkansans. It was a poor rural state where success was tied much more closely to owning land or running a business. Only 10 percent of the population had a college degree, and typically those who graduated from college left the state for better opportunities elsewhere. "He convinced people that there was a connection between education and good jobs. We hadn't all heard that very much before, and didn't know exactly what those connections were. But he talked constantly about the world economy that was coming, and how we would not be able to deal with it unless we improved education. So, he was selling education all the time," said Root.

Clinton did more than just pound the bully pulpit. He put a plan into action, quite literally from day one. In his inaugural speech he announced the formation of an education standards committee, and his decision to name Hillary chair of the cause: "I think she will have more time to exercise the sort of leadership and direction the commission needs."[72] Later he added, "This guarantees that I will have a person who is closer to me than anyone else overseeing a project that is more important to me than anything else."[73] (Based on their success with education in Arkansas, Clinton would make a similar intervention when he became president, putting Hillary in charge of health care—but with a very different result.)

Paul Root was chosen by Clinton to be his official observer on the education standards committee. His first reaction to the news that Hillary would be in charge was, "Uh-oh." Like many people, he "wasn't sure it was such a great idea." But he soon changed his mind. "The main thing I need to say about Hillary, from where I sit, is that she did her homework, she knew what she was talking about, she had high standards and high hopes for Arkansas, and she wouldn't back away from that." Root had sat on committees like this before. "Every education committee I've ever been on would start the first meeting by outlining the ideal. Then, at each meeting, they would take something away, based on the assumption they couldn't afford it. Our committee kept trying to do that, saying, 'Oh, this is great, but we can't afford it. She's outlined a Cadillac program, and we've got a Chevrolet budget.' The other committee members kept trying to pare down the first-day ideal to something they thought more realistic. She wouldn't let them. She held to it. They kept saying, 'We don't have the money to do this.' She kept saying, 'The governor is responsible for the money. Let's do our job and let him worry about the money.' She had good people on that standards committee, but they just didn't believe that they could do that much. They had never seen that much change before."

Money was the key. The Clintons knew their ambitious program would not be possible without a major increase in state revenue. Convincing people that the schools should be better was not a hard sell. Convincing them to pay for it was. It was also a risky one. Conventional wisdom had it that Clinton had lost his first reelection in large part because he raised the fee to register a car by a mere thirty or forty dollars. Yet to fund education the Clintons were proposing a huge increase in taxes. Clinton would have to convince legislators to vote for a 33 percent hike in the sales tax, from 3 percent to 4 percent—the largest tax increase in twenty-five years. Like the hike in car-tag fees, a sales tax was, unfortunately, a regressive tax measure that fell disproportionately on the poor and working class. But the Arkansas constitution required a three-fourths' majority to increase the income tax, and that was politically unachievable.

The Clintons set about building grassroots support for their education tax, even though "it was generally understood by most of the politicians in Arkansas at that time, if you vote to raise tax today, you won't be here tomorrow," said Root. It was essential to build consensus at the grassroots level, because a majority of legislators were not going to cast a vote that they thought would cost them their jobs. Hillary's educational standards committee held hearings in all seventy-five of Arkansas's counties. The strategy was to systematically go, county by county, one town hall meeting at a time, and evangelize to educators, school administrators, and parents for the cause, with the hope that they would in turn pressure their representatives to vote yes.

This was Hillary's real debut in politics. As a political spouse she had been her husband's chief consultant and worked behind the scenes, but now she was out in front in the limelight. When people saw her in action, they were generally impressed. "She tackled it and addressed it with such eloquence and with such tirelessness that she really won a lot of friends and a lot of admirers for herself," said journalist Steve Barnes. Everyone I spoke to remembers being taken aback by how articulate and passionate Hillary was. Even John Brummett, a frequent Hillary critic, acknowledged: "I'm not one of her biggest fans, but I give credit where credit is due. She worked hard and competently and built political consensus. . . . It was masterful."[74]

The Clintons succeeded in making it "more dangerous to be against improved education than raising taxes," said Root. Polls showed that Arkansans favored higher taxes if it was used to improve education. "That's the only time in my life I ever saw people demanding a tax increase," said John Robert Starr, editor of the *Arkansas Democrat*.

When her committee's report was completed, Hillary presented it to a joint Senate-House legislative committee. It was a moment of high drama. She made no small talk. Dressed in a white suit, she sat in the wood-paneled conference room facing a horseshoe formation of unsmiling men. Hillary testified with such zeal, one journalist wrote, that she had "the mien of an evangelist."[75] "I know I sound preachy," Hillary declared, "but I believe in this."[76] "We Arkansans have to quit making excuses and accept instead the challenge of excellence."[77] One legislator recalled that she spoke for ninety minutes without notes. Typically people walk in and out during hearings, but not a single person left the room. "She had us all mesmerized," said one legislator. When she was finished, one older legislator announced, "Fellas, it looks like we might have elected the wrong Clinton."[78]

The Clintons benefited from one lucky piece of timing. There was a case before the Arkansas Supreme Court that was challenging the constitutionality of the drastic differences in funding for schools in rich and poor neighborhoods. Clinton held off on all attempts at legislative reform until a decision was reached in this case. As expected, the court agreed that the existing system was unconstitutionally inequitable. The state was mandated to "equalize educational opportunities," but without any reference as to how they should pay for it.[79] The governor could reasonably argue that he was being forced to raise taxes to comply with the court's unfunded mandate. Obviously, Clinton couldn't simply equalize spending by taking money away from wealthier districts to finance poor ones, which would spark a revolt by the middle and upper classes. So new funds would have to come from somewhere. But the problem was more than inequality—the whole system was underfunded. Arkansas was at the bottom in student spending and teacher salaries. The court case became the occasion to start phase two of the ambitious education campaign: Clinton argued that the penny sales tax increase was being "forced on him" by the court.

Dick Morris polled all kinds of scenarios that would help people accept higher taxes. At the most basic level, people wanted to be sure that they got what they paid for. There was immense suspicion and cynicism in Arkansas, as elsewhere, about liberal solutions to social problems that seemed to just throw more money at government bureaucracy. These were the Reagan years, when big government was portrayed as the problem, not the solution. To gain people's confidence in the plan, it was necessary to build measurable accountability into the proposal at many levels. One such idea mandated that teachers take a test to prove that they were academically qualified to teach. Many had heard anecdotes of barely literate teachers who sent home assignments rife with misspellings. In one highly publicized example, a teacher taught about "world war eleven," because she didn't understand the roman numeral II, and obviously knew nothing about history. The proposal that teachers be required to take a test became an explosive cause célèbre among teachers. The teachers association, which had been a staunch Clinton ally, turned against him with a vengeance. The issue caught national attention, with Clinton debating the head of the Arkansas teachers association on the nationally televised *Donahue* show. Ironically, the teachers' opposition helped Clinton. By standing up to his natural ally, the teachers' union, Clinton appeared to be more than just another knee-jerk liberal. Playing against type prevented his being typecast. Dumas later called it a "Sister Souljah moment," referring to Clinton's public critique of a black rap singer for her antiwhite lyrics, which also aimed to convince voters he was a centrist, and not just a slave to his liberal base.

"No test, no tax," Clinton declared defiantly. He contends that he never would have been able to round up the votes he needed, especially from reluctant conservatives, without the teacher test. When discussing it with Dumas, Clinton named a handful of legislators who had told him that the teacher test was the specific reason they voted for the sales tax. The teacher test issue was good strategy. Morris's polls showed that the public favored it by a hefty two to one majority. In reality, after all the Sturm und Drang, the test had little impact on anything, one way or another. The actual test was very basic, and less than 3 percent of the teachers failed.

By the time the Supreme Court handed down its decision, the legislature had disbanded. In Arkansas the legislature meets only every other year for a couple of months. This timing was also fortunate. It was the end of May, and Clinton now called a special session of the legislature to meet in October just to deal with this one issue. This session lasted six weeks, and the education package was its sole focus.

I liken the Clintons' education crusade to a military campaign. General Hillary landed the troops on the beach and drove them across the state, county by county, to the statehouse in Little Rock. There, General Bill fought the hand-to-hand battle to get the bill passed by the legislature. While Hillary had been traveling the state with her committee, Clinton intentionally hung back, allowing her to take the lead. "He stayed completely out of it until the education standards committee made their recommendations and it had to be sold to the legislature," said state senator David Malone. After Hillary presented the report to the legislature, however, it was up to Bill to round up the votes. "Then he stepped back in and seemed to take over," said Malone.[80]

His chief weapon was schmoozing. He invited scores of legislators, educators, business and civic leaders, and journalists for intimate meetings in the governor's mansion for breakfast or lunch to solicit their thoughts on how to solve the education dilemma and, more important, to solicit their support. It was a compliment to be asked to such a meeting. "A meeting with the governor in this relaxed, informal setting was not commonplace for most of the attendees, however blasé their attitude about it, and they were pleased to have a hand in designing the strategy for solving such a weighty problem."[81] Of course, everyone who stopped to give the problem some thought had to agree that the schools must be improved, and that it would take money.

Clinton was extraordinarily effective in this setting. "He was incredibly persuasive," said Root. "I heard him say things I couldn't imagine a politician saying. He said, 'How much would you sacrifice, of what you have today, to ensure that your children will have a better education, and can compete better in a world economy?'

" 'Search your hearts and go home and look at your children,' " Clinton exhorted.[82]

"I'm afraid to go in a room with him by myself. I'm afraid he'll change my whole notion about things," said one legislator. "He was convincing so many people, and many of them were surprised," said Root.

At the same time, under the direction of Betsey Wright, the Clintons unleashed a massive public relations effort for their program, equal to any political campaign. Clinton went to the airwaves with radio and TV ads. He sent letters to everyone in his database, asking his supporters to contact their congressmen. They even ran phone banks at night. Betsey Wright recalled: "We bought radio ads, newspaper ads, TV ads; we did a lot of direct mail across the state. We had people doing postcards and letters to their legislators. We had them wearing the blue ribbons [a symbol of support for the program] . . . and rallied meetings across the state—all meant to snowball into the beginning of the legislative session, so that by the time those legislators convened, each of them had a constituency in their district begging them to raise their taxes for education. . . . It was a very well-planned campaign."[83]

Clinton opened the special session in October 1983 with a televised address, something which had not been done before. "The first night, we started on television, where he explained to the people all over the state exactly what he was going to try to pass. Now, that's very different, because usually you'd present that to the legislature first, but he presented it to the state. He changed a lot of legislators' minds by doing that, because they started hearing from people back home," said Root. In his remarks, Clinton called this a "magic moment" that could "change the face of the state's history."[84]

If Hillary had directed the equivalent of the D-day invasion, initiating a march across the state, this was the Battle of the Bulge, a concentrated, all-out, nonstop battle royal to turn the tide of the war. While Hillary's more systematic and reasoned style could be compared to generals like Eisenhower and Bradley, Bill's was more like the hypomanic Patton, whose basic strategy was: attack, attack, attack. It would be the longest special session in Arkansas history. It lasted "six agonizing weeks," according to Bobby Roberts, who served as one of his senior legislative assistants.[85] For those six weeks, Clinton's troops worked almost twenty-four hours a day.

Every morning at 7:00 A.M., thirty to forty Clinton aides huddled to plan the day's battles: which bills would be discussed in which committees; what talking points to emphasize; which legislators had to be wheedled. Typical of Clinton's style, these meetings were relatively unstructured, freewheeling discussions held over bad coffee in Styrofoam cups and donated fast food, with people wandering in and out constantly to smoke in the hallway.

As is so often the case with Clinton, despite all the hard work and planning, there was still a sense that things were being done on the fly. Bobby Roberts complained about Clinton's "chronic failure to be fully prepared for sessions." According to Roberts, the beginning of the 1983 special session was "particularly chaotic," in large part because some of the bills were still being written as the special session began.[86] Particularly galling to Roberts was Clinton's "distressing habit of changing his position on a particular bill" in midstream.[87] For example, he recalled listening to Senator Cliff Hoofman making an impassioned speech in support of one of the governor's proposals. Another Clinton staffer, Don Ernst, was motioning to Roberts frantically from the hallway. When Roberts stepped out, Ernst explained that Clinton had changed his mind, he didn't want to pass this bill. Roberts panicked.

"He's already testifying for the bill," Roberts said, referring to Hoofman.

"Can we stop him?" pleaded Ernst.

"It was highly irregular for anyone, especially a legislative aide, to approach any person who was testifying," wrote Roberts, "but I knew something had to be done. I got down as low as I could, and tugged on his sleeve; Senator Hoofman looked at me as if I were a two-headed dog. He leaned over and I whispered that the governor was now opposed to the bill he was testifying for. Senator Hoofman straightened up and without missing a beat, calmly announced that 'I've been telling you all the things that are good about this bill—now I am going to tell you everything that is wrong with it.' If I have ever seen murderous intent, I saw it in Senator Hoofman's eyes after the meeting ended. He unloaded his wrath on me, and headed down the hall, where I am certain he gave a repeat performance to the governor."[88]

Root said that incidents like that were not uncommon. He had been in that same position himself, arguing for a bill before the legislature without knowing that Clinton had made a deal to kill the very same bill a few minutes earlier. Fortunately for Root, the bill was defeated, so he was spared the humiliation of having to recant his earlier speech. "Things were happening so fast," he said, "and so many people were involved, that you might be called on to say something about a bill, and maybe things had changed in the last thirty minutes that you were not aware of." In fairness to Clinton, this was not simply a manifestation of being scattered or inconsistent. Constant behind-the-scenes negotiations were taking place simultaneous with lobbying efforts in the chambers. And with more than a hundred bills under consideration in a given day, it was difficult to keep tabs on a process that was continuously in flux. This was the fog of war.

Aides met with Clinton throughout the day and night to monitor the progress of the battle. "I usually tried to get home before midnight," wrote Roberts, but Clinton and several other aides seemed "to be able to go on forever."[89] And it all began again, each morning, at 7:00 A.M. "This pattern of long hours, too little sleep, too much food and drink, and too much stress continued day after day, until both our staff and the legislators were worn down," wrote Roberts.[90] "The days were long, harrowing, exhausting and exhilarating," wrote staffer Kathy Van Laningham, who claims to have "specific gray hairs" that she attributes to the special legislative session of 1983.[91]

As usual, Clinton seemed energized by the high stress. When Meredith Oakley interviewed him, he was "bouncing up and down like a tennis ball in play."[92] Oakley asked him how things were going: " 'I love it!' " he said, "with a wide grin, before grabbing the arm of a passing legislator."[93] Throughout the special session Clinton roamed the hallways squeezing arms and hugging shoulders. In the last ten days "the governor maintained an exhausting twenty-hour-a-day schedule of late-night telephone calls and one-on-one meetings with strategists and recalcitrant lawmakers."[94]

Clinton stood in the doorway of the House and Senate chambers during votes—something that was simply not done by Arkansas governors. There he could be seen directing his troops in the field, waving his arms and shouting for his legislative troubleshooters, telling them to "go run up and down the aisles" to make sure no one left their seats during crucial votes.[95] "We even had two or three guys who would go and clean out the restrooms and bring people back to the meeting in time to vote!" recalled Root.

The final vote came down to the wire. He was in a desperate struggle to get the votes he needed to pass the tax increase necessary to fund the plan. Vada Sheid, a legislator who was getting a lot of pressure from the teachers' union to vote no, recalled how Clinton cornered her in the hallway to implore her to vote yes.

"Vada, you're not thinkin' clear, you've forgotten your grandchildren have always taken priority with you," said Clinton with tears in his eyes. He told Sheid he was "dead meat" without her vote.[96] Sheid replied that she was afraid a yes vote would get her defeated. Clinton assured her it wouldn't.

"You're afraid, Vada, but I have to have one more vote to pass this thing."[97]

As it happened, she voted yes, the bill passed, and as she feared, she was defeated in her reelection bid.

In the end they required fifty-one votes in the House to get the tax increase, and they got exactly fifty-one. Clinton had needed every vote. It was a photo finish.

The changes that the Clinton education plan brought about were substantial. New standards shrank class sizes, raised teachers' salaries, and expanded course offerings to include in every school such previously obscure luxuries as physics, foreign languages, and music. Per capita spending per student more than doubled. The school year was lengthened. Student testing ended social promotion. The percentage of graduating seniors electing to attend college rose from 38 percent to 50 percent. Emphasis was put on helping children learn during the critical early years, almost from birth: There was a program to teach parenting skills to young mothers; access to preschools was increased; and mandatory kindergarten was added.

But the most significant legacy of the Clinton education crusade cannot be measured in any of these statistics. They changed Arkansans' values about the importance of education. "Not much value had been placed on education," said Dumas. "The most important thing Clinton did was change public attitudes—particularly in the rural areas—that education is important for your children." Clinton staffer Mahlon Martin said that the general populace "really embraced education as important. The changing of this mind-set was as important as anything that he did."[98]

Clinton would forever be remembered as the "education governor." Arkansas voters never stopped being grateful to the man who improved their kids' schools. He not only created opportunity for the next generation, but also inspired optimism and pride among the general population. Clinton was never seriously challenged at the ballot box again.

None of that would have been achievable without Hillary. He could not have passed the education bill without her. Not only did she take the lead and do a lion's share of the work—but like Grandma Edith, Hillary kept *his* eye on the ball.

"Education has to be right on top of the list of his accomplishments," said Arkansas journalist Roy Reed. "Now there is an example of what the guy can do when he's focused."[99]

"The older you get," Clinton told a reporter, "you get to the point where you don't want to disappoint yourself any more. You realize that the time you have is limited, and you want to live like a laser beam instead of a shotgun."[100]

PART III

The Prodigy President

Prosperity and Peace

7

It's the Economy, Genius

· A MANHATTAN PROJECT FOR THE ECONOMY ·

I t's the economy, stupid," read a hand-lettered sign posted by James Carville in Clinton's campaign headquarters. It became a mantra. Clinton promised to "focus on the economy like a laser beam."

But focusing on a problem and knowing how to solve it are two different things. Can any president fix the American economy? Many experts think not. And even if one could, there is no general agreement as to how that can be accomplished. For Clinton to keep his campaign promise, he would have to unlock this dilemma, and gamble on a theory. His presidency would hinge on guessing right.

Clinton's determination to make the economy his top priority was indicated by his creation of an "economic security council"—renamed the National Economic Council once he became president—"to do for economic policy what the National Security Council did to coordinate foreign policy."[1] Clinton put together a blue-ribbon panel of economic advisers and worked them like dogs, day and night, for over a year. When I suggested that it was like a Manhattan Project for the economy, the Clinton economic team members I spoke to readily agreed. That was exactly the way they thought of it, too, they told me.

But the analogy would be more apt if Harry Truman had taught himself nuclear physics and led the bomb-making effort personally. Clinton did not do what one would expect of a president: simply appoint a panel of experts and receive their recommendations. He intellectually mastered the problem in all its aspects, from the most abstract economic theories to the minutest line items in the federal budget. One of the many witnesses of his mastery was Alice Rivlin, a core member of Clinton's economic team. She was deputy director of the Office of Management and Budget (OMB) in 1993, and served as OMB director from 1994 to 1996, when Leon Panetta moved up to chief of staff. What she still marvels at is how fast Clinton came up to speed in his level of economic understanding, quickly becoming conversant enough with economic ideas to be able to discuss them intelligently with the best economic minds in the world. By way of example, she recalled that when the finance ministers and central bankers from twenty-two countries, called the G-22, met in Washington, Clinton did not want to just drop by the meeting; he insisted on leading it. He led an engrossing, detailed discussion for several hours before his aides whisked him away to his next event. "These high-ranking folks from various countries were just agog. They were saying: 'Our president doesn't do that.'" How many presidents can? Few Americans had any idea that they had elected a prodigy.

In 1994, Bob Woodward published a book, *The Agenda,* about the seemingly madcap process that Clinton led his team of economic advisers through in devising and selling his administration's economic strategy in the first year of his presidency. The book served to reinforce the image of Clinton as a not-ready-for-prime-time president. "*The Agenda* was marketed as the most persuasive proof yet that Clinton was an undisciplined and indecisive president leading an inexperienced and out-of-control White House," wrote George Stephanopoulos.[2] Stephanopoulos is convinced that the book did real political damage. Clinton was enraged by it.

There is no reason to believe that Bob Woodward, one of America's premier investigative reporters, distorted the facts. He had unprecedented access, and his reports are essentially substantiated by other reporters, such as Elizabeth Drew, author of *On the Edge,* a book about Clinton's first year as president, and *Washington Post* reporter John F. Harris, who wrote *The Survivor*, a book about the Clinton presidency. What I will attempt to show is that while Woodward did not distort the facts, he did, I'm sure unwittingly, distort their *interpretation*, which can be just as devastating. Clinton told Woodward that he was afraid that "you're going to make me look like a madman." He wasn't far off. On *60 Minutes*

Woodward succinctly summarized his assessment of the Clinton White House: "Chaos. Absolute chaos."[3]

Woodward was not alone in this assessment. Indeed, the word *chaos* comes up repeatedly in relationship to Clinton, particularly in his first year. Dick Morris wrote that "Clinton lived in chaos; on his best days he seemed to thrive on it. He was always at the center of a swirl of activity."[4] Leon Panetta, who was part of the economic team and then served as director of the Office of Management and Budget, admitted to me that there were times, especially when meetings seemed to drone on endlessly, that he feared that they were degenerating into "total chaos," and repeatedly asked himself, "Where the hell is all this going?"

But was it chaos? Robert Rubin, in his role as director of the National Economic Council, led the economic meetings. He wrote that "the impression of chaos seemed to me greatly overstated. . . . What might have looked messy to outsiders was actually a process of deliberate open discussion, of smart, committed people engaging in debate as a way of getting to the best decision."[5] Alan Blinder agreed, offering an explanation for this vast discrepancy in perception between journalists like Woodward and those who served on the team: The process gave the "superficial appearance of chaos," he readily admitted. Indeed, "if one peered into the room, they would see open pizza boxes, wastepaper baskets full of trash, and lots of people milling about talking at once." But there was "an underlying logic," he insisted, a method to Clinton's madness, so to speak.

Part of this discrepancy in perceptions stems from a more basic confusion about what *type* of process this really was. The usual governing process that a reporter might expect to see in the White House is characterized by businesslike meetings, with agendas, committee reports, brief discussions, decisions, and action items. But this was a *creative* process, and creativity is rarely orderly, linear, dispassionate, or time efficient. The economic team was trying to solve a macroeconomic and political problem that had never been solved before, brainstorming on how to split the economic atom. Truly, Clinton thrives in such high stress, superheated intellectual climates, and loves to draw others into his creative process. As Hillary well understood, "My husband likes to pull everyone into his creative tumult."[6] Blinder laughed when I read him that quote. "It's true! We had plenty of tumult, and it was very creative."

Despite all, Alice Rivlin believed it to be "the best decision-making process I've ever seen in government, and I've been there for a long time." Ultimately, Clinton made remarkably good decisions, Panetta agreed, even if "he went by way of Mars to get there."

· THE GAMBLE ·

Alan Greenspan, chairman of the Federal Reserve, arguably had more power over the American economy than any other single individual. Not only did he control short-term interest rates—an awesome power in itself— but even his most understated pronouncements on the economy moved markets. Alan Greenspan was the most powerful and respected Fed chairman in memory.

The chairman of the Federal Reserve is autonomous, supposedly above influence by the president, but that has not stopped presidents from trying to influence him, for the simple reason that his decision to raise or lower interest rates, and his statements about the economy, can have enormous effect on their political fortunes. George Bush Sr., for example, was convinced that he lost reelection because Greenspan raised interest rates before the election.

Would Clinton be any more successful in coaxing low interest rates and economic optimism from Greenspan? He was surely going to try. Before Clinton took office, he invited Alan Greenspan to meet with him in Little Rock, on December 3, 1992. It would prove to be a meeting of immense importance.

Greenspan wrote in his memoir, *The Age of Turbulence,* that Clinton seemed very happy to see him. "I could see why he was a great retail politician. He made me believe he really had been looking forward to seeing me."[7] Actually, Clinton was not faking it. He really was looking forward to meeting Greenspan, very much so.

"We need to set our economic priorities, and I'm interested in your outlook on the economy," said Clinton.

Greenspan was ready to make a "pitch," he wrote: "From the Fed's perspective, if he wanted to address the economy's long-term health, the deficit was the most pressing concern. I'd made that argument at the start of Bush's term, and now the problem was four years worse."[8] Greenspan emphasized the importance to the economy of reducing the deficit—something that most of the economists on Clinton's economic team had also stressed. The lower the deficit, the less money the government would need to borrow. If the government borrowed less money, there would be a larger supply of money available for loans in the private sector. According to the laws of supply and demand, money becomes cheaper to borrow when there is more of it, and so long-term interest rates would come down if the deficit was reduced. Consumers would then be able to refinance their homes at lower rates of interest, which would put more money in their pockets, which they could then save, spend, or invest. Businesses would be able to borrow more freely for capital investment and expansion, which should create jobs. If the financial markets really believed that Clinton was serious about cutting the deficit, Greenspan believed that the bond market would respond by dropping long-term interest rates. And, as the interest rates on bonds went down, people would invest less in bonds and more in stocks, and that would pump up the stock market.

Greenspan had made this speech to Reagan and to Bush (and later to the next President Bush), but none had acted on his advice. In fact, all three Republican presidents went the exact opposite way, increasing the deficit by dizzying amounts. Greenspan had been a prophet crying in the wilderness without honor in his own party—Greenspan was a Republican. "Now I know how Cassandra feels," he wrote.

Greenspan's encounter with Clinton was a shock. "To my delight," wrote Greenspan, "he seemed to pick up on my sense of urgency about the deficit, and asked a lot of smart questions that politicians don't ask." Not only did Clinton get Greenspan's gospel, but he was, Greenspan noted, a kindred spirit—a fellow wonk. "Our meeting, which had been scheduled for an hour, turned into a lively discussion that went on for almost three. We touched on a whole range of topics beyond economics— Somalia and Bosnia, and Russian history, job-training programs, education. . . . So the saxophone wasn't the only thing we had in common. Here was a fellow information hound, and like me Clinton enjoyed exploring ideas."[9]

Greenspan left the meeting thinking that Clinton really got it. He found Clinton so sincere that, if he were faking, it would be the most frighteningly impressive display of lying he had ever seen in his entire life. The irony of the situation did not escape him. Though Republicans were supposed to be the party of fiscal responsibility, the terrible deficits facing the country had been created by Ronald Reagan, a Republican president, and then made worse by his Republican successor, George Bush. Now, a

Democratic president—standard-bearer for the party of tax-and-spend liberalism—was promising to fix the problem. A *Democrat*.

Clinton came back from the meeting elated, saying his instincts told him that he could "do business" with Alan Greenspan.[10] As usual, Clinton's interpersonal instincts proved correct. Greenspan admits that while he had a "terrible relationship" with the first president Bush, under Clinton "the relationship between the Treasury and the Fed had never been better."[11] And this relationship began in that meeting on December 3, 1992.

The other thing that impressed Greenspan was the fiscally conservative economic team Clinton put together, which included fiscal conservatives like Lloyd Bentsen, Leon Panetta, Alice Rivlin (who would later work at the Fed), Bob Rubin, and Larry Summers. "What jumped out at me was that Clinton was taking a page out of Kennedy's book. All of Clinton's economic policy appointees were fiscally conservative centrists. . . . Choosing them made Bill Clinton seem about as far from the classic tax-and-spend liberal as you could get and still be a Democrat." In his memoir, Greenspan revealed that he secretly developed an unusually close working relationship with Bob Rubin and Larry Summers: "Rubin, Summers, and I met confidentially over breakfast each week for the next four-and-a-half years. . . . We'd gather at 8:30 A.M. in Bob's office or mine, have breakfast brought in, and then sit for an hour or two, pooling information, crunching numbers, strategizing, and brewing ideas. I always came out of these breakfasts smarter than when I arrived."[12]

These meetings were not a collusion between the presidency and the Fed, whose independence from the executive branch is crucial. In fact, Greenspan mentions several times in his memoir that he was grateful to Clinton for respecting his autonomy. Instead, this weekly gathering was more like a Talmudic study group (all three of the economists were Jewish), where the process of discussing and arguing over ideas was both a virtue and pleasure in itself. Implicit was the faith that through such interactive study, insights would emerge to benefit the American economy, a goal all three men shared.*

---

* That good working relationship helped Clinton make good economic decisions. The best example would be the 1995 Mexican bailout. Faced with a cash-flow crisis, Mexico was about to default on its debt payments. Greenspan wrote in *The Age of Turbulence* that the "risk was hard to overstate." A similar crisis in 1982, when Mexico defaulted on $80 billion in debt, had triggered a cascade of defaults across Latin Amer-

Clinton's advisers were deeply divided over the deficit-cutting strategy. The economic advisers were, for the most part, deficit hawks who agreed strongly with Greenspan about the central importance of lowering the deficit as a long-term macroeconomic intervention. But there were several problems with that approach. Clinton was a liberal Democrat who wanted to fund programs to help people. He had not campaigned as a fiscal conservative. His political advisers, like Paul Begala and James Carville, thought he had lost his soul and sold out the people who had elected him. It was counterintuitive to think you could help the poor and working folk by taking money away from federal programs aimed to help them. While still others, like the deputy director of the economic council, Gene Sperling, found themselves somewhere in between.

And to make matters worse, Greenspan's advice was an untried strategy—a theory. Since FDR, presidents had stimulated the economy by *increasing* government spending. There was compelling evidence that cutting the deficit could actually produce a recession, at least in the short run, because it removed government spending from the national economy. Government spending pumps up the economy, and cutting it would potentially cause the economy to contract. Blinder recalls it was his job to explain to the president the possible economic risks of a deficit-cutting strategy: "At one point, I made a remark: 'In the worst-case scenario you

---

ica, and nearly triggered a wider economic collapse. "Behind the scenes, I argued, as did Bob Rubin and his top deputy, Larry Summers, and others, that U.S. intervention should be massive and fast," noted Greenspan. Congress stalled on the issue, because it was too politically unpopular. Voters opposed it by a "stunning margin" of 79 percent to 19 percent. Rubin suggested that the administration "take matters into its own hands" by taking the unorthodox step of tapping a Treasury fund created by FDR to stabilize the dollar and use the funds to make loans to Mexico. "I pitched in to help work out the details of the plan," wrote Greenspan. "Rubin and Summers presented it to Clinton on the night of January 31. The surprise was still in Bob's voice when he phoned afterward to report the result. Clinton had said simply, 'Look this is something we have to do,' Rubin told me, adding, 'He didn't hesitate at all.'" Not only was the crisis averted, but the United States made a $500 million profit on the bailout. Cleverly, the plan put a very high interest rate on the short-term bailout loans, motivating Mexico to pay them off first, before any other debts. "The experience formed a lasting bond between Rubin, Summers, and me. . . . We became economic foxhole buddies. I felt a mutual trust with Rubin that only deepened as time passed." (Greenspan also gives the Clinton team high marks for their handling of other economic crises, such as the Asian contagion, when South Korea threatened default, an impending Russian default, and the unraveling of Long-Term Capital Management.)

could have a recession about the size of Bush's.' Now Bush had just lost his job because of that recession. And I frankly thought some of that talk might make him lose his resolve. But he never did, he never did lose his resolve." "It was definitely a gamble," said Rivlin. "How much risk were you taking by cutting the deficit?"

The essential unanswered question was, How quickly would interest rates come down? Would they come down far and fast enough to compensate for the inevitable economic contraction produced by lowering government spending? That was impossible to predict with any accuracy. It all depended on the mood and psychology of the markets—bond traders controlled long-term interest rates—and that of Alan Greenspan, who controlled short-term rates. Summing it all up, Clinton asked his economic team if he was understanding them correctly: "You mean to tell me that the success of my program and my reelection hinges on the Federal Reserve and a bunch of fucking bond traders?"[13]

All the economists around the table nodded. That was exactly what they were telling him.

At first Clinton would try to have it both ways, putting new social programs in the budget even as he tried to reduce it overall. But in the end, when push came to shove, he would give up many of those programs to bet on deficit reduction. "The deficit hawks were right," wrote Clinton. "If we didn't get the deficit down substantially, interest rates would remain high, preventing a sustained, strong economic recovery."[14] Clinton would eventually propose a budget that cut the deficit by $500 billion over four years, consistent with his promise to halve the federal deficit. Along the way he would be forced to abandon the middle-class tax cut he had promised, his economic stimulus package (which Congress defeated), as well as half the new programs for investing in education and infrastructure that were most precious to him. He was betting that if he could improve the economy through deficit reduction, tax receipts would rise and allow him to build those investments into later budgets.

As Clinton wrote: "That was a big 'if.' "[15]

It was a bank shot—an effort to help ordinary Americans not directly with programs, but indirectly by lifting the economy as a whole.

Hypomanics are risk takers in both the best and worst sense of the word. Clinton's effort to rescue the economy is a successful example of positive risk taking. Most people were, and still are, unaware of how boldly Clinton rolled the dice. "People forget now because it was so successful. It was a gamble politically and economically," Alan Blinder told me. "Our new president was a risk taker who was not content with the status quo," recognized Greenspan.[16]

"The most important domestic decision of my presidency was still one big gamble,"[17] Clinton would later write.

· THE PROCESS ·

Clinton had promised to unveil his economic proposal on February 17, 1993. They had less than a month to design a budget that would fix the American economy.

On January 29, Clinton and his team of economic advisers began a series of marathon meetings in the Roosevelt Room of the White House. They met almost every day and into the night, provoking Treasury secretary Lloyd Bentsen to describe Clinton as "the meetingest fellow I ever saw."[18] As some of the meetings stretched to 8:00 or 9:00 P.M., Alice Rivlin recalled, someone would say, "Mr. President, do you have time to go on?" Exhausted, everyone sitting around the table was hoping Clinton would call it quits, and politely encouraged him to do so. But Clinton, who didn't indicate that he had gotten the hint, would inevitably respond, "Sure, let's continue." "There'd be almost audible groans in the room," said Rivlin, "and he'd go on for another couple of hours." Aides would gripe in whispers among themselves—"I'm not sure how long I can take this"[19]—while Clinton, by contrast, would exuberantly interject remarks like "this is fun"[20] or "I love this stuff."[21] "He was having a good time," said Rivlin, but as the hour drew late she was repetitively thinking, "I wish we could do this in the morning. I wish we could wind this up now and go home." Blinder recalled feeling both excited and drained. "It was exhilarating, but it was exhausting. We were all sleep deprived."

Along with being sleep deprived, the participants were often food deprived as well. "These meetings went on for hours in the Roosevelt Room, every day, at what I thought was the worst time of day, late afternoon and into the evening. That's my low-blood-sugar time," said Rivlin. "And nobody's had anything to eat. Sometimes the president said, 'You know, we could use some food here.' And then somebody would come with big plates of cookies. Always these wonderful cookies, which you knew you shouldn't eat before dinner, but everybody was starving. Cabinet officers were grabbing those cookies! And the plate would be empty in no time at all."

Clinton surrounded himself with advisers who held sharply discrepant points of view, and encouraged them to debate in front of him. "As a decision maker, Clinton wanted his aides and advisers to present him with the widest possible range of views and alternatives," wrote Rubin. "He liked to encounter those views not just in memo form, but actually hear people on his team discuss and debate the options in front of him."[22] To some, this open process was invigorating. Begala recalled that "people came in. They argued with passion. They stated their case. The other side stated its case. The president would go back and forth. I thought, it was great. I thought, that's the way it ought to be." Blinder also believed that the sometimes rowdy discussions and passionate disagreements were a good thing, especially compared to the alternative: "That was a strength of the meetings, not a weakness, because governments make bigger mistakes when the president is kept in a bubble and only hears one opinion. Bill Clinton was hearing lots of opinions, sorting out the arguments, and reaching decisions."

Though the meetings were not without structure, their basic method allowed for a free exchange of ideas, with wide tolerance for free-association detours. "Sometimes it would kind of degenerate into a free-for-all, and people would be arguing with each other," said Rivlin. "You know, at a dinner party, when you have ten people and it breaks down into separate conversations? That would go on for a little while, and then somebody, either the president, or Gore, or Rubin, or somebody would say, 'Wait a minute, come on, we have to have one conversation here, please!' I thought if I were president of the United States, I would say: 'Shut up, you guys!'"

In this freewheeling debate, tempers sometimes flared. In one meeting, Treasury secretary Bentsen heard Gene Sperling mutter something under his breath against what Bentsen had just said. Turning in his chair, Bentsen stared threateningly at Sperling. "What did you say?"

Trying to diffuse the tension, Deputy Treasury Secretary Roger Altman joked, "Why don't we let Gene and Lloyd go out and settle this in the hall?" Clinton also gave the conflict a humorous spin: "After about three months we'll be sitting around saying, 'Whatever happened to old Sperling?'" (Bentsen, though in his seventies, was a tough old Texan, while the young Sperling was a bit of a boyish nerd.)

But after the meeting, Clinton came up to Sperling and encouraged him to keep up his dissent: "You stick at it! You stick at it!"[23] Though Clinton did not like personal discord, he thrived on debate, and he wanted to encourage Sperling not to back down, to maintain an honest exchange of ideas.

"Basically, he kind of operates best in this kind of uncontrolled environment of ideas and discussion in which people are debating issues, and he has the opportunity to be able to evaluate all those ideas, using his own chemistry," said Leon Panetta, who described it as unlike any decision-making process he had ever seen before in government. "There are very few people who can go through a process like that and pull it together to make it work. But he did."

Beyond the grueling schedule and endless discussion, what was most maddening to many was that Clinton seemed to be constantly changing his positions. To some of those in the room, it seemed as if Clinton was swinging back and forth, alternately being for and against everything that was proposed. To others it seemed as if he was moving in mental circles, viewing and reviewing the same material over and over from every angle. Yet to others still, he just seemed to be terribly indecisive. George Stephanopoulos thought that Clinton's mind was like a kaleidoscope, constantly turning to reveal new facets of a problem. In this regard Clinton's brilliance was a liability. As Nigel Hamilton wrote in the second volume of his Clinton biography, *Bill Clinton: Mastering the Presidency*, "Clinton was, and always would be, a prisoner as well as a beneficiary of his high intelligence."[24] In the infinite regress of his thinking, no issue is ever really finally resolved, as new streams of thoughts and information are forever flowing in. On a practical level it was paralyzing for the team, since Clinton didn't come to a resolution one way or another. "The worst thing about him is that he never makes a decision," said Leon Panetta.

One reason for Clinton's shifting positions was that he was consulting multiple sources beyond his team of economic advisers. "He was getting conflicting advice and trying to reconcile it. He might get a group of us technocrats in the room and say that it was a great idea to cut wheat subsidies. Then you started hearing from the wheat senators. There were cases where he would sort of say 'yes' to us, and then the next day we would hear the answer was 'no,' because someone else had gotten in there," said Alan Blinder. Some people say Clinton's final decisions are swayed by the last person he talks to, but that seems too simplistic. Paul Begala has a slightly different take. He said that Clinton "operates by sonar." He is constantly bouncing ideas off of multiple sources and navigating his way by analyzing the stream of answers that bounce back, making multiple midcourse corrections while in flight.

Another aspect that made these meetings mind-numbing was that no detail was too small for Clinton's attention. "He was a sponge for detail," recalled Blinder. They went through the budget with a fine-tooth comb, debating whether to maintain a subsidy of a few million dollars for honeybee farmers, for example. "We were having an intense seminar on government minutiae led by Bill Clinton," recalled one staff member.[25] The staff did their best to move Clinton along, but "the president resisted, hungering always for more detail. The arcana of deliberations were torture for nearly everyone but Clinton," wrote Bob Woodward.[26] "We'd be going over the numbers hour after hour, looking at every minute program," Labor secretary Robert Reich recalled. "Can we cut that? What's the consequence of cutting that? Can we get a little more money to do this? It seemed to be endless, and it also did seem remarkably academic, in a way. I mean, here's the president of the United States, the head of the free world, wondering whether, if we cut the Coast Guard by this much, would we have a little more money to go into this training program."[27]

"The federal budget is a big thing," Blinder told me. And they literally went over it "line by line. . . . He paused over a $2 million—not billion, million—line in the Commerce Department. It had something to do with minority set-asides, and he wanted to hear about it. It just piqued his curiosity. You know, $2 million is not even a rounding error (to be a rounding error, you have to figure about $50 million). But, you know, we stopped, and for five minutes he heard a Commerce Department guy explain what this program was." Even Alan Greenspan—perhaps the ultimate econometric data sponge—was impressed. "I never ceased to be surprised by his fascination for economic detail."[28]

As is often the case with Clinton, someone had to take charge to keep the meetings on track, and more often than not that was Robert Rubin. "Sometimes the president was having such a good time, talking about this and that, telling stories from Arkansas, that things would slow down," noted Alice Rivlin, and "Rubin moved it along." Rivlin noticed that when the team had conducted its 1992 preinaugural economic summit in Little Rock, Hillary had played the same role in those meetings:

"She played the disciplinarian role. She would say, 'Now, time to make a decision,' or 'Time to move on.' She was very good at that."

Predictably, Clinton drove himself into exhaustion in the service of this marathon effort. Treasury secretary Lloyd Bentsen confronted Clinton, saying that he was wearing himself out and it was impairing his judgment. Bentsen told him: "Mr. President, you want to make every decision. You can't. You've got to delegate more. It's not the quantity of your decisions. It's the quality. I've sat beside you when someone else is talking at one of these meetings, and I watch your eyes just fog over." Bentsen half closed his eyes, and in front of the president did an impression of Clinton on the verge of passing out. "You're gone. It's because you're tired. You think you can go without sleep. You can't."

Clinton admitted, "I know you're right, Lloyd." But nothing changed.[29] Begala thought that sometimes Clinton looked like a battered fighter, throwing wild punches that didn't connect, who needed someone to stop the fight. But no one had the authority to pull the president of the United States out of the ring.

"He was sleep deprived," agreed Blinder. "When someone falls asleep in the middle of meetings, you know they're sleep deprived." Yet even when he was literally passing out, Clinton's mental engine kept revving. "He would doze off now and then, but then he had the ability to snap to, and get right in the middle of the conversation. It was almost like, while he was sleeping, he was hearing this, and it was getting processed in his brain. I was quite amazed," said Blinder.

Rivlin recalled that "there were times when he would appear to nod off in a meeting. Somebody would say something, and he would suddenly say, 'No, I don't agree with that,' or 'That's an interesting point.' And you realized he was still in it!"

There were sharp divisions within the administration between the economic team, made up of deficit hawks (e.g., Panetta, Rivlin, Bentsen), and the political consultants (e.g., Begala, Carville, Stephanopoulos), who were advocates for more investments through social programs—what Clinton had campaigned on. The political consultants firmly believed that this new deficit-cutting mania was political "suicide." Clinton was ambivalent—he wanted both—and let the two camps debate. But what many regarded as a healthy debate became politically destructive to the administration, especially when some tried to win the battle by pushing their views through leaks to the press. The negative consequence of this was a public relations disaster. Rivlin thinks that the political consultants were particularly guilty of this: "The political team felt very strongly about this, and they were down and dirty about it, too. They were trying to sabotage it." Some of the maneuvering was quite personal. For example, a *Newsweek* article entitled "Dead Man Walking" cited "a source close to the president" saying, " 'Alice Rivlin, nobody pays any attention to her any more. She'll be gone by the end of the year.' " Rivlin was, needless to say, quite upset. "I inadvertently found out later who the source was. It was George Stephanopoulos. But there was a lot of that going on." So the press got stories of infighting, endless debate, and indecision.

The battle between Clinton's two groups of advisers mirrored a battle within Clinton himself, said Rivlin. "His head said 'deficit reduction' and his heart said 'promised programs.' " For example, Clinton eliminated some subsidies to farmers, but he hated having to do it. Alice Rivlin, taking off on Clinton's promise to "end welfare as we know it," made a joke: The next time Clinton campaigned, he could boast that he had "ended welfare as we know it for farmers." Clinton suddenly became furious with her: "Spoken like a true city dweller," he said coldly. "Farmers are good people. We're going to make these cuts, but we don't have to feel good about it."[30] "He dressed her down in public," said Begala, "because she wasn't showing empathy."

Clinton was so torn that the economic consultants thought Clinton needed some bucking up to maintain his budget-cutting resolve. Lloyd Bentsen asked Greenspan to meet with the president on January 28, 1993. Greenspan said firmly that the long-term outlook for continuing spiraling deficits was "financial crisis." [31]

Clinton "looked grim."[32]

"The hard truth," wrote Greenspan, "was that Reagan had borrowed from Clinton, and Clinton was having to pay it back." What impressed Greenspan was that Clinton bit the bullet. "His subsequent decision to go ahead and fight for deficit cuts was an act of political courage."[33]

The populist in his soul, and the populists among his political advisers, wanted the investments. Eventually he would have to choose his top priority, and that would be the deficit, though half his investments would survive. Clinton reasoned that doing what they could to lift the whole American economy would be a necessary precondition to making the progressive changes he really cared about. "No matter what I proposed to do in the way of investment programs, I was going to be operating around the margins of a very large economy. And that in the end, having control, some control, over the discipline and direction of the economy was going to be a precondition to making the investment programs work."[34]

In the battle between his heart and his head, "in the end, his head won," said Rivlin. "The promises were sacrificed for fiscal discipline."

To make the deficit cutting even harder and more frustrating, the numbers kept changing on Clinton, and always for the worse. Just a few days before he took office, Clinton learned that the deficit was $60 billion worse than initially expected.

After his inauguration, Clinton had a team at the Office of Management and Budget continuously recalculating the budget every time a new change was proposed, which put an unprecedented strain on the OMB bureaucrats. "Each new decision forced the Office of Management and Budget to re-estimate all the numbers. All-night sessions in the large, ornate Old Executive Office Building, where OMB officials dwelled, were becoming common," wrote Elizabeth Drew.[35] Unfortunately, the government accountants were not as adept at pulling all-nighters as Clinton; he had overloaded the federal agency beyond its capacity, with the predictable result that they made mistakes. At one stage, when they had moved a long way down the road, the OMB had to admit that they had made a slight calculation error of $60 billion. Clinton was furious; he then needed to find yet another $60 billion to cut.

It was almost expected in Washington that presidential economic plans would be based on fuzzy math bordering on fantasy, but Clinton was adamant in his demand that they refrain from using any phony numbers or accounting gimmicks. All the numbers had to be based on the most objective source—the Office of Management and Budget. When Begala suggested that they might resolve some of their budget dilemmas with a little smoke and mirrors, Clinton became incensed. "We can't lie about the deficit. Can't do that," Clinton said emphatically.[36]

"He was using scrupulously honest numbers, to the point of even going overboard to rig the numbers against ourselves," said Alan Blinder, always using the more pessimistic rather than the more optimistic estimates and assumptions.

Greenspan noted, "I was impressed that he did not seem to be trying to fudge reality to the extent politicians ordinarily do."[37] Clinton's iron-clad honesty here goes against the conventional wisdom that Clinton was a manipulator always seeking to shade the truth. However, the reasons for such scrupulous accuracy were practical as much as moral: To move the bond market and the Federal Reserve, which were central to the plan's success, "we had to acquire instant credibility," said Blinder. "Remember, the marketplace had been seeing rosy scenarios and baloney for years. They were extremely skeptical. And we had to fight that legacy. . . . Previous presidents had fudged the numbers horribly." To make matters more difficult, "we were the new Democratic kids on the block. And most of those money people are Republicans. So they were not our natural philosophical allies."

Convincing bond traders that this new budget would make the good times roll hit resistance right away. Bob Rubin, a former bond trader himself, and Alice Rivlin made a visit to the New York Stock Exchange to explain the plan. "These were his folks; he knew all of these guys. So he took the lead, but it was a hard sell. These guys were really angry. What they were angry about was the tax increase. These guys were mostly Republicans, they were all rich, and so *their* taxes were going up, and they didn't like it one bit. Bob was doing his best, but he wasn't making a sale," said Rivlin.

· THE SPEECH ·

On the night before the all-important February 17 State of the Union address, in which Clinton would unveil his plan, several Clinton staff members worked through the night; some worked through two nights (pulling all-nighters was becoming a "badge of honor" in the Clinton administration).[38] They were still making changes at 2:00 A.M. on the day of the speech. Hillary and various staffers reworked drafts all day.

Clinton continued to tinker with the speech up until the last minute, as he always did. There was a 7:00 P.M. version, an 8:00 P.M. version. At 9:00 P.M. in the limo on the way to Congress, Clinton made more changes.

When Clinton stepped up to the podium, the teleprompter was a blur; perhaps as a result of all the last-minute changes, someone had loaded the wrong version of the speech. The teleprompter issue was quickly resolved, allowing Clinton to read his latest draft, but the speech was still not in its final form because Clinton continued to rewrite the speech even as he gave it. Political adviser Mandy Grunewald, who was following along with a copy of the speech in her hand, realized with horror that Clinton was ad-libbing. "He's riffing," she said to a fellow staffer. "He's making it up!"[39]

Despite the chaotic process that surrounded the speech, Clinton seemed very much in command. The speech conveyed that Clinton was taking control of a federal deficit that everyone agreed was out-of-control: "Let's just face facts. For twenty years, through administrations in both parties, incomes have stalled and debt has exploded and productivity has not grown as it should. We've got to play the hand we've been dealt and play it best as we can."[40]

"Clinton seemed reassuringly in command, not only of the facts and figures, but he had a sense of mission," Tom Shales wrote in *The Washington Post*.[41] He was interrupted sixty times for applause. There were so many standing ovations the speech became "an aerobic activity" for the listeners. Clinton had a number of rousing and memorable applause lines: "We're going to have no sacred cows except the abiding interest of the American people"; "We must scale the walls of people's skepticism not with our word but with our deeds"; and invoking the spirit of Kennedy, "My fellow Americans, the test of the plan cannot be what's in it for me. It has got to be 'what's in it for us.'"[42] Senator David Boren said that, as the speech progressed, "he could virtually see and feel Clinton become president before his eyes."[43]

"He hit the cover off the ball with that speech," said Alan Blinder.

Much to his chagrin, Greenspan was seated next to Hillary. "In the uncomfortable glare of TV lights . . . the cameras focused on us again and again."[44] Greenspan realized that he was being used as an unwitting visual prop. "Obviously, I'd been positioned up front for a political purpose."[45] Every time the camera panned up to the gallery, showing Greenspan next to Hillary, it sent a not-too-subtle message suggesting that Greenspan was behind Clinton's plan. However, Greenspan wasn't too upset about being used. First, he was a little flattered: "I guess it was nice to know that the Federal Reserve was considered a valuable national asset after the somewhat less than favorable embrace we had gotten from President Bush."[46] More important, Greenspan really *was* behind Clinton's plan. "Clinton had broken the gridlock on dealing with the deficit," said Greenspan. To do so, "Clinton had taken an enormous risk," and Greenspan admired his courage.[47] He "deserved commendation if there was any justice in this crazy town of Washington."[48]

Clinton would later discover that he could expect little justice from the Republicans in Washington. But while Greenspan was also a Republican, "he's not a partisan person. He's an economist, first and foremost," Alice Rivlin said. And perhaps equally important, "He's a mensch"—a Yiddish term for someone who is moral, kind, and fair.

The next day the *Washington Post* editorial stated that Clinton had shown "conspicuous courage [and] presidential leadership" in presenting a "well balanced and sturdy economic plan. . . . President Clinton is betting that most Americans want their government to pay its bills and their country to invest more heavily in its people and the tools with which they earn a living."[49] Indeed, he seemed to be betting right: Polls showed that 79 percent of Americans liked the speech and supported the president's plan.

On February 19, two days after the speech, Greenspan appeared before the Senate Banking Committee for his semiannual presentation on the economy. He "commended" the president for presenting a plan that was both "serious" and "credible." If instituted, the plan would be "a very positive force in the American economy."[50] For the normally understated Greenspan, this was high praise, and the press interpreted it as such. It was his intention to support Clinton without seeming to do so too abjectly. "He found a way to endorse it without officially endorsing it," said Blinder. The message got through. *The New York Times* wrote that Greenspan had "endorsed Mr. Clinton's proposal to cut the budget deficit." "Greenspan Vows to Help Clinton," read the *Washington Post* headline, while the *Wall Street Journal* headline announced "Greenspan Takes Positive View of Clinton's Strategy."

The Clinton strategy had been to accelerate the drop in long-term interest rates by "sending a signal to the markets," said Rivlin. For Greenspan, who moved markets every day with the inflections of his voice, to give such a ringing endorsement was a megasignal, and it gave Clinton the instant credibility he needed. A large part of a national economy is a manifestation of group psychology, which affects the way the markets view the future. After Clinton's speech, long-term interest rates began to fall.

On February 23, Clinton announced proudly in a speech to the U.S. Chamber of Commerce: "Just yesterday, due to increased confidence in the plan, interest rates fell to a sixteen-year low." For the first time since the government began issuing thirty-year bonds, the rate fell below 7 percent.

And the rates kept falling. They would hit 6.37 percent by mid-August.

"The long rates came down, and more quickly than we had ever dared imagine," said Rivlin. "We were overjoyed. Even before we implemented the plan, it was working."

But the economic plan had one strength that became a weakness: It was *too* well thought out. It has been said that genius is the ability to hold two opposing ideas in mind at the same time. By that criterion, the budget reflected Clinton's brilliance, for it integrated what would seem to be contradictory aims.

As a result, it was easily misunderstood—worse yet, easily misrepresented by its opponents. Overall, the Clinton budget reduced spending—making cuts in more than 150 programs. But it also added a dizzying array of new programs, many of them related to Clinton's pet cause—education—providing cradle-to-grave learning and training opportunities, from expanding Head Start to providing college loans, and offering vocational retraining for workers who were laid off from jobs in industries that went overseas. The logic was that these investments were supposed to produce more valuable workers, which would ultimately benefit the economy in the long run.

Overall, Clinton raised income taxes—but only for the top 1.5 percent of earners. The logic, according to Gene Sperling, was that "wealthier Americans had both the greatest ability to bear the short-run costs of balancing the budget and the most to gain if our deficit reduction gamble worked."[51] While it is difficult to prove a direct cause-and-effect relationship, things did go according to plan. After the 1993 tax increase, upper-income households saw their annual *after-tax* incomes go up by $188,000 over the next four years.[52]

In contrast, Clinton actually *lowered* taxes on fifteen million of the poorest Americans, putting precious dollars back into the pockets of the working poor, many of whom were barely earning more than welfare after taxes. Clinton tripled the earned income tax credit (EITC), which is actually a negative income tax, meaning that the government gives money to the poorest workers to supplement their meager wages. "It was almost enough to ensure that anybody working full time at the minimum wage or higher would be above the poverty line. We didn't quite make that. But it was close," said Alan Blinder. So, "with the stroke of a pen Clinton lifted millions above the poverty line." In his book *The Pro-Growth Progressive,* Sperling estimates that five million working families were lifted above the poverty line. This gave them more incentive to work, and stimulated the consumer economy, since poor people spend what little money they have. During the intense negotiations and number crunching that went on when the Clinton team was crafting their budget, the question of whether Clinton could afford this tax cut, whose price tag came to $7 billion per year, came up again and again. Maybe they could increase it, but by less? Sperling wrote that Clinton remained stalwart on this promise: "President Clinton considered sacred his pledge that no parent working full-time should raise their children in poverty."[53] (Republicans, however, opposed the measure; Gingrich called it "increasing welfare spending."[54])

Raising the earned income tax credit was one of Clinton's most important and underlooked achievements, thought Blinder. While the millionaires who got their taxes increased noticed it, and many hated Clinton for it, few of the masses of working poor—not a group known for their interest in obscure issues of tax policy—had any idea that Clinton had improved their bottom line. In his 1994 State of the Union address, he introduced Faith Bowman, a beneficiary of the tax cut, who sat in the First Lady's box. Clinton joked that he could introduce Ms. Bowman as "the only one of fifteen million EITC recipients who actually knew she got a tax cut."[55]

Clinton's plan also contained a small energy tax. The BTU tax was Al Gore's baby. In addition to raising revenue, it was designed to have the added benefit of reducing consumption, and thus slowing global warming. Ultimately, because of the opposition it raised, the BTU tax would not survive, though a small four-cent tax on gasoline would, which allowed Republicans to truthfully say that everyone's taxes had been raised.

As a result of this complexity, people didn't know what to make of Clinton's budget. Was it tax-and-spend liberalism or deficit-cutting conservatism? In truth, it was both. It was Clinton's third way. But while Bill Clinton could readily hold and reconcile contradictory ideas and arguments in his head at one time, most normal mortals can't. Nor did such complexity translate well in the sound-bite culture of the news media. Integrating seemingly contradictory aims produced a mixed message. "People can't receive two messages at once," Democratic senator David Boren warned Clinton. "You've gotten them all believing they've got to get the deficit down. This is mission one, and now you're confusing them by coming in with a spending program. That mixes the message."[56]

Bob Dole informed the president that the Republicans in both the

House and the Senate were going to vote as a solid block against his proposal. Dole was honest enough to say that it was a calculated political
move. If the Republicans were on record as being against the plan, and
the economy didn't improve, they could blame Clinton. It was nothing
personal, Dole seemed to be saying. It was just business. Clinton thanked
Dole for his "candor." However, even though forewarned, he didn't anticipate how vigorously the Republicans would oppose him. He was "jolted
by the degree of resistance," wrote Alan Greenspan. "Most new presidents get a honeymoon from Congress, but Clinton got a trench war."[57]

The Republicans began attacking the plan right away. They were united
in portraying the plan as "a tax-and-spend old Democratic approach disguised as deficit reduction."[58] Trent Lott, a Republican senator from Mississippi, called it "the biggest tax increase ever proposed by a president,"
which was not true. "People don't want tax and spend," cried Pete Do-
menici, senator from New Mexico. Texas senator Phil Gramm called it
a "cradle-to-grave government paid for by cradle-to-grave taxes."[59] Scoff-
ing at the claim that only the top 1.5 percent would pay increased income taxes, House minority leader Bob Michel said, "When you hear a
Democrat call for taxes, do not ask for whom the tax rises. It will rise
for you."[60]

These attacks worked. After the initial euphoria following the speech,
polls showed that the only thing the average American knew about Clinton's budget was that it was a plan to increase taxes. A California poll
showed that 42 percent of the respondents thought that their income
taxes were being raised, though only the top 1.5 percent earners faced an
increase. Furthermore, the Republicans predicted dire economic consequences if the plan was adopted: Newt Gingrich said it would "kill jobs
[and] actually increase the deficit."[61] Phil Gramm called it "a one-way
ticket to recession." John Kasich, ranking Republican on the House Budget Committee, said it would "put the economy in the gutter."[62]

The irony was that Clinton was aiming to achieve the very fiscal discipline the Republicans declared to be central to their core values. Clinton
drew great heat from his own political advisers and the left wing of his
party for putting together what some disdainfully called an "Eisenhower
Republican" budget. But in order to pass the plan, he would have to win
with Democrats *only*. If that effort succeeded, it would be "the first time
in postwar congressional history that the majority party had passed a
major legislation with absolutely no support from the opposition."[63]

But in stark contrast to the Republicans, who moved in lockstep like a military unit, organizing Democrats was like herding cats. The scramble to line up votes for Clinton's budget would prove an apt illustration of what humorist Will Rogers once said: "I don't belong to an organized political party. I'm a Democrat."

· THE VOTE ·

On April 19, the Republicans mounted a successful filibuster against a portion of the budget plan known as the "stimulus package." Because there was a reasoned fear that cutting the budget could put the economy in recession, the administration had thrown in some efforts to stimulate the economy as a hedge to offset possible economic contraction in the first year. This afterthought was not well thought out—they didn't need it, and it was no great loss. The stimulus package was "not a thing of beauty," said Alan Blinder. "I never thought the stimulus package was very important or a particularly good idea," said Alice Rivlin. It was also a public relations disaster in two respects. First, because it outlined increased government spending, it contributed to the confusion about whether this was a budget deficit reduction package or a tax-and-spend plan, allowing Republicans to frame it as a tax-and-spend wolf in deficit-reduction clothing. In addition, the filibuster of the stimulus plan was a major political defeat. After having released his plan to major fanfare two months earlier, this was "a large political embarrassment," according to *The New York Times*.[64] Much of the public was under the impression that Clinton's entire economic package had been defeated, or soon would be. His economic plan was in "intensive care," according to Bob Dole, who was described as "gleeful" when saying this to *The Boston Globe*.[65]

Dealing with the Democrats wasn't much easier. The vote was so close that any one of the Democratic congressmembers had virtual veto power over the entire budget, especially in the Senate, where an earlier version had passed 50–50, with Gore breaking the tie. Any one of 50 senators could take the entire plan down at will. Many used this power to extort the administration for things they wanted. As a result, the budget became more laden with pork. To make matters more chaotic, several members of the administration were negotiating at once, so the right hand didn't know what the left was giving away. This ultimately led Clinton's chief congressional liaison, Howard Paster, to resign. He couldn't function as a negotiator, he said, while everyone else "freelanced."[66]

And they were freelancing in more ways than one. Administration members talked regularly to journalists, who then reported on the endless debates within the administration, greatly solidifying the notion that things were out-of-control. On several occasions senior staff even went on-the-record criticizing Clinton. All White Houses have leaks, but this one was a sieve. A well-chosen firing might have put the fear of God into the staff, but that wasn't Clinton's style. Before he took office, Ken Adelman, former head of the Arms Control and Disarmament Agency under Reagan, warned Clinton: "You will not have accountability from your cabinet members until you fire someone." Clinton blanched: "That was never my strong suit. Why can't you just fix it?"[67] Clinton would predictably forgive the leakers' transgressions. A case in point: On April 27, in a *Washington Post* article entitled "President in Trouble on the Hill," Leon Panetta was quoted as being gloomy about both the economy and the chance for their plan to pass, unless the president "defines his priorities."[68]

He apologized abjectly to Clinton, who was almost incapable of not forgiving the penitent. "You're Italian, you're Catholic. I understand," said Clinton, who knew from personal experience that hot-blooded people sometimes blurt out things impulsively that they wish they hadn't. When he did get mad enough to demand a firing, he usually rescinded it. "Clinton cries out for a bad cop," wrote columnist John Brummett, and unfortunately, "Mack the Nice," as his first chief of staff Mack McLarty was known, was the wrong man for that job.[69]

Finally, it became impossible for the administration to stay on message in the public relations war, because there were two camps in the Clinton White House working at cross-purposes. The economic advisers were pushing for deficit reduction and the political consultants stressed the more populist themes that they felt had gotten him elected: investments and taxing the rich to give to the poor. The two messages canceled each other out.

On June 9, 1993, Greenspan visited with Clinton again. Clinton's approval rating had plummeted to 36 percent, the lowest ever recorded for a new president five months into his term. Greenspan wanted to encourage Clinton to stay the course on deficit reduction. With all the political heat he was taking, especially for raising taxes, it would have been easy for Clinton to cave. But "Clinton spoke yet again with such depth and passion about his deficit reduction plan that Greenspan concluded once more that unless Bill Clinton was the best actor ever, the statements were genuine."[70]

Clinton's frustration was palpable. On June 14, from the Rose Garden, he announced the nomination of Ruth Bader Ginsburg to the Supreme Court. In her acceptance speech she mentioned her deceased mother, which brought tears to Clinton's eyes. Immediately after the announcement, ABC's Brit Hume asked Clinton if he could "perhaps disabuse us" of the perception that there has been "a certain zigzag quality in the decision-making process here."

Clinton shot back, steely eyed: "I have long since given up the thought that I could disabuse some of you of turning any substantive decision into anything but a political process. How you could ask a question like that after the statement she just made is beyond me."[71] Clinton virtually stormed off the podium, with a curt "good-bye," ending the press conference. It enraged Clinton that the press was obsessed with the process, which *was* zigzagging ("Brit just didn't know how right he was," wrote George Stephanopoulos[72]), but seemed less interested in the well-reasoned and thoroughly researched content of his plan. Part of the problem is that the press has to document process, because they write every day. As John Brummett observed: "Clinton's best side is the big portrait. There, one could see a deficit reduction plan in place, Reaganomics revised if not reversed. . . . But the daily snapshot could be most unattractive: hedging, retreat, reversal, premature compromise, and petulance." The problem for a journalist like Brummett, who had to write a column six days a week, was that one becomes "a walking Polaroid Instamatic. You are a prisoner of what is called 'process' rather than a student of what is called 'product.' In other words, you chronicle and comment on the often-messy process that Clinton follows toward a final product that is perhaps meritorious on balance."[73]

The final vote on the budget plan was "the Super Bowl," according to Bob Rubin. Clinton was plummeting in the polls. And there was a strong sense among the entire administration that if this proposal failed it would cripple Clinton's presidency. "If Clinton lost, he would be seen as powerless, be treated as powerless, and therefore would be powerless." It was "panic time."[74]

On Saturday, July 3, a meeting was called in the intimate White House solarium. The economic and political teams were both there. As per usual, they engaged in a long-winded, freewheeling debate.

Taking everyone aback, Hillary erupted in a frightening rage: "This isn't working." Her voice was sharp and direct. "We're not selling the plan. . . . Six months into it and the American people know nothing about it?"[75] Some thought Hillary was out of control, but those who knew her knew better. Her anger was "calculated and purposeful." She pointed to the economic team and said: "You're not serving him well by not knowing what they are doing." And pointing to the political consultants, she said, "And they have to know what you are doing." What they needed was a coordinated plan of attack. One clear message, pounded relentlessly into the public's consciousness, one campaign to win over Congress.

Sparked by Hillary's anger, Clinton erupted. Rising to his feet, he just started yelling.

"We need a war room to coordinate this," said Hillary. She had been setting up a war room for the fight for health care. She offered it to them. "Take the war room and do something with it," she said.[76]

Leon Panetta told me he remembered that meeting well. "It was a real come-to-Jesus meeting." Hillary was furious because "too many things were spinning out of control," he said. "At crucial moments like this, Hillary was often the de facto chief of staff," wrote Woodward. When I talked to Panetta, who would later become Clinton's chief of staff, he agreed: "If she did not feel that a chief of staff was doing the job, she would jump in and develop discipline."

Hillary's shock therapy worked. They formed a war room and went into full battle mode. The mere presence of a war room "made many in the administration feel that they were speaking with one voice, had their act together, and could engage in a tough fight," wrote Woodward.[77] "Then we pulled together, all the different disciplines and factions. We all had to sell it. We all had to believe in it, and we had to stop all the dissent and focus on one fixed goal," Begala said.

On August 5, the day of the House vote, there was still an alarming number of undecided. Every congressmember felt that they were risking their seat to vote for what the Republicans had labeled the "biggest tax increase in the history of the universe." They didn't want to say no to the president, but nor did they want to say yes. One representative, Bill Brewster, drove aimlessly around the streets of Washington, D.C., all day with his cell phone turned off, so that no one in the White House could reach him.

The vote in the House would be a true photo finish. In many ways it would be a replay of the all-important vote on Clinton's education package in Arkansas. Until the last ballot was physically cast, no one knew how it would go. It was a vote Clinton had to win, and he poured on the juice at the home stretch like only Clinton can, giving himself the whip all the way. On the phone, as Clinton called congressmember after congressmember, "he sounded like a machine gun," wrote Bob Woodward.[78]

" 'Get this person!' he instructed his secretary, Betty Currie, pointing to a name on the spreadsheet. As soon as she made the call, Clinton called out again: 'Get this person!' referring to another name.

" 'Get this person!' rapidly going down the list."[79]

At one point the flashing lights from the hold button indicated five congressmembers waiting on separate lines.

"If we don't get this bone out of our throat we can't do anything else," Clinton told one.

"I need your vote, man," he pleaded with another.[80]

Clinton made deals right and left, agreeing to almost anything—he just *had* to have their vote. "To me it looked like an oriental bazaar, with one member of Congress after the other trying to figure out what they could walk out the door with. That's what happens when you don't have a disciplined party and the vote looks like it's going to be really close," said Alan Blinder.

Clinton and his principal advisers congregated in the small cluttered study off the Oval Office to watch the vote. Everyone was tense. They still did not know if they had the votes. There was "nothing left to do— except worry," wrote Stephanopoulos. Gore, Bentsen, Rubin, and Panetta "paced around the President's desk and chomped on cookies. Clinton's nerves showed in the shredded butt end of the unlit cigar he'd been chewing all afternoon."[81]

There were surprising betrayals. Ray Thornton, a Democratic congressman from Little Rock, Clinton's *own* congressman, said he was voting no.

"I made him the fucking president of Arkansas State!" Clinton thundered.[82]

And there was a surprising hero as well: Congressmember Marjorie

Margolies-Mezvinsky, a freshman Democrat in a Republican district, who firmly believed that voting for the plan would most probably keep her from being reelected. "Her wealthy constituents would surely remember who raised their taxes," wrote Stephanopoulos.[83] But she wasn't willing to see the president of her party fail. She agreed to vote dead last. If Clinton was over the top, or definitively defeated, she would vote no. But if it was close and her vote could be decisive, she would take the risk and vote yes.

"I want you to know I'm going to be with you in this one," she said.[84] Clinton was so moved by her sacrifice and loyalty that he became teary.

At 9:55, the voting began.

By 9:56, Clinton was behind, 51–55.

By 10:00, he was ahead, 179–156.

Just as time was expiring, he was behind, 211–212.

All the Republicans had voted, each casting their ballots against Clinton. But eleven Democrats had yet to vote.

Within seconds the score was tied, 213–213.

By 10:12 he was down, 214–216, with only four votes left to go.

For a tense three minutes the vote remained the same. Nervously mouthing the same unlit cigar between his lips, Clinton placed one hand on Mack McLarty's shoulder and the other on the shoulder of George Stephanopoulos, "steadying himself like the captain on the bridge of a ship," while he hunched over the television in his study. "All his tension seemed to be pulsing into me through the knot on my left clavicle," wrote Stephanopoulos, "while I focused my energy on the little screen trying to will the yeas up to 218."[85]

As seems to happen so often with Bill Clinton, he was saved by a woman. At 10:15, Margolies-Mezvinsky, seeing that it all came down to her, did as she had promised and voted yes. As she walked down the aisle to cast her vote, she looked as if "she was walking to the gallows," said Begala. The Democrats in the House erupted into cheers, while the Republicans began taunting her, chanting, "Bye-bye, Marjorie!" knowing that she had put her seat in jeopardy with this all-important vote.

Clinton won: 218–216.

As she had predicted, Margolies-Mezvinsky lost her seat in the 1994 election. To many she is an unsung hero for this act of bravery. Begala later spoke at a Democratic dinner in Montgomery County, Pennsylvania, where Margolies-Mezvinsky is from. "I made sure that everybody knew that woman was personally responsible for helping to create twenty-three million jobs, and she's the only person that lost her job."

Once again, as in Arkansas with the education bill, it was as close to a photo finish as one could get. Clinton "whooped and threw his arms around each of his aides, one at a time giving them a bountiful Arkansas hug," wrote Woodward.[86] "The President's study erupted in a riot of hugs," wrote Stephanopoulos.[87]

The staff had teased James Carville that since he had recently become quite rich as a political consultant, if the bill passed, his taxes were going up. As a joke, Clinton bent Carville over his desk, put his hand in Carville's back pocket, and pulled out his wallet. Caught up in the ecstasy of the moment Clinton took all the cash out and began throwing it in the air, "symbolically redistributing the wealth."

Clinton went to the Rose Garden, where reporters were waiting for him. The president announced triumphantly, "What we heard tonight at the other end of Pennsylvania Avenue was the sound of gridlock breaking. . . . After a long season of denial, drift and decline, we are seizing control of our economic destiny."[88]

The vote in the Senate was also a nail-biter. It ended in a 50–50 tie, with Vice President Gore casting the deciding vote. One hundred and fifty White House staffers erupted in cheers. Some began to cry. T-shirts proclaiming "PRESIDENT CLINTON'S ECONOMIC PLAN VICTORY AUGUST 6" were passed around, as if they really had won the Super Bowl. The normally reserved seventy-one-year-old Lloyd Bentsen was pumping his fist into the air. "I've never seen such a great hard-fought victory! I've seen lots of presidents and lots of victories, but this is the sweetest!"[89]

Exhausted, Clinton climbed upstairs to the White House residence, where he met Hillary in the kitchen.

"Now," he said, "we can get on with what we really came here to do."[90]

· THE ECONOMY ·

The outcome—surely the real bottom line—was impressive by any standard. In the eight years between 1993 and 2001, the gross domestic product increased by a staggering 54 percent. Unemployment dropped from 7.5 percent to 4.2 percent, a thirty-year low, as twenty million new jobs were created. The expansion was achieved with low inflation, which was a mere 1.9 percent, the lowest in thirty years. The long-standing trend of growing income inequality between rich and poor was halted. This rising economy lifted the boats of all ethnicities and income levels. Unemployment among African-Americans and Hispanics hit the lowest levels ever recorded. The federal government went from an annual deficit of $290 billion to a surplus of $124 billion, and had paid off $140 billion in previous government debt. The stock market soared to unsustainable levels in the 1990s, powered by the irrational exuberance of Internet mania. But even after the crash of technology stocks in March 2000, the Dow Jones Industrial Average had done well, increasing 225 percent from the day of his inauguration to the end of his second term. It was arguably the longest, broadest, and most impressive economic expansion in American history.[91]

"The country had the longest period of growth in its history, massive new private-sector job creation, low inflation, higher incomes across all income groups, increased investment and productivity growth, and lower deficits, eventually followed by surpluses," wrote Bob Rubin.[92] "Every number that should go up went up, and every number that should go down went down," said Alan Blinder.

On May 5, 1998, Federal Reserve chairman Alan Greenspan told Clinton and his economic team: "This is the best economy I've seen in fifty years of studying it every day."[93]

Clinton cannot take all the credit, of course. New technology fueled a major investment boom that dramatically increased productivity in ways not seen before. As Alice Rivlin readily admits, "There was a computer revolution going on." And she said it was impossible to accurately calculate what percentage of the credit goes to the administration. "A few years ago, the Congressional Budget Office put out a paper arguing that the surplus that arrived in 1998 derived one third from policy decisions and two thirds from economic growth," wrote Rubin in his book *In an Uncertain World*.

One reason it will never be possible to quantify how much credit Clinton's policies deserve for the economic boom is that the economy is, in large part, driven by psychology. A nation, like an individual, can be possessed by a mood that may not be fully rational, but which can contribute to self-reinforcing patterns of behavior: either vicious cycles or virtuous ones. Rubin believes that Clinton increased confidence in the economy, by taking control of the deficit, which led to a virtuous cycle:

"In retrospect, the effect of the Clinton plan on business and consumer confidence may have been even more important than the effect on interest rates. In important ways the deficit had become a symbol of the government's inability to manage its own affairs—and our society's inability to cope with economic challenges more generally, such as our global competitiveness, then much in question. The view that fiscal discipline was being restored contributed to lower interest rates and increased confidence, and that led to more spending and investment, which in turn led to job creation, lower unemployment rates and increased productivity. . . ."[94]

There are still those who assert that Clinton was just a lucky beneficiary of the technology boom that took place on his watch, one which he did nothing to create. While it is true that Clinton did not invent the Internet, Clinton did grasp its economic implications even before his own economists. In 1995, "President Clinton's top economic advisers . . . worried that the president was getting carried away with his hopes for the high-tech boom," wrote Alan Greenspan. "The economists trooped into the Oval Office, and Larry Summers did a short presentation on why the tightness in the labor market meant growth would have to slow. The others chimed in. Clinton listened for a while, then finally interrupted.

" 'You're wrong,' he said. 'I understand the theory, but with the Internet, with technology, I can feel the change. I can see growth everywhere. . . .'

"At that moment, the president probably had a better hands-on feel for the economy than his economists," wrote Greenspan.[95]

One function of the chief executive is to be a cheerleader for the economy. At a White House conference on the "new economy" that included Greenspan and Bill Gates, Clinton proclaimed exuberantly:

"We meet in the midst of the longest economic expansion in our history and an economic transformation as profound as that that led us into the industrial revolution. From small businesses to factory floors, to villages half a world away, the information revolution is changing the way people work, learn, live, relate to each other and the rest of the world."[96]

Lastly, the he-was-just-lucky-to-be-there theory cannot explain away Clinton's very tangible war on the deficit. By the end of Clinton's second term, not only had the budget come out of deficit, but the Treasury was reporting record surpluses. Republicans wanted to use the money for tax cuts, while many Democrats wanted to fund more social programs.

Both Greenspan and Rubin believed the money should be used to pay down the $3.7 trillion national debt. Social Security was moving inexorably toward insolvency as the baby boomer generation aged. Paying down the debt could forestall the day when payroll taxes could no longer cover benefits and Social Security went bust. Yet, compared with tax cuts or spending increases, debt repayment was an "ugly duckling policy," admitted Greenspan, and it would be hard to mobilize the political will for it.

Yet Clinton turned the ugly duckling into a swan. He received a loud ovation when he declared in the 1998 State of the Union address: "What should we do with the surplus? I have a simple four-word answer: Save Social Security first. Tonight I propose that we reserve 100 percent of the surplus—that's every penny of any surplus—until we have the necessary measures to strengthen Social Security."[97]

"I'm amazed," Greenspan told Gene Sperling. "You've found a way to make debt reduction politically attractive."[98]

Gore ran on this issue, promising to put the surplus in a Social Security "lock box." But Gore did not become president.*

I think that Clinton's handling of the economy is very relevant to what has been called the "character issue." When it came to the economy, Clinton was nothing if not conscientious. He took great risk and expended great effort to expand the nation's wealth. "Clinton was often criticized for inconsistency and for a tendency to take all sides in a debate, but that

---

* Instead of paying off our debt, the surplus was once again replaced by deficits. When Bush took office in 2001, the CBO projected a surplus of $5 trillion between 2006 and 2015, as Gene Sperling noted in *The Pro-Growth Progressive*. The OMB's 2005 estimate for that same period was a deficit of $3.47 trillion, according to Douglas Holtz-Eakin, director of the Congressional Budget Office, in testimony before a Senate committee in February 2005. In his memoir, *The Age of Turbulence*, Alan Greenspan wrote that, to his utter horror, the statement that "'Deficits don't matter' . . . became part of the Republicans' rhetoric." Combined with a mild slowdown in the economy, the three main culprits for the red ink were: Bush's tax cuts—primarily for the wealthy; the costs of the Iraq war; and increased pork spending by a Republican Congress, which was "too busy feeding at the trough," according to Greenspan.

Under Bush and the Republican Congress, "Budget discipline in Washington gave up the ghost," added Greenspan. Greenspan was so disgusted with his own party that when the Republicans lost control of Congress in 2006, he believed that "they deserved to lose."

was never true about his economic policy," wrote Greenspan. "A consistent disciplined focus on long-term growth became a hallmark of his presidency.[99] In his biography of Hillary Clinton, *A Woman in Charge,* Carl Bernstein wrote: "Clinton had told Ted Koppel of ABC that he was going to 'focus on the economy like a laser beam,' and he made good on that promise."[100]

In the end, with the benefit of hindsight, it is now clear that Bob Woodward was just plain wrong. Those empty pizza boxes were not signs of chaos. They were signs of an amazingly brilliant hypomanic with a mission at work.

Clinton did focus on the economy like a laser, and it took off like a rocket.

8

A Thousand Welcomes

On September 13, 1993, Bill Clinton stood between Yitzhak Rabin and Yasser Arafat on the South Lawn of the White House. "Then, stepping up behind them, he placed one hand gently on their backs and prodded them together," wrote Nancy Soderberg, staff director of the National Security Council.[1] "Go in peace. Go as peacemakers," said Clinton as he physically pushed the two mortal enemies together. It is an image that is emblematic of Clinton's chosen role in the world. During his presidency Clinton appointed *fifty-five* special envoys, one to virtually every troubled region in the world. He helped avoid nuclear war between India and Pakistan, and worked to reduce tensions between Greece and Turkey. He also played a central role in resolving lesser known conflicts; for example, he helped to negotiate an end to disputes between Peru and Ecuador, and between Eritrea and Ethiopia. Anywhere on planet Earth where there was conflict, Clinton was there.

"The diplomacy of healing" is the phrase Tony Lake, Clinton's former national security adviser, used to describe the Clinton approach to foreign policy. He pointed out that Clinton was more than a peacemaker; he wasn't simply trying to stop wars. He was deeply driven to transform hostile relationships into positive ones. Said Lake, "Clinton was the most extraordinarily empathetic leader I have ever known."

In my effort to understand how Clinton was able to intervene so powerfully in so many international disputes I had to make a choice. I could survey all of his efforts across these many settings or choose to examine just one of those missions in depth as a prototype or case study. I chose the latter course, believing that one good story would be both more interesting to readers and more illustrative of the nuances than a more general review of all of Clinton's peace initiatives. I chose the Irish peace process for several reasons. First, unlike the Middle East one, it has not been well documented for American readers. Though there is a shelf of books published in Ireland and England about it, few on this side of the Atlantic ever really knew what Clinton accomplished in Ireland, in large part because it went almost entirely uncovered by the American press, which was more preoccupied with stories about scandal. Second, unlike the Middle East peace process, it has a happy ending. And finally, I reasoned that any story involving the Irish would have to be a damn good story indeed.

The Irish peace process was a long, winding road, involving many actors, in which Bill Clinton gave a brilliant performance as a peacemaker in action. I was able, fortunately, to interview most of the major participants on both sides of the Atlantic. Though I've tried to keep the story simple, I have included more than some readers may want to know about Irish politics to put the story in proper context, and some may wish to skim those parts.

If I had to summarize Bill Clinton's peacemaking technique, it would be the refrain from a popular Beatles song: "Come together, right now, over me." Though Clinton was not always in the foreground, his relationship to each of the warring parties was vital in bringing peace to Ireland. Clinton's approach to this legendary conflict, which no other American president had ever wanted to touch, was highly unorthodox and creative, and flew in the face of America's long-standing foreign policy. But, in many respects, it was just standard operating procedure for Bill Clinton—and it closely replicated his role in his family of origin. Clinton's mother, Virginia, was perpetually embattled with both her own mother, Edith, and her husband Roger. What brought them all together was their love for Bill, whose sunny and caring persona made him a master manipulator, but with a good purpose. He leveraged their love of him to bring harmony to their relationships with each other.

In a similar fashion, Bill Clinton inserted himself into Ireland's extended family feud by establishing warm, personal relationships over the course of his entire two terms (and beyond) with almost all of the leaders, winning them over with his combination of relentless charm and empathic concern, and his encyclopedic knowledge of their culture, history, and everything related to their conflict. And indeed, he manipulated them. Like a master family therapist, he repeatedly put warring parties in situations where they were virtually forced to interact in new, positive ways with people they despised.

Of course, the Northern Irish paramilitaries did not lay down their arms just because they loved Bill Clinton. The key was that the positive, trusting relationship they developed with Bill Clinton the man was *also* a relationship with the most powerful man on earth, the president of the United States. The combination of his person and his position gave Clinton enormous power to leverage for peace—a power few past presidents have realized so brilliantly. Nancy Soderberg, the National Security Council (NSC) staff director who worked most closely on Ireland, argued in her book, *The Superpower Myth,* that Clinton's technique should be a new model for America's role in the world. Dangling the carrot of America's power, money, and goodwill, Clinton made peace pay. He figured out how to invest America's political capital in ways that yielded enormous dividends for both the Irish and the American people, a win-win proposition. Clinton as peacemaker not only helped the Irish, but also served to raise America's stock in the eyes of the world—just as being perceived as a warmonger among critics of the Iraq war has served to lower it.

Here Clinton's hypomania served as a highly effective secret weapon for peace. Clinton's involvement in Ireland could be characterized as an irresistible force meeting an immovable object. Though not comparatively the most violent ethnic conflict on earth, the Irish situation was surely one of the most stubbornly intractable and enduring ones. Yet from the beginning, Clinton had the optimism to believe that the problem was fixable, and the confidence to believe that he could fix it. Clinton got people to buy into his vision in a way that only hypomanically charismatic leaders can, and helped breathe hope into a situation that few of the participants were hopeful about. Moods, as we discussed, are infectious. And in the end, Clinton's indomitable optimism prevailed over the renowned Irish pessimism.

The most dramatic example, and one of my favorite Clinton stories, can be found in his historic trip to Northern Ireland in November 1995, the first ever by a U.S. president. Clinton regards the two days he spent in Ireland as two of the best days of his presidency. For the first time anyone could remember, Irish Catholics and Protestants would come together en masse—over Clinton.

· THE PROMISES ·

It was a chilly afternoon in April 1992 in New York City, three days before the New York primary, when candidate Bill Clinton addressed a forum on Irish issues at the Sheraton New York Hotel. No one expected the governor of a small Southern state to know, or care, much about Ireland. Even urban Northern politicians with large Irish constituencies ignored the issue. No American president, not even those with Irish blood such as JFK and Reagan, had ever thought it was in America's best interest to risk alienating Britain, our closest ally, in order to get involved in this seemingly insoluble ethnic conflict.

It was certainly not an idealistic vision of world peace that brought Clinton to this conference. Before the New York primary, Clinton staffer Chris Hyland was given the general task of rounding up support among all of New York's diverse ethnic groups. As a preliminary step, he bought all the ethnic newspapers he could find in Times Square. There he ran across the *Irish Voice,* and called the publisher, Niall O'Dowd, who quickly invited Clinton to address the Irish forum.

Before the formal conference, the organizers met privately with Clinton. O'Dowd recalled: "I've spent my life interviewing American politicians about Ireland. I was just gob-smacked by how much he knew. Clinton was giving a seminar. He started back with the McBride Principles, the 1968 uprising, the start of the Troubles again, the whole history. His depth of knowledge bowled us over." Clinton's enthusiasm surprised O'Dowd as well: "He didn't want to go. He kept coming back into the room. He wanted to talk more. It was like he'd been waiting a long time for someone to ask him these questions. He *loved* talking about it. Ninety-nine percent of American politicians had no interest in Northern Ireland back then. Terrorism, IRA, not for me! It was remarkable."

Even more remarkable was Clinton's confidence. Clinton saw a problem that he felt he knew how to solve. "It was revolutionary, utterly revolutionary, for an American politician to be talking about this as something that was doable, and he made a bold pronouncement—'I know this can work, and this is what we should do'—that was unbelievable."

In fact, Clinton had long felt America should have a role in solving the conflict. Nancy Soderberg told me that even as a student at Oxford, Clinton was "watching the violence in Northern Ireland on TV and asking himself: 'Why isn't the U.S. doing something to solve this problem?'"

At the forum , Mayor Ray Flynn of Boston asked Clinton the first public question: Would he, if elected, appoint a peace envoy to Northern Ireland?

"I would," said Clinton. "I think sometimes we are too reluctant to engage ourselves in a positive way because of our long-standing special relationship with Great Britain." Clinton argued that with the demise of the Soviet Union, the British alliance was no longer a practical matter of life and death for the United States, and that created new opportunities for different types of engagements.

The crowd erupted into applause. This was revolutionary, said O'Dowd: "The fundamental point where every American politician eventually ended up was: I can't because this will offend the British."

Next, someone asked if he would support a visa for Gerry Adams. Adams was the head of Sinn Féin, the political wing of the IRA, which officially was a terrorist organization. Adams had applied for a visa seven times over twenty years and always had been refused. "I would support a visa for Gerry Adams," said Clinton, "or any properly elected official of a government recognized by the United States" (Adams was a member of Parliament at the time). "I think it would be totally harmless to our national security interests, and it might be enlightening to the political debate in this country."[2]

Now the crowd, made up almost entirely of Catholics sympathetic to the IRA, broke into thunderous applause. This was nothing short of unbelievable. After Clinton left the conference, the crowd broke out singing Irish freedom songs, and some people even began to dance.

O'Dowd remembered having a strong intuitive feeling in that very first encounter that Clinton was "the one" who would be the key to peace in Northern Ireland. "I was ridiculed by all my friends about my optimism that Clinton would do it."

If O'Dowd had an almost mystical faith in Clinton, former Connecticut congressman Bruce Morrison, another key member of a nascent ad hoc Irish American initiative, approached the problem with the slightly more jaundiced eye of a politician. He saw an opportunity to make a deal. Irish Americans were a group Clinton needed very badly to win the White House, a prize that had eluded Democrats for twelve years. In the

1980 presidential election, a significant portion of Democratic voters, known as the "Reagan Democrats," had abandoned their party to vote for Reagan. Working-class Irish Catholics, who used to be part of the backbone of the Democratic Party, made up a sizable portion of those voters. Clinton's election could rise or fall on wooing this group back to the fold. And they cared deeply about Ireland. "We were offering Clinton a deal that made political sense," Morrison said. "We were saying, 'Ride this horse to the White House, and when you get there we'll be there with you to collect.'" Shrewdly, Morrison had Clinton put all the promises he made at the New York Irish forum into writing. Morrison understood how campaign promises work—or don't. "I've made a few campaign promises myself," he said to me, almost with a wink. Immediately after the election, Irish Americans for Clinton-Gore was transformed into Americans for a New Irish Agenda, "an entity that was built around Clinton's Irish promises—nothing else, no other agenda, just to remind Clinton, day in and day out, of the promises he made to Irish America."

A few months after the meeting at the Sheraton, Nancy Soderberg, former chief foreign policy adviser to Ted Kennedy, became a foreign policy adviser to candidate Clinton. Once elected, Clinton would appoint her staff director of the National Security Council, and she would become the point woman on the Irish issue. Soderberg was very frank. If she had been advising candidate Clinton when he made these commitments, she would have argued strongly against them: "Contrary to everyone's opinion of me now, I was very much against doing all of this stuff." As Soderberg's former boss, Tony Lake, wrote in his book *Six Nightmares*, "The candidate had made this pledge without the prior knowledge of his foreign policy advisers."[3] Promises or no promises, Clinton's foreign policy team preferred he quietly drop the whole matter after the election. Some Clinton aides cynically called the Irish outreach a case of "use them and lose them."

Would Clinton keep his Irish promises?

· THE DOWNING STREET DECLARATION ·

President Clinton's involvement in the Irish peace process began a little more than two months after he took office, on St. Patrick's Day 1993, when he met with the Irish prime minister, Albert Reynolds.

Clinton immediately brought up his desire to send a peace envoy to Ireland, his central Irish promise. Reynolds was euphoric at seeing such unprecedented commitment from the newly elected president. However, Reynolds explained that he was beginning a dialogue with the British prime minister, John Major, and too many cooks at that stage would spoil the broth. Reynolds urged Clinton to put the idea of a peace envoy "on the shelf" until the timing was right.

Clinton pushed back. He told Reynolds frankly that he had made a campaign promise to appoint an envoy, and he wanted to keep it, because he didn't think he could win reelection without the Irish vote. Reynolds suggested that he appoint an economic envoy instead, and assured Clinton that they would collaborate on the Irish peace process.

"The system doesn't work," Reynolds told Clinton. "And I'm not going to work through the system. I hope that's OK with you. But, if we work together, and put the system aside—you and I'll start it." Bill Clinton did not know the true reason Reynolds was asking him to shelve the political envoy.

When Reynolds told Clinton that they would have to "put the system aside," Clinton could not have imagined how far Reynolds had already strayed outside that system. Reynolds was conducting his own highly secret negotiations with militants on both sides of the conflict, and he didn't need a third party muddying the waters.

When Reynolds was elected the Troubles were killing both people and the economy, and he was determined to bring the conflict to an end if he could. A pragmatic businessman by background, Reynolds knew that you can't make a deal if you don't talk to the decision makers. The official Irish and British policy was that they would not engage in a dialogue with "terrorist" organizations until they surrendered their weapons. As a result, they had gotten nowhere.

"If you want to know the *real* story behind the peace process, I'll tell you the real story," Reynolds said on the phone, when I called him for an interview. I met with him in Dublin at a hotel around the corner from his home. "I came to the conclusion that the governments, for forty years, had pursued a policy of not talking to the people with power, the people involved," he said. Reynolds made a bold decision. He would pursue his own secret diplomacy with the militants, outside all normal channels. "The decision makers were the military. They were the ones who could deliver. Everyone told me, 'You can't talk to these people, and you can't talk to those other people.' But you couldn't stop it any other way, either."

Through intermediaries Reynolds began negotiating with Sinn Féin. While that process has been written about, Reynolds then told me something that he claimed he had not revealed before: He also met personally with members of the Unionist paramilitary. In a scene worthy of a spy movie, Reynolds gave his own bodyguards the slip by leaving his hotel in a taxi, and then he doubled back to hop into a car driven by a Unionist militant. Reynolds, a head of state, was being driven by a terrorist to God knows where, utterly devoid of all protection. It was not just a political risk, but a physical one.

Reynolds's approach was simple and direct: What do you want? He wanted them to state their terms, and put them in writing.

They did.

The simple genius behind Reynolds's plan was to allow the two paramilitaries to ghostwrite parts of a declaration, so that they would buy into it. When Major presented Reynolds with a revised version, after taking out some of the paramilitaries' exact language, Reynolds threatened to quit the whole enterprise. It was the original language, or no deal.

Reynolds claimed that Major never knew that "paragraph five of the Downing Street Declaration was drafted by the Unionist military. That paragraph set out their views on the whole thing. Five or six or seven requirements—or whatever it was—that they wanted to see to bring it to a cease-fire. It's what they wanted, and I wanted to publish it. I published the whole paragraph five. I never changed a single word."*

---

* Paragraph 5 reads as follows: "The Taoiseach [prime minister] however recognizes the genuine difficulties and barriers to building relationships of trust either within or beyond Northern Ireland, from which both traditions suffer. He will work to create a new era of trust, in which suspicion of the motives and actions of others is removed on the part of either community. He considers that the future of the island depends on the nature of the relationship between the two main traditions that inhabit it. Every effort must be made to build a new series of trust between those communities. In recognition of the fears of the Unionist community and as a token of his willingness to make a political contribution to the building up of that necessary trust, the Taoiseach will examine with his colleagues any elements in the democratic life and organization of the Irish State that can be represented to the Irish Government in the course of political dialogue as a real and substantial threat to their way of life and ethos, or that can be represented as not being fully consistent with a mod-

Reynolds worked out a similar deal with Sinn Féin, by closely incorporating their demands into parts of the declaration, as well.

"So, really, the two paramilitaries wrote the Downing Street Declaration?" I asked Reynolds.

"Sure. There was nobody else. I mean, once they made a decision, that was it. So you had to convince them. That was my tactics."

The Downing Street Declaration is an agreement between the sovereign states of Britain and Ireland outlining the way forward to peace. What John Major did not know was that parts of the document he was signing had been written by the terrorists.

"He never quite understood the declaration," said Reynolds, with a sly smile.

The declaration, signed December 15, 1993, also did something else. "It triggered our engagement," said Soderberg. Up until that point Clinton was trying to fulfill a political promise, to be able to say to the Irish Americans: I did what I said I would. With the declaration, Clinton saw an opening—a real shot at peace.

· THE ADAMS VISA ·

For years, Adams had routinely applied for a visa to visit the United States, where the IRA had many of its strongest supporters, and he had been turned down every time. With the peace envoy idea shelved, the Adams visa issue became the focus of the lobbying efforts of the Americans for a New Irish Agenda. To force the issue, one member of the group, Bill Flynn, organized a Northern Ireland peace conference through the highly respected National Committee on Foreign Policy, and invited

---

ern democratic and pluralist society, and undertakes to examine any possible ways of removing such obstacles. Such an examination would of course have due regard to the desire to preserve those inherited values that are largely shared throughout the island or that belong to the cultural and historical roots of the people of this island in all their diversity. The Taoiseach hopes that over time a meeting of hearts and minds will develop, which will bring all the people of Ireland together, and will work towards that objective, but he pledges in the meantime that as a result of the efforts that will be made to build mutual confidence no Northern Unionist should ever have a fear in future that this ideal will be pursued either by threat or coercion."

Adams to speak at the conference. As it turned out, the entire Irish peace process would ride on this one seemingly simple decision—to give a visa or not. But the decision was anything but simple.

Clinton wrote in his autobiography: "The State Department warned against it. Warren Christopher and the State Department, including our ambassador to Great Britain, Ray Seitz, were strongly opposed to issuing the visa, arguing that since Adams wouldn't renounce violence, it would make us look soft on terrorism and that it would do irreparable damage to our vaunted 'special relationship' with Great Britain, including our ability to secure British cooperation on Bosnia and other important matters. The Justice Department, the FBI, and the CIA agreed with State. The unanimous opinion was entitled to great weight."[4] In a nutshell, wrote Soderberg: "Letting a known leader of a key terrorist organization into the United States was strongly opposed by every relevant department of the U.S. government."[5] A decision to give Adams a visa "would enrage the president's cabinet."[6]

The CIA, FBI, and Justice Department were even more strongly against it than the State Department. There was no issue to consider here: Sinn Féin was a terrorist organization—end of story. "Throughout the coming months and years, they did all they could to convince us that Sinn Féin and the IRA were both one and the same—and irrevocably committed to terrorism," Lake wrote in his memoir.[7] However, despite the strong unanimity of the intelligence chorus, Soderberg was skeptical about whether American intelligence really knew what was happening on the ground in Ireland: "Don't forget, these are the guys who missed the fall of the Soviet Union."

Only the NSC team working on Ireland—Lake, Soderberg, and Soderberg's assistant, Jane Holl Lute—saw a risk possibly worth taking. Clinton describes the Adams visa issue as "the first important issue on which my foreign policy advisers could not reach a consensus."[8]

In addition, Clinton had to weigh how the Republicans could use the issue against him. Clinton risked looking soft on terrorism, something a young Democratic president seeking reelection—who had been portrayed by Republicans as a liberal, draft-dodging, pot-smoking anti–Vietnam war protester who was incapable of leading the military because all he cared about was filling it with gays—could ill afford.

Yet the biggest political consideration of all was the Irish American vote—a must-have for Clinton to be reelected. The White House probed Brian O'Dwyer, one of the Irish American leaders from Americans for a New Irish Agenda, to assess how much damage it would do to Clinton with Irish American voters if he didn't grant the visa.

The O'Dwyer family has been a mainstay of New York politics going back to the days of Tammany Hall. Brian's uncle, William, succeeded the legendary Fiorello H. LaGuardia as mayor of New York in 1946. And his father, Paul, served as president of the New York City Council from 1974 to 1977. When I met with Brian in his law office at the firm of O'Dwyer and Bernstein, I noticed that their surprisingly modest offices, practically adjacent to City Hall, were located on a street officially designated "Paul O'Dwyer Way." Waiting in the law firm's lobby, I saw a portrait of Paul O'Dwyer, who was notable for wildly bushy salt-and-pepper eyebrows that came to pointed peaks, a feature his son has inherited.

Brian O'Dwyer said, "I remember there was a day I was called down to the White House, and sat down with people from the public policy portion. I was told that the visa was not going to be given, and asked, would I go back to the community and sell that.

" 'No, I would not,' I said.

"And not only would I not do that, but I would cease all contact with the White House, and stop being any sort of liaison with the Irish American community. . . . They were giving me a lot of crap, frankly, and I said: 'I'm not going to put up with it. Let's be clear for this community.' Then they understood that the community was serious about it. Bill Clinton understood that that community had faith in him, and that faith would have been breached had that visa not been issued."

Finally, beyond the domestic political calculus, there still was yet another kind of calculation. How could the visa issue be leveraged to achieve the ultimate aim? Peace. In exchange for the visa, the White House wanted something in return. From the outset it was integral to the White House plan to not give things away, but to demand movement toward peace in exchange for concessions. "If you simply give these things away, then you're not adjusting the odds in your favor. You're not getting anything in return," explained Lake. "We would have no leverage."

What Clinton settled for was a mostly symbolic gesture: a written statement by Sinn Féin stating that they were committed to a peaceful political solution to the conflict. "We didn't just give the visa away. We used it to get a statement from Adams on violence," said Lake.

On January 30, 1994, Clinton had to make a decision one way or another. The peace conference was to begin in two days. In a conference call with Lake and Soderberg, Clinton reiterated all the arguments his cabinet had made against the visa, and Lake and Soderberg refuted each one, point by point. Soderberg argued that, whatever happened, the visa was "a win for the president." If it helped foster a cease-fire, Clinton's actions would be vindicated. "If Adams failed to deliver a cease-fire after Clinton had risked such political capital on him, then Clinton would be in a strong position to turn Irish America against Adams and undermine the IRA."[9]

Jane Holl Lute, the third member of the NSC team working on Ireland, was also in favor of the visa, but for a different reason. She remembered being asked by Clinton: "Why do you want this?"

"Because no one expects you to," said Lute. "Not even Adams. Everyone expects you to say no. So there's a card you have to play. And if you say yes, everyone will have to recalculate, including Adams."

To change the status quo, Lute believes that you have to do the unexpected. "People make plans based on expectations. If you fulfill their expectations, their plans don't change. But when you do the unexpected, you force everyone to alter their plans, including yourself, by the way. And that's OK." The other person who agreed with this analysis was Adams, who said of his visa: "It was a change that now everyone had to react to. It shook up the status quo."

In the end, "There were only three people in the administration who were for the Adams visa: Tony, Nancy, and me," Lute said. Then she corrected herself: "Well, there were four people, ultimately, who thought it was a good idea—and only one of us mattered." That one, of course, was President Clinton.

Finally, Clinton said simply: "Let's do it."[10]

The Boston Globe would call it "a case of classic Clinton, of a president who brooded and temporized, and weighed the political ups and downs, and then followed his heart down a risky path."[11] "It was a gut thing," said George Stephanopoulos. "When it's a close call, you take the extra step for peace."[12]

With this one decision, wrote Lake, "the president had taken a step into territory no American president had ever entered before."[13]

"It was the beginning of my deep engagement in the long, emotional, complicated search for peace in Northern Ireland," wrote Clinton.[14]

Adams in New York

When Gerry Adams arrived in New York on January 31, 1994, he was stunned by the reception: "I was surprised by the furor my visit created. It was an education. The British government's hysterical handling of the issue had insured that my visit was a huge international media story. I didn't quite realize how big until I landed in New York. There were television crews there from all over the world."[15] "The media didn't know what to expect," said a Republican congressman, Peter King, a longtime friend and supporter of Adams. "They seemed to think he would come through the door with a gun on each hip. Here was a guy who had been confined to West Belfast, and they treated him like Elvis."[16]

"I did more interviews than I could count in the next two days," wrote Adams, including broadcasts with Phil Donahue and Charlie Rose. "One of the most important interviews was with Larry King."[17] At that time it was actually against the law in England to broadcast the voice of Gerry Adams. Nothing could more concretely express the fact that Sinn Féin literally had no voice. To make the ban even more bizarre, when Adams's words were quoted on the news, they were read by an actor whose full-time job was being the Adams voice-over. Often, when Adams met people for the first time, they would say: "You talk totally differently than on TV."

"Tonight," began King, "the New York visit of a man so controversial his very voice is barred from British television."[18] To avoid breaking the law, the British media had to black out transmission of CNN. The CNN incident made the ban look ridiculous. *The New York Times* wrote, "Censorship and visa blacklists are not the answer. Clinton was right to let Americans hear and question Gerry Adams."[19] "Actually, I think that, in a strange way, the most important thing that happened was Larry King being jammed," said O'Dowd. "Suddenly, here's Larry King being jammed. Larry King! It just showed how idiotic the whole thing was. We can't have Gerry Adams talking. Imagine what he might say to us. Oh my God, he's talking! . . . Then they saw how insane it was. Because if you're going to block Larry King, where does that take you? Within two weeks, the ban was gone."

Adams came off as the "Irish Nelson Mandela." And indeed, in his memoir Adams devotes an entire chapter to meeting Mandela, whom he calls his "role model." Bearded, professorial, and charismatic in a mild-mannered way, he presented himself as a man of peace who "wanted to see an end to all violence." He had been shot, interned, and beaten up, but of the loyalists who had attempted to murder him, Adams said to Larry King, "I would shake their hands to move the situation forward."[20]

At the peace conference in New York, on February 1, 1994, Gerry Adams made a revolutionary statement, which was broadcast around the world:

"It is our intention to remove the gun from Irish politics."[21]

Most historians of the Irish peace process argue that the peace process could not have gone forward if Bill Clinton had not granted a visa to Gerry Adams. The visit changed the equation. Now the IRA's foes had to reckon with a cause that had a voice, a visible charismatic leader, and the attention of the United States, while the IRA had to deal with the fact that now they did have a viable alternative to violence.

· CEASE-FIRE ·

It could have been a scene from a John Le Carré novel. On a foggy summer evening in Dublin, Niall O'Dowd stood in front of the office of the *Irish Independent* waiting for an agent of the IRA. Out of the mist emerged an attractive woman who asked him, "Do you think Dublin will win on Sunday?"[22] Recognizing the code words, he handed her a secret document, and they walked off in different directions. All that was missing were the trench coats.

The secret document O'Dowd handed to the beautiful stranger was a new set of Irish promises that O'Dowd had hammered out with the White House through secret back-channel negotiations. Clinton could not be caught talking to the IRA without major embarrassment, so O'Dowd became a self-appointed go-between. To create two degrees of separation, O'Dowd spoke to Trina Vargo, a member of Ted Kennedy's staff, who in turn spoke to Soderberg and Lake. If the IRA were to declare a cease-fire, what could they expect in return from America? According to the Irish journalist Conor O'Clery, who wrote a book, *Daring Diplomacy,* about Clinton's role in the Irish peace process, "The commitments carried considerable weight with the IRA."[23]*

On August 25, 1994, O'Dowd and his small group returned to Ireland to meet with Sinn Féin. "The army is going to call a complete cessation," Adams told them. He was beaming. O'Dowd had never seen Adams look so upbeat. "The mood was one of great joy," he recalled.[24]

But, Adams added, there was still one more condition that needed to be met before they could declare the cease-fire: "If not, the army feels there is no way they can go forward."[25] The IRA needed to make sure their political base in America—the people who had supported the IRA through all the Troubles—was on board with the decision. They couldn't afford a schism within their own organization. And to accomplish that, they wanted to send over someone who would have total credibility with even the most militant of the Irish Catholic Republicans: Joe Cahill.

Cahill was a "hard man" who represented the armed struggle. He had been sentenced to death in 1942 for shooting a Northern Irish policeman (his sentence was commuted at the last minute). When the IRA split in 1969, he became a leader of the Provisional IRA, the more militant faction. His notorious credentials and his long-standing relationship with the IRA's hard-core American supporters made him the logical person to sell the cease-fire to the American IRA base ("It was a bit like Nixon going to China," Tony Lake said[26]). But the same "credentials" that made him the perfect emissary for the IRA made him a nightmare for Washington.

Reynolds called Nancy Soderberg to lobby for the Cahill visa. "You'll just have to break every rule in the book," said Reynolds.

---

* "The list of attainable goals included: unrestricted access to the U.S. for Gerry Adams and other Sinn Féin members; parity of treatment with other Northern Ireland leaders in Washington; early release or the transfer to Ireland of IRA prisoners in the United States and the end of FBI surveillance; the opening of a nationalist office in Washington; United States government support for the peace process with the aim of getting Washington to act as guarantor of any agreements in Northern Ireland; and the promotion of Irish-American business and investment in the North of Ireland. . . . Also implicit was the promise of considerable financial backing . . . for the development of Sinn Féin," wrote O'Clery.

"I don't see this one running for you," Soderberg said.[27]

Clinton called Reynolds from Martha's Vineyard, where he was on vacation.

"Nancy has been bringing me up-to-date with this. It's extremely difficult. Did you read this man's CV?" asked Clinton.

Reynolds burst out laughing. He didn't need to read a CV. Everyone in Ireland knew who Joe Cahill was.

"What did you expect, a parish priest? You know this thing has been going on for hundreds of years in Ireland. You can't go fix it in half an hour. But I'm absolutely certain this is going to bring a cease-fire. If we get no visa, I don't think we'll have a cease-fire. That's my honest opinion," said Reynolds.

"Are you sure?" asked Clinton.

"I am," replied Reynolds.

On the afternoon of Tuesday, August 30, 1994, Joe Cahill arrived in New York. O'Dowd's secret Sinn Féin contact had told him the cease-fire would be declared the next day, after Cahill's arrival.

"At what time?" O'Dowd asked.

"Listen for the Angelus Bell."

The Angelus Bell was a Catholic call to prayer that was broadcast on TV at noon. At noon on Wednesday, August 31, a breathless reporter came on the TV to report the news, a scratchy recording from a female IRA volunteer announcing the cease-fire.

Clinton called Reynolds immediately. "The President was the first one on the phone. He said 'Well done!' He said he always believed it would happen."[28]

When I spoke to Reynolds, twelve years after the cease-fire was declared, I asked him if he thought, with the benefit of hindsight, that there was any chance that the cease-fire would have come anyway, without the Cahill visa.

"No chance," he said.

Six weeks later, on October 13, the combined loyalist Protestant military command announced their own cease-fire. Reynolds told me that in his secret negotiations with the Unionist paramilitary, he had asked them point-blank: What would it take for you to declare a cease-fire? They told him that if the IRA declared a cease-fire and held it for six weeks, they would follow suit, and six weeks to the day at noon, that is exactly what they did, delivering on their promise to Reynolds. They offered "the loved ones of all the innocent victims over the past twenty-five years abject and true remorse," a note of apology that stunned everyone.[29]

For the first time in anyone's memory a ray of optimism shone down upon the bleak Northern Irish landscape. As the Irish Nobel Laureate poet Seamus Heaney put it, the cease-fire was: "A space in which hope can grow."[30]

· FAMILY THERAPIST TO THE WORLD ·

With the cease-fire, for the first time, it was politically acceptable to talk to all the parties involved in the conflict. Clinton took full advantage of this opportunity in two ways. First, he had intensive interactions with all the factions. And second, he hosted and sponsored events that forced them to interact with each other. Both of these interventions would be familiar to any family therapist. Salvador Minuchin, one of the founders of family therapy, believes that the therapist's first job is to *join* with each member of the family: He must connect with them, make them feel understood, and forge an alliance with them. The therapist's next task is to *restructure* the family, often accomplished by assigning tasks to family members that force them to interact in unfamiliar ways, thus helping to break up reified relational patterns. For example, the therapist might prescribe a task that allows habitually embattled family members to experience surprising mutually "pleasurable transactions."[31] Ethnic conflicts are like extended family feuds, and Bill Clinton, with his foreign policy of healing, served as a kind of family therapist to the world, instinctively employing joining and restructuring techniques.

Joining

Clinton established an open-door policy for all of the Irish parties—a door open so wide that it was excessive by everyone's reckoning. A U.S. president's time is one of the most valuable commodities on the planet. Yet Clinton lavished attention on the Irish as if he had all the time in the world. Excessive generosity is a common hypomanic trait. In their expansive exuberance hypomanics feel beneficent, and see no reason to limit the expression of their bighearted impulses. We will turn to how Clinton spent that time in a moment, but the very fact that he gave so much of it made a powerful impression on all the protagonists. In fact, the Republicans and Unionists alike used the same word—ridiculous—to describe this largesse. Gerry Adams said, "I have to say that he was very giving of his time. . . . It was almost ridiculous. The governors of states couldn't get in to see the president as easily as we could." Reg Empey, one of the leaders of the Unionists, was likewise taken aback: "It did get out of hand. When you consider the scale of the problems the United States was facing, even we could see that the enormous commitment of time the administration was putting into this was ridiculous." Dick Spring, Ireland's foreign minister, noted: "There was very much an open door toward the Irish government." Though protocol would dictate that he meet with the secretary of State, a minister at his level, "Any time that I went to Washington, there was always an understanding that I would meet with the president himself. He was always available." Even on the day of the nail-biting congressional vote on NAFTA, when Clinton was frantically trying to round up votes, Clinton made time to meet with Spring, who happened to be in town. Ireland's special treatment "was quite a talking subject amongst my European colleagues, even at the prime ministerial level." Heads of state were asking Spring, "Can you help us to meet the president of America?"

As Ireland's family therapist, Clinton's toughest job was to join with the Unionists. From the Unionist point of view, his involvement in the peace process was entirely unwelcome. Since they were committed to remaining part of Britain, any interference in this British "internal affair" was a threat to a status quo to which they were deeply committed. Much worse, American politicians were perceived as being beholden to the powerful Irish American vote, which was almost monolithically Catholic and sympathetic to the Republican cause of seeking to unify the North with the rest of Ireland. For the Unionists, the Adams visa was so shockingly outrageous that it only confirmed their worst suspicions about Clinton. But, whether they liked it or not, the Unionists had to deal with the reality that Clinton *was* involved. The equation had changed, and no interest group could afford to let their views go unheard by the eight-hundred-pound gorilla that had entered the room, and thus forfeit the ear of the American president to their enemies.

So the Unionists came to the White House to meet with Clinton, but they came in a defiant and suspicious frame of mind. One of the Unionist politicians who visited the White House was David Trimble, then leader of the Ulster Unionist Party (UUP). (Trimble would later be a corecipient of the 1998 Nobel Peace Prize for his role in the Irish peace process.) I met Trimble in the restaurant at the Europa Hotel in Belfast. He is now Lord Trimble, and a member of the British House of Lords. He wore a classic gray suit and a blue tie with white polka dots. His manner was formal, even a bit stiff, as is his reputation.

"Clinton was viewed with considerable suspicion here," he said, "particularly amongst Unionists. We knew that he was coming from a background which made him better informed and possibly potentially more sympathetic to the Nationalists' position than to ours. And our reaction to that was to say: 'All right, we are going to engage with this chap from the point of view of trying to ensure that there is balance in the approach that was taken.'"

The first time Trimble met with Clinton, he insisted that the British ambassador accompany him, to literally be at his side, to make sure there wouldn't be a ray of daylight between the Unionists and the UK.

Predictably, Clinton melted much of this resistance. Trina Vargo, who was a foreign policy adviser for Senator Edward M. Kennedy, told me: "The Unionists wanted to hate him, but he's such a likable guy, he can seduce anybody. So I think they didn't know what to do. They thought he was the enemy. They wanted to go home and say, 'He's the devil.' But how do you do that when you just really like the guy?"

Nancy Soderberg said, "The Unionists just had such a high bar of distrust for us to overcome. They never thought that we would be even-handed. That we were, just stunned them, stunned them."

How did Clinton succeed in joining with the Unionists? I posed this question in my interview with Sir Reg Empey. Empey now leads the UUP, and at that time was second in command under Trimble. I met with him at the party's headquarters in Belfast. Empey has graying strawberry-blond hair that betrays his Scottish descent. (The Protestant Irish of Northern Ireland are sometimes called "Scotch Irish," because most have Scottish ancestry.) Despite his dignified, formal manner, I quickly realized that he was, in fact, quite friendly and down-to-earth. Like Trimble, Empey had started from the assumption that Clinton was on the Republican side: "I think most Unionists would've regarded American policy as being a bit hostile, on the grounds that it was overly influenced by what is called the Irish American lobby." In contrast, the Scotch Irish had no ethnic political lobby in America. "In domestic terms, we were of no value to him." After the Adams visa, the impression they had had that the United States was biased against them was heightened dramatically, said Empey. "We were shocked initially, to be honest, by the visa."

How did Clinton overcome these objections?

He was charming, of course. "I have to say he was a very engaging person. He has great charm and interpersonal skill," said Empey. "You always felt relaxed with him. With Clinton, you could almost have put your feet on the table and not have felt in any way out of place." The image of Sir Empey putting his feet on the table under any circumstances seemed intrinsically out of place, and it made me smile. Empey mentioned Clinton's personal commitment to the peace process: "He took a decision to say to his administration that he wanted this done. He was the first to get his feet wet in what was really a quagmire at the time. He genuinely did want to do this, there's no question or doubt about that. There was more than simply from the teeth out." And Empey felt there was something infectious about Clinton's vision of peace. "He could see a way, there's no doubt about that. And he tried to encourage other people to buy into that vision, which they did to a large extent."

But most important of all, Clinton was *empathic*. He listened. He genuinely wanted to understand the story from the Unionist point of view, said Empey. "Clinton gave us a hearing and attention which had not been made available to us in the past. Under the Clinton administration, Unionists began to feel that their views were being taken into consideration seriously for the first time." And Empey was also taken aback by Clinton's fund of knowledge about their issue: "He had quite a command of the detail. He had a lot of the minutiae at his disposal, which was really astonishing for someone in his position. And that showed his interest was genuine."

Jane Holl Lute was serving as assistant secretary-general of the United Nations in charge of all peacekeeping operations when I met with her in her large office at the top of the UN overlooking the East River. She believes that Clinton epitomizes the two most important skills of a great peacemaker. First: "A deeply genuine and authentic ability to empathize, not only with the position of each side, but with the aspirations of those sides. You can't fake that. You have that or you don't." Second: "You must master factual details about the conflict," what she called "mastery of the brief." "Conflict happens somewhere and involves somebody. So you can't stay theoretical. You have to know the facts, and the facts as they bear on what parties can do and what they simply cannot do." When a peacemaker demonstrates both empathy and mastery of factual detail, said Lute, it makes each party in the conflict feel, at a gut level: "I get you. I get this."

It is interesting to note that Gerry Adams, chief representative of the opposite side of the conflict, had a very similar impression of Clinton: "Bill Clinton was enthusiastic about the peace process. I was impressed by his commitment. In time, as I got to know him, I was impressed also by his grasp of detail, the personalities, the politics, and the strategies involved."

The first time Clinton met Adams, he shook his hand, and ended the meeting by waving his fist in the air and saying: "We're going to make this thing work! We're going to make this thing work!"[32] It was reported incorrectly in Irish newspapers that Clinton had given Adams an IRA victory salute, but the mistake is telling. Clinton joined with each side so thoroughly that one could imagine he was on everybody's side.

Restructuring

In 1994, Bill Clinton began a new annual tradition of holding an Irish party at the White House on St. Patrick's Day. The rollicking first St. Patrick's Day party, which ended with Clinton, Reynolds, and John Hume, an Irish Catholic civil rights activist, in a kick line singing "When Irish Eyes Are Smiling," was essentially an all-Catholic affair.

When St. Patrick's Day 1995 rolled around, the political landscape and Clinton's role in it had changed dramatically. The cease-fire had been in place for six months, all-party peace negotiations were expected to commence, and it was clear that Clinton was engaged in the process. Clinton now saw the White House party as a vehicle for bringing the two sides together. Despite living only a few blocks away from one another in the small provincial city of Belfast, members of these warring factions had, with few exceptions, never spoken, much less attended a party together. The Unionists in particular were reluctant to do it now, but Clinton had put them in a bind: When the president of the United States invites you to the White House, can you say no?

Elizabeth Bagley, one of the organizers of the St. Patrick's Day event, said of the Unionists: "They were all invited, and they came, reluctantly. At first they had refused. . . . They hated Clinton for granting Gerry Adams a visa. But they realized that if they were invited to the White House they ought to go." Again, if for no other reason, neither side wanted to cede America to the other. Gary McMichael, leader of the Ulster Democratic Party (UDP), a party associated with one of the Unionist paramilitaries, expressed the dilemma this way: "The decision to attend was not taken lightly. But we felt for too long that loyalist views had not been heard openly. . . . The IRA propaganda machine must be challenged."[33]

At the St. Patrick's Day party, the Unionists stayed as far from Gerry Adams as humanly possible, never acknowledging the presence of a man they regarded as satanic. "They would be at opposite ends of the room," Brian O'Dwyer said. But Clinton, performing his family therapy intervention, actually orchestrated these events with the intention of forcing the warring parties into physical proximity. "The dances being done in the White House to keep them next to each other were incredible," O'Dwyer said. The result was a slight thaw, according to Bagley, and probably not coincidentally, alcohol helped break the ice. "I think that Clinton's St. Patrick's Day celebrations were a really important way of bringing the Irish factions together. They were drinking, and if you have a few drinks, everyone gets a little warmer. Even David Trimble, who is not the warmest person in the world, to say the least, you saw him with a few smiles on his face, and by the end of the evening he was smiling quite broadly."

But as talented as Clinton is at bringing people together, it wasn't an easy sell. For example, one day, in a secret, unofficial meeting, Clinton brought David Trimble and Gerry Adams upstairs to the White House residence, hoping to facilitate a more human interaction between them.

"He tried at one point to broker a little tête-à-tête between myself and David Trimble," Adams told me. "He took us to his private quarters, and told us about how this desk had been used for a hundred years, and how so-and-so had used this office, and it was all very dazzling."

Clinton then intentionally left the two of them alone in the room, leaving an awkward silence that he hoped they would be forced to fill with ordinary polite conversation.

Adams tried to warm Trimble up. There was a huge crystal decanter of some fabulously expensive, rare whiskey on the desk, and Adams said: "Oh, I'm going to take a drop!"

Conspiratorially, Adams urged Trimble to join him in helping themselves to a little of the president's whiskey.

"I couldn't possibly," Trimble said, looking away.

When word of the secret meeting leaked out, Trimble was embarrassed, and had to repudiate it, claiming that "the meeting wasn't engaged in properly."

The most memorable restructuring intervention made by Clinton was an
Irish economic conference held in Washington. When Bill Clinton first
met with Albert Reynolds, on St. Patrick's Day in 1993, Reynolds had
proposed that Clinton appoint an economic envoy to Ireland, rather than
a peace envoy. In January 1995, Clinton did so, appointing George Mitchell to that position, and Mitchell organized an economic conference at
the Sheraton Hotel in Washington, from May 24 to 27, 1995, to promote
American investment in Ireland. Again, it was an invitation the parties
could hardly refuse. What politician doesn't want to bring jobs to their
district? Unemployment in Northern Ireland was 13 percent, and in the
troubled neighborhoods where the violence was the worst, it had reached
as high as 80 percent.

Capitalism, as it turns out, can be used as a potent force for peace.
"Economic enticement" became a standard part of Clinton's peacemaking modus operandi, wrote Soderberg.[34] And capitalism can create strange
bedfellows. Suddenly, everybody could see new opportunities in which
cooperation across traditional boundaries could produce wealth. "The
whole strategy" of the conference, said Soderberg, was to "convince them
of a win-win strategy." Up until then virtually everyone had thought in
zero-sum terms. More jobs for Protestants meant less for Catholics. "The
idea was to create a bigger pie, so everybody can have a bigger slice," said
Bruce Morrison, one of the leaders of Americans for a New Irish Agenda.
Various cross-border relationships that would have been inconceivable
now represented joint economic opportunities.

Sir Patrick Mayhew, British secretary of State for Northern Ireland,
gleefully announced that there were unparalleled opportunities for "match-
making," and startled some clergy present by concluding his pep talk
with a quote from Shakespeare: "Let nature take its course . . . let copu-
lation thrive!"[35]

Everyone I spoke to agreed that the most significant impact of the event was not its economic consequences. Mitchell's assistant, Martha Pope, who organized it, said, "The economic conference was important not so much for the possibilities of economic investment in Northern Ireland, but because some of the parties attending the conference were in the same room for the first time. . . . Ironically, though Ireland is a very small place, about the size of Maine, with a mere two million inhabitants, the Catholic and Protestant communities are very insular. If you remove them from this isolation, then new ideas seem more possible. The economic conference gave the parties a chance to come together in a neutral way. It provided an opportunity to safely interact and exchange ideas." Sir Reg Empey said, "While it was all totally commercial, at the end of the day, bringing people together was part of the deal. Clinton brought together all the different political parties and traditions; something that had never been done before and would have been unachievable here. It was a groundbreaking event, really. The starting pistol for the peace process went off at that event."

What is frequently recalled are the informal interactions that took place in the bar. Family therapist Salvador Minuchin prescribes tasks that force warring parties to share *pleasurable* transactions (and indeed most people find drinking to be pleasurable). "All these people who would never talk to one another at home were sitting around the bar drinking. It was wild. You know, it worked. It got them to realize that the other side doesn't actually have horns," said Soderberg. There was "an extraordinarily cheerful atmosphere in the hotel bars," wrote Conor O'Clery, and "unlikely groups from Britain, Northern Ireland and the Irish Republic joined in songs and cocktail chatter."[36]

In some instances the conference forced adversaries into situations so comic that they could have been drawn directly from a stage farce. For a case in point: Sir Patrick Mayhew, the British official in charge of running Northern Ireland, had always refused to meet Gerry Adams. But the conference presented Mayhew with a dilemma. As Adams wrote, "How could Mayhew and I be in Washington in the same hotel at the same conference and not meet—even accidentally in the corridor? Was he going to hide behind the potted palm trees?"[37] The scene, as it unfolded, was almost that absurd. Civil servants inspected the elevator before Mayhew entered, and then stood guard to make sure he didn't encounter Adams in it. Even the Unionists, the group most naturally opposed to Mayhew acknowledging Adams, couldn't help but laugh. "It was almost like a Whitehall farce," said Empey. "Everybody was laughing at it. Oh yes, it was tremendous sport." The conference changed the dynamics: Now, rather than being embarrassed by meeting Adams, Mayhew was being embarrassed by his efforts to *not* meet him. To avoid becoming a laughingstock, Mayhew bowed to the inevitable and publicly shook hands with Adams, an event that would have been unthinkable only a few weeks earlier.

The conference ended with a reception under a large tent on the White House lawn. Thunder crashed and the skies released a deluge of pouring rain. Sticking together under one big tent was the only way to keep from getting drenched.

"We are all here in a very large tent in more ways than one," said Clinton.[38]

· THE BEST TWO DAYS OF HIS LIFE ·

Flying to the Rescue

On November 21, 1995, after twenty-one days of isolation at an air force base in Dayton, Ohio, Richard Holbrooke, the assistant secretary of state, and his team, along with representatives of Bosnia, Croatia, and Serbia, came to an agreement to end the Bosnian war. It was a historic accord.

A mere seven days later, Clinton was in the air, headed for Northern Ireland on yet another peace mission. A president of the United States had never visited Northern Ireland before, which made the visit an event in itself. And Clinton wasn't just coming to visit Northern Ireland: He was coming to save it.

The timing of the trip couldn't have been better. "The peace process was in trouble," wrote Gerry Adams. George Mitchell agreed: "As plans for the president's trip moved forward, the peace process seemed to be moving backwards."[39] The British had stalled, insisting that the IRA decommission all of its weapons before negotiations could begin, something it adamantly refused to do. The IRA felt it had already made a historic concession by granting a cease-fire, against the wishes of its more hard-core members. With the peace process stymied, the IRA hawks were becoming restless. Adams and his peace wing were starting to appear as though they had been taken for fools by the Brits. The cease-fire was hanging by a thread.

Dick Spring, who served as Ireland's minister for foreign affairs under both Albert Reynolds and Reynolds's successor, John Bruton, had come up with a plan to break the logjam—a "two-track" plan—in which political negotiations and decommissioning negotiations would take place simultaneously, rather than either one being contingent on the other. "Invariably, any initiative you came up with brought one crowd in the door and the other crowd went out the door," Spring told me. Twin track was an inspired initiative that could keep both groups at the table, by giving each side a process they considered a precondition for moving forward. Bruton, who had been pushing the British to accept the two-track plan, used the imminence of Clinton's visit to apply even more pressure. The British were concerned that if Clinton's trip produced nothing, it could be a major embarrassment to their biggest ally. Clinton had a succession of phone calls with Major the night he flew to Ireland, urging him to accept the two-track approach. It was literally launched "while Clinton's plane was in the air," said Bruton.[40] As they landed on British soil, Major said " 'OK,' " Soderberg recalled. There was a burst of applause aboard Air Force One when they got the news. Clinton presented Tony Lake with a bottle of champagne for his role in "midwifing" the breakthrough.

In London, John Major harrumphed that America had had nothing to do with the agreement, though later, with Clinton standing by his side, he conceded that the imminent arrival of the president had "concentrated the mind."[41] Spring doesn't think there was any question: "Clinton's visit was definitely the crucial element in the British accepting the twin-track approach."

Despite fears that the Adams visa would wreck the alliance, America's relationship with Britain survived, as Clinton had predicted, and the two countries worked together to secure peace in Bosnia. As Clinton flew across the Atlantic for his groundbreaking visit to Northern Ireland, thirteen thousand British and twenty-five thousand American servicemen were preparing to deploy to enforce the Dayton peace agreement. Clinton stopped first in London, where he turned on the charm. Addressing a joint session of Parliament, Clinton recalled the shared sacrifice of the two nations in two world wars. To honor the alliance, America's newest destroyer, the most powerful ever, would be named after Winston Churchill, Clinton announced to sustained applause. "On a score of one to ten, the relationship jumped from four to six just then," said an American diplomat.[42] Alluding humorously to their recent disagreements,

Clinton harkened back to the War of 1812, when the British burned the White House, parts of which still have scorch marks.

"Now, whenever we have the most minor disagreement, I walk out on the Truman balcony and I look at those burn marks, just to remind myself that I don't dare let this relationship get out of hand again," said Clinton, to much laughter.[43]

The next day Clinton flew to Northern Ireland. "It was the beginning of two of the best days of my presidency," Clinton wrote.[44] Veteran correspondent Helen Thomas, who has been covering the White House since the Kennedy years, said, "No president had two such good days at home or abroad."[45] When Clinton called Ted Kennedy he didn't put any qualifiers on it. According to Trina Vargo, Clinton said simply: "These are the best days of my life."

The trip was a love fest. Even veteran Clinton staffers claimed that they had never seen more adoring crowds. More important, the trip was transformational. With the acceptance by the British of the two-track approach, Clinton had rescued the peace process, and with his charisma, Clinton ignited a national mania for peace unlike any Ireland had ever seen.

Shankill Road

Not everyone in Northern Ireland was happy about Clinton's visit. "You have the two communities in Northern Ireland. The Catholic Nationalist community was overjoyed to see him coming, because they thought it meant that what was happening in Northern Ireland was swinging in their favor," Conor O'Clery told me. But for the same reason, the Unionist community was hostile and suspicious, viewing Clinton as beholden to the Irish American lobby, and thus far from neutral. Clinton's visit put the Unionists in an impossible position, he said. "As far as the Unionist community was concerned, they couldn't ignore a person of such overwhelming importance."

Every gesture, every movement, and every word on this trip was superbly choreographed to make both communities feel as if Clinton was on their side. Over the course of the short visit, you could see the momentum building, with larger and larger crowds meeting Clinton at each stop.

In Belfast, Clinton stopped first at Shankill Road, a center of Protestant Unionism that had been the scene of a terrorist attack in 1993 that killed ten people. Clinton visited Violet's fruit shop, next door to Frizzell's fish store, which had been bombed by the IRA, because they mistakenly believed a Protestant paramilitary group was meeting upstairs. "We knew there was real skepticism in the Protestant community about whether Clinton was there on behalf of all the people or one community," said Clinton's press secretary, Mike McCurry, who accompanied Clinton on the trip. "I think that guided the decision to go to Shankill first."[46]

The stop was unannounced. Clinton just got out of the limo and started shaking hands, much as if he were running for office, talking to people in the street, buying things in the shops. "I wanted them to know I was working for a peace that was fair for them, too," he wrote.[47] When planning his trip, the British had balked at this idea of a walkabout. "Walking on the Belfast streets, they insisted, was too dangerous."[48]

"Think of this from a security standpoint. If you are the Secret Service," said Bruce Morrison. "This was both a physical and a political risk. No shots got off, thank God, but he was in a battle zone, on the peace line, where people had been killed. So there was physical risk. It was not a war zone like Iraq, but he wasn't in the Green Zone, either." Clinton had waved off their warnings, insisting he wanted to meet "real people" before giving his address. As a concession to the security team, he wore a bullet-proof trench coat.

The initial response from the Shankill community was far from welcoming. Press secretary Mike McCurry, following three cars back, felt uneasy: "You could tell the motorcade had crossed the line. There was a noticeable chill in the air in the Protestant section. It was very, very eerie."[49]

Footage of the brief stop shows people looking dazed at first—no one had known Clinton was coming. But as he worked the crowd, smiling and shaking hands, they warmed up. In one instance he reached up to shake the hand of a young boy on his father's shoulders, a gesture beamed to every television set in Northern Ireland.

Violet Clarke, the shopkeeper who sold Clinton a piece of fruit, said, "I know the road was on the map for bad reasons, but this put it on for good reasons. I think people on the Shankill thought he was for the Nationalists, but once they heard him speak and everything, I think their views changed."[50] Clarke put up a sign: "President Clinton shops here."

A stern Edith Cassidy. Clinton's aggressive, controlling, and protective grandmother raised him for the first four years of his life and served as the prototype for Clinton's relationship with Hillary, who would also structure his life. *Courtesy of Bill Clinton's 1st Home Museum, Hope, Arkansas*

Made-Rite
ICE CREAM

Clinton's grandfather, Eldridge Cassidy *(at right),* in his grocery store. He kept bootleg whiskey, supplied by Roger Clinton, behind the apples. His store was one of the few places where blacks and whites shopped together. *Brad Markel/Liaison/Getty Images*

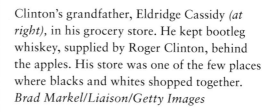

The young Virginia Cassidy. Virginia was the prototype for Clinton's future lovers. There is a physical resemblance between her and Monica Lewinsky. *Courtesy of Richard Fenwick*

Bill, Virginia, and Roger, Jr. "Bill was father, brother, and son in this family. He took care of Roger and me," wrote Virginia. *William J. Clinton Presidential Library*

Miss Mary's Kindergarten. Clinton *(center)* embracing Joe Purvis with his left arm and George Wright, Jr., with his right. It was an "open secret" in some circles in Hope that George Wright, Sr., was Bill's true, biological father, which would make George, Jr., his half brother. *Courtesy of Donna Taylor*

Young Clinton dressed as a cowboy. *AFP/Getty Images*

Clinton shaking hands with JFK. "I made sure I'd get to shake his hand even if he only shook one or two," wrote Clinton. The handshake became part of Clinton's personal mythology. Virginia said she'd never seen him so excited about anything in his life. "When he came back from Washington, holding this picture of himself with Jack Kennedy . . . , I knew right then that politics was the answer for him."
Arnold Sachs/Getty Images

A tale of two brothers. In 1978, Clinton was attorney general while his brother fronted a rock band and would later be caught dealing cocaine.
© *Stewart Mike/Corbis Sygma*

Campaign poster for Clinton's 1974 run for Congress. Clinton lost by a slim margin, but in the process became a political star in Arkansas, and four years later he would become governor. *Clinton House Museum, Fayetteville, Arkansas*

A pair of shoes worn by Clinton during the 1974 campaign have holes in the soles. "A force of nature," he campaigned around the clock in an effort to personally meet each voter, wearing out his shoes and his staff, but not himself. *Courtesy of Johnette Taylor*

Bill and Hillary staring into each other's eyes on their wedding day, October 11, 1975. *William J. Clinton Presidential Library*

After he lost his first reelection bid in 1980, it looked like the boy governor had "a great future behind him." But Clinton earned his title, "the Comeback Kid," on Election Day 1982, when he recaptured the governor's mansion. *AP*

Clinton addressed a special session of the Arkansas legislature about his education initiative in 1983. Bill put Hillary in charge of the effort, and they worked together as a team to get it passed. © *Sygma/Corbis*

Bill coming out of the voting booth with young Chelsea. *AP/Danny Johnston*

Bill and Hillary pose with the Birthday Club, a group of Virginia's friends who met once a month for drinks, her version of therapy for a late life depression. Fourteen years after her death, the club still meets to honor her memory and have a good time. *Courtesy of Johnette Taylor*

Virginia Clinton Kelley dressed from head to toe in campaign regalia, 1992. Like her son, she loved a political campaign.
Courtesy of Johnette Taylor

Clinton and his staff preparing for his address to a joint session of Congress on his economic plan, November 15, 1993. Clinton met night and day with his economic advisers in a swirl of activity. "It was exhilarating, but it was exhausting," recalled Alan Blinder.
Robert McNeely/Whitehouse

Hillary congratulating Bill after his economic address to Congress, February 17, 1993. Among those who have observed the Clintons up close, there is almost unanimous agreement that they genuinely love each other, though aspects of their marriage remain mysterious. *Robert McNeely/Whitehouse*

Clinton and his team crowding around a small TV in the White House to watch as the House of Representatives voted on Clinton's economic proposal, August 5, 1993. It was the "Super Bowl," according to Robert Rubin. Clinton won by one vote in the final seconds. *Robert McNeely/Whitehouse*

Campaigning for reelection, October 31, 1996. "Clinton wants to pour everything into you, even if it's for five seconds on a rope line," said Paul Begala, who noted that one of his techniques was to make eye contact and physical contact at the same time, even though it meant he had to reach blindly for the next hand. *Robert McNeely/Whitehouse*

Clinton was chronically exhausted, and many of his errors can
be attributed to fatigue. "Every important mistake I've made in
my life I made when I was tired," said Clinton. A fountain of
hypomanic energy who cannot tolerate inactivity, Clinton drives
himself beyond his limits. © *Dan Habib/Concord Monitor/Corbis*

The peacemaker. Clinton pushing Yitzhak Rabin and Yasser
Arafat to shake hands on the White House lawn, September 13,
1993. The image epitomized Clinton's politics of healing.
William J. Clinton Presidential Library

On Shankill Road, a Protestant Belfast neighborhood. Clinton successfully reached out to Northern Ireland's Protestant community despite its suspicions. *AP/Tim Ockenden, PA*

Clinton shook hands with Gerry Adams on the Falls Road in the heart of Catholic Belfast. "That handshake empowered Adams, empowered him to make peace," said Bruce Morrison. *Martin McCullough/REX Features*

Clinton lighting the Christmas tree in Belfast's Donegall Square. The peace process was the domain of politicians until seventy thousand Catholics and Protestants began singing "Silent Night" in response to Clinton's Sermon on the Mount–inspired speech. "This was the moment that peace began." *AP/Joe Marquette*

Clinton waved to tens of thousands of people holding American flags in Derry, November 30, 1994. *AP/Tim Ockenden, PA*

Monica and Bill in the White House. Contrary to the way it has been portrayed, the couple had a real romance. To Clinton, Monica represented his lost mother, who had passed away the year before, and he repeatedly told her how much she reminded him of Virginia, while she was shocked that the most powerful man in the world seemed like a lost little boy. *AP/OIC*

"I did not have sexual relations with that woman," said Clinton denying the sexual relationship with Monica Lewinsky on national TV, January 26, 1998. In a moment of panic, his mind went blank and he couldn't recall her name. "That statement caused him more lasting damage than any other of his presidency," wrote Sidney Blumenthal. *AP/Greg Gibson*

Preparing to give videotaped grand jury testimony, Clinton looked grimly determined. He could no longer deny the affair, but he ate up the clock with long speeches that confounded his questioners.
AP/Greg Gibson

Clinton and Nelson Mandela, his hero, role model, and father figure, in Johannesburg, July 19, 2007. Like a dutiful son, Clinton faithfully visits Mandela in South Africa each summer on Mandela's birthday. *AP/Jerome Delay*

Pandemonium broke out in this restaurant (seen in the background) when Clinton got up from the table in Lusaka, Zambia, July 21, 2007. "Now you see what the Clinton experience is really like," a veteran photographer said. *Author's Collection*

Clinton on stage in Tanzania, announcing the introduction of new antimalarial drugs now available at low cost through contracts negotiated by the Clinton Foundation, July 22, 2007. "Not one soul should ever die of malaria. Nobody," he proclaimed. *Reuters/Emmanuel Kwitano/Landov*

Clinton hugging a girl at the City Year Event in a school in Johannesburg, South Africa, July 19, 2007, right before the author got to ask his one question. *Author's Collection*

Mackie

Clinton's next stop was a factory owned by the Mackie Corporation. Protestant owned, Mackie had a history of discriminating against Catholics in its hiring practices, but through conscious self-correction it had achieved an integrated workforce. Physically, it was located on the boundary between the Protestant and Catholic neighborhoods, essentially sitting on the "peace line" that divides the two communities. Symbolically, it represented a setting where Protestants and Catholics were able to work together—an example of progress. Yet, it was also well known that some of the workers were members of the IRA and Protestant paramilitaries when they were off the clock.

Eleven-year-old David Sterritt, a Protestant, and nine-year-old Catherine Hamill, a Catholic, both read letters welcoming the president and supporting peace. Catherine's memorable letter blew everyone away. Looking like the perfect child from central casting, with an angelic face and long blond hair tied with a yellow ribbon, little Catherine stood on a wooden box to reach the microphone.

When Catherine was six months old, Protestant gunmen had broken into her home and murdered her father in front of her. Yet, now she called for peace and reconciliation:

"My name is Catherine Hamill. I live in Belfast. I love where I live. My first daddy died in the Troubles. It was the saddest day of my life. I still think of him. Now it is nice and peaceful. I like having peace and quiet for a change instead of people shooting and killing. My Christmas wish is that peace and love will last in Ireland forever."[51]

Clinton put his right arm around Catherine, squeezed her shoulder gently, and put his cheek on her head. "This is one of those occasions where I feel that all that needs to be said has been said."

"There wasn't a dry eye in the house," said Jamie Lindsay, a member of Clinton's advance team.[52] That twenty-eight-second sound bite was played and replayed on Irish television all day long, and it became one of the enduring memories of the trip. Indeed, during my visit to Ireland, twelve years after Clinton's visit, numerous people recalled Catherine's speech almost as if she had given it yesterday.

Clinton spoke after Catherine: "In the land of the harp and the fiddle, the fife and the lambeg drum, two proud traditions are coming together in the harmonies of peace." He thumped his bully pulpit, waving a finger and shaking a closed fist. "Only you can decide between division and unity, between hard lives and high hopes." Then he uttered a twist on the IRA's slogan, "Our day will come":

"You must say to those who would still use violence for political objectives: 'You are the past, your day is over.'"

Clinton stood face-to-face with members of the Protestant and Catholic paramilitaries, literally looking them in the eyes, and challenged them to choose peace.

In this boldness, however, there was also an embedded humility. Clinton well understood that, ultimately, the choice was not up to him. Many times during the trip he would use phrases like "if you choose to walk the path of peace, we will walk with you." Jane Holl Lute also believes that great peacemakers have the humility to "never lose sight of who really owns the issue."

"At the same time," said Clinton, "those who renounce violence are entitled to be full participants in the democratic process."

One man, Cedric Wilson, a follower of the confrontational Unionist leader Ian Paisley, shouted out, "Never." Wilson was locally famous for coining the slogan "Ulster says no" that could be found spray painted on walls all over Protestant neighborhoods, along with other slogans, such as "not an inch" and "no surrender."

"Those who showed the courage to break with the past are entitled to their stake in the future," Clinton continued.

Once again, Wilson shouted out, louder this time: "Never!"

But Clinton held his own against his heckler. He pointed in Wilson's direction, saying that leaders must make compromises for peace, and "risk the backlash."

He concluded: "Peace must be waged with a warrior's resolve—bravely, proudly, and relentlessly—secure in the knowledge of the single greatest difference between war and peace: In peace everybody can win."

Clinton got a standing ovation that lasted a minute, and would have gone on longer had he not left the stage. The Mackie speech had an instantaneous national impact. Suddenly, members of the Unionist community changed their minds about Bill Clinton. "The speech influenced the whole trip," said the CEO of Mackie, Pat Dougan, who saw virtually every one of his workers bring their families to the Belfast town square where Clinton lit the town Christmas tree that night.[53]

David Trimble noted that the Mackie speech was the turning point:

"On his first visit here, I think the most significant thing that he did was the speech that he delivered at Mackie's in West Belfast, which had a whole lot of messages, basically to Irish Republicans, telling them to put violence behind them. There are a lot of Unionists who were going to ignore the Clinton visit until then. The warm reception that he got at city hall that evening was a response to that speech."

Falls Road

Clinton then traveled to Falls Road, the heart of Belfast's Catholic community—the complement to his walk on the Shankill Road. Furious negotiations had been going on between Sinn Féin and the administration, right up until 2:00 A.M. on the day of the trip, about how and where Clinton would meet Gerry Adams, and whether Clinton would publicly shake his hand. "Getting to that point was a nightmare," Richard McAuley, Adams's longtime communications director, told me. It was "quite a head butting," agreed Adams.

To learn more about that stop, I traveled to Falls Road, a gritty working-class area of row houses, pubs, and dingy shops. When I arrived in the late afternoon, the streets were filled with bright-faced young girls—many with red hair, pale skin, and freckles—walking home from school in their maroon Catholic school uniforms.

Sinn Féin's headquarters is covered with mirrored glass—obviously a security precaution. I was buzzed into a tiny vestibule, where a middle-aged man was watching a security camera. Behind him there was just enough room for a couple of simple metal chairs.

I met Adams in a conference room on the third floor. The walls were unadorned except for a few posters celebrating various revolutionary struggles around the world.

I was surprised by how drab Sinn Féin's offices were. The day before I had met with Sir Reg Empey in the Ulster Unionist headquarters, which looked like a small embassy: It was a modern building with sleek glass walls surrounded by a manned security gate. At the UUP, a polite blond secretary with a chipper British accent had offered me fresh brewed coffee in a fine china cup that was ringed with gold, along with a matching plate that held pieces of Scottish shortbread molded into coats of arms. The contrast was a bit of a shock. The scuffed and dingy mustard-colored walls at Sinn Féin looked like they hadn't been painted since Bill Clinton's Oxford days. The dirty maroon indoor/outdoor–style carpet looked equally old. The instant coffee I was offered in a chipped mug was undrinkable. When I went to the bathroom the toilet didn't flush, but instead ran continuously. The only hand towel available was a wet cloth rag.

To meet with me Adams had been forced to tear himself away from a high-level meeting at Stormont, the Northern Irish Parliament's building. Thus, I was surprised to see him dressed in a work shirt and jeans. He told me that Clinton's presence on Falls Road was "hugely important" for a "stretch of the road that had seen so many funerals, so much disaster, so much vilification and demonization."

Rumors about the president's arrival had been flying, and thousands of people had begun massing around Falls Road. The largely Protestant Royal Ulster Constabulary (RUC), the police force responsible for crowd control, became worried, since the RUC and the Catholic community had a long history of violent clashes. The police had the delicate job of keeping the crowd at bay without provoking the Catholic population. Fortunately, the atmosphere was jovial rather than confrontational. "There wasn't any raw antagonism. It was more like some sporting event," said one American who was present.[54]

However, there was almost a crisis. At one point the president's parked limo blocked the crowd's view of him. "The crowd thought they were being obstructed and began jumping the barriers," recalled a policeman. "It was overexuberance . . . more push and shove than fists flying."[55] Nonetheless, "chaos threatened." Officers grabbed a firm hold of each other's belts to form a human chain to resist the surge of the crowd. Adams recalled that there "was some shoving and pushing with the citizens and the RUC. I remember actually saying to the people, 'Calm down.' And to the cops, 'Back off.'" Wishing to avoid the negative publicity a melee would create, the Secret Service said to the RUC commander: "Think CNN."[56]

By design, Clinton just "happened to" run into Gerry Adams at a bakery on Falls Road, near the corner of Falls and Springfield roads, a location popularly known as "hijackers corner," because vehicles were regularly taken and burned there during the unrest. It was also a few doors down from Sinn Féin headquarters.

"Hi, ya, Gerry," the president said, with a smile.

"*Céad mile fáilte,*" Adams said, a traditional Irish greeting that means "a thousand welcomes."[57]

Clinton told Adams that he had been up till 5:00 A.M. reading his book, *The Street,* a book of short stories about the Falls Road community. Clinton said it gave him a better appreciation of what Catholics had been through.

"Now I know where you get your inspiration from," Clinton said.[58]

And then they shook hands.

This handshake had also been the subject of intense negotiations. Clinton had shaken Adams's hand before, but by design, no photos had been taken. It's a little like the old adage: If a tree falls in the forest, and no one hears it, did it really fall? If the president shakes your hand, but no one sees the image of it, did it really happen? At the precise moment when Clinton was about to shake Adams's hand, a truck pulled up, blocking the view of the photographers from the press. Sinn Féin's people are convinced to this day that it was intentional. "A vehicle parked itself very conveniently in front of the press," Adams said. Nancy Soderberg adamantly denied that the truck was parked by American agents with the intention of obstructing the view of the news media. "No, I've never heard that. That's not true," she said.

Fortunately, the Sinn Féin men were prepared for such contingencies. McAuley pulled out a cheap Instamatic camera and shot the president shaking hands with Gerry Adams. The next day his amateur photo was on the front page of *The New York Times* and a host of other papers around the world.

Clinton went into the bakery, where they gave him some traditional Irish bread. "You couldn't see anything else, only him. He just seemed to be so big he filled the place," said one customer.[59] When Adams went back to the bakery the next day, the list of breads that had been presented to Clinton, including treacle (dark Irish soda bread made with molasses) and barmbrack (fruit bread), were now listed on the menu as "by appointment to the President."

The bakery was even renamed "Clinton's."

Clinton stopped next at a furniture store, where one customer, Evelyn Meredith, spontaneously kissed him, saying, "I'm glad you came." Meredith recalled that "I just automatically put my hand around him and kissed him. The security men nearly died."[60]

Indeed, Adams noted that the "Secret Service was going bananas as he walked about talking to people."[61] When a bartender at McDermott's bar gave Clinton a free pint of Guinness, the agents stepped in quickly and spilled it into the street before Clinton could take a sip. (Nobody can give food or drink to the president. It could be poisoned.)

All around in the streets there was a carnival atmosphere. People were gleefully shaking hands with everyone in the Clinton entourage, including British diplomats who normally would not have been welcome on Falls Road. "They'd have shaken hands with anybody. They even shook hands with me," noted Lord Mayhew, with some astonishment.[62]

Like the visa, the handshake with Clinton "greatly empowered Gerry," said Bruce Morrison, who was there with O'Dowd as a leader of Americans for a New Irish Agenda. There was an unstated contract implicit in the handshake: "Clinton was reaching out, and taking risks, and he had expectations. That handshake was valuable to Gerry Adams, and Clinton expected him to use that for good, to make progress. I'm basically empowering you, Clinton was saying. I'm telling you that you have a friend in high places. For what? For making peace. That's the message, and it's personal. It can't be delivered by some underling. Only the president can really do that."

But the emotional high over the handshake was short-lived. In a humorous reminder that all politics is local, Morrison recalled: "It was the funniest thing. Gerry had just shaken hands with the leader of the free world, and we were walking down the street, and this little old lady starts complaining to Gerry about the mistreatment that she's getting in the factory where she works. She just starts going at Adams: 'What are you going to do about this, Gerry? I can't put up with this, Gerry.'

"And I'm thinking, this is Gerry's world. He had just been at the mountaintop, and now he's down in the gutter, trying to solve problems in this little, narrow, Republican, nationalist community in West Belfast."

Perhaps it was that, or the grueling all-night negotiations that had preceded this moment, but afterward Adams and McAuley just felt drained, suffering perhaps from posthandshake letdown.

But the main reason they felt deflated was that the peace process, bogged down by the British demands over decommissioning, was in more trouble than anyone realized. As Bruce Morrison put it, "Gerry Adams's fundamental message was: If something doesn't happen quickly that puts this foolish decommissioning thing aside, and gets some activity that vindicates the cease-fire, it's not going to last."[63] Adams said that "the peace process at that time had been stretched like a piece of elastic and was coming more and more to the snapping point. Our hope was that the visit would kick-start a process ready to collapse."[64]

By the time I left Sinn Féin headquarters it was dark outside. McAuley briefly showed me around the neighborhood. Before we parted we stood together on Falls Road, helpless against the implacable winter wind that was whipping through us.

"You have to remember where we were," McAuley told me, looking up at the night sky. "We were in a very dark place in the process at that point. The president was, to use an old television cliché, like the Seventh Cavalry coming over the hill to the rescue."

Derry

Clinton's next stop was the Northern Irish city of Derry, hometown of John Hume, the father of the nonviolent Republican movement. (Hume would share the 1998 Nobel Peace Prize for his role in the Irish peace process.) Clinton went to Derry largely "to pay homage to Hume," said Ed Emerson, one of the American trip planners.[65]

I also went to Derry to meet with Hume. On the way to Derry road signs tell you you are approaching Londonderry—a name only used by Protestants. However, on each sign the word "London" had been covered with spray paint, presumably by a Catholic. From the crest of a hill you come upon the River Foyle, and see a small city rising across the water that is dominated by a huge stone cathedral. Derry is 90 percent Catholic. The Catholics live on the side of the river where the town is found, and the Protestants live on the other side.

Derry was also a significant stop for a historic reason. In 1968 the Troubles came to the world's attention on TV, when a Catholic civil rights march there degenerated into a violent confrontation between protesters and police. That march was meant to be a nonviolent protest. "We started the civil rights movement in the 1960s, inspired by the civil rights movement of the United States," Hume told me. Like Clinton, Hume's personal role model was Martin Luther King.

Because of his commitment to nonviolence, Hume has always been the acceptable alternative to the IRA for American politicians concerned about Ireland. Though Hume has met annually in Washington with every president since Reagan, he says Clinton was the first American president to really take an interest in Northern Ireland.

The American event planners had been anxious about attendance at the event, uncertain that people would show up. As she was driving to town from the airport with the president, it became apparent to aide Susan Brophy that they needn't have worried. "I'd never seen anything like it. We were weaving through the streets, and the farther you got into the city, the bigger the crowds. There were people as far as the eye could see. The president loves to be warmly received, and he was absolutely overwhelmed. He was elated. It was impossible for him to be happier than he was."[66]

Hume reminisced about the day of Clinton's visit: "The very fact that somebody of the international status of the president of the United States would come to our area to encourage peace obviously gave enormous encouragement to the peace process. I've always argued that the vast majority of our people from both sections of our community were against the violence and the division and wanted peace."

When they got to the Derry town hall, "they were extremely exhausted," said John Kerr, mayor of Derry. "At one stage the president put his head down on Hillary's shoulder. He was very tired."[67]

But as Clinton heard the roar of the crowd his adrenaline started flowing. "We were walking toward the front door and you could hear the people's cheers grow louder. When we got to the steps the daylight hit us, and we saw there were thousands of people in that tiny square. It was an overpowering experience," said Jim Lyons, who succeeded George Mitchell as the U.S. trade envoy to Northern Ireland.[68] Clinton wasn't tired anymore. The hypomanic extravert became like a stallion bucking at the starting gate. Clinton's advance man for the Derry trip, Ed Emerson, remembered that he couldn't hold Clinton back. "I had my hand on his chest, literally trying to keep him back from going out too soon. The crowd was so out of its mind, he was charged up to get out of there." John Keanie, the man introducing him, had only begun to utter his first words when Clinton started marching to the podium. "The second John Keanie spoke the president started walking. I couldn't hold him back, he was so excited."[69]

Guildhall Square was overwhelmed by a mass of twenty-five thousand people. "The people of the city were hugely honored that their city would be recognized by an American president. Virtually the whole population of the city came out to welcome him," Hume told me. Thousands of people waved American flags. The Derry town council had scoured all of Ireland and England for every American flag they could find. ("Where in the world, today, would you find thousands of people waving the American flag?" asked Elizabeth Bagley, an American diplomat who worked with Clinton on the Irish peace process.)

"I'm proud to be here in the home of Ireland's most tireless champion of civil rights, and its most eloquent voice of nonviolence, John Hume," said Clinton. "I've had John Hume to the White House a couple of times, and last time I said to him, 'You can't come to the White House one more time until you invite me to Derry,'" a line which caused Hume, who was sitting next to Clinton on the stage, to laugh loudly with delight.

Clinton again issued his challenge of hope. "Are you going to be somebody who defines yourself in terms of what you are against or what you are for?" And he reiterated that America was ready to lend its resources to the nation and politicians who worked for peace. "The time has come for the peacemakers to triumph in Northern Ireland, and the United States will support them as they do."

Quoting from Derry-born Nobel Prize–winning poet Seamus Heaney,* Clinton said:

> *"History says. Don't hope*
> *On this side of the grave.*
> *But then, once in a lifetime*
> *The longed-for tidal wave*
> *Of justice can rise up.*
> *And hope and history rhyme."*[70]

---

* I corresponded with Seamus Heaney to ask him about Clinton's quoting his poetry in the Derry speech. "It was a singular honor and no empty gesture," wrote Heaney, "since he spoke the lines by heart . . . with an inwardness and insight that would have left most professors of literature in the shade. The next evening I brought him a handwritten copy of the stanza which he subsequently had framed and hung in the Oval Office." It now hangs in Clinton's private office at the Clinton Foundation in New York.

After the speech, as Clinton walked among the crowd, he got pure rock star treatment. One woman pitched herself over a railing into the president's arms before the Secret Service could grab her.

"They even tried to pull my wedding ring off," said Clinton.[71]

When I asked Hume how things have changed in Derry since Clinton's visit, he said: "The atmosphere in the streets has been totally transformed. As you arrived here today, you wouldn't have any reason to be aware that there was ever any kind of conflict. Years ago, you might have been stopped and searched. Now there's total peace in the streets."

Belfast Town Hall

The first couple ended the day in downtown Belfast's Donegall Square for the official lighting of the Christmas tree outside city hall, a large elegant building crowned with a copper dome. Once again, security was a nightmare. Donegall Square is ringed by tall buildings, which provide dozens of potential vantage points for a sniper. The Secret Service insisted that the president be surrounded by bullet-proof glass and the light in every window be kept lit, to illuminate any gunman wishing to hide in the darkness.

The majestic forty-foot white pine that Clinton would light was a gift to the people of Belfast from Al Gore's home state of Tennessee. However, because of a labor dispute, the importation of American timber was banned by British law and, as absurd as it seemed, bureaucratic red tape threatened to derail America's Christmas present. One British official described the "diplomacy over the bloody Christmas tree" as the lost episode of *Yes, Minister,* a hit British TV comedy series about the workings of the UK government. "By the end, the notes on it were half a foot thick, with every agency having to have a say."[72]

Lord Mayhew said the whole incident made him "extremely angry."

"Their bloody Christmas tree is going up and I don't care. Any trouble you can blame me. Now get it up," he commanded.[73] And up it went.

No one was sure how many people would come. All week mostly Protestant listeners had been calling radio shows protesting that the majority of people in Belfast resented the president's interference. Originally, the Power Rangers had been scheduled to light the tree. One poll showed a majority favored the Power Rangers over Clinton.

But crowds began lining up at ten in the morning in the frigid cold. "There was magic in the air that ended up drawing people like magnets," said a Washington official.[74] Eighty thousand jammed the square and the surrounding blocks as far as the eye could see.

As surprising as the size of the crowd was, its composition was even more so. Brian O'Dwyer, one of the leaders of Americans for a New Irish Agenda, remembered that "it was the two communities coming together, basically for the first time. A common rally, where there wasn't a Protestant section and a Catholic section, where they were mingling together, was unthinkable, almost like a break in the color line."

Belfast-born rock star Van Morrison energized the crowd by singing his anthem "Days like This." He also sang a love song specially requested by Clinton, and dedicated to Hillary. In the ecumenical spirit of the occasion, Morrison, a Protestant, was accompanied by Belfast singer Brian Kennedy, a Catholic. A mood of elation was rising in the crowd. Kennedy recalled that "the buzz I felt from the audience defies words. People were hugging and crying and there was a sense of celebration in the air."[75] The people just radiated "sheer joy," Tony Lake told me. "It was overpowering."

Bill and Hillary stood onstage together. Hillary read excerpts from letters written by two children who stood behind her—once again a Catholic girl and a Protestant boy—pleading for peace. She ended by saying, "Let us remember that we seek peace most of all for our children."[76] Bill put his arms around the shoulders of both children.

Clinton then threw the switch to light the tree, and Cathy Harte, the Catholic girl, said in wonder: "It's beautiful."

"Yeah, you're right. It's beautiful," responded Clinton, looking down on her with a smile.[77]

Clinton began his speech by poking fun at the Power Rangers controversy. "Now, to become president of the United States, you have to undertake some considerable competition. But I have never confronted challengers with the name recognition, the understanding of the media, and the ability in the martial arts of the Mighty Morphin Power Rangers."[78] The crowd erupted in laughter. No one appeared to be missing the Power Rangers now.

On a more serious note, Clinton read from a letter he had received from a fourteen-year-old girl from County Armagh: "Both sides have been hurt. Both sides must forgive."

The most powerful moment came at the end, when Clinton, ad-libbing, used the occasion of Christmas to tap into the common faith in Christ that Irish Protestants and Catholics share, but virtually never acknowledge. Clinton ended by quoting from the Sermon on the Mount: "Jesus, whose birth we celebrate today, spoke no words more important than these: 'Blessed are the peacemakers, for they shall inherit the earth.' Merry Christmas, and God bless you all."

"It was practically a religious experience for people. It was that strong," said O'Dowd. "I saw Martin McGuiness. I've known Martin for years, and I have never seen a man so moved. Joe Cahill, the old revolutionary, came over and hugged me with tears in his eyes."

"He tapped into all the right notes," said Dick Spring, "because there is a basic underlying Christianity in the country, which obviously had been ignored in the context of the conflict."

Clinton was more than just quoting the Sermon on the Mount; he was a Christ-like prophet *giving* the Sermon on the Mount, preaching to a multitude who were being collectively illuminated and transformed in the hearing. There had always been a messianic streak in Clinton. Hypomanics are prone to messianism, and for Clinton it has been one of the most potent forces motivating his behavior. The young boy who walked to church alone, and who delivered the speeches of Martin Luther King in his living room, had been dreaming of a moment like this.

"He was the only man in the world who would come and save us," O'Dowd thought, as he witnessed Clinton preaching to the throng.

Spontaneously, the crowd of Catholics and Protestants, who had never sung a hymn together in their lives, began singing "Silent Night."

"Usually historical moments aren't clear until later," said Soderberg. "This one was clear as it was happening."[79] This precise moment, when the crowd began singing "Silent Night"—this was the moment of salvation.

"They're all singing 'Silent Night' together on Christmas, sharing a common Christian tradition, which they had, but no one had ever acknowledged that before," said O'Dwyer. "The feeling was: 'This is the moment when peace will begin.'"

Most of those present shared the feeling that this was the true turning point. "It was more than just a great party," wrote Belfast journalist

David McKittrick in his column the next day. "It may turn out to be a truly historic turning point, for in a single day almost all of the lingering doubts about peace were swept away."[80]

Up until that night the peace process had been the domain of bickering politicians. But Clinton "reached out to the public over the heads of the politicians," said Mo Mowlam, the woman who would succeed Sir Patrick Mayhew as Britain's secretary of State for Northern Ireland, under Tony Blair.[81] The rally revealed that there was a silent majority who wanted peace. One Irish journalist dubbed the elated pro-peace crowd the "Clinton majority."

That moment in the Belfast town square "fundamentally altered the equation in Northern Ireland," said Lake. Before Clinton's visit, "political leaders probably felt that they had to make the case to their own constituencies for why they had to compromise. Now I think the burden of proof is on those who don't want to compromise for the sake of keeping the peace."[82]

"It was as if the people were saying: 'What's wrong with you politicians? We want peace. We're ahead of you. Catch up with us,'" said Nancy Soderberg.

It is interesting to note that Clinton actually misquoted the Sermon on the Mount, which reads: "The meek shall inherit the earth" and "the peacemakers are the children of God." But Clinton combined the two lines by saying that "the peacemakers shall inherit the earth." A misquote is rare for Clinton in general, since he has a nearly photographic memory. And it was particularly unusual for him to misquote the Bible, since he has been studying the scriptures for years, and had underlined at least a dozen Bibles. Yet one could view this as a Freudian slip, which is to say, it was not a random slip of the tongue, but one which revealed the speaker's underlying intent and feelings. Clinton's entire message to the Northern Irish politicians was that the peacemakers will be politically victorious (inherit the earth), while those who cling to violence will be swept from power, because the people want peace.

Walking hand in hand with Hillary, Clinton bid the crowd farewell. "His eyes moistened," he waved, saluted, and applauded.[83]

When they finally got back to their hotel at midnight, Clinton couldn't unwind. "He was on a high," one staffer recalled.[84] He and Hillary went down to the bar where his staff was drinking. Jim Lyons recalled that he was "physically shot," but at the same time "pretty emotionally charged."

When Lyons and some others prepared to go across the street to drink more, they had to respectfully decline Clinton's request to join them; he was obviously in need of rest. "In some ways he's like your oldest child," said Lyons.

"We had to say to him: 'You have to go to bed.'"[85]

Bill and Hillary returned to their suite, but it was obvious that the president was nowhere near sleep. "He was so full of energy that night he wanted to bounce off the walls," said McCurry. "We left him and the First Lady sipping whiskey, probably about two in the morning."[86] The next day, while leaving for Dublin, the president confessed that he'd had a little too much to drink. "I was stunned, because a hangover is something Bill Clinton's maybe only had two or three times in his whole life," said McCurry.[87]

If Clinton had altered the equation in Ireland, Ireland altered the equation within Bill Clinton, too. Virginia's maiden name, Cassidy, is a common Irish name, and she had described herself as descended from "poor Irish farmers."[88] But if Clinton had any sense of himself as Irish, it was theoretical at best, until he went there and discovered his roots. On this trip, "Clinton became Irish," said Niall O'Dowd. "I don't think he started out Irish, but he ended up Irish. I saw it happen in front of my eyes." Elizabeth Bagley said that after the visit "all of a sudden he had Irish blood and talks about being Irish."

I think that Gerry Adams got it right when he said to me, with a wink: "Clinton and Ireland have a love affair. And his visit here was the consummation of the affair."

But it was more than just a love affair. On this, one of the best days of Bill Clinton's life, he finally had a chance to be the Christ-like transformational figure he had long dreamed of being.

The Bomb

Ten weeks after Clinton's visit to Northern Ireland, on February 9, 1996, the IRA cease-fire was broken by a bomb at Canary Wharf in England. Two people were killed, hundreds were injured, and millions of dollars of property was destroyed. The IRA claimed responsibility.

The cease-fire was over.

The peace process had, indeed, been in trouble when Clinton arrived in Ireland. In fact, it would later be learned that the IRA had begun constructing the bomb while Clinton was in the country. What Gerry Adams knew about that bomb, and when he knew it, will probably never be known, but when he said that the peace process was in trouble during Clinton's visit, Adams knew what he was talking about.

David Trimble met with Clinton soon after the bombing: "When he came into the room, he looked like a man whose feelings were a bit raw. Referring to Canary Wharf, I described the actions of the Republicans as being 'just plain stupid,' and he broke in and said, 'Yeah they were damn stupid.'

"It's the only time I heard him use language of that nature."

"We all felt sick," said Soderberg. "It was one of the lowest days in my life."[89] Jim Lyons, U.S. trade envoy to Northern Ireland, "took a walk and cried."[90]

Why did it happen? No one outside the IRA knows for sure (and they aren't talking). But the most straightforward explanation was that the IRA had lost faith, what little it had had, in Britain's good faith. Over a year after the cease-fire was declared, the political peace negotiations that the IRA felt it had been promised had yet to start. As George Mitchell wrote, "The IRA had declared a ceasefire in August 1994 in the expectation that inclusive negotiations would begin. Now, eighteen months later, there were no negotiations in sight."[91]

"I think there was huge frustration. I thought that more would happen a lot quicker," said Soderberg. "Whatever they did, there was always another obstacle. Understandable frustration, but, you know, the answer isn't to go drop a bomb."

Clinton's approach toward the IRA had been: I'll take a step forward (e.g., the Adams visa); now you take one, too. In contrast, Britain's stance toward the IRA appeared to be: You took a step forward. Good. Now take another one. "Throughout the process they created new hurdles to cross and standards to be met," said Bruce Morrison. It seemed like they kept moving the goalposts.

The sad irony is that just three weeks after the Canary Wharf bombing, London, at last, scheduled all-party peace talks to begin June 10, 1996. Now, ironically, Sinn Féin would be disqualified from participating in the long-awaited peace talks.

St. George in Purgatory

In May 1996, the governments of England and Ireland turned to George Mitchell to chair the all-party peace negotiations. Mitchell, who had been Clinton's economic envoy, now became the peace envoy Clinton had promised Irish Americans before the election. In the 1995 negotiations, kicked off by the acceptance of the two-track peace process, Mitchell had led a committee on decommissioning. In that capacity he had impressed everyone with his skill, patience, and fair-mindedness. His committee generated the Mitchell Principles, which declared that any party that wanted to enter into negotiations would have to publicly commit themselves to the principles of democracy and nonviolence, and these principles became accepted as the basis for entrée into the all-party peace talks.

It never escaped anyone's mind that Mitchell was Clinton's appointed representative, informally involving the United States as the mediator in the dispute, even though it was repeatedly emphasized that Mitchell was an "independent chairman." While overall this was an asset, some Unionists had never overcome their suspicion that Clinton was in the pocket of the Republicans. Reverend Ian Paisley, an evangelical Protestant minister who led the Democratic Unionist Party (DUP), the second largest Unionist party, was the most provocative and recalcitrant of the Unionists. He combined radical anti-Catholic religious fundamentalism with political guerrilla theater. Among the nation's major politicians, Paisley had stood alone in completely rejecting Bill Clinton's involvement in the peace process. He met with Clinton only reluctantly when he visited Northern Ireland, and then only to tell him: "I feel like kicking you out after your actions today. Ulster people are saying: 'Mind your own business or you'll get a bloody nose.'

"It wasn't very easy," said Paisley proudly, "telling the world's strongest man to his face that you'd like to put your boot in his backside."[92]

Because Paisley's party threatened to walk out if he walked into the meeting room, Mitchell watched the negotiations he was supposed to be chairing on closed-circuit TV. After two days of this, at midnight, on Tuesday, June 12, Sir Patrick Mayhew announced, "We're going in," which to Mitchell's ears sounded uncomfortably "as though we were embarking on a military invasion of foreign territory."[93]

Mitchell entered the room to a "bizarre scene." He was surprised to see an Irish government official occupying his chair. As he got closer, the official got up and explained that he was guarding the chair for Mitchell to prevent a member of the DUP from occupying it.

As Mitchell took his chair, Paisley stood up and shouted, "No, no, no, no," and led a walkout of his entire party.

The talks had not even begun and one major party had walked out, while another, Sinn Féin, was locked out. (They showed up anyway, however, Gerry Adams, Ken McGuiness, and thirteen Sinn Féin delegates tried to gain entry, and were denied. The news showed grim pictures of them standing at the locked gate.)

It wasn't going well, to say the least. Nor did it get much better. All agree that Mitchell had the patience of a saint to put up with the nonsense that droned on for *two years*.

"If anything he was too fair a chairman," said David Trimble.

These were "excruciating discussions," said Reg Empey, who also sat through them. "Mitchell was sitting here listening to the most appalling amount of minutiae, and whining, and churning, and going on, day in and day out. I could never understand what he was doing here."

Two things moved the talks forward. The first was the election of Tony Blair, who took office in May 1997. Blair and Clinton liked one another, and shared a basic centrist liberal worldview. Blair also shared Clinton's vision for a negotiated peace in Northern Ireland. Equally important, Blair was elected with one of the largest majorities in British history, which gave him political capital to spend. In contrast, John Major, who always seemed to be putting the brakes on the peace negotiations, had only been clinging to power by the narrowest of majorities. He specifically needed the votes of the Northern Irish Unionists in Parliament to survive politically, making him all but hostage to their demands to see the status quo maintained.

Clinton also made it known to Blair, almost as soon as he was elected, that facilitating the Irish peace process was a top priority. According to Bruce Morrison, Clinton went to one of Blair's first cabinet meetings after he became prime minister and talked about Ireland, in May 1997. Clinton said: "I want this."

Morrison recalled: "When Blair came in, that's when the marching orders changed to: 'Find a solution rather than a problem.'"

Blair signaled to Sinn Féin that he was serious about a settlement, but renouncing violence would be their ticket of admission to the peace process. "The settlement train is leaving," Blair announced in a public statement to Sinn Féin. "I want you on that train. But it is leaving anyway, and I will not allow it to wait for you. You cannot hold the process ransom any longer. So end the violence now."[94]

Sinn Féin got the message. The second essential breakthrough came on July 20, 1997, when Sinn Féin announced a new cease-fire, making themselves eligible to join the all-party talks.

The Deadline

Mitchell may have had the patience of a saint, but it was not infinite. Enough was enough. He set a deadline. Mitchell had spent two years in Irish purgatory, literally making no money (he had nobly refused a salary) and, worst of all, separated from his wife and new baby. He promised his wife, Heather, he would be back by Easter. He was going home.

"Mitchell knew that these guys could talk for the rest of time," said Morrison. "The real thing that Mitchell did was draw a line and say: 'We're going to do it or we're not. I'm not sitting over here the rest of my life.'" Adams knew that Mitchell wasn't kidding. He showed all the signs of "gate fever," the agitation a prisoner feels as his release date comes up.

But they were still far from an agreement, and personal relations had not thawed. Members of the UUP had refused to speak directly to any of the Sinn Féin negotiators.

"Trimble had not uttered one word to us," wrote Adams.

"I tell a lie," Adams corrected himself. "He actually had said two words to me. We met in the toilet one day. There was no one else there. 'We can't keep meeting like this,' I said in an effort to break the ice. 'Grow up,' he said."[95]

I asked Trimble about this men's room encounter with Adams. "That is not quite accurate. He saw me going in, and he ran in after me. He pursued me, and tried to accost me, and I am using that term purposefully, because to us, people being accosted in the toilet has a certain ring. So he tried to accost me in the toilet, and I told him to grow up."

When my interview with Adams was over, I said that I had one last question: "History needs to know," I said. "What really happened in that urinal? Did you follow Trimble in or did you really have to go?"

Adams laughed heartily.

"It was a call of nature, I can assure you," he said, shooting me a sly smile.

Good Friday Agreement

Everyone knew that Thursday, April 9, 1998, was do or die—the final night of negotiations. Some would have preferred die. That night Ian Paisley, in a last-ditch effort to block an agreement, led hundreds of supporters to the gates of Stormont, where the negotiations were being held. When denied admission, they broke through a gate and surged up a hill, carrying British flags to the statue of Edward Carson, a legendary Unionist leader. They called UUP leader David Trimble a "traitor."

But as Paisley tried to speak he was interrupted by loud, rude heckling. "Go home" they chanted. "Go home."[96]

That was a stunning statement of how public sentiment in Northern Ireland had changed. While Mitchell watched the scene taking place outside on TV, an Irish official standing next to him captured the meaning of the moment: "Once he would have brought thousands, tens of thousands with him. Now he has a few hundred. And look at those loyalists. Many of them thought him a god. They went out and killed, thinking they were saving the union. Now they've turned on him. It's the end of an era."[97]

Inside Stormont, everyone stayed up all night, and into the next day, while Clinton shuttled back and forth between the parties by phone all night, grabbing an hour or two of sleep here and there. The hypomanic deal maker was in his element. "I had been up most of the night before, trying to help George Mitchell close the deal. Besides George, I talked to [the Irish prime minister] Bertie Ahern, and to Tony Blair, David Trimble, and Gerry Adams twice, before going to bed at 2:30 A.M. At five, George woke me with a request to call Adams again to seal the deal," wrote Clinton.[98]

Clinton's first phone call to Gerry Adams came at 1:00 A.M. Irish time. They were stuck on the prisoner issue, a highly emotional and contentious issue on both sides. To the IRA, their people in prison were prisoners of war, and if the war was ending, they should be released. To the British they were murderers—not the sort of people you just let out the door if you don't want to be portrayed as soft on terror. They were working on a compromise that would involve early release. "I asked the president to use his influence to make the British understand the importance of this," wrote Adams.[99]

At 2:30 A.M. Irish time, Clinton had a long talk with Senator Mitchell.

"They're saying it's not looking so good." That's the message Clinton was getting from Mitchell, Morrison told me.

At 5:00 A.M. Clinton phoned Adams again for an update. Adams wrote, "He told me he would do everything he could to work through the remaining issues."[100]

At 8:15 A.M. (3:15 A.M. Washington time) Mitchell received a phone call from Clinton. "I was surprised to have him calling me in the middle of the night, Washington time, but knowing him, I shouldn't have been," Mitchell told me.

"What are you doing up so late?" Mitchell asked.

"I can't sleep. I want to know what is happening. I want to help," said Clinton, who then phoned Trimble, Hume, Adams, and others. "They were impressed that he would stay up all night to follow the negotiations, to talk with them."[101]

At 9:45 A.M., Adams called Clinton. Adams was embarrassed when he realized that it was 4:45 A.M. in Washington. He had obviously woken the president, who must have dozed off for a few minutes. Adams apologized. Clinton said not to worry.

It now looked like Sinn Féin was close to saying yes.

But fear lingered over whether the British would follow through on their agreements. Clinton assured Adams: "He was prepared to do all he could to guarantee any agreement. He told me if I was asking for help in getting an agreement implemented, the U.S.A. was ready to help."[102]

This was perhaps *the* crucial factor in Sinn Féin's saying yes. As Morrison put it, "Adams had to deliver the militants in his own movement. And in order to deliver them, he had to say: 'We've got this external force—the superpower—on our side, to keep the British in check when they try to walk from the deal.'"

Indeed, Adams told his friend Congressman Peter King, whom he spoke to that morning, that Clinton's intervention had made the difference. "One of the main reasons they agreed was because Clinton has assured them of continued U.S. involvement," said King.[103]

Dick Spring likened Clinton's role as "guarantor" to someone cosigning a loan for a party whose own credit is poor, and indeed the British had a bad credit rating with Sinn Féin.

Adams told me that because Clinton had showed "good faith" and "been active in getting them this far," his assurances counted for a lot: "It was important to be able to say to yourself that at least you have someone who is coming on board saying, 'Look, we were with you on this.' It's a comfort to know that there's somebody there that you can go to."

As Nancy Soderberg pointed out, the necessity for an American guarantor was not specific to the Irish peace, and could serve as a model for other peacemaking efforts as well. "While neither side trusted commitments made to each other, any commitments made to the United States, especially the president, could be trusted."[104]

At the same time, both Tony Lake and Soderberg emphasized that it would be a mistake to overstate America's power as guarantor. "In the end, we can't make anybody do anything. Gerry Adams would ask for 'guarantees' of British concessions in return for his considering new moves—something only the British themselves could provide. It is always essential that an 'honest broker' be clear about what that role can provide—and what it cannot," wrote Lake.[105]

Soderberg told me that the British would call her and ask, "Can you guarantee that Adams is going to do this?"

To which she would reply: "No, but here's what he told us, and if he backs off that commitment, he's going to have hell to pay with his supporters on the Hill and across the country, because he's made this commitment to us."

In turn, Adams would call her and ask: "Can you guarantee me the British are going to do this?"

And Soderberg would reply: "No, but here's what they've told the United States of America they're going to do.

"While the two sides might not trust each other, they do trust the United States, and they trust the fact that there is a great cost to breaking the commitment to the United States," said Soderberg.

For the Unionists, the final sticking point in the agreement was hypothetical: What if the IRA failed to decommission their weapons? They didn't want to feel they were trapped in a marriage with Sinn Féin if they turned out to be unfaithful. It was too late to change the text of the agreement. The only solution anyone could envision was a side letter of assurance from Tony Blair that if that were to happen the agreement would be "reevaluated." Blair was at Stormont staying up all night, too. It was in the early morning that Trimble and Blair discussed the letter.

"It was after that meeting with Blair that I took a phone call from the president," Trimble told me. "The telephone call began in a rather formal way, with him saying that an agreement could be hugely beneficial to Northern Ireland, for both of us. And I basically interrupted him, and said: 'Look, Mr. President, let me bring you up to speed. We've got a problem, and we've got a potential solution to the problem,'" and Trimble explained the need for the letter.

"I'll get that across right away," said Clinton.

The moment of Clinton's call was so uncanny—the same moment the UUP was discussing the letter option—that the UUP members concluded that their room must have been bugged. And, to this day, many of them are certain Clinton was being fed information by an American agent listening in. "It may have been coincidence, it may not have been, I don't know," said Reg Empey. "We came to the conclusion that the room was bugged because Clinton's phone call came through just at the critical moment." The UUP got their letter. It was circulated to the other parties, and no one objected.

"I assume Clinton's intervention helped secure that. That was very helpful. Very significant," said Trimble. "Clinton came on the phone, and he obviously did intervene," said Empey.

At 4:45 in the afternoon on Good Friday, Trimble called Mitchell: "We're ready to do business," he said.

Mitchell hurriedly gathered the parties to vote. In his book, Mitchell wrote that as Senate majority leader he had learned never to postpone a vote on a contentious bill once he had reached an agreement. Don't allow time for doubts and second guesses to creep in. At 5:00, only fifteen minutes after Trimble's phone call, the vote took place.

Friday, April 10, 1998, was "one of the happiest days of my presidency," wrote Clinton.

Mitchell had done the heavy lifting. But on that last night, Clinton was the closer. In his book on the Irish peace process, *The Far Side of*

Revenge: Making Peace in Northern Ireland, Deaglàn De Bréadun wrote: "In important ways and at key moments, the peace process had been Clinton-driven."[106] Good Friday was one of those key moments. It was "extremely unlikely," said Spring, that the parties would have reached agreement without the Clinton phone calls. Spring, a former rugby champion—his team won the 1979 Rugby Union Cup for Ireland—used a sports analogy to describe Clinton's role in the process as the clock ran out in the final minutes of negotiations: "He was the catalyst that pulled people across the line."

But considering it further, Spring offered a more spiritual analysis: "There was a big leap of faith required. And I don't think it was possible to get people to make that leap of faith without the intervention of one Bill Clinton."

That Easter the Irish rose from decades of deadly conflict to a new life—saved by their faith in Clinton.

A Twenty-Two-Minute Standing Ovation

On September 11, 1998, five months after the Good Friday Agreement, Ken Starr's report to Congress recommending the impeachment of the president was released on the Internet by the House of Representatives. Tens of millions of people read in humiliating pornographic detail every sexual act that had taken place between him and Monica Lewinsky. It was one of the lowest days of Bill Clinton's life.

By sheer coincidence Clinton was scheduled, on that same day, to receive the first Paul O'Dwyer Peace and Justice Award, named in honor of Brian O'Dwyer's father. who had died the year before. The award was bestowed by Brian, who shared with me Clinton's frame of mind on that day: "I was inside the White House with him. It was his first public appearance, him and Hillary, after the report came out. It was pretty devastating to him. What would have been a rather routine affair turned out to be a major media event. Every single camera in the United States was there in the background, waiting for Clinton to be booed. I was in the White House with Clinton and my family, and it was very obvious that he was very reluctant to go out. He was dreading this first public appearance."

Some even wondered if Clinton would have the guts to show his face. Clinton emerged, looking nervous and tentative, uncertain of what kind of reception he would receive. As soon as he appeared, O'Dwyer recalled, "The audience started cheering, and gave him a twenty-minute standing ovation. A *twenty-minute standing ovation*. I get chills even thinking about it." I thought perhaps O'Dwyer had exaggerated. In fact, it was a slight understatement. "It was twenty-two minutes, to be exact," Elizabeth Bagley told me. Someone had timed it.

Niall O'Dowd remembered clapping so long and so hard that "my hands were sore." The next day his hands were literally black and blue. "He comes in, and we just clapped, clapped until we dropped, and then we clapped and hollered some more. And every time he opened his mouth, we did it again."

Before their eyes, Clinton became transformed. "People around him say that that was the beginning of the turnaround for him," said O'Dwyer. "In that moment he knew that he could succeed, that he could stay. The Washington insiders and the Republicans can do anything they want to him, but the people were for him."

"Thank you very much. Thank you. Well, I have loved this, but you must be exhausted. I want to say, Hillary and I have been over there just lapping this up. We don't want this to ever end . . . Hillary and I will never forget what you've done for us today," said Clinton with emotion.[107]

"That was very important for him. That was his first encounter with the public after the impeachment recommendation. The Irish will never forget, ever," said Trina Vargo, the woman who had served as an intermediary between the Clinton administration and Niall O'Dowd in the early stages of the peace process. "They were saying, 'Even if everyone else is going to abandon you, we're not.'"

"It was like the ultimate moment," said O'Dowd, "because on one hand you have the forces of evil trying to bring this guy down. All the media was there, hoping for some kind of catcalling. The Irish American audience just went insane. This was our hero's tale. Here was a guy, our champion, our hero. And now he has been wounded and we had to stand up for him. We loved this guy, and we didn't give a shit about impeachment."

Bagley believes that Clinton sensed another emotion from the Irish American audience.

"He felt our *defiance*. How *dare* they? They don't call us the fighting Irish for nothing. We were the underdog, and Bill Clinton was there for us. He was our champion, and now we'd do it for him. He realized then that he was going to survive, because the people wanted him. And that's what counted. Every man and woman in that audience knew that the impeachment was wrong. . . .

"They knew it was a *crucifixion*."

PART IV

Impeachment-gate

9

The Horse-Whipping

The worst presidential decision I ever made" is how Clinton would later describe his choice in January of 1994 to appoint a special prosecutor to investigate him. Even on the face of it that would seem like a self-destructive thing to do. Why willingly give your enemies a club to beat you with?

One close associate told me that Clinton said bitterly in private: "I should be horse-whipped for that decision. I weakened the presidency."

Horse-whipped? What an interesting choice of words—and thus a potentially revealing one. As we discussed in the section about the three stages of Roger, Clinton has an unconscious drive to recapitulate his abusive family, a deeply masochistic need to be whipped, to triumph over his whipper, and ultimately to forgive and be reconciled with him. Only by understanding this dynamic pattern can we make sense of Clinton's deeply irrational decision: By appointing a special prosecutor, he was unconsciously reenacting an old script, surrendering himself for a whipping.

Clinton knew there was nothing to Whitewater. The so-called "scandal" surrounding this Arkansas real estate deal was so murky that few people in America, even if they read the newspaper every day, could explain what the Clintons were alleged to have done wrong. Eight years and $64 million worth of investigation would prove that, in fact, they had done nothing wrong: The Clintons were passive investors who lost their money to a con man, as they had claimed all along.

The Clintons had dinner one night with their friend Jim McDougal, who suggested they kick in eighty thousand dollars for an investment property on the White River. This was before anyone knew that Mc-Dougal, a beloved former college professor, was becoming severely ill with a manic-depressive disorder. McDougal made a variety of failed investments that he attempted to cover up through fraud—none of which had anything to do with the Clintons. "The only mistake we made is who we went into business with," said Clinton.[1]

In addition, Clinton knew this faux scandal had been birthed and kept alive through the artful collective actions of a group of people Hillary Clinton would famously call a "vast right-wing conspiracy." Dignifying this plot by appointing a special prosecutor was an abuse of both himself and the judicial process, making the decision all the more unjustified and ill advised.

The real origins of the Whitewater probe began with Pittsburgh billionaire Richard Mellon Scaife. Scaife had a long history of funding right-wing covert operations going all the way back to the Nixon administration (he reportedly gave over a million dollars, some of which ended up in a shady slush fund that paid for the break-in at the Watergate hotel complex and other "dirty tricks"). Since then the "Daddy Warbucks of the conservative movement," as Scaife has been called, spent hundreds of millions of dollars building up conservative think tanks and organizations and creating his own right-wing media empire.

Scaife spent millions of dollars on a secret smear campaign against the Clintons known by the code name "The Arkansas Project," embedded inside the conservative *American Spectator* magazine. Scaife sent operatives into Arkansas to dig up dirt on Clinton. He didn't care whether it was true, only whether it could stick, according to David Brock, who worked for the Arkansas Project.

In Arkansas, Scaife's agents found David Hale, a corrupt judge who had been arrested for running a multimillion dollar scam on the Small Business Administration. Hale saw Bill Clinton as his get-out-of-jail-free card. After his arrest he suddenly claimed that he had valuable information to trade for leniency: Bill Clinton, he maintained, had been his co-

conspirator in a fraudulent loan to Jim McDougal. According to Hale, "The Governor came over and shook hands with me and asked if I was going to be able to help he and Jim out." As this conversation almost certainly did not take place, it should be no surprise that there were no documents, witnesses, or evidence of any kind to support this claim. Yet "virtually the entire long investigation of Whitewater flows from one single purported conversation between Hale and Clinton in 1986," wrote Jeffrey Toobin in *A Vast Conspiracy*.[2]

Seeing his potential as a tool to get Clinton, The Arkansas Project adopted Hale, providing him with money, a car, a place to live, and an attorney, Ted Olson, to whom we will return later. The Arkansas Project then launched a publicity campaign, putting Hale in touch with reporters from *Time, Newsweek, The Washington Post,* and other national publications. Hale's most intensive contact was with *New York Times* reporter Jeff Gerth, who flew to Arkansas twice to meet with him. Gerth broke the original Whitewater story, based largely on these conversations, spawning the investigation.

So, why would Clinton give credence to this dirty-tricks operation by appointing a special prosecutor, knowing that typically most people assume a crime has been committed if a special prosecutor is appointed? Clinton had help in making this suicidal decision from some of his key advisers, particularly George Stephanopoulos, who insisted that acceding to the demand for a special counsel was the only way to put the scandal behind them. "It was a huge mistake," Clinton told one reporter. "Terrible mistake, but it followed all the conventional wisdom. I wound up being for it. Everybody was for it."[3]

But that's not accurate. Not everybody was for it.

Hillary was dead set against appointing a prosecutor, and she fought the decision vehemently. She reminded Clinton's inner circle that she had worked on the Watergate investigation and knew what a real scandal was. Appointing a counsel when there was no legal basis for suspecting wrongdoing was an abuse of the process.

"Bill's staff trooped in to lobby me, one after another, each delivering the same familiar message: I would destroy my husband's presidency if I didn't support their strategy. Whitewater had to be pushed off the front pages so we could get on with the business of the administration, including health care reform."[4] The advisers were spectacularly wrong, of course. Hiring a special prosecutor had the exact opposite effect. As Leon Panetta said, "You appoint a special counsel, and suddenly you lose total control of what is happening on an issue."

Hillary's primary ally in this internecine struggle was White House counsel Bernie Nussbaum. The "tightly wound," frank-talking fifty-six-year-old New York lawyer had managed the staff of the House Judiciary Committee during the Nixon impeachment investigation, and Hillary, just fresh out of Yale Law School, had been one of his staff members. (He had laughed at her twenty years ago when she told him that her fiancé, Bill, would be president someday, provoking her to storm angrily out of his car.) Nussbaum argued forcefully against the special counsel, warning that he would become a "roving searchlight" with "an inevitable institutional mandate to indict *someone*."[5]

Clinton recalled that "Nussbaum was distraught, predicting that whoever was appointed would be frustrated when nothing was there, and would keep widening the investigation until he found something someone I knew had done wrong."[6] Nussbaum's advice was: "Don't feed the beast."

Many of Clinton's advisers thought Hillary was paranoid. White House counsel Abner Mikva was not alone in calling her "the center of paranoia" in the White House.[7] Leon Panetta admitted to me that his first reaction was "maybe this is paranoia," but his initial reaction had been wrong, he conceded. "Hillary's instincts were always to fight and to not simply give in. She felt in the end that they would pay an even higher price if they didn't hang tough," he said. And later events would prove her instincts right.

"Requesting a special prosecutor is wrong," said Hillary.[8]

On Tuesday, January 4, 1994, at a senior staff meeting, George Stephanopoulos was arguing that they had to appoint a special counsel. The only dissenter in the meeting was Bernie Nussbaum.

When White House lawyer Joel Klein was sent to broach the matter with Hillary, she "shut him down."

Two hours later chief of staff McLarty and political adviser Harold Ickes tried approaching Hillary again: "The answer was still no."

While the participants in the meeting were griping about what a mistake Hillary was making, she unexpectedly walked into the room, which then went dead silent. "I think this is a meeting I ought to be at," she said.[9]

A little unnerved, Stephanopoulos looked directly at Hillary and made his case. "Well, I might as well go on with what I was saying: Assuming we did nothing wrong, the best thing is to have a special counsel say so. There's an air of inevitability to this. . . . Congress will keep the drumbeat going." Stephanopoulos tried to appeal to her interest in passing health care reform. "This is going to kill health care if we don't get it under control."[10] Stephanopoulos thought this final argument was the coup de grâce. He was wrong.

"If we were tough as the Republicans, we'd band together and beat them back," she replied.[11]

Her eyes began to tear. And she lashed out at Stephanopoulos, who she thought was always the first to capitulate at the first whiff of scandal. During the New Hampshire primary, he privately counseled Clinton to drop out of the race when the Gennifer Flowers story hit. She reminded him of that and began to cry. "You *never* believed in us. In New Hampshire . . . If we wouldn't have fought, we would never have won. *You* gave up on us." Stephanopoulos had to admit, "I knew why Hillary's words wounded me so deeply. They were true. I never showed it to the world, but I did give up in New Hampshire."[12]

Hillary paused, her voice fell, and she continued to cry.

"We were out there alone, and I'm feeling very lonely right now. Nobody is fighting for *me*."[13]

Stunned, no one knew quite what to say. Harold Ickes made one more plea for the special counsel.

"I don't want to hear anything more," Hillary snapped. "I want us to fight. I want a campaign now."[14]

The need to fight became Hillary's recurring theme over the next few days, and her contempt for staffers urging compliance grew. "JFK had real men in the White House," she chided them.[15]

The next morning Stephanopoulos brought it up with Clinton. "Hmm, makes some sense," he said in a noncommittal way before going back upstairs to the residence to change, where he discussed it once again with Hillary. A few hours later Mack McLarty and Harold Ickes walked into Stephanopoulos's office looking "chastened and pale. . . . 'You can all keep talking about this if you want,' said Ickes, 'but it's useless. We're not doing a special counsel.'" He added that Hillary was "really angry" at Stephanopoulos.[16]

For the moment, it appeared that the move to request a special counsel had been rejected, by both Clintons. Yet six days later, Bill Clinton would decide to appoint one. What happened to make him change his mind? Psychotherapists often look for what we call *precipitants*, environmental events that trigger dysfunctional behavior. There is a glaringly obvious and important precipitant here: the death of a parent.

While Virginia was vacationing in Las Vegas, Clinton had anxiously called his mother's hotel room several times but hadn't gotten an answer. On January 5, Clinton had finally reached her at home the night she returned from the trip. "She laughed and said she had been out day and night, having the time of her life in her favorite city, and she didn't have time to sit around and wait for the phone to ring."[17]

Late that night, Bill and Hillary's phone rang. "The sound of a telephone ringing in the middle of the night is one of the most jarring in the world," wrote Hillary. "It was Dick Kelley calling to tell Bill that his mother had just died in her sleep at her home in Hot Springs."[18]

Bill and Hillary were up for the rest of the night making phone calls to friends and family. That morning when they turned on the *Today Show,* Bill saw a report of Virginia's death. "The President's mother died early this morning after a long battle with cancer." The news report "made her death seem terribly final," wrote Hillary. Then Bob Dole and Newt Gingrich appeared on the screen, and Dole began talking about Whitewater: "It to me cries out for the appointment of a regulatory, independent counsel."[19]

"I looked over at Bill's face. He was utterly stricken," wrote Hillary.[20]

Dole continued his hectoring for two days, including the day of Virginia's funeral. "Clinton couldn't believe it," wrote Bob Woodward. "Political attacks on the day of his mother's death and then again on the day of her funeral were unforgivable."[21] Bob Dole, to his credit, would later write Clinton a letter of apology. But his timing, in a perverse way, was excellent. At this uniquely vulnerable time, Clinton was even more prone to acting out an unconscious script he wasn't aware of.

The pressure to pick a special counsel continued to build. On January 10, eleven key Democratic senators, including Bill Bradley, Joseph Lieberman, John Kerry, and Daniel Patrick Moynihan, urged the appointment of a special counsel.

On Tuesday evening, January 11, Clinton spoke with Hillary and his advisers on a conference call from Prague. Hillary wrote: "It was the middle of the night in Europe. Bill was worn out and exhausted after days of hearing nothing but Whitewater questions from the media. He was also heartbroken about losing his mother, the one steady presence throughout his life and his chief cheerleader, offering unconditional love and support. I felt sorry for him and wished he didn't have to deal with such a crucial decision under these circumstances. He was terribly hoarse, and we had to lean in close to the black batwing-shaped conference phone to hear his voice."[22] George Stephanopoulos found it eerie that this was the first time they had ever met in the Oval Office without Clinton physically present; instead, he was this disembodied and tired voice coming from the speakerphone.

Stephanopoulos argued that the presidency would be stalled until they got this out of the way. "This will be over in six months," he said.

Nussbaum forcefully disagreed. "I've lived with this institution. It's an evil institution." The prosecutor's whole reputation depends on making this one case. "You will create a roving spotlight that will examine your friends and anyone you've ever had contact with."

Others countered that the investigation could be restricted to Whitewater. Nussbaum interrupted. They didn't understand the pressure a special prosecutor feels to get something on someone. "Your friends, your family will be chased to the ends of the earth."

"Goddamn it, Bernie," Clinton's disembodied voice said. "I can't give a press conference without being asked about this." He added: "I can't take this."

Clinton was frustrated that even while he was in Eastern Europe pursuing a historic expansion of NATO, he was being hounded by press questions about Whitewater. Clinton usually made rational decisions, but "I can't take this" is not a rational reason to take such a momentous step. Clearly his judgment was impaired at this moment in time.

"If you create a special counsel it will last as long as your presidency and beyond," predicted Nussbaum.

Even James Carville, normally the more combative of the advisers, sided with Stephanopoulos. "Get somebody. Have Reno appoint somebody. It's just a pile of shit, you know, it'll all blow over."[23]

Nussbaum became increasingly agitated. "I don't think so," he said. Stephanopoulos accused him of being hysterical. Nussbaum realized at this point that he *was* hysterical.

Hillary recalled that "after several heated rounds back and forth, Bill, exhausted, had heard enough. I wrapped up the meeting asking only

David Kendall [the Clintons' personal attorney] to remain for a few more minutes with the President.

"The room was quiet for a moment, and then Bill spoke.

" 'Look, I think we've just got to do it,' he said. 'We've got nothing to hide, and if this keeps up, it's going to drown out our agenda.'

"It was time to fold my cards," wrote Hillary. " 'I know that we've got to move past this,' I said. 'But it's up to you.' "

Hillary knew the signs. Clinton was tired, and this is when he was most likely to make a bad decision. He needed to rest and review the issue in the morning.

" 'Why don't you sleep on the decision? If you're still willing to do it, we'll send a request to the attorney general in the morning.'

" 'No,' he said. 'Let's get this over with.' "

Hillary wrote, "I felt terrible. He had been pushed into a decision he didn't feel comfortable about." And she would forever regret not standing her ground. "I wish I had fought harder."[24]

Looking back, Bill Clinton wrote, "Perhaps I did it because I was completely exhausted and grieving over mother." Begala agrees it was a terrible decision, and that it was a product of grief and fatigue. "He just lost his mom. He was exhausted and grief-stricken. Then he flew to Russia, literally from the funeral, to meet with Yeltsin. That's a hard trip. . . . He was beat down. He was at sea. . . . It was horrible."

He was exhausted. He wasn't thinking straight. But it was more than exhaustion. Virginia's death caused Clinton to temporarily regress, strengthening the unconscious need, which had always been deep in Clinton's psyche like an undertow, to re-create the dynamics of his home life. With Virginia gone, the psychological pressure to reenact his lost childhood relationships must have been intense. To submit to one more whipping resonated with a compelling gut feeling he couldn't articulate; in spite of his better judgment, it just felt right. Virginia had done the same all their lives, sticking with Roger, even remarrying him after they divorced.

In that regressed moment, Clinton was on Air Force One physically, but psychologically he was back in his family home in Hot Springs. When Clinton said he should be horse-whipped for appointing a special counsel, he probably didn't realize that unconsciously it was his desire to be horse-whipped that had motivated him to appoint one in the first place.

The psychodrama inside Clinton's unconscious was about to be played out on the national stage: Roger Clinton, the abusive older man who dispensed the whippings, would be played by Ken Starr. Virginia, the exuberant lost love object whom Clinton had long been desperately seeking and now longed for more than ever, would be played by Monica. And Edith, his fierce protector, would be, as always, played by Hillary.

The next day Hillary broke the news to Nussbaum.

"This is a great tragedy," said Nussbaum. "Why are you going to put your head in that noose?"[25]

· THE CONTRACT ON CLINTON ·

Once appointed, a special counsel is accountable to no one. There are no checks and balances on his power, no mechanism for oversight. The unchecked power of the special prosecutor is an example of the law of unintended negative consequences. While the statute had been written in the Watergate era to protect the prosecutor against undue interference—a reaction to Nixon's firing of special prosecutor Archibald Cox—for that same reason, the law left open the danger of a runaway prosecutor.

In theory, the prosecutor was beyond partisanship since he was chosen by a three-judge panel selected by the chief justice of the Supreme Court. But as Antonin Scalia noted in 1988 when hearing arguments against the special prosecutor law in *Morrison v. Olson,* the law had no safeguards or oversight to stop the panel of judges from intentionally choosing a prosecutor who would abuse his discretion.

"What if they are politically partisan, as judges have been known to be, and select a prosecutor antagonistic to the administration?" he asked prophetically. "There is no remedy for that, not even a political one," Scalia exclaimed.[26] "The context of this statute is acrid with the smell of threatened impeachment."[27] According to Scalia: "Therein is the most dangerous power of the prosecutor; that he will pick people he thinks he should get, rather than cases that need to be prosecuted. With the law books filled with a great assortment of crimes, a prosecutor stands a fair chance of finding at least a technical violation of some act on the part of almost anyone. In such a case, it is not the question of discovering the commission of a crime and then looking for the man who has committed it. It is a question of picking the man and then searching the law books or putting investigators to work, to pin some offense on him."[28]

Ted Olson, then an assistant attorney general in the Reagan administration, argued before the court that the special counsel statute was unconstitutional. Olson had been a target of an independent prosecutor for allegedly lying to Congress. (The prosecutor concluded that he had given testimony that was "disingenuous and misleading," but did not find sufficient grounds to charge him with criminal wrongdoing.[29]) This is particularly ironic because Olson would become one of the pivotal players in the behind-the-scenes campaign to impeach Clinton, using the very mechanism he had once tried to abolish.

Olson was, and still is, one of the top Republican lawyers in the country, "an architect of the conservative legal movement," according to *The Washington Post*. He successfully argued *Bush v. Gore* before the Supreme Court, became George W. Bush's solicitor general, and was on his short list for both the Supreme Court and attorney general. David Brock, who worked for the Arkansas Project, had been a frequent visitor to what he called the "Olson salon," a small group of highly placed Washington insiders who met weekly at Ted Olson's home with the explicit purpose of coordinating their actions to "get Clinton." Regular participants included Robert Bartley, editor of the *Wall Street Journal* editorial page, Supreme Court justice Clarence Thomas, former Supreme Court nominee Robert Bork, Judge Laurence Silberman, and an old law partner of Olson's: Ken Starr.

The initial organizational meeting to set up the Arkansas Project was held in Olson's downtown Washington, D.C., law office, supporting Brock's claim that the Arkansas Project operated "in conjunction with, but outside the official GOP."[30] (During his Senate confirmation hearing for his post as solicitor general, Olson denied any knowledge of the Arkansas Project. "He perjured himself," said reporter Joe Conason, co-author of *The Hunting of the President*. The Arkansas Project's own financial records show payments of $14,341 to Olson's firm in 1994. In a letter to the Judiciary Committee, Ralph Lemley, a longtime adviser to Ron Burr, cofounder of the *American Spectator*, the conservative magazine that operated the project, wrote that Olson's denials were "contrary to my firsthand knowledge of what really happened. . . . Ted Olson was an integral part of the project.")

To Ted Olson and his salon, Scalia's constitutional nightmare was a dream come true. A partisan special counsel would allow them to finally get Clinton.

When Clinton came into office, the special counsel statute had elapsed. In January 1993, three days before Clinton took office, Nussbaum met with Bush's outgoing White House counsel, William Barr, who had one piece of advice: "We killed the independent counsel statute. Take my advice; don't breathe new life into it. As a Republican, I'd love to see you live under it, but as an American, I can tell you it would be bad news if you get that thing going again." Even though Clinton had promised to renew it, Barr said, "Let the Republicans take the hit for it."[31] Republican presidents from Nixon to Bush had been forced to deal with protracted investigations. Clinton could avoid the same simply by letting the dormant law lie fallow.

When Democratic leaders in Congress indicated they could put the renewal of the act on the back burner, Nussbaum told Clinton to jump at the chance.

"No, nah, Bernie," Clinton said. "This is good. And I promised it during the campaign."[32]

After the law's expiration, the only mechanism for appointing a special counsel was for Clinton to ask his own attorney general, Janet Reno, to appoint one. Reno chose Robert Fiske, a Republican, who thus was not inclined, either in appearance or reality, to be biased in favor of the president. Plus, he had a sterling reputation for fairness, thoroughness, and tough-mindedness.

Fiske first investigated the death of Deputy White House Counsel Vince Foster, a close friend of the Clintons who had committed suicide in Fort Marcy Park in Virginia on July 20, 1993. Bizarre rumors had surfaced in the right-wing press that Foster, Hillary's former partner in the Rose law firm in Arkansas, had been murdered because he knew too much about Whitewater. It was even alleged that the Clintons might have ordered their friend's execution.* Both the park police and the FBI had

---

* Richard Mellon Scaife's media machine was one of the driving forces behind the bizarre conspiracy theory about Vince Foster's death. Scaife called Foster's death "the Rosetta Stone to the Clinton administration." "Listen, [Clinton] can order people done away with at his will. He's got the entire federal government behind him," said Scaife in an interview with John F. Kennedy Jr. ("Who's Afraid of Richard Mellon Scaife?" *George,* January 1999). Scaife added that "God, there must be 60 people [associated with Bill Clinton]—who have died mysteriously." The irony was that Scaife himself had been suspected of ordering a murder and making it look like suicide. In the 1960s, Scaife backed a local candidate for attorney general,

ruled it a suicide, yet suspicions about his death voiced by Republican lawmakers had kept the otherwise tepid Whitewater drama hot. Dole had referred to Foster's "alleged suicide." And Gingrich had said, "There's a lot there that is weird."[33] (Congressman Dan Burton had actually carried out target practice in his backyard to determine if the angle of the bullet really could have credibly been self-imposed.) Fiske had four of the top pathologists in the country review the data, and all four strongly concurred it was suicide.

On June 30, 1994, five months after beginning his investigation, Fiske issued two reports. The first stated that Vince Foster had indeed committed suicide. The second declared more broadly that no crimes had been committed in the White House.

Ironically, in assigning blame for Foster's death, Fiske cleared the Clintons but pointed a finger at the *Wall Street Journal* editorial page (and by extension its editor, Olson salon member Robert Bartley), which had stridently called for the investigation in the first place. Fiske numbered among the factors that contributed to Foster's suicide "mean-spirited and factually baseless" editorials in *The Journal*. Foster had become profoundly upset in response to this series of editorials attacking his character, including a rare

---

Robert Duggan. When federal prosecutors began investigating Duggan, he absconded, eloping with Scaife's sister. Scaife was, understandably, enraged. Six months later, Duggan was found shot to death, and several feet from his body was a shotgun, cleaned of fingerprints—a classic gangland-style slaying. Scaife insists it was suicide—though how a man could shoot himself with a shotgun and then, after fatally wounding himself, wipe the gun clean of prints and throw it away from his body has never been explained. Dick Thornburgh, the federal prosecutor who had jurisdiction over the case and who would later become the Republican governor of Pennsylvania, didn't seem interested in investigating Scaife. "It should have piqued Dick Thornburgh's curiosity, but it didn't seem to," noted reporter Joe Conason (author interview with Conason, October 11, 2006). Journalist Gene Lyons spoke to one reporter in Pittsburgh who "was quite convinced that he was murdered, with Scaife being the obvious suspect, but he had no proof" (author interview with Gene Lyons, October 4, 2006). While the authorities exonerated Scaife, his sister did not. She never spoke to her brother again till the day she died because she was certain that Scaife was responsible for her husband's death, according to Conason, who has confirmed this with people who worked for Scaife. Whether or not any of these allegations are true, it is thus more than ironic that Scaife would become the chief proponent driving the rumor that Vincent Foster was murdered by the Clintons, who made it appear like suicide. This could be a projection: accusing the Clintons of something he was alleged to have done.

full-page editorial entitled "Who Is Vince Foster?" One more in the series was published the day before Foster killed himself, suggesting that it may have been a precipitant. His suicide note plainly states that these editorials helped drive him over the edge: "The *WSJ* editors lie without consequence," he wrote, lamenting, "I was not meant for the job or the spotlight of public life in Washington. Here ruining people is considered sport."[34] If those editors had any remorse for possibly having driven a man to his death with baseless, mean-spirited words, there was no evidence of it. *The Wall Street Journal* published an editorial on August 6, seventeen days after Foster's death, stating that the nation would probably "never know" all of the reasons for Foster's depression. Robert Bartley told a *Boston Globe* reporter that "the text of Mr. Foster's note suggests that he was deeply distraught over a variety of issues. At this time, we have nothing to add to our last editorial of Aug. 6."[35]

In a tragic irony, Clinton signed the law renewing the independent counsel statute on June 30, the very same day Fiske issued his report exonerating him. But before Clinton signed it, he said to his new chief of staff, Leon Panetta: "Do I have to?"[36]

Panetta said he did. Clinton's own administration had pushed for the renewal of the act, and it had passed by a 3 to 1 margin. Now would not be the time to change his mind and oppose the law. That window of opportunity had been shut. "I remember when there was the extension of the special counsel law and he indicated that in signing it he might be asking for some real trouble," Panetta told me.

Clinton said aloud, "I may be making a terrible mistake."[37]

How true. With that signature he transferred power over his fate to William Rehnquist, chief justice of the Supreme Court. In essence he was signing a contract authorizing a hit on himself. Scalia's nightmare scenario was about to unfold.

Attorney Mark Tuohey served as a consultant to Fiske and then stayed on to become deputy counsel under Ken Starr. When I interviewed him in his Washington, D.C., office in 2007, Tuohey told me that before Fiske was replaced by Ken Starr, he was about to finish his investigation, concluding that there had been no wrongdoing by the Clintons. According to Tuohey, "Fiske was very far along. He was close to wrap up" on all the issues related to alleged misdeeds by the Clintons in office: the Vince Foster death, Travelgate (a controversy surrounding the firing of several White House travel office employees), and Filegate (a firestorm provoked by the unauthorized release of several hundred FBI background files). Prosecutions of Jim McDougal and Jim Guy Tucker in Little Rock, on charges not related to the Clintons, were all that remained. An honest, thorough investigation had cleared Clinton. And that should have been the end of that.

For the right wing, Fiske's finding that the Clintons were innocent was an inconvenient truth they refused to accept. Conservatives claimed that Fiske, a Republican, was a Clinton stooge. Conservative *New York Times* columnist William Safire called it a "cover-up," and demanded that Fiske be fired. The *Wall Street Journal* editorial page also accused Fiske of being complicit in a "cover-up," declaring his investigation to be nothing but "political damage control."

Still, by all objective accounts, Fiske was doing an excellent job. "The criticism of Fiske was wholly unfounded in my book," said Tuohey. "Fiske was a class act," said another lawyer on Starr's Office of Independent Counsel staff, who asked that his name not be used.

The day after Clinton signed the special counsel act back into law, Janet Reno requested that Fiske be retained, "so that he may continue his ongoing investigation without disruption."[38]

Lauch Faircloth, Republican senator from North Carolina and one of the Clintons' most vociferous right-wing enemies, immediately jumped on Reno, declaring it "highly improper" for her to recommend Fiske's renewal.[39] Faircloth made a speech on the Senate floor demanding "a new, truly independent counsel."

Supreme Court chief justice William Rehnquist was responsible for choosing the three-judge panel that would in turn have the power to choose the special prosecutor. This was one of the chief reasons the Clintons were anxious about renewing the independent counsel law. Hillary believed that Rehnquist "despised" her and Bill and was sure that Rehnquist would "screw" them.[40]

People have long forgotten William Rehnquist's 1971 confirmation hearing, but there had been grave concern the Nixon appointee might be a conservative ideologue. He had been a supporter of the ultraconservative 1964 Republican presidential contender, Barry Goldwater; had ties to the John Birch Society, an extremist right-wing group; and had written a memorandum in favor of school segregation when he was a Supreme Court clerk. Rehnquist had also been a leading force in the founding of the Federalist Society, a fraternal legal organization for conservatives, funded in large part by Scaife, which counted among its members Ted Olson and Ken Starr.

The special counsel statute recommended that the chief justice give "priority to senior circuit judges and retired justices," but it did not actually require Rehnquist to do so. Ignoring the statute's explicit guidance, Rehnquist chose David Sentelle to lead the panel, a forty-eight-year-old who had served only seven years on the bench.

As former head of the North Carolina Republican Party, and a protégé of Lauch Faircloth and Jesse Helms, Sentelle had earned a reputation for being one of the most extreme conservatives on the federal bench (he even named one of his daughters Reagan). In short, his main qualification was that he was a partisan.

Like many of Clinton's enemies, Sentelle was part of the embittered segregationist wing of the Republican Party. When he was confirmed Sentelle had refused to resign from his whites-only club. In his contribution to the 1981 book *Why the South Will Survive,* Sentelle argued that country music mainly appealed to whites, or, as he put it, "the long historied, little-loved descendants of the people who built half of the civilized world—the Anglo-Saxons." Southern segregationists had special hatred for Clinton—a fellow Southerner turned race traitor in their eyes for his enthusiastic support of civil rights.* As far as Sentelle was concerned, America was under attack by liberals like Clinton. In 1991, he wrote that

---

* The man who put Judge David Hale in touch with the Arkansas Project was Arkansas politician Justice Jim Johnson. Johnson was an old-style segregationist and the founder of an organization called the White Citizens Council. In his failed run for governor of Arkansas in 1966, Johnson was officially endorsed by the Ku Klux Klan, and he was at the core of the anti-Clinton underground in Arkansas, which was composed of embittered segregationists. Segregationists had once ruled in Arkansas. Longtime governor Orval Faubus made national news when he personally stood on the schoolhouse steps to block African-American children from entering Little Rock High School in 1957. The defeat of Johnson in 1966 was the permanent turning point in racial politics there. "The segregationists lost," Arkansas journalist Gene Lyons told me, "and they kind of disappeared from public sight, but they didn't go away, and they never got over it. They were just a defeated, disgraced, embittered group of people who hated the winners. And Clinton, for a number of reasons, in their minds became a symbolic figure who incarnated everything that they hated." The local headquarters for the Arkansas Project was a bait-and-tackle shop on the shore of Lake Katherine near Hot Springs, owned by Parker Dozhier, a white supremacist with close ties to Johnson.

"leftist heretics" were scheming to turn the United States into a "collectiv-
ist, egalitarian, materialistic, race-conscious, hyper-secular, and socially
permissive state."[41]

In mid-July, Sentelle lunched with Jesse Helms and Lauch Faircloth.
They all later denied that they discussed the choosing of a special counsel, claiming that they had talked only about "old friends, western-style
clothing, and prostate problems." But in later Senate testimony Sentelle
admitted that the topic of who should be special prosecutor *had* come up
over lunch, and it was agreed that he would pick a Republican "who had
been active on the other side of the political fence."

They were hiring a hit man.

On August 5, the panel of judges rejected Janet Reno's request to retain Fiske, arguing that it "would not be consistent with the purposes of
the independent counsel act. . . . It is not our intent to impugn the integrity of the Attorney General's appointee, but rather to reflect the intent of
the Act that the [independent counsel] be protected against the perceptions of conflict [of interest]. . . . The Court therefore deems it in the best
interest of the appearance of independence . . . that a person not affili-
ated with the incumbent administration be appointed."[42]

Ken Starr, the man they chose to replace Fiske, was not just a conservative, but an active member of what David Brock called the "anti-Clinton
jihad." Starr had been one of the heavy-hitting right-wing Christian lawyers advising the lawyers in Paula Jones's sexual harassment suit against
Clinton, generously forgoing his five-hundred-dollar-an-hour fee for this
labor of love. This was no secret. He had been a frequent guest on TV
news programs championing Paula Jones's cause. He had even offered to
file an amicus brief in support of her case with the Supreme Court, on
behalf of an antifeminist organization called the Independent Woman's
Forum, a conservative group funded by Richard Mellon Scaife and
founded by Riki Silberman, wife of Judge Laurence Silberman, a central
member of the Olson salon.

Sentelle chose him, according to David Brock, because he would be "a
reliable anti-Clinton partisan."[43] "By the time he was named independent
counsel, he had long ago signed on with many of the people who wanted
Bill Clinton destroyed," wrote Toobin.[44]

Five months before he was appointed special prosecutor, Ken Starr
ran into James Carville at the U.S. Air Club at National Airport. Carville

didn't know Starr, and had no idea who he was. With "undisguised glee," according to Carville, Starr came up to him and said: "Your guy's going down. He's gonna get rolled. He's a crook."[45]

Carville mentally dismissed this stranger as another "goofy Clinton hating type."[46] When Carville saw the face of the man named to replace Fiske on TV, he instantly recognized him as the crazed man who had accosted him at National Airport.

Carville went nuts. "Wait a minute! Just wait a Goddamn minute!"[47]

"From the day he was appointed, I knew this guy was trouble," Carville told me. "I wanted them to fight this guy. Fuck this."

Carville wanted to publicly attack Starr as a partisan, to expose the politicization of the office from the very get-go, and Hillary agreed. In hindsight, this would have been the better strategy. Instead the administration followed the advice of newly hired White House counsel Lloyd Cutler, who recommended against antagonizing the new prosecutor. "They had Lloyd Cutler. He's a decent guy. But Washington lawyers, they don't want to rock the boat," Carville told me.

"We have no reason to doubt the fair-mindedness of Ken Starr," Cutler told the press.[48]

Bill Clinton agreed that Starr's appointment should be fought, but thought a campaign coming from the White House would look bad. Clinton was frustrated: Why weren't fellow Democrats rallying to protect him?

"Where are the Democrats to attack the appointment?" he asked. "Who will attack? Only the Republicans know how to attack."[49]

In the end Clinton chose not to fight, and once again I must wonder if he was not still unconsciously playing out his inner script. This man was brought in for the express purpose of whipping Clinton, and yet the president passively submitted to it.

Dick Morris wrote that, at the time, he thought Clinton was paranoid when he claimed that "Senators Helms and Faircloth were out to get him. They had put Judge Sentelle on the bench, and Chief Justice Rehnquist, a Nixon-Reagan conservative, had chosen Sentelle to head the three-judge panel. Sentelle had chosen Starr, who was out to get him. Helms, Faircloth, Sentelle, Starr, and the system—all of the above were out to get him, he said."[50]

But that's exactly what happened.

Clinton would later say that Starr was not "an independent renegade," but rather "an instrument of a grand design."

"Starr did just what he was hired to do."[51]

· THE BOX IN THE ATTIC ·

For over two years, Ken Starr hit one dry well after another. Whitewater went nowhere. Paradoxically, with each passing month, the frustration of not finding a crime to convict the Clintons of only strengthened Starr's conviction that the Clintons were guilty and fiendishly clever at hiding their crimes. He was certain that "some grander conspiracy was sure to be uncovered, just over the horizon."[52]

On January 4, 1996, Starr thought that he had finally found the smoking gun he had been looking for, proof that the Clintons were masterminds behind a massive cover-up. On that day White House assistant Carolyn Huber found a cardboard box on a card table in the book room of the White House residence. The book room was the equivalent of the president's attic. The box sat amid rows of other boxes, gifts, pictures, chairs, old shoes, and coat hangers. When Huber saw what was inside the box, she froze with panic.

The box contained billing records from the Rose law firm relating to Hillary's work for Madison Savings and Loan, a bank run by Jim Mc-Dougal. Starr had long ago subpoenaed all Rose billing records, but this box had been missing—until now. Quantitatively, this missing box represented less than 0.1 percent of all the documents that had been requested and delivered. Tens of thousand of pages had been submitted in response to at least twenty separate document requests. In moving this mountain of paper, it was not only plausible but inevitable that some documents would be misplaced.

When they told Bill Clinton about the discovery of the records, he didn't see the problem. The White House took the initiative of bringing the discovery of the papers to the attention of the Office of Independent Counsel (OIC) as soon as they resurfaced. Logically, no one could conclude that this was an attempt to obstruct justice. "Why would we be producing them now, if we had been trying to hide them and obstruct? That doesn't make any sense,"[53] said Clinton. If they had been determined to hide the billing records, they could have destroyed them or simply not notified Starr of their discovery.

Hillary was scheduled to begin the tour for her book *It Takes a Village*. However, the firestorm created by the box in the attic overwhelmed media coverage of her book. On January 8, William Safire declared in his column in *The New York Times* that Hillary was a "congenital liar." He predicted "jail terms" for all those who helped hide the "damning records."[54]

On January 22, 1996, Ken Starr issued a subpoena for Hillary to testify before the grand jury. He could have taken her testimony at the White House, as he had done three times before, but he wanted to haul her before the grand jury like a common criminal, forcing her to do the humiliating perp walk past the cameras outside the courthouse.

The Starr media machine pronounced that the first lady was on the verge of indictment. "A top official with the investigation" told *New Yorker* writer Jane Mayer that the odds of Hillary being indicted were "fifty-fifty."[55]

Before her testimony, Hillary was *fingerprinted* at the White House.

For Hillary this was the psychological nadir. The public humiliation, the unfairness, were too much to bear. "I can't take this anymore," Hillary said. "How can I go on? How can I?"[56]

Screwing up her courage, she waded through the crowd of reporters outside the courthouse with as much dignity as she could preserve.

Inside the courtroom Starr's prosecutors questioned her for four hours: What did she know about the missing box, and when did she know it? But, strangely enough, they didn't ask her one question about the contents of those "damning records," not one.

Why?

Because there was nothing even remotely damning in the billing records. Just the opposite. Hillary had always claimed that her work for Madison had been minimal, a few hours a month. And the records showed exactly that. The papers were *exonerating*.

I was able to interview an attorney who worked for Ken Starr in the OIC. He had never before given an interview, and he was very nervous about talking to me, fearing retribution from his Republican colleagues if his identity became known. He wanted no record that could connect him to his comments. He refused to let me tape-record him, and wouldn't communicate by e-mail, which leaves a record, or by phone, which could be taped covertly. To have our secret meeting, I had to fly to a location I won't disclose. I got in the tongue-in-cheek habit of calling him Deep Throat, after the famous ultrasecret source who tipped off Woodward and Bernstein about Watergate. My "Deep Throat" gave me access to the firsthand observations of an insider in Starr's office. However, unlike the Deep Throat of Watergate fame, my source simply served to reconfirm and reinforce the well-known public record of Starr's demeanor and actions as Whitewater special prosecutor.

In Carl Bernstein's 2007 biography of Hillary, *A Woman in Charge*, he revealed that Hillary was genuinely terrified she would be indicted by Ken Starr. Indeed, David Kendall, who served as the Clintons' private attorney, told Hillary that "her indictment was a strong possibility, that Starr would stop at nothing."[57]

Hillary had good reason to worry, Deep Throat told me:

"We had her indictment in the computer ready to go. It wasn't a question of if, but when. We had a betting pool in Starr's office on the day we would indict Hillary."

· KEN STARR UNRESIGNS ·

Mark Tuohey, Starr's deputy prosecutor, told me that by the time he left the OIC in the fall of 1995, it was his impression that they were ready to wrap up the investigation. "The final conclusions were drawn, and most of the investigative work was completed by the time I left," he said. Like Fiske before them, this second investigation had found nothing: "What we concluded was that there was no wrongdoing—period—by the Clintons or anybody else." Sam Dash, Starr's ethics adviser, told Starr: "He had nothing."

"Zero plus zero plus zero equals zero," said Dash. "Your job is over," he told Starr. It was time to "close up shop."[58]

Deep Throat said, "It was obvious that there was nothing there. The guy [Clinton] wasn't venal. He obviously didn't give a shit about money. He didn't even own a house. He lived on a meager government salary. The guy didn't have a pot to piss in. This is not the portrait of someone who is financially corrupt."

Though in reality Starr had nothing, he had kept the investigation in the news cycle for years by constantly claiming that he was on the verge of a major breakthrough. On October 12, 1995, a month after Tuohey left Starr's office believing that the investigation was over, *The Washington Post* reported that Ken Starr had written a letter to the Whitewater committee claiming that his "investigation had reached a critical phase."[59] A year later, with no more to show, Ken Starr told an audience at the Detroit Economic Club that his investigation was at a "critical juncture now."[60] On December 2, 1996, *Newsweek* reported that according to Starr the Whitewater probe was at a "critical stage."

One reason for the smoke and mirrors was that, even if they couldn't pin anything on Clinton, the appearance of scandal might be enough to stop him from being reelected. However, in 1996, after Clinton was re-elected, even Ken Starr was finally ready to throw in the towel. On February 17, 1997—Presidents' Day—he announced that he would be leaving the independent counsel's office to take a job as dean of Pepperdine University's law school and its new School of Public Policy. Even Ted Olson admitted that his friend wouldn't be quitting "if he was about to embark on a prosecution of historic proportions."[61]

Five days later Starr would rescind his resignation.

It was discovered that Starr's Pepperdine job was funded, in its entirety, by a million-dollar contribution from Richard Mellon Scaife. "In effect, Starr's salary will be coming out of Scaife's pocket," noted James Carville. It certainly looked like Scaife was providing his man with a golden parachute, and this embarrassing exposure of Starr's link to the vast right-wing conspiracy caused him to issue a public denial: "I have never met or talked with Richard Mellon Scaife. I have had no arrangement—implicit, explicit, direct, or indirect—with him."[62]

But far more wounding to Starr were the cries of outrage that came from his conservative allies, who saw him as jumping ship in the middle of battle. In a column entitled "The Big Flinch," William Safire blasted Starr as a "craven . . . wimp" with a "warped sense of duty" who had brought "shame on the legal profession."[63] Senator Arlen Specter complained to Starr that his departure would have a "devastating" impact on the investigation. Starr was now a victim of his own false advertising. As he had led his allies to believe that he was on the verge of taking Clinton down, they now demanded that Starr deliver on his false promise.

Saying he had been "humbled," Starr rescinded his resignation on February 22, 1997.

"I hope and I know he hopes this will be a hiccup and the investigation will go forward," Ted Olson told *The Washington Post*. "I think he grew a lot this week."[64]

In his letter rescinding his acceptance of the position, Starr wrote that as much as he would have liked to go to Pepperdine, "the work of the office however has expanded considerably, and the end is not in sight."[65] Some critics pointed out that Starr actually only deferred his acceptance of the position—making the conflict-of-interest issue with Scaife still a potential problem. In response, Starr then wrote a second letter permanently rescinding his acceptance of the Pepperdine job. But his permanent rescission would, in fact, prove to be only temporary. At the time of this writing Ken Starr holds the position of dean of Pepperdine's law school, the job that he turned down in February 1997. I e-mailed him there requesting an interview, but he did not respond.

On February 23, 1997, the *Chicago Sun-Times* reported, "Ken Starr decides to forgo Pepperdine University and return to his investigation, claiming his investigation has reached a critical phase."[66]

Now Starr was like a trapped animal, desperate and dangerous. He had no case, yet nothing less than Clinton's scalp would satisfy his right-wing supporters. "After Starr had been shamed into staying at his post, his zealous determination to find any criminal wrongdoing by the Clintons became manic," wrote Jeffrey Toobin.[67]

"By hook or by crook, they were going to make the case for impeachment," Deep Throat told me. "They made that decision early on."

Having hit a brick wall in their efforts to prove corruption, the OIC began investigating more fertile ground: Clinton's sex life. Just three weeks after Starr rescinded his resignation, a gossip column in the *New York Post* reported that Starr's men were "closely questioning Arkansas state troopers" who had guarded Clinton "about his personal life." *The Washington Post* reported that "FBI agents and prosecutors working for independent counsel Kenneth W. Starr's Whitewater investigation have questioned Arkansas state troopers in recent months about their knowledge of any extramarital relationships Bill Clinton may have had while he was Arkansas governor." The OIC's official explanation for this new tack was that women Clinton may have had sexual relations with might know something about Whitewater, a transparent cover story. "The nature of the questioning marks a sharp departure from previous avenues of inquiry in the three-year-old investigation, which began as an examination of the Whitewater land development project," wrote *The Washington Post*. Trooper Roger Perry is quoted as saying: "In the past, I thought they were trying to get to the bottom of Whitewater. This last time, I was left with the impression that they wanted to show he was a womanizer."[68]

Starr's office called it their "trooper project." It was more than ironic. The first attack on the Clintons by the Arkansas Project had been an article by David Brock that alleged that Clinton had used state troopers to procure women for him for sex. The OIC was now not just colluding with the Arkansas Project, it was *becoming* the Arkansas Project. The crossbreeding of these two entities produced a monster akin to a highly treatment-resistant strain of a deadly virus that the body politic could not defend against. This Arkansas Project was armed with the full power of the state. David Brock, who broke the original Troopergate story, was just a journalist; Ken Starr had an army of prosecutors, the FBI, an unlimited budget, and a grand jury at his disposal.

In 1949, George Orwell wrote a dystopian novel about a bleak possible future entitled *1984*. In his imagined fascist future world, sex is a crime against the state, and personal behavior is monitored by an army of sex police. His heroes are two lovers caught by the authoritarian government, and tortured into betraying one another. The president and his mistress were about to be captured by the real sex police.

Had Orwell known then what we know now, he might have entitled his novel *1998*.

10

Monica and Bill
A Romantic Tragedy

· SEX AND THE CHARACTER ISSUE ·

I know. This is the chapter everyone has been waiting for—or perhaps dreading. The Monica sexual scandal was flogged by the media so relentlessly that we overdosed on it. A sex scandal is like a car accident: You just can't turn your eyes away, even if you want to. It grabs your attention. And for a year, it seemed, we could attend to nothing else. But attending to something is not the same as understanding it. Perhaps, now that we've recovered from our Monica hangover, we can review what happened in a more thoughtful manner.

I would like to tell you the story of Monica and Bill just one more time, but in a way that you have not heard it before. It is, believe it or not, a very human and even poignant story. It is the story of a love affair.

But before turning to Monica and Bill's story, it is important to first address the broader issue of Clinton's sexuality, and see what it tells us about his character. I have become convinced that much of the conventional wisdom regarding Bill Clinton and sex is deeply flawed.

Bill Clinton's sexuality is as complex as the rest of his personality. Is Clinton a morally reprehensible user of women? Or is he an addict, powerless over his sexual desires? Or is he a hypomanic with a big libido and reduced impulse control? Or, as I suggested in the first chapter, is he acting out his inner Virginia, having witnessed and internalized her serial infidelity? Or, as I suggested in that same chapter, is he perpetually, unconsciously seeking the lost Virginia of his youth, the exciting party girl who left him in the care of his more reliable Hillary-like grandmother? Or is he simply a normal male with abnormal sexual opportunity? Any and all of these explanations can be true simultaneously, as I will try to demonstrate.

Issues surrounding Clinton's sexual behavior, both in general and relative to Monica in particular, have been closely linked to what has been called the "character issue." We have a clear picture in our minds as to what a male serial adulterer is like: someone who heartlessly seduces, exploits, and discards women, using them for his own pleasure with reckless disregard for their feelings. He feels no anxiety, guilt, or remorse about the lies he tells, the rules he breaks, or the people he hurts. It's clear to anyone that people with these traits are not good people. Technically, they demonstrate signs of what we call antisocial personality disorder. Across their lifetimes people with this condition have a fundamental disregard for the rights and well-being of others, whom they view as targets to be exploited. Many womanizers, even if they don't meet the full diagnostic criteria for antisocial personality disorder, still evidence what psychiatrists call "features" of the condition in their character (personality disorders are part of the family of disorders that used to be called "character disorders"). But even mere features are pure poison to character. Most therapists believe that antisocial features, never mind a full-blown antisocial personality disorder, make a patient untreatable—quite literally beyond our saving.

Does Clinton's womanizing point to such antisocial features in his personality? Intuitively, many people would say yes, but I will argue that this is not a correct diagnosis, for at least three reasons. First, Clinton's pattern of illicit relationships in general, and with Monica in particular, does not show the wanton disregard for human feelings we normally associate with womanizers. As hard as it might be to imagine, I will show that Clinton truly cared for Monica. Second, I will show that Clinton's pattern of lying about sex is much more consistent with an addictive disorder than a personality disorder. Being an addict, even when it causes you to do bad things, is not the same as being a fundamentally amoral person. And finally, a few words about male sexuality. I will ask my readers to join me in a thought experiment. What would most men do if they could have sex with virtually *any* woman they wanted?

I. Womanizer with a Heart

Clinton's pattern of adultery does not fit the description of an amoral user of women described above. It is quite different, and for that matter, most unusual. Clinton tends to form mutually felt, caring, romantic attachments with multiple women, many or most of whom he maintains lifetime relationships with even after the sexual relationship is over. Like a chess grand master who can play twenty-five games at a time, he can love many women at one time (including Hillary). Such emotional multitasking would be beyond most people's capacities, but Clinton is not most people.

Jerome Levin, a psychologist who wrote a book about Clinton's alleged sexual addiction, *The Clinton Syndrome,* noted that Clinton does not fit the classic sex addict pattern in one important respect. The attitude of most sex addicts, Levin told me, can be "crudely summarized" as "find them, feel them, fuck them, and forget them." In his research Levin came to the same conclusion as I: "His flings were relationships." Clinton appears to form close emotional bonds with most of the women he sleeps with, and maintains them (Ron Addington told me that some of their biggest campaign contributions in 1974 came from Bill's former lovers). As I mentioned earlier, when I discussed this with his lifetime friend Rose Crane, she gave me a sly look and said, "Bill Clinton never says good-bye." He doesn't want *to* say good-bye. He loves them, and *doesn't* leave them.

This may be the real reason why why Clinton was able to get away with so many affairs. Despite a massive infusion of money, journalists, private eyes, and subpoenas, Clinton's enemies came up with comparatively little evidence for what they knew was a long history of philandering. Why weren't more scorned women eager to seek their revenge on this cad who had used them, especially when they could have made millions by coming forward? Betsey Wright said this of her former boss's many affairs: "Either they didn't happen, or these women are very loyal." Obviously, they did happen, which raises the question: How many lotharios can honestly claim an army of former lovers who are still loyal to them?

Therapists spend a great deal of their time assessing and aiming to improve patients' capacities for deep, authentic, mutually felt intimate relationships. Many psychologists consider this to be the single most important dimension of psychological development, a fundamental measure of both mental and moral health.

There is a paradox here. From the perspective of a psychologist assessing Clinton's character, the presence of real emotional involvement with Monica is an important mitigating factor in evaluating how harshly we should judge his behavior. However, from the perspective of a spouse, it would actually be much more hurtful to Hillary if Bill had indeed had loving feelings for Monica. The classic defense of the philandering husband caught in the act is: "It was just sex. It didn't mean a thing." Lucinda Franks, who interviewed Hillary for *Talk* magazine, explained how Hillary coped with Clinton's pattern of infidelity: "She put these transgressions in a box called lust: it had nothing to do with his profound relationship and love for her."[1] Thus, most likely to protect his marriage, Clinton never challenged the conventional wisdom that he had merely used Monica as a sex object. The great irony here is that to protect Hillary's feelings and his marriage, Clinton may have had to pretend to be a bigger cad than he really was. When he was asked on *60 Minutes* why he had the affair with Lewinsky, his only answer was, "Because I could.

"I think I did something for the worst possible reason—just because I could. I think that's the most, just about the most morally indefensible reason that anybody could have for doing anything. When you do something just because you could . . . I've thought about it a lot. And there are lots of more sophisticated explanations, more complicated psychological explanations. But none of them are an excuse."[2]

Monica later said that what hurt her the most was that it was never acknowledged, either by the press or publicly by Clinton, that they had had a real relationship. "It was a mutual relationship," Lewinsky told Larry King, both "physically" and "emotionally."[3]

Later in this chapter we will review the relationship with Monica, and readers can judge for themselves: Was Clinton just having oral sex or was this a true romance for both parties?

I will argue that Clinton seems to be as addicted to romance as he is to sex. Perhaps that's one of the secrets to his amorous success.

II. When Good People Do Bad Things

The assessment and treatment of personality disorders has been my area of specialization for twenty-five years. As part of my training I completed a postdoctoral fellowship at New York Hospital–Cornell Medical Center, where Otto Kernberg—one of the world's top experts in this field—served as medical director and clinical guru. I have been responsible for teaching psychiatric residents at Johns Hopkins Medical School how to diagnose and treat personality disorders for twenty years, and given something close to a hundred workshops on the topic across the country. In short, my expertise is assessing defects in character.

If Clinton were truly antisocial according to the American Psychiatric Association's *DSM-IV* criteria, the antisocial behavior would need to have manifested itself clearly in childhood and adolescence. "The essential feature of Antisocial Personality Disorder is a pervasive pattern of disregard for, and violation of, the rights of others that begins in childhood or early adolescence and continues until adulthood."[4] I combed through Clinton's developmental history, looking for even the most subtle signs of antisocial features. In addition to reading every published Clinton biography, I interviewed seven of Bill's schoolmates and one of his high school teachers. I found no such evidence. None. In fact, what I found was the polar opposite. The profile that emerged of Bill Clinton was that he was practically the perfect kid. If the Hot Springs class of 1964 had been asked to nominate the graduate *least* likely to be accused of having a character problem as an adult, it most likely would have been Bill Clinton.

The most distinguishing characteristic of antisocial people is their *lack of empathy*. It's easier to do bad things to people if you don't feel their pain. Empathy, according to those who have studied moral behavior, is the fundamental psychological foundation upon which moral structure is built. Clinton, as we have seen, is off the charts on empathy; his cup runneth over with feelings for his fellow man. As you might predict, children who are high in empathy tend to be supermoral adults. Such *altruistic personalities* naturally seek to help others, even when it involves sacrifice or risk and no promise of reward. They are preoccupied with helping humanity. This is *pro*-social behavior, which, as the name implies, is the opposite of antisocial behavior.

From childhood to his current save-the-world work at the Clinton Foundation (which we will explore in the final chapter), Clinton has been a model of the altruistic personality. At eight years old, Clinton brought a boy he met at a bus stop home for Thanksgiving dinner when he learned the boy had no meal to go home to—a classic example of altruistic behavior. And, as I discussed, he took care of his younger half brother like a father, without ever being asked. When Clinton was eleven he began secretly sending part of his allowance every week to Billy Graham. There was no glory in this for him because no one knew about it. He just did it as a good work. "I never told my parents or friends about that." To help strangers he gave not just his money, but his time, volunteering at places like the local hospital, for example. He won numerous awards from local community organizations and was often asked by local civic groups to speak at their functions or chair their fund drives. While most young men revere sports figures, Clinton's heroes and role models were people like Martin Luther King.

What about breaking rules? Did young man Clinton show a pattern of getting in trouble? Not only didn't he have a pattern of breaking rules, I was hard-pressed to find a single example of his breaking one. The Hot Springs class of 1964 was pretty square and wholesome, but even by these standards Clinton was exceptional. One peer described him as "disgustingly responsible."[5] School friend Carolyn Wilson once screamed at Bill: "Don't you ever do anything wrong? You're a teenager. . . . You're supposed to do things wrong!"[6] Wilson told reporters that anyone looking for evidence of misbehavior in his teenage years would come up empty. "You won't find anything bad about him." She was right. Schoolmate Michael Muldoon told me that Bill Clinton "never got into trouble." He couldn't remember one incident. "He did everything right, and never did anything wrong," classmate Phil Jamison told me.

David Leopoulos recalled that "the worst thing Bill and I ever did was throw acorns at cars." Even that minor mischief was put to a stop when a man got out of his car and chased them home, which led to a stern lecture by Virginia. A few times Bill made crank calls to the madam of the local bordello, Maxine (this was Hot Springs, after all). "I was with him when he made the crank phone call, cracking up," said Leopoulos. "But yah, that's as far as it went. I can't think of anything else wrong that he ever did. I know it's hard to believe, but it's the truth."

As unbelievable as it sounds given his reputation for tardiness as an adult, nobody could even remember young Bill having a problem with lateness. "If you were ten seconds late, you had to go to the principal's office," said Jamison. "If Clinton had a lateness habit, it would have been obvious."

There was one incident of misbehavior that Maraniss wrote about: "One day Clinton, Jamison, and Ronnie Cecil escorted their teacher [a new physics teacher] to the equipment closet in the back of the room and locked him inside. He banged and pleaded to be let out, but they pretended the lock was stuck and talked among themselves till the bell rang."

When I had lunch with Phil Jamison at the Ritz-Carlton in Pentagon City, near Washington, D.C., I sprung this incident on him, thinking, "Aha, at last, I've caught young Clinton red-handed." But my excitement was premature. "I don't actually remember which one of us shut the door, but it wasn't Bill, that I can tell you for sure. Bill wasn't the ringleader. We were. We did it. He was just there." True, Clinton didn't spring up to free the teacher either, but that would have made him a teacher's pet.

According to teachers as well, he was the ideal kid. "Young Bill Clinton was one of those students that history teachers pray to have in their class," said Paul Root.[7] Virgil Spurlin, his music director and mentor, spoke very directly to the character issue when he said: "He always let his Christian character and beliefs take priority in his dealings with others. He never disappointed me. Not one time."[8]

Was young man Clinton faking it? Some have suggested that his apparent goodness was mostly a facade, what some psychoanalysts have called a "false self." Biographer Nigel Hamilton puts forth this view, suggesting that Clinton's appearance of goodness was "goody-goodness," an exaggerated caricature of goodness adopted for defensive purposes. "Billy had drawn on the mantle of churchy goodness, charm, precocious sociability, and striving for excellence at school. Once assumed, the mantle of goodness, he found, became him, inspiring widespread approval; indeed, it became a second skin rather than apparel, since he could never take it off again."[9] Clinton himself admits that he emphasized the caring, happy, gregarious aspects of his personality, sometimes to hide the deeper feelings of anger and shame that simmered beneath. "I was raised in a culture where you put on a happy face and don't reveal your pain and agony," he said.[10] No one was more conscious than he that he looked more perfect than he truly was. Thus, for defensive purposes, Clinton did overemphasize this aspect of himself. That much is true. But that is very different from saying his good self was false.

Kids can pick out a Goody Two-shoes in a second, yet none of Clinton's peers saw him that way. "Bill was no Goody Two-shoes," said Jamison. Tommy Caplan's first impression of his new Georgetown roommate was that indeed he must be a goody-goody. "There ain't nobody anywhere in this world this good—nobody." But when he got to know Clinton, Caplan had to admit he was wrong. "Until I saw how genuine he is, I could not trust him. . . . I just did not believe a human being could be this good."[11] "Bill wasn't trying to be a goody-goody," Leopoulos told me. "He was just good."

So, what happened? How did Beaver Cleaver become Slick Willy? "The most popular theory among mental health professionals was that the President was a sex addict," wrote Gail Sheehy.[12] This is one area where the conventional wisdom is not wrong. Hillary's pastor, Reverend Ed Mathews, who provided informal pastoral counseling to the Clintons, had no doubt that Clinton was a sex addict. He revealed that Clinton himself believed this: "It's a sickness, just like drug addiction or alcoholism, and he knows that."[13] Indeed, Clinton himself obliquely acknowledged as much when in the mid-eighties he had to attend family therapy sessions as part of Roger Jr.'s court-mandated drug treatment. "We're all addicted to something," Clinton said to a close friend who understood that Clinton was talking about his sexual compulsion.

Is sexual addiction a real addiction? The psychiatric profession has not entirely agreed one way or another on this question, but clearly there are behavioral similarities between sex addicts and substance addicts. What makes sexual excess an addiction? The addict feels out of control, unable to resist the impulse. He does it more and more, centering increasing amounts of his life around the addictive behavior, and taking escalating risks, despite the potential for destructive consequences. "Repeated efforts to quit" is one of the diagnostic criteria for addiction. As we shall see when we tell the Monica story, Clinton was desperately conflicted about the affair and tried to break it off several times. He confessed to her that their relationship was part of a pattern of behavior he had been struggling to control for many years. In simple terms, Monica was a relapse.

In addition to behavioral similarities, there is a common underlying neurological basis to sexual and chemical addictions. Food, sex, and addictive drugs work on the same reward centers in the brain.[14] There is a pleasure center in the oldest part of the brain that we find, not just in humans, but in almost every species. Whatever vehicle they use to stimulate that reward center—sex, drugs, or bungee jumping—the addict becomes addicted to the high itself, which has a final common pathway in this part of the brain.

Does addiction cause people to do bad things? Yes. "All addicts lie," a friend who goes to AA told me, and he's right. Addicts must lie to actively maintain their addiction and keep functioning. The need for secrecy and deception with sexual addiction is particularly high, for obvious reasons. Studies of alcoholics show that an astoundingly high 80 percent commit antisocial acts. If you test people who are actively alcoholic or drug addicted on a psychological test called the Minnesota Multiphasic Personality Inventory (MMPI), as a group they score very high on the "psychopathic deviance" scale, a measure of antisocial traits. "The question is: Is it causative or consequential?" asked Jerome Levin. "Are they alcoholics because they're no good to begin with? Or, under the pressure of addiction, do good people start to do bad things?"

Levin argued that the data suggests that "in approximately 80% of the cases it's driven by the addiction. If you look at average MMPI psychopathic deviance scores for people who get into recovery, they come close to approximating the scores of the general population, with the notable exception of about 20 percent of the addicts, who really have antisocial personality disorders. I think that's absolutely the case with people that suffer sexual addiction or compulsion. Probably a lot of the antisocial stuff you see is secondary to the addiction."

When people bring up the character issue, they are almost always making reference to Clinton's excessive sexual behavior, and his lies about it. But if Clinton were one of the fundamentally dishonest 20 percent, he would have manifested his antisocial traits by adolescence, at the latest. Thus, the only logical conclusion is that Clinton's sexual addiction has led to immorality, but he is not a fundamentally immoral person—just the opposite.

Addictions are also progressive. Over time, an alcoholic drinks more, functions more poorly, and behaves more recklessly. Indeed, this was Clinton's pattern, with his sexual acting out peaking during the end of his tenure as governor: "As the 1980s wore on, his marital delinquencies became more frequent and flagrant," wrote Sheehy. His acting out increased. He became "very careless."[15]

In 1989 the Clinton marriage hit its nadir. For the first time Hillary was discussing divorce with her close friends. And "this was the first time she acknowledged knowing about the affairs," a close friend said.[16] In the summer of 1989, Bill and Hillary had a "come to Jesus meeting," in which Bill repented. "In the end, they made a commitment to work and save their marriage," said Betsey Wright, who believed that Bill didn't *want* to be unfaithful. Hillary's minister, Reverend Mathews, said, "At that point maybe they did get some counseling."[17]

When the Lewinsky affair was revealed, Hillary harkened back to that 1989 watershed: "I thought this was resolved ten years ago." Possibly alluding to his having worked on the sexual issue in some kind of therapy, she said, "I thought he had conquered it. I thought he understood it. But he didn't go deep enough or work hard enough."[18]

III. A Normal Male with Abnormal Sexual Opportunity

The primary mission of every organism is to propagate its genes. Once you accept this basic evolutionary premise, the mysterious war between the sexes starts to make a lot more sense—and so does Clinton's sexual behavior. A male is hardwired for promiscuity. To maximize his reproductive success—the only scorecard nature cares about—the male wants to spread his seed around as widely as possible. Males are programmed to take advantage of sexual opportunities—not to turn them down. That's not to imply that males don't have the opportunity to make choices consistent with their values and commitments. Biology does not have to be destiny, but underestimating its power would be a mistake.

On the other hand, females, it has long been thought, need to be more selective for precisely the inverse reason. They are limited in the number of offspring they can bear, so indiscriminate promiscuity would be self-defeating to their reproductive success. They are looking for a mate, not just a date, and a mate who will both provide good genes and provide protection and resources for the growing child.

Interestingly, however, relatively recent research among supposedly monogamous species of both animals and humans has found surprisingly high rates of female infidelity. When females do cheat, they are most likely to do so at a time when they are fertile, and it is almost always with a male who is more dominant than their mate. Power is "the ultimate aphrodisiac," as Henry Kissinger once said. What's going on here? It is often in the female's reproductive interest to have sex surreptitiously with a more dominant male—who presumably has better genes—and let her cuckolded mate provide resources to raise the offspring. A pair of researchers in Britain performed genetic tests on every man, woman, and child in a block of flats in Liverpool, and found that more than 20 percent of the children had not been fathered by their supposed biological fathers. They repeated the test in a more affluent neighborhood and got the same results.[19] It is the most basic of equations. Powerful men attract women, including married ones, for very sound evolutionary reasons. "You can argue that Clinton's behavior is just alpha male behavior," conceded Levin. Thus, it is no coincidence that Clinton's sexual career really took off when his political career did.

Bill Clinton has always been attractive to women. In high school, girls were constantly slipping notes to his friend Rose Crane, wondering if he liked them. Carolyn Staley, who lived next door, noticed that when her friends visited her they parked their cars near the hedge separating her house from Clinton's, hoping he might spy them from his window. Even in high school Clinton had his uncanny ability to connect and make a girl feel special and appreciated: "Whenever you were with Bill, I don't care who you were, he had a way of making you feel like you were the only one on this earth," said one woman who dated him. He was always a mesmerizing talker. Virginia Clinton recalled, "He always had the girls carrying his books home for him after school, and he'd be giving lectures and talking to them about the things they'd learned at school."[20] But at the same time Clinton isn't remembered by his classmates as someone who dated more than average, and when he did date, he often brought his little brother along.

At college and law school he was known as someone who could juggle a lot of girlfriends, but again, he didn't stand out because of that.

When Clinton was a student at Oxford, preparing for a political career, he anticipated that his sexual prospects might change, and he worried about how it might affect him. He told a female friend: "Politics gives guys so much power and such big egos they tend to behave badly toward women. I hope I never get into that."[21] He was right to worry.

It was the *combination* of Clinton's considerable personal charms and political power that dramatically multiplied his sexual temptations. Everything changed in 1974, when he ran for Congress. He became a minor celebrity, and masses of women developed crushes on him. His campaign volunteers were disproportionately young female college students, and the girls treated Clinton like a "rock star" and "worshipped the ground the man walked on," recalled one woman.[22] "There were a lot of young women. I guess you'd call them groupies today," said Jim Daugherty, who served as one of Clinton's drivers during the 1974 campaign. One reporter who visited the Clinton campaign headquarters was struck that the mostly female Clintonites seemed "like members of a cult. . . . These are the kind of people who stand in the rain at high school football games to distribute campaign leaflets. The workers are influenced by the Dexedrine-like effects of campaigning white line fever. . . . They constantly mutter the candidate's name in hushed tones: 'Bill thinks, Bill feels, Bill does . . .'"[23] Once Bill Clinton became a candidate in 1974, "all of a sudden all those women appeared," a Yale Law School classmate recalled. Putting it crudely, "for the first time in his life he could have all the pussy he wanted."[24]

After losing the 1974 campaign, Clinton would become governor four years later—the official alpha male of Arkansas. It is not a coincidence that it was during the period when he was governor that his sexual activity hit its peak. Clinton's power, in combination with his charm, intelligence, and warmth, made him sexually irresistible to a large number of women. "Women would just swoon. He really is irresistible to women," said Ann McCoy, who worked as his assistant in the governor's mansion. Women hurled themselves at Clinton, literally. "Keeping the Van Buren County rodeo queen from throwing herself in the back of the limo was always a problem for the staff," Arkansas journalist Gene Lyons told me.

It is interesting to note that the demographic group who judge Clinton's sexual behavior most harshly is not that of women, but of middle-aged white males. One has to wonder if there is not some element of sexual jealousy, at least unconsciously, in their disapproval. Sexual competition for mates between males is serious business. From an evolutionary point of view, it is as important as physical survival itself, perhaps more so. How could normal males not be jealous? As Gene Lyons put it: "One day I finally understood why so many of these old guys hated him. I was in a restaurant and Bill Clinton just strutted in, and that really is the right word, he strutted. And there was just something about the look on his face that said, 'I'm getting all the nooky,' and then I understood: Of course they hate him."

In 2006, I gave a talk about hypomania among entrepreneurs to a Southern business group. When I mentioned to one of the organizers that

I was working on a biography of Bill Clinton, the man suddenly became stiff and the tone of his voice became stern: "Some of us have the moral fiber to control ourselves."

I remember looking at this straitlaced, gray-haired, unremarkable-looking man and thinking sarcastically: "I can only imagine what a daily temptation that must be for you." I'm not trying to belittle this man, or suggest that he never had his chances to commit adultery, which he may have forgone for all the right reasons. But I can assure you that rodeo queens were not throwing themselves into the back of his car on a daily basis.

Can we judge Clinton without walking a mile with his libido? What would most men do if they were irresistible and could have sex with almost any woman they wanted? While an admirable moral minority would consistently resist such constant temptation, I think we can all agree that most men would fail this test, at least some of the time. Even though they might feel terribly guilty about it, they would have sex with multiple women for the simplest reason of all:

Because they could.

· MONICA AND BILL ·

We've heard the salacious stories, but how many people truly understand the real relationship between Bill and Monica? Of course, only two people know what really took place: Bill and Monica. And here we are fortunate, in that one of them wrote a memoir about the affair. Many reviewers dismissed Monica's book as coming from the point of view of a dramatic young girl in love, fantasizing about her relationship with the president. But I don't think that's fair. The book is thoughtful and penned (as told to) by veteran biographer Andrew Morton, who is certainly no hysteric. Most important, the book is rich enough in factual detail that the readers can form their own opinions. In this regard it's important to note that even the most hostile book reviewers did not accuse Monica of factual inaccuracy. As a psychologist who listens to people's stories all day long, I'm constantly having to separate reality from fantasy. One of my tricks is to ask a lot of very concrete, standard journalistic who, what, where, why, and when–type questions, till I can create a mental video depicting who did and said what to whom, and how the interaction transpired over time. People don't tend to lie about those sorts of details. As far as I know, only once in my career did I have a patient actually make up elaborate stories from whole cloth that fooled me entirely. But if it's hard to fool one therapist, imagine how much harder it must be to fool the whole world. Surely, if Monica had made up stories in her memoir she would have gotten caught. As with Virginia Clinton's memoir, a careful reading can tell us a lot even with the distortions and evasions. Fair warning to the reader: We will need to review some of the details of what took place between them sexually to understand the true meaning of this relationship.

When the world learned of the relationship between Monica and Bill the question on everyone's mind was: "How could he have done something so stupid?" The core of the Clinton enigma. In this chapter we've already reviewed some of the reasons. Because he was hypomanic, a sex addict, the child of a serial adulterer, and a powerful man who could. As a psychologist, there is another question I always ask when someone develops a symptom, acts out, or relapses: Why now? Was there any precipitant that could have triggered the behavior?

One possibility was the death of Virginia.

The last time Clinton saw his mother alive, she was leaving for a trip to Las Vegas. As Clinton kissed Virginia good-bye he thought: "She was a marvel, still beautiful at seventy, even after a mastectomy, chemotherapy treatments that took all her hair and forced her to wear a wig, and daily blood transfusions that would have put most people in bed."[25] Clinton's comment on her beauty, even in this rather ghastly state, is striking. Virginia had always been his elusive erotic ideal. He spent his early years longing for her, admiring her loveliness, thinking of her every time the phone rang or the train whistle blew.

"I knew it was coming, but I wasn't ready to let her go."[26]

Clinton lost his mother again, this time for the last time.

Eighteen months later he would meet a young girl who bore a striking physical resemblance to Virginia (the more psychologically minded members of the press commented on this often), and whose exuberant energy reminded Clinton of her spirit as well. More than once Clinton would tell Monica that she reminded him of Virginia.

Admittedly, eighteen months between Virginia's death and the start of the relationship with Monica might appear to strain the word "precipitant." Normally a precipitant is closer in time to the behavior it provokes. But this was such a profound loss for Clinton, and one that reopened his deepest early wounds, that I'm certain it influenced his state of mind. This major life event made him uniquely vulnerable.

If Clinton saw his mother in Monica, Monica saw a needy little boy in Bill. More than once, Monica describes her impression of Clinton as a "lost little boy," an odd description for a man more than twice her age who also happened to be the most powerful man on earth. Intuitively, Monica had a powerful sense that there was a role reversal at some level between them, even as she was at a loss to explain it. What Monica sensed, but couldn't articulate, was that psychologically the ghost of Virginia inhabited their relationship powerfully. Monica was Virginia, and Clinton was the little boy who longed for her.

When the young intern came to Washington, in the summer of 1995, she was awed to be at the White House, but she couldn't understand why "tons and tons" of women working there had crushes on Clinton. He had a "big red nose and coarse wiry-looking gray hair" and he was "an old guy."[27] However, that impression changed the first time she met him in person. When the band struck up "Hail to the Chief" and Clinton appeared: "I remember being very taken aback. My heart skipped a beat, my breathing came a little faster, and there were butterflies fluttering in my tummy. He had a glow about him that was magnetic. He exudes sexual energy. I thought to myself: 'Now I see what all the girls are talking about.'"[28]

On August 9, she had her first contact with him, on a rope line. He "gave me the full Bill Clinton." When it was time to shake her hand "the rest of the crowd disappeared and we shared an intense but brief sexual exchange. He undressed me with his eyes." She said the president later told her what he was thinking in that moment: "I knew that one day I would kiss you."[29]

She met him again not long afterward, on the White House lawn at his forty-ninth birthday party. "He looked deep into my eyes and I was hooked." As he moved off, his arm casually, but intentionally she thought, brushed against her breast. Monica hung around the party till almost all the guests had left. As the president turned to go, Monica impulsively blew him a kiss, and he threw back his head in laughter.

It was the government shutdown in November 1995 that created the circumstances that facilitated their relationship. The White House was down to a skeleton staff, and there was the giddy atmosphere of a slumber party. Monica was one of the few federal employees allowed to work because, as an intern, she was unpaid. Interns were not normally allowed to enter the center of power, where the most senior members of the administration worked, but they were short staffed. So on November 15, Monica found herself working in the office of the chief of staff. Clinton passed her desk several times that day.

In a bold act, now famous, Monica made the first move. When she was sure no one else was looking, she put her hands on her hips, and with her thumbs lifted her jacket to show him a fleeting glimpse of her thong panties. Flashing a sex addict with thong panties is a bit like waving a red flag in front of a bull. It was a temptation Clinton would fail to resist.

Later that evening Monica passed by the office of George Stephanopoulos. Clinton was there alone, and said to her: "Come on in here for a second." They chatted for a while, making conversation, and then Monica blurted out: "You know, I have a really big crush on you."

She recalls that he "hesitated for a moment." We can only speculate about what passed through Clinton's mind in that moment of hesitation, but it was most likely some thought warning him that what he was about to do was wrong and risky.

"Come into the back office," he said.[30]

Monica's memory of their first embrace is no doubt colored by her own romantic feelings, but it is nonetheless revealing. "I remember looking at him and seeing such a different person than the one I had expected to see. There was such a softness and tenderness about him, his eyes were very soul searching, very wanting, very needing, and very loving. There was, too, a sadness about him I hadn't expected to see."[31] While the reader would expect Clinton to be warm and exciting, it is a bit of a surprise to us, as well as to Monica, to discover that he is also needy and sad.

They talked. Clinton told her that she was beautiful, and that her energy lit up the room. He asked if he could kiss her. It was "soft, deep, romantic. It was wonderful." Two thoughts competed for her attention: "I can't believe this is happening" and "What an incredible, sensual kisser!" While he stroked her face and hair, Monica told him that she had participated in an affair with a married man before, and she understood the rules. "I didn't want him to be worried. I wanted him to be comfortable with me. I wanted him to trust me."[32]

Later that night, at 10:00 P.M., they met again in Stephanopoulos's office. This time, their kissing became sexual, and Monica, as we all later learned, began giving him oral sex. During the encounter the president took a call from a congressman while Monica was pleasuring him, an incident that naturally led to many jokes when it was revealed by Starr. "People have made it seem so demeaning for me but it wasn't, it was exciting and the irony is that I had the first orgasm of the relationship."[33] This passage is revealing in several respects. First, it is important to note that Monica did not feel demeaned by her relationship with Clinton, rather it was the public ridicule that was intolerable to her.

Finally, there's a very important piece of information to consider: Clinton did not allow himself to have an orgasm with Monica on this occasion, nor would he for many months. More than any other single fact, this is telling evidence that Clinton was deeply conflicted about what he was doing. We have rarely heard how intense a struggle he waged against his impulses, how guilty he felt, and how often he tried to apply the brakes. "The spirit is willing but the flesh is weak," wrote St. Paul, "and I do the very thing I will not to do."

Sins of the flesh, the most common of human failings, are just like that. Like St. Paul, Clinton was doing the very thing he tried to will himself not to do, and so in this weird way he both did it and didn't do it, by receiving oral sex but denying himself an orgasm with his partner. All of this would make perfect sense to Freud, who saw all neuroses as the expressions of inner conflict, and all symptoms as "compromise formations" between an impulse—usually a sexual one—and an internal prohibition.

There was another indicator that the relationship was about more than sex. Gift giving would become an important part of their relationship. Monica took it upon herself to spruce up Clinton's image, and shopped for hours to buy him a silk hand-stitched Zegna tie from Italy. She left it with his secretary, Betty Currie. Monica was pleasantly surprised when Currie called her to Clinton's office while he was visiting Ireland. Clinton had had a picture taken of himself wearing the tie, and Betty said he wanted her to know that he "loved" it. When he returned he had her come to the office, and he signed the picture: "To Monica Lewinsky, Thanks for the nice tie, Bill Clinton." He complimented her on the weight she had lost. "He could be so adorable," she said. "The sweet-little-boy side to him was the part I fell in love with."[34]

January 1996 would be the most intense period in their relationship. On January 7, Washington was socked with a blizzard. Clinton called Monica at home that morning, and they arranged to meet. Their assignation in the Oval Office felt like their "first date."[35] They were once again intimate, in the bathroom of his inner office. While Ken Starr would focus in humiliating detail on their sexual contacts, Monica says it was the emotional side of the relationship that mattered most to her. "I told him he was like a ray of sunshine that made plants grow faster and that made colors more vibrant."

In their next meeting, Clinton said something that surprised her:

"You have no idea what a gift it is to me to spend time with you and talk to you. I cherish the time we spend together. It's very lonely here, and people don't really understand that."[36] We could simply dismiss this as idle flattery, but I think that is incorrect. Clinton could have said any one of a million flattering things, and so his specific choice of words is revealing. Clinton describes longing for her out of a deep feeling of loneliness. The Virginia-shaped hole in his heart was a vacuum crying out to be filled, just as it had when he first lost her as a young boy. It was this part of him that hungered for Monica. On this occasion she was once again struck: "There was such a little boy, a childish quality about him."[37]

Indeed, in his exuberant appreciation of her, Clinton acted more like a "lovesick teenager" full of "boyish ardor" than president of the United States. He frequently complimented her on her beauty, her energy, and her mind, and seemed fascinated and amused by everything she had to say. When she passed by the Oval Office returning from the staff mess, Clinton waved enthusiastically at her. Other visitors, thinking he was waving at them, waved back. When she got to her desk he called her just to say how good she looked.

At one point Monica asked in a lighthearted way if his real interest wasn't just sex. The president's eyes *filled with tears*, she said. The idea seemed to shock and hurt him. " 'I don't ever want you to feel that way,' " she reported him saying. " 'That's not what this is.' "[38]

We might expect a practiced philanderer to deny that his only interest was sex. He might offer a compliment, a reassurance, a hug. But to *cry*? This suggests that Clinton's real emotions were certainly involved. Even professional actors find it highly difficult to cry on demand. More specifically, it reveals the part of Clinton that felt most connected to Monica, the needy inner child. When she dismissed the relationship as mere sex, even in a lighthearted way, Clinton felt a childlike sense of loss, and had a childlike emotional response.

Monica continued to buy him ties, and his wearing them became a hidden form of intimate communication between them. Invariably, after they had been together, the next day he would wear one of her ties.

"I love it when you wear one of my ties," Monica said, "because then I know that I am close to your heart."[39]

At a rally in Virginia, someone asked him where he got his tie, and he responded, "A girl with a lot of style gave it to me."[40]

But even as he acted like a teenager in the grips of puppy love, Clinton suffered the guilt of an older married man. On Presidents' Day Clinton told her that they had to end the affair. He said that he just felt too guilty, and didn't want to hurt Hillary and Chelsea. He wanted to work at his marriage. And he didn't want to hurt Monica.

"I don't want to be like that schmuck up in Oregon," he said, comparing himself to the married man who first broke Monica's heart. It wasn't that he didn't like her. "You know, if I was twenty-five years old and not married, I'd have you on the floor back there in three seconds right now. But you will understand when you get older."[41] He gave her a farewell hug and promised they would still be friends.

In the ensuing weeks Monica intentionally used the "well-worn feminine tactic of feigning lack of interest to stimulate attention."[42] She greeted him with formal reserve when she saw him in the hall, and the gesture had "the desired effect," because he began calling her, and six weeks after he broke up with her, they were back together. Repeated efforts to quit is one of the signs of addiction, and Clinton would repeatedly try to quit the affair with Monica.

To those who worked in the White House, it certainly seemed like this young intern was spending too much time around the president. It was common that young female staffers wanted to get too close to Clinton. They were called "clutches," and Monica appeared to be one of them. Evelyn Lieberman, deputy chief of staff, told Monica's boss, Tim Keating, "I want her out of here," citing her "overfamiliarity" as the reason for transferring her out of the White House.[43] On April 5, 1996, Keating told her she was being transferred to the Pentagon. Monica went home and cried herself to sleep. "I was hysterical all weekend," she recalled. "All I did was cry and eat pizzas and sweets."[44]

Clinton was upset, too. On April 7, he complained to Monica with the plaintive tone of a boy who had lost his mother: "Why did they have to take you away from me?"[45]

On the surface this helpless cry seems out of place. Surely the most powerful man in the world could have worked something out if he was determined to meet his lover. But psychologically, it makes complete sense: Clinton was unconsciously repeating his relationship with Virginia through Monica, and being abandoned in a way he could not control was part of that script.

Though they had no physical contact for ten months, the emotional intensity of their relationship did not abate. Clinton called Monica often and spoke with her long into the night. They also engaged in phone sex on about half a dozen occasions. This, too, was obviously a compromise formation, a way to both be sexual and not be sexual at the same time—a kind of safe sex. For the most part, however, it seems that it was the emotional bond that kept Clinton calling. The content of their conversations covered "everything under the sun." Clinton confided intimate things about himself. "We're a lot alike," he told her, "because we both had pain in our childhoods." This chapter in the relationship with Monica is the most concrete proof that Clinton was not simply using Monica for sex, because he wasn't getting any. Clinton was getting romantic stimulation from their phone calls, which suggests both that he truly had feelings for her, and that, as stated earlier, Clinton is as much addicted to romance as he is to sex, if not more so.

Andrew Morton, who wrote Monica's as-told-to memoir, noted that this period in their relationship smashes many of the myths about Clinton. "So when, in emotional disarray, Monica Lewinsky left the White House in April 1996, it would have been natural, if there is truth in the persistent rumors that he is a serial seducer, for him to have effortlessly closed the door on that episode in his life. With Monica Lewinsky banished to the Pentagon, Clinton could have suavely moved on to the next intern, or whoever, to take his fancy. That he did not do so offers a different perspective on the character of the man and the nature of the relationship."[46] More than as "a mere sexual plaything," Clinton had "a deeper need" for Monica.[47]

Even in this phase of their relationship, Clinton was reliving a significant part of his childhood. When he was a youngster, for two years the phone was his primary mode of contact with the mother he longed for so desperately. Every time the phone rang in his grandparents' home, he urgently hoped it was Virginia. And for ten months the phone was

Clinton's only link to Monica. He called every four to seven days in the first few months after Monica left the White House, until the reelection campaign made that frequency of calling unfeasible.

"He was so good about calling," wrote Monica.[48]

When Monica asked Clinton if it was painful for him to be facing his first electoral campaign without his mom, Clinton appreciated her sensitivity, and once again commented on how much Monica reminded him of Virginia: "She would have liked you," he told her, "you are very much alike."[49]

On occasion they would see each other at public functions. At one event in May 1996, as he was leaving the room, he pointed to her and mouthed: "I miss you." (Amusingly, a former male staffer standing next to Monica thought Clinton was talking to him, and said he missed him, too.)

The other reason that Clinton had passively accepted the forced separation from Monica is that he was trying to control his sexual acting out. On one occasion in September, the president phoned from Florida during the reelection campaign. Monica asked when they were going to consummate their relationship properly by having sexual intercourse. Clinton responded that he was not going to have sex with her. Again, Clinton was struggling to maintain his sexual boundaries while staying emotionally close to Monica—the opposite of how the relationship has been portrayed. Monica was hurt and angry. Clinton became angry in return. "If you don't want me to call you anymore, just say so."[50]

Monica stopped pushing the issue.

For Valentine's Day, Monica put a quote from *Romeo and Juliet* anonymously in *The Washington Post,* dedicated to "Handsome," her nickname for Clinton. Monica's allusion to Shakespeare's romantic tragedy about two lovers who come to grief because of outside political forces was more prescient than either of them could have realized.

Yet one more time, Clinton tried to end it, this time saying he didn't want to hurt her: "You have been hurt so much by so many men. I don't want to hurt you all like the other men in your life have."[51]

But the conversation continued, and they ended up having phone sex again.

Clinton had invited Monica to the White House to attend his weekly radio address on February 28, 1997. She wore a sexy dark blue dress. For the first time in ten months they were alone together. The sexual tension must have been incredibly intense. They exchanged gifts. He handed her a small box decorated with gold stars. Inside was a blue glass hat pin he had promised her. But the gift Monica would treasure most was a copy of *Leaves of Grass* by Walt Whitman.

They retired to the bathroom, where they kissed. And he pulled away.

"I don't want to get addicted to you," he said, acknowledging that he was battling an addiction. "And I don't want you to get addicted to me."

"It was much too late for that," thought Monica. She was deeply in love.

One of the most telling aspects of this year-and-a-half-long affair is that Clinton—the sex addict—had yet to experience an orgasm with his lover. If this relationship was just one more transitory casual pleasure, Clinton would have to be considered the most inefficient Don Juan in history. Monica told Clinton that she "cared about him," and desperately wanted him to trust her enough to share this intimate experience with her. Ironically, that night would be the night that Clinton would finally allow himself to let go, and this one moment of release would spell their doom.

Monica went home on cloud nine. But Clinton later said, in his grand jury testimony, "I was sick after it was over, and I was pleased at that time that it had been nearly a year since any inappropriate contact had occurred with Ms. Lewinsky. I promised myself it wasn't going to happen again."[52]

When Monica got undressed that night, she threw her blue Gap dress in the back of the closet. She lived on twenty-five thousand dollars a year in an expensive city. Why pay for dry cleaning now, when she could defer the expense until she needed to wear it again? She claims that she did not save the dress as a trophy, as some suggested. She certainly could never have imagined that this dress would be the smoking gun that would prove their affair.

The next time they met Clinton had injured his knee, and was hobbling around on crutches. Monica had assembled a "get well" pack of presents: a new tie; *Vox,* a novel about phone sex; a medallion with a heart cut out of it; and a framed copy of her Valentine's Day ad.

Clinton had been growing increasingly anxious about the possibility of detection and told Monica that they needed to be careful. Throughout the affair she had told him that she would never tell anybody, that she would always protect him. He reminded her that if she were ever questioned about it, she should say that they were just friends.

When it was time to go, Clinton seemed endearing as he hobbled over to her on crutches, kissed her forehead, and began to serenade her. Looking deep into her eyes, he crooned the first line of the classic "Try a Little Tenderness": "She may be weary."[53]

On Saturday, May 24, 1996, Monica arrived at the White House bearing gifts. She and Clinton retired to his back study. Monica thought they were going to "fool around," but Clinton said they needed to talk. He was breaking off the affair, this time for good. Monica was devastated, but Clinton was relieved. He explained to Monica in some detail his personal history with sexual addiction, why this tortured him so deeply, and why he needed to stop. Pouring out his heart, Clinton shared the "anguish in his soul."

"It was not right for him, or his family, nor did he believe it was right in the eyes of God. He went on to describe the pain and torment that having an extramarital affair gave him as a married man."[54] He told Monica that since he was a child he had lived a double life, as most children from abusive backgrounds do. None of his friends even knew about Roger's violent drunken rages. After he married in 1975, when he was twenty-nine, his secret life continued. "The number of his affairs multiplied and Clinton became increasingly appalled at himself, at his capacity not only for deceiving others, but also for self-deception. By the time he reached the age of forty, he was unhappy in his marriage and hated what he was doing to himself and others, the struggle between his religious upbringing and his natural proclivities ever more pronounced."[55] Clinton told her about the turning point in his life, when he had considered divorcing Hillary and leaving politics forever. The torment of constantly having to deceive others had become intolerable. "If I had to become a gas station attendant to live an honest life and be able to look at myself in the mirror and be happy with who I am, that's what I was prepared to do," she reported him saying.[56]

But instead of leaving Hillary to live an honest life, Clinton had decided to resolve the crisis by quitting his sexual acting out instead: "At that stage in his life, feeling miserable, downcast, and directionless, he had made a momentous decision—it would, he believed, be better for his beloved daughter if he and Hillary stayed together and worked on their marriage. He said that since then he had tried to make his marriage work."[57] Clinton even adopted one aspect of the AA method to manage his addiction. One of AA's very effective dictums is "one day at a time." It's more manageable to decide each day that you won't drink that day than to promise you will never drink again. In keeping with that method, Clinton "kept a calendar on which he marked off the days when he had been good."[58]

As painful as it was to lose him, Monica was deeply moved. "I could see on that day and at that time that this was really a struggle for him and it was painful to talk about," said Monica. "It reminded me of my own struggles with weight."

"I cried and he cried too."[59]

Clinton said that he wanted to remain friends. "If you and I are just friends, I can tell them to go to hell and you can come here and spend time and it won't matter what they think because nothing is going on. I want you to do whatever it is you want to do. I want you to be happy. I can be a very good friend for you and help you in a lot of ways that you don't even realize." Though devastated, Monica was relieved to see Clinton did not want to sever the emotional connection between them. "I had the overall feeling that he still wanted me in his life, still wanted me to be a friend."[60]

Monica would stay in bed and cry all weekend. Clinton, too, was sad, but he was also relieved. He had taken back control of his life. Yes, he had slipped off the wagon, but that was over now, and he was back on track. He could look himself in the mirror without feeling like a liar. He could stop worrying about getting caught and damaging his presidency and hurting his family. Life was no longer out of control.

If only he knew. Three days after the emotional breakup, the Supreme Court ruled that the Paula Jones lawsuit could proceed. The real nightmare for the lovers, and the nation, was about to begin.

· THE PERJURY TRAP ·

When Monica was banished to the Pentagon, she was lonely, depressed, and needy. Even her therapist had abandoned her, albeit unintentionally, by moving out of town. The only person she had to confide in was a new coworker at the Pentagon: Linda Tripp.

History often turns on the most improbable events. Neither Clinton nor Lewinsky could ever have imagined there was a spy inside their relationship. The stunningly cruel and gratuitous betrayal by Tripp would change American history and finally put Bill Clinton in the clutches of his enemies. "You have to wonder what kind of human being could do this," Monica said of her ex-friend.[61] Tripp's motives have been a subject of debate. A holdover political appointee from the Bush administration, she had never liked the Clintons and had dreamed of writing a "tell-all" book about them.

Monica thinks she was jealous. Tripp, who was nicknamed "the witch" by the press for her unfortunate physical resemblance to the classic fairy-tale villain, would later tell the grand jury that the reason she had been forced to leave the White House was that Bill Clinton had been attracted to her, which made Hillary jealous. One can only call this a sexual delusion of grandeur. Tripp had to envy this young woman who was actually living her fantasy, and that envy may have made her want to destroy her trusting young friend.

During his tenure as president, two groups of men were out to destroy Bill Clinton. The first was a trio of right-wing attorneys, George Conway, Jerome Marcus, and Richard Porter, who had taken control of the Paula Jones lawsuit. They were not her official lawyers but they provided ongoing consultation behind the scenes. The three men called themselves "the elves."[62] Back in 1994, chief "elf" George Conway told David Brock that "the Jones team was planning to grill Clinton under oath about his consensual sex life, and hopefully catch him lying about it—a deliberate perjury trap."[63] A perjury trap is an abuse of legal process in which you put someone under oath for the sole purpose of trying to trap or trick him or her into testifying falsely.

The second group hunting for Clinton was Ken Starr and his OIC prosecutors whose Trooper Project had yet again yielded nothing. Clinton's former loves are loyal, as I stated earlier, and the OIC had not found a single woman willing to inform on him.

One phone call from Linda Tripp would bring these two groups of conspirators together, armed with the perfect perjury trap.

Both Clinton and Monica were shocked and dismayed to see Monica's name on the witness list for the Jones lawsuit. How could the Jones lawyers have known about her? Even more disturbing to both of them: Why were there specific questions about the stone bear and blue hat pin that had passed between them as gifts? Who could have obtained such specific information? It never occurred to Lewinsky that Tripp was informing on her. And out of embarrassment, she never told Clinton she had confided their secret to a friend, since she had promised to tell no one.

Clinton never actually told Lewinsky to lie in her Jones lawsuit affidavit. In part, that was because he didn't have to. The rules had been well established before Monica's name came up on the witness list: deny, deny, deny. And perhaps Clinton was also smart enough to know what line not to cross. This comparatively minor distinction—Clinton wanted her to lie in her affidavit, and knew she would, but never instructed her to do so—would prove decisive in the effort to remove Clinton from office. Tripp had begun recording her conversations with Lewinsky and regularly tried to goad her into incriminating the president. Monica repeatedly said Clinton never explicitly told her to lie in her affidavit, even as she readily admitted that she was planning to.

It's against the law in Maryland, where Tripp lived, to record a phone conversation without the consent of both parties. When Tripp told her lawyer that she had been illegally taping her phone calls with Monica, he rightfully told her to stop. Instead, Tripp decided to get a new lawyer and turned to Lucianne Goldberg, a conservative literary agent to whom she had been shopping a book idea about exposing the Clinton White House. On December 23, 1997, Goldberg called Jerome Marcus, one of the "elves." He agreed to find Tripp a more ideologically simpatico attorney.

He also wanted to listen to those illegal tapes.

The elves would connect Tripp to both the Paula Jones lawsuit and the OIC investigation, and things would progress rapidly from there.

On January 8, 1998, two weeks after Goldberg called him, Marcus had dinner with Paul Rosenzweig, a former law school classmate who happened to work for Ken Starr. The other two elves, Conway and Porter, attended as well. At an exclusive French restaurant the elves told Rosenzweig about Linda Tripp, Monica, and the latter's new connection to the Paula Jones lawsuit.

On Friday, January 9, Rosenzweig told his boss, Jackie Bennett, Starr's deputy director and right-hand man, about the conversation.

On January 12, Starr gave Bennett the go-ahead. Word was passed through Goldberg that Tripp should call Bennett, who stayed late on Monday, January 12, waiting for her call. "To the true believers who remained on Starr's staff, it was as if they had spent three years and five months waiting for Tripp's call."[64] When she called, Bennett told her to stay put; he was coming over right away. He arrived at her home at 11:45 P.M., and they spoke almost till dawn. Though the OIC had yet to receive authority to expand their investigation into Clinton's sexual life, or into anything having to do with the Paula Jones lawsuit, Bennett quickly decided to have the FBI wire Tripp and begin officially recording her conversations with Monica. In one conversation, later called the "sting tape," Tripp keeps leading the conversation in the direction that would help the OIC make the case that Clinton had urged Monica to commit perjury. Monica talked about the false affidavit she was about to sign in the Jones case denying a sexual relationship with Clinton, adding that technically it was not a lie, since they had never had intercourse. She said nothing about Clinton's urging her to lie. In fact, when Tripp suggested it, Monica denied it.

The OIC still did not have authorization to investigate this matter. That was about to change. At 10:00 P.M. on January 14, Bennett paged Assistant Attorney General Eric Holder, who was at a basketball game, saying he needed to see him urgently.

On January 15, according to Jeffrey Toobin, Bennett met with Holder, along with two new special prosecutors, Bruce Udolf and Mike Emmick. Bennett explained that they had explicit evidence that Lewinsky was planning to lie about her relationship with the president and that "the effort" at providing a false story in the Jones case "seems to go back to the President."[65] "In fact, the sting tape contained evidence to contradict all these assertions," wrote Toobin.[66] At that point Udolf, the only member of the staff who had actually listened to all the Tripp tapes, contradicted Bennett, saying that the allegations against the president were vague. But Bennett quickly cut him off. "We think it's real, and it involves the White House."[67]

Had the collusion between the Jones team and the OIC been known to Holder, the OIC would never have received permission to expand their investigation. Bennett claimed that "we've had no contact with plaintiff's attorneys."[68] Yet in 1999, Starr's successor, Robert Ray, would admit that these contacts indeed had taken place. Bennett would defend himself by saying that he had contact with the elves—Marcus, Porter, and Conway, who were assisting Jones's lawyers but were not her official lawyers of record. Bennett also failed to reveal that Starr himself had worked on the Jones case pro bono before becoming the independent counsel.

Based on this at best misleading information supplied by Bennett, permission to expand the investigation was granted.

· TERROR IN ROOM 1012 ·

On January 16, 1998, Monica went to the food court of the Ritz-Carlton Hotel near the Pentagon to meet her friend Linda Tripp for lunch. While they were there, Monica was confronted by FBI agents, who demanded to speak with her.

They took her to room 1012.

Special prosecutor Mike Emmick walked into the room. He started talking about Ken Starr's investigation, and Lewinsky was dumbfounded. What was he talking about, and why was he talking to her? "What on earth has he got to do with me? All I'm trying to do is cover up my affair with the President—what's my little relationship got do with him?" She soon found out. "We are prepared to charge you with perjury, obstruction of justice, subornation of perjury, witness tampering and conspiracy," he said. "You could spend up to twenty-seven years in jail."[69]

Monica collapsed into hysterical tears. "I find it difficult to describe the raw openness, the fear I felt. It was as if my stomach had been cut open and someone had poured acid into my wound. I just felt an intense stinging pain and an overriding terror. It was surreal. I couldn't understand how all this was happening."[70] Monica fell apart, crying, rocking, hugging herself—but she was determined not to betray her lover. She sobbed hysterically for ninety minutes.

"If I have to go to jail, I will do so to protect the President," she thought. "I can't do this. I can't turn him in." But at the same time, she had a competing thought: "I couldn't bear to go to jail. I would come out an old lady and no one would ever want to marry me. I would never have the joy of getting married and starting a family. My life would be over."[71]

The only alternative she could imagine at that moment was suicide. "I thought there is no way out other than but killing myself." The room had sliding glass doors, and she considered throwing herself to her death. "If I killed myself, what happens to everyone else in this investigation? Does it all go away?" she asked.[72]

The prosecutors kept emphasizing that their concerns were "time sensitive," that they needed her to cooperate that very day, or she would go to jail for twenty-seven years. Repeatedly, "she was faced with the choice of twenty-seven years in jail or immediate cooperation."[73]

Why time sensitive?

They were baiting a perjury trap for Clinton, who would be giving his testimony in the Paula Jones lawsuit the very next day. A perjury trap is an abuse of prosecutorial power in which the "prosecutor, frustrated at his inability to indict the suspect witness for a substantive crime, purposefully seeks to induce the witness to testify in a manner that the prosecutor knew would be contradicted by sufficient independent evidence, thereby subjecting the witness to prosecution for perjury."[74]

"They set me up," Clinton later said to Mike McCurry, his press secretary. "They brought me in there because they were convinced I was going to lie about Monica. . . . They were going to try to get me to perjure myself."

If Clinton had known that Monica was in the clutches of Ken Starr, he might have offered different testimony in his deposition in the Jones case. But as far as Clinton knew, Monica had denied the relationship, and he would, too. How could anyone prove an affair that both parties denied?

Monica had the presence of mind to ask to speak to her lawyer, Frank Carter, and though Monica pleaded to speak to Carter several times, she was told that if she did it might tip off the "alleged criminals" (i.e., Clinton), and her chance to escape jail would be lost. What they really feared was that Clinton would be alerted to the perjury trap they were setting for him. According to Deep Throat, it was essential to their plan that Monica not communicate with anyone who could tip off the president, and thus, they had to prevent her from talking to her attorney.

During the interrogation, Lewinsky, who is Jewish, kept drawing strength from the story of Hannah Senesh, the Hungarian-Jewish student who sacrificed her life because she refused to cooperate with the Nazis. Lewinsky recovered some of her composure, and told them that if she couldn't call her lawyer or her mother, then she was leaning toward not cooperating.

Jackie Bennett, affectionately known around Starr's office as the "thug" ("whatever works" was his motto), played their ace. "You should know that we are going to prosecute your mother, too, because of the things you have said she has done. We have it all on tape." In fact, there was nothing even suggestive of a crime by Monica's mother on any of the tapes, but Monica hit a new level of terror and disorientation. "I still have nightmares" about that day, said Lewinsky, "the sense of being trapped and drowning."

They had broken her. "In her heart, Monica conceded that she was no Hannah Senesh," wrote Morton.

By the end of the evening the prosecutors felt they had sufficient mental control over Lewinsky to allow her to call her mother, and to wander the food court of the hotel, where she bumped into Linda Tripp, who was casually shopping after turning in her friend. Lewinsky thought of calling the president to warn him, but by now she was out of her mind with fear. She was so paranoid that she thought the homeless woman near the pay phones was an FBI agent.

She wanted to warn the president. But she didn't. "She feared she might be arrested or the phones might be tapped. She sent no warning."[75]

The next day Clinton testified that he had never had sexual relations with Monica Lewinsky. That he had never been alone with her.

The perfect perjury trap slammed shut on Bill Clinton. After years of dry holes, the vast right-wing conspiracy had their man at last.

11

High Noon

When Bill Clinton was in first grade, the classic movie *High Noon* was released. He went to watch it over and over again. As a boy, "I saw a lot of movies, and especially liked the westerns," he wrote. "My favorite was *High Noon*—I probably saw it half a dozen times during its run in Hope, and have seen it more than a dozen times since. It's still my favorite movie."[1]

Gary Cooper plays Marshal Will Kane, the town sheriff. The back story is that Kane captured and brought to justice Frank Miller, leader of a murderous gang that had been terrorizing his town. Miller was supposed to hang, but mysteriously he has been pardoned.

The movie begins on Kane's wedding day to Amy, played by Grace Kelly. As the newlyweds sit together in their coach and buggy, getting ready to leave for their honeymoon, the news comes that Frank Miller is out of prison and arriving on the noon train to meet his gang. Together they plan to kill Kane and take back the town. The townspeople urge Kane to flee, as does his new wife, a pacifist Quaker. Kane takes their advice and rides away with his new bride. But then he has a change of heart and decides he must turn around and face Miller and his gang. Amy says that if he returns to fight, it will be without her. She vows to leave town on the same noon train that brings Miller back.

High Noon was one of the first movies ever made set in real time— between 10:00 A.M., when Kane gets the news that the Miller gang is coming, and the penultimate confrontation at high noon. The tension builds masterfully, as Kane goes from one friend to another seeking help, only to discover that the upstanding members of this town are all too afraid to help him. Before the final confrontation, a masterful tracking shot looks down on the eerie abandoned windswept street where Kane is standing alone.

In the climactic gun battle, Kane kills two of the men, but a third outlaw gets the drop on him, and it looks like the end. Then a shot rings out, and instead of Kane falling, the bad guy falls, and we see Amy holding a rifle. Despite her fury at Kane, she has returned to save her man.

Frank Miller, the head of the gang, is the last bad guy left standing. He takes Amy hostage and demands that Kane come out and throw his gun down in exchange for Amy's life. Kane agrees to comply, grimly facing his fate. But just as he comes out into the open street, the scrappy Amy, with a gun to her head, claws Miller's face, distracting him just long enough for Kane to shoot him.

Kane and Amy mount the same wagon where we found them just two hours before. Kane throws his sheriff's star in the dirt—good riddance to this faithless town. And the couple rides away.

In the end Amy was the only one who stood by Kane. *High Noon* is one of the few westerns ever made in which the main character is saved by a gun-toting *woman*. Throughout the movie the haunting soundtrack sings: "Do not forsake me, oh my darling, / On this our wedding day." And indeed, she did not.

From a psychological point of view, we can see why Clinton loves this movie. As a young boy he felt alone, heroically facing down his abusive stepfather. Clinton had his own high school high noon moment when he physically confronted Roger, proclaiming that if he wanted to hit anyone, he'd have to go through him. And as an adult, he has faced many enemies who wanted to do him in. "I loved this movie because from start to finish Gary Cooper is scared to death but does the right thing anyway. . . . Over the long years since I first saw *High Noon,* when I faced my own showdowns, I often thought of the look in Gary Cooper's eyes as he stares into the face of almost certain defeat, and how he keeps walking through his fears to do his duty. It works pretty well in real life too."[2]

At a deeper unconscious level I think that there is another reason the film resonates with Clinton: Kane is saved by his *wife*. As I have said, in Clinton's psyche Hillary is a stand-in for Grandma Cassidy, the tough, gun-toting (literally) mama who was his fierce protector when he felt forsaken by his mother. Hillary has proved to be a protector every bit as fierce as Grandma, indeed more so, and that's one of the reasons Clinton loves her and can't imagine life without her.

There is another interesting aspect of *High Noon*. It was intended as a political allegory about, of all things, facing a vast right-wing political conspiracy. It was written and produced by Carl Foreman, an Austrian Jew, who was not credited in the original film because he had been blacklisted. The movie is an allegory for the failure of intellectuals to stand up to McCarthyism.

Bill and Hillary Clinton would live a modern-day version of this movie. Together the first couple would face down a gang of bad men who were both bent on their destruction and aiming to take over the town. Though wounded by her husband's infidelity, Hillary would fight back, foiling the evil plot and saving her man.

· A WEEK IN JANUARY ·

On Wednesday, January 21, 1998, *The Washington Post* dropped a bombshell. The four-column headline read: "Clinton Accused of Urging Aide to Lie." Up until that day few Americans had heard of Monica Lewinsky; indeed, almost no one in the White House even knew who she was. Susan Schmidt, who wrote the article, was one of Starr's most-favored reporters, and his office had leaked this information to her (the article cites "sources close to the investigation," a code for Starr's office, twenty-four times), creating a scoop that hit with the force of Pearl Harbor. It shockingly informed the readers of audiotapes, surreptitiously recorded by Linda Tripp, in which Lewinsky told of an affair with the president and said he urged her to commit perjury. "Lewinsky described Clinton and Vernon Jordan directing her to testify falsely in the Paula Jones sexual harassment case against the President, according to sources."[3]

In fact, there were no tapes of Lewinsky saying she was urged to lie. *That was a lie*, expertly fed to the media by Starr's office. To the contrary, at least one tape existed in which she explicitly said he did *not* tell her to lie.

At 5:00 A.M. on January 21, Monica Lewinsky stepped into the hallway of her Watergate apartment and picked up her copy of *The Washington Post*. When she saw the headline, "time seemed to stand still." Her life was now changed forever; what she would refer to as the "endless waking nightmare" had begun.[4] "Everyone was talking about him having to resign. I couldn't believe that. I was still very much in love with the President, very protective of him," said Lewinsky. "There was a sense of frustration because these charges were simply not true. He never told me to lie."[5]

Clinton and Lewinsky had an understanding from the beginning that they would both lie if anyone asked them about their relationship, which is intrinsic to the nature of affairs—but that was before the relationship became a matter of legal inquiry. Throughout the entire ordeal, Lewinsky would be utterly consistent in her contention that Clinton never instructed her to lie in her affidavit. The OIC bullied Monica and resisted offering her an immunity deal for over six months because she never varied on this point. If Clinton did not tell her to submit a false affidavit then, Deep Throat told me, "That meant there was no obstruction of justice case, no case at all." All they had was an affair. "The case was never anything more than it appeared to be—that of a humiliated middle-aged husband who lied when caught having an affair with a young woman from work," wrote Jeffrey Toobin.[6]

Starr's office leaked this lie to *The Post* as part of a systematic misinformation campaign aimed at misleading the nation into believing Clinton had been caught committing a crime. "The reporters went on to repeat several falsehoods that the Starr team fed them," wrote Toobin, adding that "all of this misinformation had a distinct purpose: to persuade official Washington . . . that Starr had a strong case."[7]

Deep Throat said, "Starr is a liar. I often saw him lie on TV, lie to reporters, lie to Congress, and lie to my face."

Another former prosecutor who worked in the OIC said: "Ken is capable of saying anything."[8]

While the focus of this book is Clinton's psychology, it is also important to understand the psychology of his adversaries, to appreciate the context in which Clinton was operating. Starr and many of those who participated in the campaign to get Clinton lied easily and often, according to many observers, and evidently felt genuinely self-righteous in doing so because they believed Clinton to be so evil that the ends justified the means. These are features of a character disorder, *malignant narcissism*, described by Otto Kernberg, which combines three types of personality pathology: narcissism, paranoia, and antisocial features.

Like all narcissists, malignant narcissists desperately crave admiration and public glory. Starr was "obsessed with his public image," Deep Throat told me, adding that the walls of Starr's office were covered with pictures of him "shaking hands with every famous ass he ever kissed." Typical of most narcissists, malignant narcissists see themselves in idealized terms. It was widely noted that Starr wore his religious piety on his sleeve in a self-righteous manner. "You cannot defile the temple of justice," Starr declared when asked why he was pursuing the case against Clinton so doggedly, implicitly putting himself in the role of Jesus, who cleansed the Temple by driving out the moneylenders (by whipping them, coincidentally enough).

Paranoia creates a sense of threat from a person or group the pathological narcissist experiences as evil. "Ken thought Clinton was the anti-Christ," Deep Throat said. Even when the malignant narcissist is confronted with contradictory information, these paranoid distortions are not amenable to change. Given that Starr was convinced that Clinton was evil, no amount of exonerating evidence could dispel this fixed idea. "The more the evidence seemed to exonerate Clinton, the more enraged he became at him," said Deep Throat. "Starr was under the impression that there was a lot of lying and covering up, even if he couldn't put his finger on it. He assumed there was a crime there somewhere, even though he didn't have any evidence."

Another feature of paranoia is projection. In order to maintain the experience of themselves as all good and their enemies as all bad, malignant narcissists must project all the unacceptable parts of themselves onto those enemies. Thus, they will consistently accuse them of doing bad things that they are in fact doing (even as they deny doing them). For example, Starr was obsessed with the idea that the Clintons were inveterate liars, in contrast to himself—a guardian of truth. Yet, as widely reported, he was constantly lying.

If a person feels threatened by a supposedly evil enemy, aggressive behavior toward this malevolent adversary is morally justified as mere self-defense. When antisocial traits are added to the mix, the malignant narcissist is willing to lie and violate both rules and the rights of others without compunction in the service of his or her supposedly righteous cause. The malignant narcissist feels heroic for lying, cheating, and destroying people's lives in his battle against evil.

For a number of reasons, grand jury secrecy is considered to be one of the foundations of the legal system.* Not only did Starr's office breach grand jury secrecy, but the scale on which information was systematically leaked was breathtakingly unprecedented. "This was the greatest abuse of grand jury process in American history," said Deep Throat. "Never before has there been such a systematic exposure of grand jury material, on such a large scale, for so blatantly political a purpose." In a move he would later regret, Starr basically admitted that his office had leaked information to reporters when he was being interviewed by journalist Steven Brill, who was researching an article entitled "Pressgate" about Starr's illegal leaks of misinformation, and the press's complicity in the process. Wouldn't those leaks be illegal? Brill asked.

Starr offered what Brill called a "stunning rationalization" that reveals much about how the mind of a malignant narcissist works: "That would be true, except in the case of a situation where what we are doing is countering misinformation that is being spread about the investigation in order to discredit our office and our dedicated career prosecutors. . . . I think it's our obligation to counter that kind of misinformation."⁹

In the inverted internal world of the malignant narcissist, he experiences his victims doing to him the bad things that he is actually doing to them: Starr was not *countering* a misinformation campaign from Clinton; he was *running* one against the president.

Second, because he felt attacked by Clinton, Starr felt justified in breaking the rules; this is hardly a sound legal argument. Even if Starr's contention was true, it wouldn't justify *his* violating the law. But psychologically,

---

* From the American Bar Association Web site: "Rule 6(e) of the Federal Rules of Criminal Procedure provides that the prosecutor, grand jurors, and the grand jury stenographer are prohibited from disclosing what happened before the grand jury, unless ordered to do so in a judicial proceeding. Secrecy was originally designed to protect the grand jurors from improper pressures. The modern justifications are to prevent the escape of people whose indictment may be contemplated, to ensure that the grand jury is free to deliberate without outside pressure, to prevent subornation of perjury or witness tampering prior to a subsequent trial, to encourage people with information about a crime to speak freely, and to protect the innocent accused from disclosure of the fact that he or she was under investigation."

the malignant narcissist feels justified in doing anything to someone he or she imagines is threatening them.

Starr's office systematically leaked misinformation to his favored reporters, in order to see the lies printed the next day with the authority of fact. Starr's "illegal leaks were holding virtually the entire press corps in his thrall," wrote Sidney Blumenthal in his book *The Clinton Wars,* because they were actually dependent on those leaks to write the scandal stories that became their bread and butter. The tastiest morsels were doled out to favored reporters like Susan Schmidt, who had dropped the January 21 bombshell.

According to Deep Throat, Starr's chief deputy, Jackie Bennett, was essentially a full-time press officer "leaking to reporters constantly." He was especially "sweet" on Susan Schmidt and also close with Starr's allies on the *Wall Street Journal* editorial page. "He was on the phone with Schmidt and Micah Morrison from *The Wall Street Journal* every day, usually more than once a day."

This was a new low in journalistic standards, according to veteran journalist Marvin Kalb, who wrote *One Scandalous Story: Clinton, Lewinsky, and Thirteen Days That Tarnished American Journalism*: "Until the breaking of this story, the *Washington Post* had rigorously abided by its two-source rule, imposed by Ben Bradlee during the Watergate scandal. . . . During the first few days of the Lewinsky scandal, the *Post* often disregarded its own rule."[10] According to one study, only 16 percent of *The Post*'s reporting on the Lewinsky affair relied on named sources. Even worse, this new low suddenly became the benchmark for the profession as a whole. According to a study by the Committee of Concerned Journalists, only 1 percent of the national stories relied on two named sources, and 26 percent relied on one. The remaining 73 percent cited only a single anonymous source (aka Bennett at the OIC) or cited no source at all.[11] In other words, most of the coverage was, in essence, an OIC press release filled with misinformation.

It was Monica 24/7—all Monica, all the time. Never before had anyone seen such media frenzy. "For the second time in the last quarter of a century, *The Post* had launched a journalistic assault against a sitting president and everyone—*everyone*—wanted in, " wrote Kalb.[12] But the methods used to research these two stories couldn't have been more different, according to Bob Woodward, who broke the original Watergate story in *The Washington Post.* As he told Steven Brill, "The big difference between this and Watergate is that in Watergate, Carl [Bernstein] and I went out and talked to people whom the prosecutors were ignoring or didn't know about. . . . We were able to look these people in the eye and decide if they were credible. . . . Here the reporting is all about lawyers telling reporters what to believe and write." In "Pressgate," Brill wrote that "Watergate spawned great reporting. The Lewinsky story has reversed the process." In Watergate, the press served its traditional function: being "a *check* on official abuse of power," whereas in this story, the press "became an *enabler* of Starr's abuse of power."

On the first day of the crisis, Tim Russert suggested on MSNBC that Clinton might resign within days. "The next forty-eight to seventy-two hours are critical," he said, adding that if the president lied, "he's going to have to leave this town in disgrace."[13] The next day Russert added, "I believe impeachment proceedings will begin on the Hill if there is not clarity given by the president over the next few weeks." "His presidency is dead," said George Will on ABC's *This Week,* on Sunday, January 25, 1998. "He cannot survive," William Kristol agreed. "I think his presidency is numbered in days," predicted Sam Donaldson, adding that it was quite possible that Clinton "will resign, perhaps this week."[14] "If he's not telling the truth," said Ted Koppel that night, "he's cooked."[15] Even former senior staffer George Stephanopoulos, now an ABC commentator, publicly wrote off his old boss: "Is he telling the truth, the whole truth, and nothing but the truth? If he is, he can survive. If he isn't, he can't."[16] (Hillary had been right: George had always been the first to abandon ship at the whiff of scandal.)

The panic was palpable inside the White House the day the story hit. Chief of Staff Erskine Bowles said: "I think I'm going to throw up." The next day he told Clinton's senior adviser, Sidney Blumenthal, that "he wouldn't have anything to do with managing the scandal and he didn't want to hear about it." Bowles "took time off," and "his absence on those first few days created an instant vacuum at the center" that only served to ratchet up the level of panic.[17] Blumenthal described what it felt like: "Within the White House there was no organizing focus, no strategy, no one calling meetings, and we had a growing sense of standing on a beach waiting for a tidal wave."[18]

At noon Clinton spoke to Dick Morris—the only person Clinton leveled with about the Lewinsky affair.

"You poor son-of-a-bitch," said Morris. "I know just what you're going through. I've been there." In 1997 Morris's own career had been derailed by a sex scandal.

"Oh God, this is just awful," said Clinton, in a "lifeless" voice.

Oh God, have I fucked up this time is what Morris heard.

"It occurred to me that I may be the only sex addict you know," said Morris. "And maybe I can help you."

"Ever since I was elected, I've tried to shut my body down, I mean sexually, and sometimes I just failed," indicating once again what a protracted struggle Clinton had waged with his sexual impulses. "This woman, I didn't do what they said I did, but I did do something and I don't know if I can prove my innocence."[19]

"There's a vast capacity for forgiveness in this country," Morris reassured him. "The one thing you've got to avoid is getting trapped like Nixon into a rigid posture of denial."[20]

At that point Clinton was contemplating simply going to the public, confessing, apologizing, and getting it over with. In retrospect that is exactly what most people wish he had done. But Clinton was in a state of panic, too.

That day Sidney Blumenthal got a call from Betty Currie: Clinton needed to see him. Blumenthal was a trusted adviser and, perhaps more important, one of Hillary's closest friends. This bombshell would have both political and marital consequences. When Blumenthal entered the Oval Office "I saw the President alone, standing, his gaze distracted. He started pacing slowly behind his desk and then in front of it. He rearranged knick-knacks, touching some and slightly moving others." Blumenthal found "a man who was beside himself." He had seen Clinton upset before, "but I had never seen him this off balance before."

Clinton told Blumenthal that he wanted to explain to him about Monica Lewinsky. He portrayed Lewinsky as a "troubled person." "He told me he had been trying to help her." This is the story he had told Hillary, and Hillary had already confided as much to Blumenthal. Blumenthal launched into a speech about how Clinton couldn't allow his compassion to entwine him with troubled people. "That's how I am. I want to help," said Clinton.[21]

Then the conversation took what seemed like an odd turn. He said he had been speaking to Dick Morris, who had told him that "if Nixon at the beginning of Watergate had delivered a speech on national television explaining everything he had done wrong, making it public, he would have survived."[22]

In retrospect, this was a crucial moment in the president's deliberations. He was considering doing what, in hindsight, all agree he should have done: quickly take the air out of the scandal by admitting to the affair—his only real misdeed—asking America's forgiveness, and moving on. One of Clinton's problems was that he could not openly discuss this option with his advisers without telling them the truth. Yet, in an elliptical way, he was trying to do just that. Blumenthal immediately asked the logical question: "What have you done wrong?"

"Nothing," Clinton replied. "I haven't done anything wrong."

"Then," Blumenthal said, "that's one of the stupidest ideas I've heard."[23]

Unfortunately, Blumenthal failed to see the implied question that Clinton was virtually begging him to answer: If, for argument sake, I *had* done something wrong, then would it be better to say so?

With that line of inquiry cut off, Clinton gave Blumenthal his false version of the relationship. "He said she made sexual demands on him and he rebuffed her." (That was sort of true. He had refused her requests for intercourse.) He said he had told Monica, "I've gone down that road before, I've caused a lot of pain, and I'm not going to do that again." (That was sort of true, too, only he said it after they had begun a sexual relationship and he needed to end it.) Then Clinton told a complete lie. He said she had responded by threatening him. If he did not have sex with her, she threatened, "she would tell others they had had an affair."

"I feel like a character in a novel," Clinton said. "I feel like someone who is surrounded by an oppressive force that is creating a lie about me and I can't get the truth out. I feel like the character in *Darkness at Noon*," referring to a famous novel by Arthur Koestler, about a Bolshevik facing a purge trial.[24]

Blumenthal would later learn that this was the most detailed story the president had given to anyone. To other aides he had given "uncomplicated brief denials." Blumenthal later realized that Clinton had told him this elaborate story "because of my relationship with Hillary. He knew we would share information. . . . I was close to Hillary, and there was nothing more important to him at that moment than protecting his marriage." Thus, Clinton was using Blumenthal to reinforce his efforts to hide his adultery from his wife. (Almost comically, one of the articles of impeachment declared that Clinton had attempted to obstruct justice by telling this tall tale to Blumenthal. "Not in my wildest dreams did I imagine that my listening to him telling me what he did was, as the House managers later claimed, part of an obstruction of justice. That was absurd.")[25]

Unwisely, Clinton kept several prearranged appointments for TV interviews on day one of the crisis. Of course the scandal became the focus of all the questions, and Clinton's responses seemed tentative and evasive. At first he tried to slide by by using the present tense, denying a current relationship without explicitly denying a past relationship.

"There is no improper relationship," Clinton said to Jim Lehrer on the *News Hour.*

"What does that mean?" Lehrer asked.

"Well, I think you know what it means. It means there is not a sexual relationship, an improper sexual relationship, or any other kind of improper relationship."[26]

The press seized on the strategic use of the present tense, and press secretary Mike McCurry delicately told the president that people expected him to deny the Lewinsky relationship in the past tense as well.

Sidney Blumenthal placed a phone call to David Brock. Brock had worked for the Arkansas Project, but after a crisis of conscience he had repented of his role in the "vast right-wing conspiracy," and become a double agent of sorts, informing on his former colleagues. Brock told Blumenthal about the Paula Jones–OIC collusion, and Blumenthal shared what he learned with Hillary. "The two of them spent hours together, fitting together the pieces of the conspiracy. It had the advantage of considerable underlying truth," wrote Bernstein.[27] Indeed, this was the band of usual suspects—the Scaife-funded right-wing zealots who were out to destroy the Clintons by any means necessary. Regardless of what Clinton had or had not done with Monica—and at this point Hillary believed his denials—this was one more battle in a very long war.

By happenstance, that very night a dinner was held at the White House to honor those who had contributed to the White House Preservation Society. On the guest list was none other than Richard Mellon Scaife. Of course, his idea of restoring the White House was to liquidate its current occupants, and now he was there to gloat. Blumenthal and

Hillary joked about who should sit next to Scaife at dinner—the whole situation was so absurd they had to laugh. "We spent a lot of the day just joking about Richard Mellon Scaife," said Blumenthal.

"Clinton and the First Lady mingled with the guests as though they didn't have a care in the world," wrote Blumenthal.[28] But nothing could have been further from the truth.

Clinton spoke to Morris again at 11:30 P.M. Morris had taken a quick rudimentary poll with a small sample, and came back with bad news:

"Well, I'm wrong. You can't tell them about it. They'll kill you."[29]

The public could tolerate his admitting to an affair, but not any hint of his lying about it under oath. Some 35 percent thought he should go to jail if he had lied. The perjury trap was tightening around Clinton's neck like a noose.

"You didn't ask them about capital punishment, did you?" Clinton asked in the spirit of gallows humor.

But Morris was not joking. "They're just too shocked by this. It's just too new. It's just too raw. They're just not ready for it."[30]

The implications were grim. Clinton saw only one path to survival: lie, lie, lie. "That flat denial, not clever evasions, would be necessary to save his presidency left him badly demoralized," wrote Harris.[31]

"Well, we just have to win then," Clinton told Morris.[32]

But he was by no means sure that he could win. Earlier that morning Clinton had confided in a friend that "he doubted his presidency would survive the week," according to Bernstein.[33] He feared a stampede in which Democrats, urged on by the press, would join Republicans in asking for his resignation.

Clinton's advisers had been strongly pushing the president to make a more emphatic denial. "You've got to be so fucking indignant that you're almost seething," said Clinton attorney Bob Bennett.[34] On January 26, in the Roosevelt Room, Clinton clenched his jaw, glared at the camera, and pointed his finger, saying, "I want you to listen to me. I'm going to say this again: I did not have sexual relations with that woman. . . . Miss Lewinsky. I never told anyone to lie, not a single time—never. These allegations are false. And I need to go back to work for the American people."[35]

"This was the performance his advisers had been hoping for but it was not strictly a performance," wrote John F. Harris. "His rage was real. As he finished speaking he pivoted almost violently away from the lectern and out of the door. His body was literally shaking."[36]

Monica, who was watching on TV, was glad he had denied the relationship, because she didn't want him to have to resign. But "I was very hurt when he said 'that woman.'"[37] Though the phrase conveyed contempt, it was not intentional. Clinton explained to an adviser afterward, "I blanked out on her name."[38] Clinton had never experienced stage fright before, but he did on this day. It was, in part, a Freudian slip. Freud argued that slips of the tongue are not random mistakes, but rather reveal unconscious feelings and wishes. At that moment Clinton no doubt wanted to forget about Monica altogether.

"That statement caused him more lasting damage than any other of his presidency," wrote Blumenthal.[39]

In the first few days of the crisis Clinton was off balance and in shock. When John Podesta, who would succeed Erskine Bowles as chief of staff, greeted him in the Oval Office on Friday, January 23, day three of the crisis, "the president's face was heavy and drawn, his frame almost physically deflated as he slumped in his chair." For the first time, it seemed entirely possible to Podesta that "his presidency might be over."[40]

But by the end of the week, Clinton was ready to fight. "If they want me out of this office," he told his staff, shaking his head, "they are going to have to carry me out feet first."[41]

Clinton amazed his staff, many of whom seemed poised for nervous breakdowns themselves, with his iron resolve to fight back, and by using the best weapon at his disposal: being presidential. While it would have been understandable if Clinton had become distracted by the crisis, Clinton's focus on the presidency, paradoxically, seemed to increase, prompting much speculation about what in Clinton's psychological makeup allowed him to do this. The Freudian defense mechanism "compartmentalization" suddenly became part of the popular lexicon. "From an early age, he developed a capacity to block out unpleasant aspects of his life," wrote biographer David Maraniss in a front-page analysis published in *The Washington Post* on January 25, 1998.[42] Indeed, that defense mechanism seemed to be serving Clinton well now.

Hillary was ready to fight, too: "As the pressure intensified, Hillary was already planning how their presidency could be saved. She knew she was once again the key to their potential survival."[43] Clinton's State of the Union speech was scheduled for the evening of January 27, just six days after the bombshell. That morning Hillary appeared on the *Today*

Show, and from this interview the phrase "vast right-wing conspiracy" was burned into the cultural lexicon.

"I think everybody ought to just stop a minute here and think about what we're doing. I'm very concerned about the tactics that are being used and the kind of intense political agenda at work here," said Hillary to Matt Lauer. "This is what concerns me. This started out as an investigation of a failed land deal. I told everybody in 1992, 'We lost money.' It's taken many years, but it's true. We get a politically motivated prosecutor who is allied with the right-wing opponents of my husband. Who has literally spent four years . . ."

"Spent thirty million," said Lauer.

"Spent more than that, now. But looking at every telephone call we've made, every check we've ever written, scratching for dirt, intimidating witnesses, doing everything possible to try to make some accusation of my husband.

"Bill and I have been accused of everything, including murder, by some of the very same people who are behind these allegations," people, she noted, who would like to "undo the results of two elections."

Lauer pointed out that she was criticizing Starr. "It's not just one person," Hillary explained. "It's an entire operation."[44]

"I do believe that this is a battle," she continued. "I mean, look at the very people who are involved in this; they have popped up in other settings. This is the great story here, for anyone willing to find it and write about it and explain it, this vast right-wing conspiracy that has been conspiring against my husband since the day he announced for president. A few journalists have kind of caught on to it and explained it, but it has not yet been fully revealed to the American public. And actually, you know, in a bizarre sort of way, maybe this will do it."[45]

When asked if Clinton had "caused pain in their marriage," Hillary replied: "You know, we've been married for twenty-two years, Matt, and I have learned a long time ago that the only people who count in any marriage are the two who are in it. We know everything there is to know about each other, and we understand and accept and love each other." Hillary was supporting Clinton's denial of the affair, but she was also sending a message similar to the one she had sent when the Clintons went on *60 Minutes* after the Gennifer Flowers story broke. Clinton's issues with marital fidelity were *their* business.

Hillary struck back by calling out Starr and his allies publicly on what they were doing in secret. But the general public watching this interview didn't have any idea who or what she was talking about when she referred to a vast right-wing conspiracy. The press had failed to report the story, and even after Hillary's *Today Show* challenge, they continued, with a few notable exceptions, to leave the plot to bring down the president unreported. In fact, Hillary would be widely mocked for what sounded like paranoia, especially when the truth about the Lewinsky affair emerged. Actually, "she was closer to the truth in her complaint—alleging secret coordination between the independent counsel and right-wing Clinton opponents—than all but a few people knew at the time," wrote *Washington Post* reporter and Clinton biographer John F. Harris.[46]

Nonetheless, Hillary's *Today Show* performance helped rally the troops back in the White House. Woodward wrote that "it was one of Hillary's strongest television performances, and it made major news. If she had settled accounts with her husband, why should anyone else dwell on it? With the single interview she had managed to refocus media attention on Starr." It was a morale builder: "Top Clinton aides almost danced in the corridors of the White House."[47]

"I guess that will teach them to fuck with us," said Hillary defiantly when she returned to the White House from the television studio.[48]

According to one of the OIC prosecutors, Brett Kavanaugh, Starr was "very mad at Hillary" for her comment about the right-wing conspiracy, which had obviously hit a nerve: "The next day Starr was furious. He told his deputies that in his opinion the first lady had almost threatened potential witnesses. She was sending a message: This is war and anyone perceived to be hostile will be killed. He had to be calmed down," wrote Woodward.[49]

By what possible logic could Starr believe Hillary to be *threatening witnesses*? Only by understanding the psychology of malignant narcissism can we make sense of this seemingly inexplicable outburst. Malignant narcissists lean heavily on the defense of projection. Like a movie projector displaying an image on a screen, malignant narcissists project their own destructive impulses and behaviors onto the objects of their hatred, accusing their victims of doing what they are actually doing. Over and over again the key to translating Starr-speak is to reverse the pronouns. Who was threatening witnesses? Not Hillary, but Starr. We certainly have the example of Monica's brutal interrogation, where they even threatened to jail her mother (they would later threaten to audit her father, as well, unless she gave them what they wanted against Clinton). This one incident was part of a pattern of intimidating witnesses. While we don't have space here to cover the details of the trials run by Starr in Arkansas, Max Brantley, editor in chief of the *Arkansas Times*, said that Starr's deputy counsel Jackie Bennett routinely "screams at and berates witnesses. He's a schoolyard bully."[50] Steve Smith, one of Clinton's three chiefs of staff in his first gubernatorial administration, was found guilty of a misdemeanor unearthed in the Whitewater investigation. According to Smith, Starr's team encouraged him to lie to a grand jury about Clinton's involvement in Whitewater. They even prepared a script and wrote out a false statement for him: "They kept trying to get me to say things that weren't true. They told me to sign a document they had written that was simply not true."[51] When Smith refused, they "said that they were going to subpoena my mother who was seventy years old and knew nothing."[52]

While most of these abuses took place outside public awareness, Starr's jailing of Susan McDougal for her refusal to give what she claims would have been false testimony against the Clintons captured national attention. "Parading Susan in shackles was actually one of his adversary's biggest mistakes," wrote senior journalist Helen Thomas. "As the pictures flashed around the country, the public began to rebel against Starr."[53]

But Starr was not wrong to be upset by Hillary's frontal assault. She saw herself as being in a "death struggle" with Starr. From that day forward Hillary and Blumenthal unleashed a systematic campaign to expose Starr's misbehavior to the media. The decision to fight Starr in the media "represented Hillary's thinking at its most clearheaded. She wasn't wrong that Starr was trying to stretch the law and use his almost unlimited powers to indict her—or seek the impeachment of the president. But if he knew he was going to be more carefully scrutinized, and if more outrage among Democrats on Capitol Hill could be stirred by demonstrating his excesses," wrote Bernstein, "it might constrain him."[54] Starr would later haul Blumenthal before the grand jury, accusing him of obstructing justice for speaking to reporters about Starr's own illegal methods and his connection to the president's right-wing enemies.

That same evening it was Clinton's turn to counterpunch in his State of the Union address. Should the president mention the scandal? "I and everyone else on the political staff were against his doing so," wrote Blumenthal. "Separating what Clinton was doing as President from the scandal became a basic strategy. It also clarified a basic truth: what Clinton had done was a personal indiscretion that had no bearing on his conduct of public policy."[55]

Just before he left the White House, Clinton's Arkansas friend Harry Thomason told him: "Just remember, you've got the biggest balls over there. Just go over and kick their butts."[56]

As Clinton walked into the House of Representatives, it struck Blumenthal that the president was "preternaturally calm." In sharp contrast, the "nervousness of the Democrats milling in the chamber was palpable," as was "the smugness of the Republicans."[57] Blumenthal was scared, too. As he stood in the back of the chamber, waiting to hear the president speak, he felt "like a Union soldier on Little Round Top before the battle of Gettysburg."[58]

Clinton came out strong: "For 209 years, it has been the president's duty to report to you on the state of the union. Because of the hard work and high purpose of the American people, these are good times for America. We have more than fourteen million new jobs, the lowest unemployment in twenty-four years, the lowest core inflation in thirty years, incomes are rising, and we have the highest home ownership in history. Crime has dropped for a record five years in a row, and the welfare rolls are at their lowest levels in twenty-seven years. Our leadership in the world is unrivaled. Ladies and gentlemen, the state of our union is strong."

The Democrats clapped loudly.

"For three decades, six presidents have come before you to warn of the damage deficits pose to our nation. Tonight, I come before you to announce that the federal deficit, once so incomprehensively large that it had eleven zeros, will be simply zero."

The applause was tumultuous, from both parties.

"Now, if we balance the budget for next year, it is projected that we'll then have a sizable surplus in the years that immediately follow. What should we do with this projected surplus? I have a simple four-word answer: Save Social Security first. Tonight, I propose that we reserve 100 percent of the surplus—that's every penny of any surplus—until we have taken all the necessary measures to strengthen the Social Security system for the twenty-first century. Let us say—let us say to all Americans watching tonight, whether you're seventy or fifty, or whether you just started paying into the system, Social Security will be there when you need it. Let us make this commitment: Social Security first. Let's do that—together."

Even as they clapped loudly at this line, many Republican lawmakers were befuddled. They would prefer to use that money for tax cuts. With that one phrase—"Save Social Security first"—a trillion dollars went from their side of the ledger to the Democrats. Somehow, once again, a politically weakened Clinton was taking control of the budget agenda.

Clinton went on, issue after issue, receiving 104 ovations.

"We burst back into the White House and ran up the stairs to the state dining room, where the rest of the staff and a couple of hundred supporters welcomed us. The President clasped his hands over his head to raucous cheering. The polls were already rolling in. Support for the President's speech was above 80 percent," wrote Blumenthal.[59] Six out of ten Americans thought the country was moving in the right direction, and 67 percent approved of his job performance. As for the sex scandal, the majority believed that something had happened between Clinton and Lewinsky, but the same number thought that Clinton's enemies were "conspiring" to bring down the presidency, and that Starr was "more interested in hurting Clinton than determining whether crimes had been committed."[60]

During a week when the media predicted Clinton would be resigning within days, the first couple fought as a team for their survival, and won. The state of *their* union was surprisingly strong, but by summer it would fray to the breaking point.

· HIGH NOON: THE ELECTION OF '98 ·

August 15, 1998, was possibly the worst day of Bill Clinton's life. For eight months he had lied to Hillary, his advisers, and the nation about his affair with Monica. But now, knowing that Monica had come to an agreement with Starr to tell the truth about the affair, and that a DNA sample had proved it was his sperm on Monica's blue Gap dress, Clinton would have no choice but to testify truthfully before the grand jury in two days. There was no room to run. Nowhere to hide.

Early that morning Bill Clinton had to wake up his wife and tell her the truth. According to Hillary, Bill "paced back and forth" by the bed before his confession. When he finally got to the point, Hillary "could hardly breathe."

"What do you mean? What are you saying? Why did you lie to me?"

"I'm sorry. I'm so sorry. I was trying to protect you and Chelsea."

"I was furious and getting more so by the second . . . I was dumbfounded, heartbroken, and outraged . . . ," wrote Hillary.[61]

By some accounts, according to Sheehy, Hillary "lunged at him and gave him a blow," shouting, "You stupid bastard!"[62]

Clinton tried to minimize the impact by stressing that he never actually had intercourse with Monica, but whatever reassurance Hillary could take from that, if any, was undermined by the further revelation that this relationship had gone on for over a year.

Then they had to face the question of how to tell Chelsea. "When I told him he had to do this," wrote Hillary, "his eyes filled with tears."[63]

Some believe that Hillary knew about the affair, but it seems more likely that she maintained her denial to the end. Linda Bloodworth-Thomason and her husband were staying in the private White House quarters the morning he told her. She said, "Anyone who thinks Hillary knew what happened before the two of them had their conversation wasn't there that weekend." Linda recalled that she thought it was great that Hillary "smacked him upside the head."[64] He had betrayed her, lied to her, lied to the nation and all their advisers, publicly humiliated her, and put their presidency at risk.

Clinton was spared the indignity of having to make a perp walk to the courthouse for his August 17 testimony, but that was about the only one he avoided that day. He was allowed to testify from the White House, with the proviso that the OIC could videotape his grand jury appearance—a highly unusual request his lawyers should have objected to. It seems obvious now that they were making the tape for the premeditated purpose of being able to later release it publicly (also an unprecedented move) to humiliate Clinton. "Someone on the grand jury might be absent that day" was the alleged reason, though as Jeffrey Toobin points out, it seems hard to imagine that any of the grand jurors might have anything more pressing to do that day than listen to the testimony of the president of the United States, and even if they were absent for some reason, standard procedure in such cases is for them to read the transcript.[65] "Though Starr, Robert Bittman, and his staff denied it, the only reasonable interpretation of their insistence on videotape was to embarrass Clinton."[66]

By agreement there was a four-hour time limit, and Clinton did a

masterful job of eating up the clock, giving long speeches about how un-
ethical the investigation had been. And the prosecutors were surprisingly
inept in their questioning, wasting much of their allotted time pursuing
absurd blind alleys that only further revealed their paranoia. Certain
that he was "dressing to obstruct justice," they asked Clinton if he had
been sending a secret message to Monica, urging her to lie, by wearing
on the day of her grand jury appearance a striped Zegna tie she had given
him as a gift.[67]

"My personal feelings and political beliefs were on a collision course,"
Hillary later wrote. As far as her marriage was concerned, her feelings
were too ambivalent to sort out at that point. "Although I was heartbroken and disappointed with Bill, my long hours alone made me admit to
myself that I loved him." Nonetheless, "what I still didn't know was
whether our marriage could or should last." On that front, they had
agreed to attend regular marital counseling, which they did for approximately a year.

But she had no mixed feelings about battling their enemies. "I hadn't
decided whether to fight for my husband or my marriage, but I was resolved to fight for my President. . . . Bill's Presidency, the institutional
Presidency, and the integrity of the Constitution hung in the balance,
[and] I knew what I did and said in the next days and weeks would influence not just Bill's future and mine, but also America's. . . . I believed Bill
was a good person and a great President. I viewed the independent counsel's assault on the Presidency as an ever-escalating political war, and I
was on Bill's side."[68]

On September 15, she sat down with a delegation of congresswomen
in the yellow Oval Room. They wanted to see "how I was holding up and
what I was planning to do next. Once they realized that I was serious
about standing up for the Constitution, the President, and the Democratic Party, they asked me to get out and campaign for them."[69]

Hillary Clinton knew that the battle to save the Clinton presidency
would take place at the polls in the election of 1998. The Republicans
were making the election a referendum on impeachment, and so would
she. "The only way to avoid impeachment was through a strong showing
in the November elections," wrote Hillary.[70] And she was right. Hillary
thrust herself into the campaign "with the fury of a prairie wife fighting
off Indians."[71]

She barnstormed the country, visiting twenty-seven states, making over a hundred appearances. "I spent the fall crisscrossing the country on a campaign marathon," wrote Hillary.[72]

Hillary Clinton poured every ounce of her strength into winning elections for Democrats. "She was on fire," said Senator Barbara Boxer's daughter, Nichole.[73] "'Energized' is the word most often used to describe her," wrote Mary Leonard in *The Boston Globe*, calling her "a one-woman campaign machine."[74] She was "a tornado on the hustings."[75] "She's full of fire and brimstone," said a retiree in Florida who heard her speak.[76] Indeed, Hillary was traveling from town to town "preaching the Democratic gospel" as if the salvation of the world depended on it.[77]

Paradoxically, in the wake of the Monica scandal, Hillary Clinton's popularity soared. Where she had once been viewed as a political liability by the Democrats, with an approval rating of 42 percent, the lowest ever for a first lady, she was now the most popular political figure in America, with a sky-high approval rating of 72 percent. As the victim of her husband's infidelity, she garnered a sympathy that most people had not felt for her before.

But it was her dignity in the midst of the public humiliation, and her strength in defiantly battling the forces that had attacked them both, that really won her admiration. She had been victimized but she was no victim. "If I could shake her hand and give her a hug, I'd tell her I'm proud of her for holding her head up high," said a secretary in Milwaukee.[78] "She's behaved with such dignity under the most trying circumstances," said a woman in New Rochelle, "she's royalty."[79]

Women had complicated, varied, and often conflicted feelings about Hillary for staying with a man who had cheated on her. It seemed like such an unfeminist thing to do. And yet, there is something about the bond between husband and wife that people intuitively feel to be sacred. And loyalty is a trait we value highly. In truth, we all have ambivalent relationships with our spouses and family, but the impulse to defend them against external attack is hardwired in our brains, the same way a mother bear will defend her cubs. America got it. "She's been through a lot, and voters know that and they respect the loyalty she has, and I think that has made her more effective," said Colorado governor Roy Romer, Democratic National Committee chairman.[80] Certainly her ability to put her personal pain aside and fight for what she believed in made her seem like the ultimate team player. Perhaps most important, she was not passively accepting Clinton's behavior, but instead was taking active control over their joint political destiny, going from victim to potential victor. Republican strategist Rich Galen said that what Americans admired is that "she stoically went through this Monica stuff and has come out shining—and come out swinging."[81]

And there was another very important message that her presence on the campaign trail communicated. If she could forgive Clinton (to whatever extent she actually had) over what was really a private matter between them, then the rest of the country should be able to move on, too.

Most candidates were afraid to have Bill stump for them, unsure if it would help or hurt, and for the most part he confined himself mostly to private Democratic Party events. However, there was no such ambivalence about hosting Hillary. She was the most sought-after figure by Democratic candidates across the country. Newspapers described her as "the party's deadliest weapon against Republicans." "There was no one even close to being in demand like Hillary Rodham Clinton as a campaigner," said Senator Robert Torricelli, Senate Democratic Campaign chairman.[82]

David Gergen, among others, has noted that the Clinton marriage sometimes has the quality of a seesaw. When one is down, the other rises higher, in the delicate power balance between them. Clinton's new low facilitated a new high for Hillary, who had replaced her husband as the Democrats' "campaigner-in-chief."[83]

At a Democratic rally in Jacksonville, Florida, where she was to speak, five thousand tickets were "snapped up in a day." Hillary's "impassioned stump speech" was interrupted over a dozen times with "cheers, applause, and standing ovations."[84] In Allentown, Pennsylvania, she was "often interrupted by whistles and applause."[85] In Des Moines, she "fired up a cheering rally of more than a 1,000 people."[86] And so it went, in town after town.

For the most part, Hillary's message was about the issues, proclaiming that Democratic candidates cared more about education, health care, and the environment. But her presence alone was a stand against impeachment. She frequently raised the issue, though usually indirectly. "Does this state, does this country care more about progress over partisanship? Or are we going to give in to the sideshow running Washington? The choice is yours."[87]

While Hillary was campaigning for Chuck Schumer in New York, her foot swelled up so badly "I could barely put my shoe on."[88] "When her foot became badly swollen during a campaign stop in New York, a blood clot was discovered behind her right knee and she was put on blood thinners," wrote Bill Clinton. A blood clot is a serious, even potentially fatal, condition. "Dr. Mariano wanted her to stay in bed for a week, but she kept going, giving confidence as well as support to our candidates. I was really concerned about her, but she was determined to push on. As angry as she was with me, she was even more upset about what Starr and the Republicans were trying to do."[89] Hillary defied her doctor's advice. "I was determined not to cancel any of my campaign stops."[90]

She was a veritable "avenging angel," wrote one columnist, taking a special aim at the men who had tried to take her and Bill down.[91] For example, she "poured her heart" into Chuck Schumer's campaign; he was running against her chief Whitewater Senate tormentor, New York Republican Al D'Amato. She made eight trips to New York, including one on the final day of the campaign.

The entire election hinged on one word: turnout.

For that reason, "I urged people to vote as if their lives depended on it," wrote Hillary.[92] And indeed, her urgency was palpable and infectious. In Jacksonville she urged, "Talk to every person you know—call them on the phone, e-mail them on your computer, stop them on the street—and tell them this is no ordinary time, no ordinary election." She even told them to change the message on their answering machines, urging everyone to vote.[93] In New York she said, "There is a lot at stake in this election, as much as an election can have. Become a pest. Anyone you know, whatever age, please ask them to vote."[94] In Des Moines she told a cheering crowd, "This is a close election, this is a dead heat, and every single vote counts."[95] At a rally of twenty-five hundred mostly black voters on the South Side of Chicago, Hillary's "gospel-tinged message" was: "All souls to the polls. Staying home is not an option." Her voice rising higher, she implored them: "It's just not a choice. You have to vote this year because this is no ordinary election."[96] *The Washington Post* noted that Hillary was so fired up at the Chicago event that even the charismatic Jesse Jackson, who stood by her side, "seemed almost subdued compared to the First Lady."[97]

The Republicans analyzed the election the same way. "GOP Sees Low Turnout as Key to Victory" read one headline.[98] Republicans were "privately excited that low turnout could lead to big election wins."[99] Republicans believed that turnout would be at or below historic lows; indeed, *The Washington Post* reported that "experts say voter turnout this Election Day could be the lowest in decades."[100] The theory was that Democrats would be so disgusted with Clinton's behavior that they would just stay home. Newt Gingrich proclaimed that the GOP would pick up thirty to forty seats.

Clinton, the consummate political strategist, had figured out that voter turnout among African-Americans would be the key, one way or another. Voter turnout is tradionally lower in midterm elections than it is in presidential election years, but past experience had shown that the degree to which turnout was reduced was not equal for both parties. Key parts of the Democratic base, particularly African-Americans, voted in much lower numbers during midterm elections than did members of the Republican base. As a group, blacks almost uniformly supported Clinton—his approval rating in the black community was an astounding 90 percent. In the wake of the 2008 Democratic nomination fight, in which Clinton was accused of "playing the race card" in his disparaging remarks about Obama's victory in South Carolina, likening it to Jesse Jackson's victories there, it's easy to forget how strongly African-Americans supported Clinton. But African-American support would only help the Democrats if they actually cast their ballots.

Republicans knew that a low minority turnout was crucial for them. An article in the *Los Angeles Times* reported that the Republican National Committee, and isolated local Republican committees across the nation, had strategized about how to suppress the black vote, including having poll monitors with video cameras stationed in black neighborhoods to intimidate voters. Clinton publicly condemned the plan, which the Republicans denied, in his radio addresses.

The ultimate question was, would African-Americans vote or stay home? There was a kind of poetic justice in this. A portion of Clinton's enemies were segregationists who saw Clinton as a race traitor for his support of civil rights. It was fitting that Clinton would live or die by the African-American vote.

The Democrats targeted a lot of their TV and radio ads, direct mail, speaking engagements, and phone bank activity directly at African-Americans. In New York, for example, the state's Democratic Party assembled a get-out-the-vote operation focusing on seven hundred heavily black districts across the state where turnout had been historically low, using a "7-touch" plan meant to ensure that every registered voter received seven contacts from the party, through phone calls, personal visits, or literature. The Democratic Congressional Campaign Committee distributed flyers in black communities that featured a sour-faced Gingrich with the words: "Newt Gingrich and his Republican friends don't want you to vote on Tuesday, November 3rd. Stand up and prove them wrong!"[101]

The Democrats also employed a new electoral technique to get out the vote that had never been used before: prerecorded automated calls from both Bill and Hillary targeted at Democrats, especially minorities. Hundreds of thousands of people heard Hillary Clinton say: "Hello, this is Hillary Clinton. The Republicans are hoping that voters will stay home on Election Day. We can't let them get away with it."[102] Millions of people got these calls and, research showed, the calls were very effective. "People were excited to receive those calls," said Robin Brand, the Democrat in charge of the get-out-the-vote campaign in Washington State. "One woman actually thought she had a conversation with Hillary Clinton."[103]

For the Democrats, the key to increasing African-American turnout was to make this midterm election a presidential election. This midterm election "is about as presidential as you can get without having the actual Clinton name on the ballot," said Representative Charles B. Rangel, a New York African-American Democrat.[104] Rangel, who organized a national bus tour to get out the African-American vote, said: "There is no question that the African-American community strongly supports the President and strongly opposes anything that could be perceived as an effort to drive him out of office."[105] "This was the first time African Americans had the opportunity to do something in support of the President," said Elijah Cummings, an African-American congressman from Maryland. "People are fired up."[106] In New York they distributed flyers in heavily black neighborhoods that said: "The Republicans want to impeach our President. Say NO and send the Republicans a message."[107]

Particularly telling were the sentiments among black pastors. The black church had been at the heart of the civil rights movement in America, but black evangelicals had sometimes felt drawn to the social conservatism of the Republican Party. Not in this election. Clinton was being pursued because "he was a little too black for white America," said the Reverend Sandy Reed, an assistant pastor at Zion Baptist Church in Philadelphia. "The Republicans want to get him at any cost." In the previous two elections Reverend Charles W. Quann, minister of the Bethlehem Baptist Church, had supported the Republican incumbent in his area, Pennsylvania representative Jon D. Fox. But now, angry over the "witch hunt" against President Clinton, he told his eight-hundred-member congregation: "The Republican Party has no agenda for us other than to pull back the pages of history. This is the pulse of many African Americans. We've had enough."[108]

Another person who played an unwitting supporting role in energizing the Democratic base was Newt Gingrich. In one of the biggest electoral miscalculations in modern times, Gingrich decided that the Republicans were being "far too gentle with Clinton."[109] In the final days before the election he decided to run $10 million worth of ads across the country featuring the Monica scandal. In one Newt-inspired ad a woman complained indignantly: "It was wrong! He lied to us for seven months."[110] In another, two mothers talk under their breath: "What did you tell your kids?"[111]

The ads were the height of hubris, given that national polls had shown for months that the electorate was sick of the Lewinsky scandal. Though they were disgusted with Clinton's behavior, they approved of how he was handling his job, and disapproved of how the Republican Congress was doing its job, precisely because they saw impeachment for exactly what it was: a partisan grab at power that was interfering with the work of governing the nation. Depending on the poll, between 62 percent and 68 percent of respondents opposed impeachment, disliked the GOP's handling of the scandal, and wanted them to simply "drop the whole matter."[112]

The ads backfired, making the campaign a $10 million get-out-the-vote drive for the Democratic base paid for by the Republican National Committee. Republicans lost more seats than they won in the districts where the ads were run. "A serious and potentially historic blunder" is what Democratic National Committee chairman Steve Grossman gleefully called it.[113]

On election night Clinton had planned to watch the election returns over pizza with a small group of friends in the White House movie theater. Instead, he sat at Chief of Staff John Podesta's desk and began clicking around the Internet. Clinton had never used a computer on election night before. "He was so excited that he could follow election results precinct by precinct all over the country. Talk about a kid in a candy store. He has instant access to early returns and this was a man who knew every congressional district by heart," wrote Terry McAuliffe, who was with him that night.[114] Clinton never left Podesta's chair all night. Instead they brought the pizza party into Podesta's office.

"D'Amato defeated!" shouted Clinton.

A cheer went up.

"Faircloth defeated!" Clinton announced.[115]

Another cheer. The atmosphere was becoming festive. The defeat of Clinton enemies Faircloth and D'Amato were particularly sweet.

Clinton was euphoric.

By midnight "the mood in the room changed dramatically as it became clear we were actually going to pick up seats in the House," wrote Terry McAuliffe.[116]

"Mr. President, I think we have finally shut impeachment down," McAuliffe said.

Clinton hugged everyone. He was ecstatic.

"Black Turnout Proves to Be Key for Democrats" read headlines across the country the morning after Election Day.[117] The pollsters and pundits had been wrong. "What we had all over the country was a phenomenally large African-American vote," said commentator Robert Novak on CNN. "The Clinton strategy worked. It has made the margin of difference in state after state."[118] "The sleeping giant of black voting power awakened," wrote columnist Mary McGrory.[119] It was particularly striking in the red state South: "The turnout of black voters just killed us in many Southern states," rued Representative E. Clay Shaw of Florida.[120] In North Carolina "turnout helps tip the scales." John Edwards of North Carolina was elected to the Senate "buoyed by a heavy turnout of black voters."[121] In South Carolina 30 percent of blacks voted, as compared to only 19 percent in 1994. In one inner-city precinct in Baltimore voting rates were four times greater than they had been in 1994. The Republicans had wanted to make the election about Clinton, and they succeeded. Representative Maxine Waters of California, head of the Congressional Black Caucus, said African-American voters came to the polls because they were mad about impeachment: "It became obvious that they were out to get Bill Clinton. That played a role in this."[122]

Despite the fact that the Republicans had outspent the Democrats by $100 million, for only the second time in the twentieth century the president's party gained seats in a midterm election. The last time was two years after FDR was elected, when the populace still blamed Herbert Hoover and his party for the Depression. To find the last time a president's party won seats in his sixth year in office, one has to go back to 1822 and the administration of founding father James Monroe. In short, this historic victory was a total rebuke of the Republican power grab. Both Bill and Hillary Clinton have written that if more Democrats had run on a firm anti-impeachment message the Democrats might have retaken control of the House. "Many of them didn't do so because they were afraid," wrote Bill Clinton.[123] As it was, the Republicans clung to a mere five-seat majority.

The Republicans had completely misjudged the mood of the nation about impeachment. *The Economist* defined the mood of the American electorate as "defiant."[124] The returns were "a slap in the face" to pro-impeachment Republicans, according to *The Philadelphia Inquirer*.[125] "The elections are over, and the people have spoken: Keep Bill Clinton in the White House," trumpeted the *Orlando Sentinel*.[126] Or as *Washington Post* columnist Mary McGrory put it succinctly, the American people had one message: " 'Leave him alone.' "[127]

The media understood that the American people were sending a message: "Forget about impeachment, Ms. or Mr. Lawmaker, and get back to work" was how one ABC commentator put it.[128]And the implication was that if they didn't, they could well be next to get the boot: "Sure the impeachment train is still rolling, but in exit polls and key races voters flashed a warning signal about Congress's handling of the presidential scandal: Caution! Sharp Curb Ahead! Proceed At Your Peril," wrote Sandy Grady in the *Arkansas Democrat-Gazette*.[129] At least some Republicans got the message. As one Republican lawmaker put it: "The voters were saying 'put a fork in impeachment.' "[130] It's done. (And while you're at it "Stick a fork in the GOP revolution—it's done," read another headline.[131] And indeed, soon after this defeat, Newt Gingrich would resign both his speakership and his seat in Congress—another Clinton foe beaten in the election of 1998.) "As the returns came in," reported *The New York Times* the day after the election, "many party leaders appeared to be backing off from the impeachment inquiry."[132] "There's no doubt that Republicans are getting wobbly kneed as a result of Tuesday's vote," wrote Cokie and Steve Roberts in the *Daily News*. While publicly the Republicans were still blathering on about having "their Constitutional duty to fulfill, privately, they say they will act sooner rather than later, calling fewer witnesses rather than more, and try desperately to get the whole business over with."[133]

The prevailing metaphor among both Democrats and the press became that "the impeachment train has lost steam," as the *Arkansas Democrat-Gazette* put it.[134] Of course, the trial would go forward, but after the election of 1998 the result was never again in doubt. Bill Clinton would remain in office. He would survive.

The next day, Bill Clinton gave a victory speech: "The American people sent us a message that would break the eardrums of anyone who was listening," he said, calling the election a victory of "progress over partisanship."[135]

But "the big winner" in the election was Hillary. "Hillary Clinton is finally being seen as the political force she has always dreamed of being. She owns the party now," wrote McGrory.[136] *Newsweek* gave her an up arrow, calling her the "superstar vote getter of 1998."[137] "Give'em-Hell-Hill was the party's biggest asset," read *The Oregonian*.[138]

Hillary was even featured on the cover of *Vogue* magazine, the first time a First Lady had graced the cover of this fashion magazine in its 110-year history, a decision the editors said was mandated by Hillary's "exuberant, triumphant campaign barnstorming."[139] On the cover she looked "poised, elegant, and aristocratic" wearing a burgundy Oscar de la Renta evening gown in the red room of the White House, in a photo shot by famed celebrity photographer Annie Leibovitz.[140] *Vogue* editor Anna Wintour said it was her intention to portray Hillary as "very classic and regal, almost like British royalty."[141] Wintour pronounced her "woman of the year."[142] Hillary had finally bloomed, as both a politician and a woman. ("Long gone is the dowdy brunette with Coke-bottle glasses and a goofy butterfly blouse of two decades ago," declared *Vogue*.[143])

The election of 1998 was Hillary's moment, her debut as a national political figure in her own right. Hillary had shown "strength under enormous pressure," said presidential historian Doris Kearns Goodwin, adding: "Maybe it's going to be her turn next."[144] Indeed, Hillary would soon thereafter become a senator from New York and then a presidential candidate.

It is ironic, but also fitting that Hillary began her star turn by playing a familiar supporting role: Bill's protector, his Edith. As extraordinary as the impeachment crisis was, psychologically, being saved by his woman felt perfectly normal to Clinton. First Edith, and then Hillary, had protected him his whole life, though this was the most dramatic example of all.

If Hillary had not fought back, Bill Clinton would probably have been forced from office. Like Kane in *High Noon,* Clinton would have been a dead man had his wife not saved him.

In *High Noon,* Grace Kelly not only saves her man but the town, and I would suggest that if you live in the town called America, you owe Hillary a debt of thanks—regardless of whether you love her, hate her, or feel something in between. No, this is not a partisan outburst on my part. It's a statement of patriotism. The plot to reverse two national elections and remove Clinton from office was not just an attack on Hillary's husband: It was an attack on America and her Constitution. The Founding Fathers had nightmares imagining scenarios like the impeachment of Bill Clinton. The scandal I've called Impeachment-gate was one of the most serious constitutional crises in American history. Newt Gingrich said that his Republican revolutionaries were impeaching Clinton, not because he had committed a high crime or misdemeanor, but "because we can."[145] If this new standard for the impeachment of a president were to become acceptable, America wouldn't be America anymore. We'd be just another banana republic.

The resolution of the crisis came down to an old-fashioned street fight between a couple and a gang of thugs. The right-wing conspirators came after her man. And Hillary blasted them. Lucky for us she didn't miss. Democracy dodged a bullet on Election Day, 1998.

PART V

Africa: July 2007

12

Healing the Sick

When Bill Clinton left the White House, he was not a happy man. Bill Clinton's diarist, Janis Kearney, used the word "depression" to describe his mood.[1] While some postpresidential letdown is perhaps inevitable, Clinton had to deal with three sad facts. First, he was handing the White House over to George W. Bush rather than his chosen successor, Al Gore, at least in part because of the fallout from the Lewinsky scandal.* Second, Clinton was not allowed to fade away gracefully: There was a firestorm of coverage about last-minute pardons Clinton made to some dubious characters, including fugitive billionaire Mark Rich, and there was a spate of false rumors that received wide media play about the Clintons stealing furniture from the White House, which enraged Clinton. And finally, though Clinton would always be proud that he had

---

* Gore blamed Clinton for his defeat, but Clinton, in turn, blamed Gore for blowing the election. Out of his extreme disdain for Clinton's behavior, Gore excluded Clinton from the campaign—both as a stump speaker and a strategist—and, worse yet, didn't even run on the successful record of the popular Clinton-Gore administration. "Al, no one will think you had an affair with an intern if you run on our record," an exasperated Clinton told the vice president. In truth, they were probably both right. Had it not been for the scandal, Gore would have become president. And if Gore had run on their record, promising to stay the course, instead of trying to reposition himself as a flannel-shirt-wearing, outside-the-beltway populist, he most probably would have won as well.

fought and survived his high-noon battle against his right-wing enemies (impeachment was "an egregious abuse of the Constitution and the law and history of this country, and I should get credit for standing up to it," he said[2]), he could not escape the reality that impeachment had put a black mark on his second term, one that would never be fully erased from the minds of most Americans or the history books.

Clinton bounced back, as he always does. He wrote an overly long memoir, opened a presidential library, and, for the first time in his life, began making money, digging himself out of debt and becoming a millionaire from his speeches and book advance. But Clinton being Clinton, he needed a mission that was larger than life. He needed to be saving the world, and doing it on a world stage. Hence, Clinton formed the Clinton Foundation, a charitable organization that aims to tackle the planet's biggest, most intractable problems. And Clinton being Clinton, he is actually making progress toward solving some of them.

According to Leon Panetta, the former president is leading what amounts to "a government in exile" composed of people "who have basically decided it's their responsibility to deal with the problems of the world."[3] The paradox of Clinton is that even though he sometimes fails to accept responsibility for the problems created by his own behavior, he has always assumed responsibility for the problems of the world. His fundamentally altruistic nature drives him to help those in need. His hypomanic grandiosity makes him feel destined to help on a monumental scale. And his energy, intelligence, and charismatic leadership skills make him capable of actually pulling it off. Clinton claims to have some project going "in virtually every country in the world."[4]

No problem has been more massive or intractable than AIDS, particularly in third-world places like Africa. Worldwide, twenty-five million people have died of AIDS. It was estimated in 2006 that in Africa alone one hundred million people would die by 2025.[5] Clinton, through the work of his foundation, is changing those numbers. "When asked what has been his most important work since leaving the presidency, Bill Clinton answers, eradicating AIDS in Africa," wrote Carol Felsenthal in her book about Clinton's postpresidential life, *Clinton in Exile*.[6] "It gives me a chance to save more lives quicker," said Clinton.[7]

Every summer Clinton journeys to Africa to review the work of his foundation, and to visit with his friend Nelson Mandela. I went to Africa to see firsthand what Clinton has made of his postpresidential life.

I also went to meet Bill Clinton. Because I am not a journalist, I have not had the opportunity to follow him on the campaign trail or in the White House. And Clinton does not give interviews to biographers. This trip would be my one chance to experience personally the man I had been doggedly pursuing for two years. I went to Africa on a safari of sorts, but the big game I was hunting was Clinton.

· JULY 18, 2007 ·

The Activist

I arrived in Johannesburg two days before Clinton. In that time there was one man I really wanted to talk to. Though you've probably never heard of Zackie Achmat, he is one of the most famous people in South Africa. The charismatic AIDS activist was described in a 2003 *New Yorker* profile as "the most important dissident in the country since Nelson Mandela."[8]

"I hope your book isn't a hagiography of Clinton," was the first thing Achmat said when we met. Only after he told me his story did I understand why, but we will return to that in a moment.

Achmat's universally recognized trademark is a black T-shirt with HIV POSITIVE written in bright letters, which he wears almost constantly. The only way to destigmatize AIDS, Achmat believes, is for people with HIV and AIDS to come out of the closet. The idea for the shirt originated in 1998, when a woman named Gugu Dlamini was murdered after openly declaring her HIV-positive status on a TV broadcast—one of the first people in South Africa to do so.

Achmat told me, "When Hitler invaded Denmark and went after Jewish people, it was the king of Denmark who said that every Danish citizen should wear the star of David. And for us, we encourage everyone to wear this HIV POSITIVE T-shirt, to create openness and to help break the stigma. I believe in the power of assertion and being open. What we are saying is that we are here and we have a right to exist."

Achmat makes no attempt to hide his past as a male prostitute. "I want to give Bill Clinton a little bit of advice on sex life: be as open as possible. No one can say to me, 'You've had sex in toilets since you were a child.' I don't do it now, of course, because I don't want to. It's not newsworthy, because I've said it myself. Be open about your life. It's human. We all make mistakes."

When *Vanity Fair* published an issue on Africa in July 2007 that featured the most important global figures responsible for determining the fate of Africa, Achmat was profiled. He is featured wearing his HIV POSITIVE T-shirt while standing on the beach with his black dog, Socrates. The ocean is behind him, the sun is beginning to set, and Achmat's brown skin (he is of Malaysian heritage—what South Africans call "colored," as opposed to black) appears to be glowing, as he looks at the camera with an expression of mildly amused serenity. "He radiates charm and vigor," Alex Shoumatoff wrote in the article.

I arranged to meet Achmat at a gathering organized by Archbishop Desmond Tutu and Nelson Mandela to announce the inauguration of a new initiative: the Global Elders. Drawing on the African tradition of resolving problems through the collective wisdom of a tribe's elders, Mandela and Tutu were trying to expand that model on a world scale: They gathered twelve elder statesmen of the highest moral authority to collectively exert their powers of persuasion to resolving the world's most dire problems. None of the elders aspired to political office any longer, and so it was hoped that they could be truly independent in their moral voice. In addition to Mandela and Tutu, the council included former president Jimmy Carter, former UN secretary-general Kofi Annan, and former Irish president and UN Commissioner for Human Rights Mary Robinson. Three of the ten were Nobel Peace Prize winners.*

The event was held in an auditorium connected to South Africa's Supreme Court. To emphasize the difference between the old and the new South Africa, the modern court building was erected next to an infamous symbol of injustice, Old Fort prison, where black dissidents had been

---

* Other Elders included: Ela Bhatt, founder of India's Self-Employed Women's Association; Gro Brundtland, former prime minister of Norway; Fernando H. Cardoso, former president of Brazil; Graça Machel, board member of the United Nations Foundation and wife of Nelson Mandela; Lakhdar Brahimi, former foreign minister of Algeria; Li Zhaoxing, former foreign minister of China; and Muhammad Yunis, founder of the Grameen Bank and winner of the Nobel Peace Prize for his use of microcredit in the third world.

imprisoned, tortured, and executed; the abandoned prison is now a museum. A who's who of South African society waited with us outside the security entrance for this invitation-only event, while we were serenaded by a chorus of young people singing African chants. Everyone, it seemed, wanted to greet Achmat, from members of the media to political figures. As a concession to the formality of the event, Achmat wore an unbuttoned black blazer over his trademark HIV POSITIVE T-shirt.

Afterward, we retired to an outdoor café. For an agitator, Achmat doesn't act very agitated. Instead, he has a warm, relaxed manner. He has "mellowed," he says. During the Soweto student uprising of 1976—the equivalent of the Boston Tea Party in the struggle against apartheid—students revolted and boycotted school. Achmat, a student at the time, took things a step further. He burned down his school.

"I *tried* to burn down the school," Achmat corrected me. "I only got as far as the administration block, which I suppose was the most important part," he laughed conspiratorially. "It's my most important political lesson. Because it taught me what impatience was in politics, and what impatience should not be in politics. It committed me to a position of nonviolence, without becoming a pacifist." Achmat was jailed five times, but was never tried, for his subsequent peaceful protests against apartheid.

A new day seemed to be dawning for South Africa when Nelson Mandela was released from prison in 1990. For Achmat, who had poured his soul into the cause, and for thousands like him, it was a moment of elation. However, just as his nation was facing a new beginning, Achmat's doctor told him his life was coming to an end. He had tested HIV positive, and his doctor said he probably had only six months to live. Achmat became severely depressed. He locked himself in his house, watched movies, ordered in food, and waited for death. After six months, when he realized that he wasn't dead, he thought, "Maybe I should leave the house."

From that moment on, Achmat went from being an anti-apartheid activist to an AIDS activist. Since 1994 he has been a key force in the movement to drive down drug prices for AIDS patients. When he began, antiretroviral (ARV) treatment cost $10,000 a year, far beyond what even middle-class people in South Africa could afford. The price tag was a death sentence for virtually every infected African. To Achmat, this was a call to arms. In 2000, in a well-publicized act of protest, he flew an illegal shipment of generic drugs into South Africa. A local newspaper cartoon entitled "The Mark of Zackie" depicted Achmat dressed like Zorro, swinging on a rope, and carving a Z on the chest of a fat man labeled "Big Pharmaceuticals."[9]

Achmat formed a political organization: the Treatment Action Campaign (TAC). In partnership with the AIDS Law Project, they mounted numerous lawsuits against the government and drug companies. "The major aim of TAC was to get drug prices down," he says.

His primary opponent in this mission, quite shockingly, turned out to be the *Clinton* administration. After Mandela became president, his health minister, Nkosazana Clarice Dlamini-Zuma, pushed through Parliament a bill called the Medicines Act. This law declared it legal for South Africa to import lower-priced AIDS drugs from third-world countries and opened the door for the possibility that South Africa would begin manufacturing generic AIDS drugs—in defiance of United States and European patents. Backing the drug companies, the Clinton administration put South Africa on a trade sanctions watch list on April 30, 1999, something Achmat finds to be sadly ironic: "It had taken the U.S. Congress and presidency probably about thirty years to put racist South Africa on the sanctions watch list. And it took a Democratic Congress and president three years to put a democratic South Africa on the sanctions watch list for wanting to make medicines affordable to its people."

Achmat appealed to AIDS rights groups in the United States to join him in protesting the action. On June 16, 1999, in Carthage, Tennessee, Gore declared his candidacy for president. Suddenly, a dozen people from the group AIDS Coalition to Unleash Power (ACT UP) interrupted his speech and began chanting, "Gore's greed kills!" The vice president looked aghast. The protesters continued to hound him all along the campaign trail. At his next stop, New Hampshire, the protesters managed to be seated behind Gore, and they unfurled a large GORE'S GREED KILLS banner behind him, which produced a devastating image for television. They continued to dog him in New York, Philadelphia, and Washington. In one city they hid overnight under the VIP bleachers so that they could be front and center when Gore spoke. "Everywhere Gore went, there ACT UP followed, chanting, 'Gore's greed kills.'" Achmat laughed. It was a public relations disaster for a left-wing Democrat, especially among African-Americans, a core part of the Democratic base. "The message was: 'You're killing Africans.'" Suddenly, the political power of big pharmacy companies paled compared to the damage a few committed activists could inflict with their vocal shaming techniques.*

Three months after the Gore's Greed Kills campaign began, the Clinton administration abruptly changed course. On September 17, 1999, U.S. Trade Representative Charlene Barshefsky announced the removal of South Africa from the trade sanctions watch list. On December 1, at the World Trade Organization meeting in Seattle, Clinton announced, "The United States will henceforward implement its health care and trade policies in a manner that ensures that people in the poorest countries won't have to go without medicine."[10]

While many AIDS activists I have spoken to will never forgive Clinton for his initial opposition to generic AIDS drugs for the third world, Achmat is generous in his assessment. While he has no doubt that Clinton's initial reversal was the act of a politician responding first and foremost to political pressure, Achmat believes that Clinton had a "genuine conversion." In the tradition of St. Paul, once Clinton saw the light, he didn't just cease his persecution of those seeking to bring generic AIDS drugs to Africa, but joined the movement, and became its chief evangelist. Clinton is now the most visible figure on earth associated with the cause. The only thing that still bothers Achmat is that Clinton has never publicly apologized for his first position, though he has come close. In 2006, a *New York Times* reporter who accompanied Clinton to Africa, asked him about the issue. Clinton "conceded that his administration fought too long to protect the patent rights of pharmaceutical companies against countries trying to make or import cheaper AIDS medicines."[11] Of his earlier trade policy, Clinton said, "I think it was wrong."†

---

* In fact, the issue may have had more effect on the 2000 election than most people realize. Ralph Nader became involved, coauthoring two letters to Gore, one in 1997 and the other in 1999, protesting the U.S. trade stance on AIDS drugs. Gore answered neither letter. According to Jamie Love, who coauthored both letters, Nader said to him, "I can't believe Gore is blowing me off. Doesn't he realize I might run against him?" According to Love, this issue was a major factor in Nader's decision to run. Not only did Gore's nonresponse make him mad, but it served as a perfect illustration of Nader's contention that Democrats and Republicans were alike in protecting corporate interests over consumers. Had Nader chosen not to run, Gore would have become president.

† Unfortunately, almost as soon as Clinton stepped out of TAC's way, Nelson Mandela's successor, former deputy president Thabo Mbeki, who took over the presidency in 1999, became the new stumbling block. Mbeki shocked the entire

When Clinton left office, there was no general international consensus on whether aid agencies should go the generic drug route or work with brand-name companies. The UN, for example, took the route of negotiating with brand-name companies, probably because their richest member states, like the United States and countries in the European Union, have big pharmaceutical industries—and thus big investments in protecting intellectual property. In May 2000, Peter Piot, executive director of UNAIDS, and Secretary-General Kofi Annan announced what *The Wall Street Journal* called a "landmark response to the AIDS crisis."[12] After three years of negotiating, Piot was able to win an agreement by five brand-name drug makers to reduce their prices for AIDS drugs to the third world by as much as 90 percent. It was a stunning breakthrough achieved through years of public shaming and haggling with the drug industry, and made even more effective by the increasing threat that the world might bypass Big Pharma altogether and go generic. However, while a 90 percent reduction in cost sounds like a dramatic step forward, the problem was that, even at those drastically reduced prices, the drugs were out of reach by third-world standards. As the article notes, "For most, even the new prices will remain too high."[13] For example,

---

world when he took the bizarre position that HIV does not cause AIDS, and that ARVs should not be distributed in South Africa because they are harmful. "Mbeki wrote this denialist letter to Clinton, a long lunatic rave, which the Clinton office really thought was a forgery and a fake because it was so crazy!" Achmat said. Now Achmat was forced to take on his own government with lawsuits, protests, and high-profile acts of civil disobedience, ironically a government led by his own party, the ANC.

Achmat is best known for being the first person in history to mount a "drug strike." Though he could afford ARV treatment, Achmat announced, "I will not take expensive treatment until all ordinary South Africans can get it on the public health system. That probably means I will die a horrible death, even though medical science has made it unnecessary." Achmat fell ill in 2002, and Nelson Mandela himself went to Achmat's sickbed on July 27, pleading with him to accept treatment (he refused). "It meant everything that he came to visit me when I was sick," Achmat told me. Mandela left Achmat's bedside, calling him a "role model," and saying that he "had a case to take up with President Mbeki." Up until that point, Mandela had avoided publicly criticizing his successor's AIDS policy.

In 2003, when the government was beginning to move toward granting access to ARVs through the public health system, and Achmat was becoming seriously ill, he ended his strike.

Achmat has been nominated for a Nobel Peace Prize.

GlaxoSmithKline agreed to reduce the price of Combivir from $16.50 per day to $2.00 per day, but because it needed to be combined with a protease inhibitor, the final cost was between $5.00 and $7.00 a day—a bargain by American standards but well beyond the reach of people who live on an average of $2.00 a day and have no health insurance.

In 2002, the year the Clinton Foundation (CF) first became involved in the AIDS drugs issue, the picture was getting clearer. Two years after the UN's 2000 "landmark agreement," it was obvious that the reduced brand-name approach was not working: Only fifty thousand Africans—1 percent of those who needed ARVs—had them.[14] Not only were the drugs still too expensive, but the process was inefficient: Each drug company was negotiating separately with each country over each drug, while eight thousand Africans were dying of AIDS each day.

The international pendulum was swinging toward generic drugs. At its annual meeting in 2001, the World Trade Organization (WTO) met in Doha, Qatar, and issued the "Doha agreement," officially sanctioning the use of generic AIDS drugs by poor countries.

In 2002, generic drug manufacturers in India, such as Cipla and Ranbaxy, began producing generic ARVs in significant amounts at vastly reduced prices for groups like Doctors Without Borders. As prices dropped to an annual cost of five hundred dollars per patient—and there was no reason to believe that they could not fall lower from there—there was an abrupt realization that people could be helped for close to *a dollar a day*.

"For a thousand dollars a year, the world was going to let them die," said Jamie Love, director of the Consumer Project on Technology. "But for a dollar a day, not to save them was obscene." Suddenly, global AIDS relief seemed not only feasible, but a moral imperative. At these prices, first-world countries could afford to just buy the drugs outright and donate them to poor countries for free. The international community, perhaps for the first time, mustered the political will to really tackle the problem of AIDS drugs for poor countries. The result was the creation of the Global Fund in 2002, a unique multinational organization formed to fight AIDS, tuberculosis, and malaria around the world.

Thus, when CF got involved, all the right conditions were set for a huge market in generic AIDS drugs to take off. There were suppliers: Indian companies that could produce cheap generics in large quantities. There was demand: tens of millions of infected patients. And there were buyers: international aid agencies like the Global Fund, with hundreds of millions to spend. It was at this auspicious moment that Clinton stepped in to speed up forces already in motion.

Negotiating directly with Indian producers like Cipla, CF aggregated the group buying power of the entire African market, and then leveraged that mass buying power to bring down prices, much like Wal-Mart does. The fact that payment was guaranteed with hundreds of millions of dollars in international aid was also an essential part of the formula, allowing these companies to avoid many of the normal costs of doing business. There would be no marketing, no unsold inventory, and no unpaid bills. In 2003, CF negotiated its first contracts. With small profit margins but huge volume, these Indian drug companies are making good money providing the third world with cheap, life-saving drugs—a win-win situation.

As of today, CF has brought the annual price of treatment down from $500 to $120. Pediatric drugs have been an area of special concern for Clinton, since only a minute fraction of children in Africa were being treated. CF worked with suppliers to combine multiple pediatric medicines into one pill, bringing the price down from $600 to $60. "Children are alive in numbers we couldn't have imagined a couple of years ago because of what he's done," said Peter McDermott, chief of HIVAIDS at UNICEF.[15]

By 2007, the Clinton Foundation claimed to have helped 750,000 people in sixty-nine countries get low-cost ARVs that had been purchased through agreements it had negotiated, and Clinton aimed to expand that number to 2 million by the end of 2008. Overall, in 2007, 1.34 million Africans were on ARVs, comprising 28 percent of the total population who are estimated to need them. Still, it's a real glass half empty–half full problem. Almost 30 times more people are getting help than in 2002, yet, 5,800 Africans still die of AIDS each day.

Clinton says it was a direct personal appeal from Nelson Mandela that made him take up the challenge. "At the International AIDS Conference in Barcelona, in 2002, Mandela asked me to devote my foundation's attention to the epidemic, and in particular to the millions of HIV-positive people living in nations unable to afford life-saving anti-retroviral drugs for their citizens." In response, that same year, "I started the Clinton HIV/AIDS initiative."[16] Like Clinton, Mandela was criticized for not having done enough about AIDS while he was in office. He embraced the cause after his term had expired. One obvious influence on Mandela's change of heart was that his only living son (he had lost another boy to a car accident) contracted AIDS, to which he succumbed in 2005.

To understand how deeply Mandela's plea affected Clinton, one needs to look at the history of the Clinton-Mandela relationship, and perhaps even more important, the psychological meaning Mandela has for Clinton. Along with people like Martin Luther King, Mandela has a prominent place in Clinton's pantheon of personal heroes. Clinton feels a deep personal connection to all his larger-than-life role models, and has since he was a child. But where some of these connections are in personal myth and fantasy, Clinton has a real relationship with Mandela, which makes it all the more precious to him. In the same Africa issue of *Vanity Fair* featuring Achmat, there is an article about Mandela, written by Clinton, entitled "A Man Called Hope." It begins: "At my Harlem office, the headquarters of the Clinton Foundation, several portraits are clustered together on a prominent wall, next to a small conference table I use to meet with staff and guests."[17] These include a daguerreotype of Abraham Lincoln, a picture of Martin Luther King the night before he was assassinated, and no less than three pictures of Mandela, which Clinton says he "treasures."

During the course of his presidency, Clinton said, he became friends with Mandela. "I think the connection that he made with Mandela during his presidency was a very, very important emotional connection," said Achmat. That connection deepened in the spring of 1998, when Clinton made a historic trip to Africa. It was the most extensive trip to the continent ever undertaken by a U.S. president, a fact Clinton reminds people of regularly when he is in Africa. At a moment of great emotional vulnerability—Clinton was feeling hunted and devalued at home, in the midst of the impeachment nightmare—the uncomplicated mass adulation he received in Africa was a balm to his spirit. This sea of adoring people (a million in South Africa alone) was a psychological oasis in the desert. This reaction strengthened Clinton's personal connection to Africa, just as the adoring throng in Ireland had brought that country closer to his heart.

During this 1998 visit, Clinton had a profound personal experience with Mandela. The moment was captured in a photograph that he displays in his home, "a picture of Mandela walking arm and arm with me outside his old jail cell on Robben Island."[18] On September 21, 1998, the media began broadcasting Clinton's humiliating grand jury testimony around the clock. It was at a White House reception for African-American leaders held the next day, with Mandela standing next to him, that Clinton told the story of their Robben Island walk. Clinton recalled that he had said to Mandela, " 'I know you invited your jailers to the inauguration, and I know how hard you've worked on this. But weren't you angry one more time when you were walking down that road?' He said, 'Yes, briefly, I was. And then I remembered, I have waited so long for freedom. If my anger goes with me out of this place, I will still be their prisoner, and I want to be free.' "[19]

"I want to be free," said Clinton emotionally, to the audience, his soul in obvious torment. Since childhood, Clinton had been struggling to achieve the capacity to forgive, beginning with his abusive stepfather—what I called the "third stage of Roger." In this, Mandela is his ultimate role model.

Nine years later, in his *Vanity Fair* article about Mandela, Clinton tells the story of the Robben Island walk again, and admits that "I've told this story a thousand times, and I'll keep telling it for the rest of my life."[20]

At the time, Clinton was feeling persecuted by his Republican tormentors, and he identified with Mandela, who had endured and transcended a far worse twenty-seven-year persecution in prison. Achmat believes that Mandela's example made Clinton feel: "You can survive this. You can get through it." Indeed, Clinton has said privately that without Mandela's example, he might not have survived psychologically.

The fact that Mandela was standing by him, literally, on this terrible day in September 1998 meant a great deal to Clinton. Mandela said, "We are aware of the national debate that is taking place in this country about the president, and it is not our business to interfere in this matter. But we do wish to say that President Clinton is a friend of South Africa and Africa, and I believe the friend of the great mass of black people, and the minorities, and the disabled of the United States. Few leaders of the United States have such a feeling for the position of the black people and the minorities in this country. We have often said that our morality does not allow us to desert our friends. And we have got to say tonight, we are thinking of you in this difficult and uncertain time in your life."[21]

According to *The New York Times*,[22] "President Clinton, clearly moved, smiled during Mr. Mandela's remarks, and appeared at one point to wipe away a tear."*

Achmat believes that Clinton sees Mandela as a father figure. "We all do," he added. "For many of us in the liberation movement, we didn't have close relationships with our own fathers, and the leaders of the movement became our father figures." Growing up, Clinton experienced a similar paternal vacuum—he never knew his biological father—and as a result he has been searching earnestly for father figures all of his life. Clinton sought out men like Virgil Spurlin, his devout Christian high school band director—strong moral men he could become close to, admire, and with whom he could identify. But in general, Clinton's father figures were as much a product of his imagination as they were real people. Clinton speculated that he was better able to cope with his alcoholic stepfather than his half brother Roger because "knowing my father was someone else, someone I thought of as strong, trustworthy, and reliable, gave me more emotional security."[23] In fact, Bill Blythe, the man Clinton believed to be his biological father, was none of these things. This was Clinton's idealized fantasy about who his father was. But to cope with his chaotic family, Clinton said, "I had to construct a whole life inside my own mind."[24] In his imagination he could be the secret heir of larger-than-life figures like Kennedy and Martin Luther King. I don't mean to suggest, of course, that Clinton fantasized in a concrete way that he was their biological child. But in some spiritual or existential way he felt that he was their successor, heir of their mantle, and carrying on their work. The search for these role models is a large part of what drove eight-year-old Billy Clinton to walk to church. To find himself, young Clinton sought out idealized father figures, both in the pew and in the Bible.

---

* A more rousing speech at the same event was made by none other than Bernice King, daughter of Clinton's other hero, Martin Luther King. She compared Clinton to David, who committed adultery with Bathsheba and yet remained God's anointed one, able to achieve redemption through repentance. "None of us is perfect, because we have all, everybody, from the highest to the lowest, from the news media to Capitol Hill, from the pulpits to the pews, we have all sinned and fallen short of the glory of God," said King. "I wish to say that it's time, I think, for us to leave our president alone." CNN reported on September 22, 1998, that, in response, "the audience, including the first lady, responded with rousing applause and a standing ovation, as some people chanted, 'Leave him alone, leave him alone.'" After King spoke, "people were cheering, screaming, crying. It was phenomenal," said Paul Begala.

Mandela is the ideal father figure for Clinton for another reason: He is the exact opposite of Roger Clinton. We could even call him the anti-Roger. Roger Clinton regularly exploded into violent outbursts. Since childhood, Clinton has struggled for ways to control his own frightening temper. "Because of the way Daddy behaved when he was angry and drunk," he wrote, "I associated anger with being out of control, and I was determined not to lose control. Doing so could unleash the deeper constant anger I kept locked away because I didn't know where it came from."[25] Clinton has had mixed success with his efforts to lock away that anger. Throughout his life he has had problems with episodic explosions of rage that in many ways resemble those of his stepfather. Many who have been on the receiving end of these eruptions describe it as an experience they would never forget, as I discussed earlier. Even as he consciously repudiated Roger's violence, Clinton could not help but unconsciously internalize the man he called Daddy all his life. Yet, from a young age, Clinton has endeavored to walk the path of forgiveness as his road to anger management. Young Clinton showed an unusually mature ability to forgive his stepfather when he reconciled with him at the end of his life. Clinton has always hungered for a paternal role model who could guide him on this path, and Mandela has been that model for the adult Bill Clinton.

When Clinton left the presidency, it was his intention to do good on the international stage, like Jimmy Carter, but the form that would take was entirely unclear. It was neither inevitable nor expected that universal access to HIV/AIDS medicine would become his focus. Clinton put his mind to *this* task and his shoulder to *this* wheel because his father figure asked him to do it. "Madiba [Mandela's affectionate nickname—an honorary title adopted by the elders of his clan] doesn't ask something of you very often, but when he does, you do it," said Achmat. "Bill Clinton's love affair with Nelson Mandela . . . is central to understanding his work in South Africa," wrote Carol Felsenthal.[26] It is mind-boggling to consider, but close to a million people may be alive today, and several more millions tomorrow, in large part because of Bill Clinton's unresolved father issues, and the path he has chosen to resolve them.

· JULY 19, 2007 ·

Clinton Day 1: Johannesburg, South Africa

Faithfully, Clinton visits Nelson Mandela every year on or near Mandela's birthday. It's an unusual tradition for two former heads of state: Visiting the old man on his birthday is more what one would expect from a dutiful son. Clinton's insistence on this thoughtful but unprecedented ritual is his way of enacting the fantasy that, on some plane, he really is Mandela's son and heir.

The morning of July 19, we were at the Mandela Foundation, a bright modern building made of blond wood and glass behind a heavy security gate in Johannesburg. In the lobby was a large rectangular white birthday cake with the cover of the local newspaper reproduced on the icing: "Happy 89th Birthday, Tata!" read the headline, and a large picture showed Mandela smiling. July 18, the day before, was Mandela's actual birthday. It was a marathon national celebration, beginning with the Global Elders event and ending in a soccer stadium, where tens of thousands came to cheer him.

Everyone from the press bus became giddy when it was announced that we would each have a photo taken with Mandela. I had imagined veteran journalists to be jaded by celebrity, but as we waited in the hallway to meet him, they seemed really excited—which says something about Mandela's star power. When we got to the room I was shocked to finally see Clinton up close, standing next to the seated Mandela.

This moment I had been waiting for for so long—meeting Clinton for the first time—was slightly surreal. In the flesh, Clinton actually seemed to glow, as if he were under high-intensity klieg lights. Was I hallucinating? I mean, he really seemed bioluminescent. I know some people claim to see auras, but I've never seen one, at least not until now perhaps. What can I tell you? The man glowed.

I wondered later if others had ever perceived this phenomenon. A Google search for "Clinton" and "glow" yields seven hundred thousand hits, but most people don't mean it literally, though they don't mean it entirely metaphorically either. For example, according to London's *Sunday Times,* "with his silver hair and trim physique . . . Clinton, 61, *positively glows* these days."[27]

I wondered if this altered perception was some sort of idealizing projection; maybe people who like him experience this hysterical hallucination. But none other than R. Emmett Tyrrell, founder and editor in chief of the *American Spectator* (the magazine that housed the Arkansas Project), has seen it, too. Speaking about Clinton's inauguration, Tyrrell wrote, "I saw a golden halo encircling the head of the gently smiling leader. It was not unlike the halo that painter Fra Angelico used to confer on Biblical notables back in the fifteenth century, and it remained with the president for hours." Tyrrell tried to laugh it off, but not very convincingly: "To this day, I do not know if it was a genuine manifestation of Divine approval, or merely another of the technical marvels pulled off by Gary Smith, producer of the American Gala, as the rites were called." Obviously, Tyrrell believes it was the result of manipulation. But he saw it. "I am sure if Clinton had but looked into one of the myriad of television monitors glowing nearby, he would have seen that halo and been pleased."[28]

I walked toward Clinton. It was thrilling to be face-to-face, and then hand in hand, with the man I had been pursuing for two years. Clinton shook my hand briefly, not saying very much, and only making fleeting eye contact—not what I expected after hearing about how he pours his soul into you during five seconds on a rope line. But then I noticed that he was gazing instead at Mandela, with a protective look of concern. Many people had mentioned Mandela's failing health to me, and Clinton seemed preoccupied with how visibly frail he appeared.

We were ushered into a small, intimate, modern auditorium decorated with simple portraits of ordinary African people. Mandela seemed tired. I imagined the previous day had simply tired him out. He sat sphinxlike next to Clinton, and did not speak.

This was the second time I had heard Clinton speak in person. The first was in November 2005, at Hofstra University, in a large college gymnasium with thousands of people, at a conference on the Clinton presidency that I attended when I first began my research on this book. But today was the first time I had heard him up close. I was no more than a dozen rows away from the stage. What makes him so effective at public events, I wondered? It was a part of the Clinton puzzle I would try to answer on this trip.

With the eighty-nine-year-old Mandela in failing health, Clinton must have been conscious of the fact that this could well be the last birthday they spend together. So the speech he gave on this occasion was very important to him personally, even though it was barely mentioned in the press, since it wasn't tied to any newsworthy event. He referred multiple times to Mandela's legacy, as if he were eulogizing the great man in his presence, while he was still alive. Psychologically, the speech revealed much about the nature of Clinton's identification with Mandela.

"Every year I try to come to Africa to review the work of my foundation," said Clinton, *"and because I want to see my friend . . . the inspiration of much of what I have done."*

This is the speech's theme: Clinton has been inspired by Mandela, who is like a great father dispensing wisdom to him, his worthy son. If Clinton has done great things, it is because Mandela has been his model and guide. Clinton told the story of how Mandela made him an African AIDS fighter.

"When we closed the AIDS conference in Barcelona in 2002, Madiba and I both said we wished we had done more when we were in office. . . . And then he did something I will never forget. There was a young woman from the Asia-Pacific region, some island nation, and he said he was going to personally see that she got her medication, and he looked at me and said, 'That's the sort of thing you ought to do.' . . . I had no clue what to do. And then—almost as if he had set it up—the medical doctor who was the prime minister of St. Kitts and Nevis in the eastern Caribbean came up to me and said, 'We have no denial problem. We have no discrimination problem.' I said, 'What is your problem?' He said, 'Money and organization.' I said, 'Well, what do you want me to do about it?' And he said, 'I expect you to fix it.'"

As described earlier, Clinton dedicated himself to bringing affordable AIDS drugs to Africa because he had been asked to in 2002 by Mandela. Almost as if Mandela had set it up, a Caribbean medical doctor tells Clinton flatly that he expects him to fix this seemingly insoluble massive global problem. In other words, in Clinton's mind Mandela gave him a great commission: Fix it.

And, Clinton is proud to report, he *is* fixing it.

"This year we are working in twenty-five countries, selling medicine in sixty-nine countries, for three quarters of a million people. [Applause.] That is just one more thing I owe to Madiba." Clinton likes to talk

about his accomplishments, as he did here. But even as he boasted of these phenomenal numbers, he quickly reminded us that this is just one more thing he owes to Mandela.

More broadly, Mandela has been an inspiration to his *"personal and political journey."* Though imprisoned by whites for opposing apartheid, Mandela forgave his captors and openly embraced whites as part of the new, black-led South Africa. In Clinton's view Mandela's imprisonment was a transformative, purifying experience, through which Mandela had achieved the realization of two great truths. First, that the human family is *"interdependent"*: *"Whether you like it or not, we are bound together. Divorce is not really an option."* Second, and most important, *"our common humanity is more important than our differences."*

Clinton made a bold claim: All the world's worst problems could be solved if we were all just more like Mandela: *"You cannot name an issue in the world where there is conflict, where the root of it is not flawed thinking and feeling. What he [Mandela] purged out of his heart and mind, in the long years he was in prison, is still a virus running rampant in the world today that claims more victims than AIDS. And it is in the mind and heart of every person in this room. . . . Every time you pick up the paper for the next month and you read about some conflict somewhere, where somebody's doing something stupid, ask yourself, Isn't it because they believe our differences are more important than our common humanity?"*

It is almost as if Mandela had overcome the root problem of original sin, and the way to salvation is to follow the path of Mandela. The truth of Mandela can set us free. Just as Christ is believed by Christians to have died on the cross for our sins, so believers don't have to if they accept him and endeavor to follow his example. In a similar fashion, we don't need to personally pass through the same crucible of suffering Mandela did, if we are willing to learn from his example: *"We have to fund and build and maintain a tribute to the life and legacy and practical implementation of Madiba's work,"* said Clinton. *"Because what he went through in all those years in prison is what we all have to go through, and we can't possibly all go to jail to do it."*

Clinton, to pursue the metaphor, is the evangelist for the Mandela gospel, the St. Paul to Mandela's Jesus, if you will. Clinton is driven to achieve a place among the great souls who have changed history. George Saunders, one of the reporters on the bus who wrote a *GQ* cover story about

Clinton's 2007 trip to Africa, calls this Clinton's "lineage pleasure. . . . The pleasure he gets from seeing himself as part of a long line of workers-against-injustice (Gandhi, King, Mandela, etc.)."[29] As I've tried to show, what Saunders calls lineage pleasure has been one of the most powerful and abiding motivations in Clinton's life since he delivered the speeches of Martin Luther King in his living room.

At one point in this speech Clinton adopted the call-and-response rhythm of a black preacher. Three times he asked a variation of the same question, and each time he gave a slightly different version of the same answer. To drill home his point, his voice became slightly sterner, like an authoritative father, while he wagged his finger up and down, and focused his eyes on the audience:

"Why was there ever apartheid in South Africa? Because the people who perpetuated it thought our differences were more important than our common humanity. Why was there ever such discrimination in the American South, where I lived? . . . Because everyone was taught to think in terms of who you were better than . . . Now, think about every headline in the world today that is a troubling headline. Why can't they make peace in Iraq? Because the Sunnis and the Shiites prefer to fight each other. . . . Why in God's name are they fighting? Because they think their differences are more important than their common humanity, even if they hurt themselves."

Quite literally, the fate of the entire world depends on whether we embrace Mandela's truth: *"It is the most important part of his legacy. Because it is at the heart of every single problem our children and grand-children will face. It will determine whether the twenty-first century is the world's most peaceful, prosperous, and interesting time, or just one long nightmare of interdependence."*

I believe that the frankly spiritual tone of this speech was no accident. Clinton invoked God only once, but it was no throwaway line. Toward the end of the speech Clinton said that Mandela's survival of his long imprisonment was part of a divine plan: *"He did live, and I believe God ordained it for a reason."* To the believer, the pantheon of moral giants that Clinton is claiming as his lineage is an exclusive club of heaven-sent prophets. Clinton is a man who began his journey to the White House by walking to church alone when he was eight years old.

Perhaps for that reason, Clinton invoked two more men he feels con-nected to, both martyrs to the gospel of shared humanity. *"Gandhi died when I was a little boy, murdered by a fellow Hindu who thought Gandhi was a traitor for believing that his common humanity with the Muslims and the Christians and the Jews and the Jains and the Buddhists was more important than his differences. . . . One of the people I loved most in life, Yitzhak Rabin, was murdered by a fellow Israeli who thought he was a traitor because he believed that the children of Israel and the children of the Palestinians had a common humanity that should allow them to live together; they should share the land and share the future."* Rabin has also been described as a father figure for Clinton, and Clinton was, by all reports, devastated by his assassination. As biographer John F. Harris wrote, "Clinton placed Rabin in an elite group, which included South Africa's Nelson Mandela, of leaders of truly historic scale. More than one of Clinton's advisers observed that the president seemed to regard the gruff Israeli as something of a father figure."[30] Clinton truly has a deep need to attach to older men who can serve as role models for the world-changing great soul he feels he is meant to be.

In concluding, Clinton looked warmly at Mandela and said, *"And now, in the grace and beauty of his later years, he doesn't even have to say anything for us to know that you look better, you feel better, and you live better if you feel our common humanity is more important than our differences. That is the legacy the rest of us must keep alive forever. Thank you very much."*

With that Clinton walked over to Mandela, who was still sitting in his wingchair, bent down, and gave him a hug. Mandela's smile was warm and genuine. *New York Times* reporter Celia Dugger, who witnessed Clinton's birthday visit to Mandela in 2006, wrote that "Mr. Clinton and a frail Nelson Mandela clutched each other's hands like a long-lost son and his beloved father."[31] This is no casual metaphor. "Clinton definitely thinks of Mandela as a father," said Achmat. "And I think Mandela thinks of him like a son, too."[32]

The School

The school was in a poor neighborhood in Johannesburg, though not the poorest of the poor. It was a residential neighborhood filled with houses with rusted corrugated-metal roofs and iron bars around all the windows and doors, painted cheerfully in now faded pink, lavender, and light blue. Curious onlookers on the sidewalk pointed eagerly at our bus as we pulled up.

This event was a celebration of a program called City Year, in which college-age youths volunteer a year of their lives to work with the needy, in this case with poor schoolchildren. The program originated in Boston in the 1980s, and Clinton says that it was his model for AmeriCorps— his domestic Peace Corps program aimed at promoting volunteerism at home. In his 2007 book, *Giving,* Clinton wrote that he was "particularly proud" of having founded AmeriCorps.[33] With the support of the Clinton Foundation, the City Year program had been exported to South Africa, and now has two hundred volunteers.

When he arrived at the school entrance, Clinton was met by an honor guard of youths wearing bright red-and-black City Year jackets and khaki pants, assembled in two lines along the path to the front door. Clinton stood with his hands behind his back, smiling, as they chanted, clapped, and danced for him, and then he clapped appreciatively. He shook their hands as he made his way to the door, where he was met by the program director and principal, and shook their hands, too. Then Clinton put his arm around one City Year youth, looked forward, and flashed a classic open-mouthed grin of utter delight.

In the entryway a couple of dozen elementary-age boys and girls in school uniforms stood in three neat rows. Clinton bent down to shake their hands, and then stood behind the group, his arms around three or four children, grinning more than ever. Many people have written about the undeniably genuine delight Clinton displays in such situations, but I was just now witnessing it for myself for the first time.

We next moved into the courtyard playground, where a crowd of adults and children mobbed the president. A troupe of red-jacketed City Year volunteers were chanting and performing an exuberant African dance, swaying and jerking with joyous enthusiasm. Everything seemed to explode into a rhythm of chanting, singing, clapping, dancing, shouting, and a high-throated bird call sound that serves as the South African version of a cheer.

Secret Service agents nervously tried to gain some sense of control. Somehow I became separated from the press contingent, and the Secret Service refused to allow me to descend the stairs into the courtyard. I found this incredibly frustrating. Later I learned from watching the journalists that there is an art to balancing your need for proximity with the Secret Service's need to control it. The journalists never directly opposed the Secret Service, or got into a power struggle with them, but neither did they obey them. None of the press people I was traveling with would have stood dumbly on the portico as I did, wishing they could be in the courtyard. You just find another route to flow toward Clinton, pretending you didn't hear the agent when he told you to "stand here" or "stay back." It is almost a dance. The Secret Service agents, for their part, pretend they don't see the reporters going exactly where they had been told not to go. It all makes more sense if you visualize how fluid the situation is: Clinton is always in motion. The agents form a perimeter around him and together work like a wave to push everyone back. Then Clinton moves, the perimeter re-forms, and another wave flows. To follow Clinton you must navigate the waves.

We all moved into the assembly hall. Clinton ascended to the stage and sat in front of several rows of City Year youths. A large City Year banner, with a bright red sun surrounded by yellow-and-black diamonds, hung from the podium. To express appreciation, members of the audience would wave their arms above their heads in a circle whenever someone said something particularly stirring, and then break into the bird call.

Clinton was introduced by a girl named Faith, who told a brief but moving story about how City Year had changed her life. Being introduced by young people with inspirational stories is part of the Clinton formula. (He did it in Ireland with great effect.) Clinton understands, as I noted earlier, people's insatiable thirst for stories.

Whenever possible, Clinton mentioned that 750,000 people are now on the reduced-price ARVs negotiated by the CF. At one point, he said excitedly, "What I think about is that that's 750,000 more stories that will unfold, which otherwise would never have happened." What a strange metric. Number of lives saved equals number of stories told. I got the genuine impression that Clinton would be eager to hear all 750,000 if he had time.

As Faith spoke, Clinton sat in rapt attention, smiling admiringly.

"In the past, I did not have much hope for my life," she said. "I used to feel that I am not good enough, before I met that special someone who took the time to listen to me. And that person is Shannon [her City Year volunteer]. City Year has taken me up from the dark and brought me to the light side of the world. She has taught me how to live my life in a positive way as a teenager. And she, too, had experienced the disappointment and regrets of making choices, especially in a world full of peer pressure and influence. Because of Shannon, I now know that there is hope. And I know that no matter what I do, I should never give up. Thank you, City Year."

Stories of transformation like this are what excite Clinton the most. I could almost hear the tune of "Amazing Grace" playing in my head as Faith described how she once was lost and now she's found. Without explicit reference to God, this story resembled the classic Christian conversion narrative that Clinton heard hundreds of times in Arkansas churches while growing up. The parallel is hard to miss. Chris Stamos, a philanthropist involved in Clinton's work in Africa, said that every time he hears Clinton give a speech in Africa, "It's almost like being in a Baptist church."[34] To me this was not surprising. As I've described earlier, I believe that, in his own mind, Clinton is on a religious mission. He is "like a revivalist at a tent meeting," according to Vartan Gregorian, president of the Carnegie Corporation.[35] "I really see this guy as a preacher," said Susan Davis, chair of the Grameen Foundation USA.[36] George Saunders asked Clinton about the "Christian basis for the work he is doing in Africa." Clinton responded with passion:

> There are an enormous number of admonitions in the Christian New Testament where Jesus says we should pay attention to the plight of the poor, the ill, the imprisoned, those with physical handicaps; that we should not judge, but extend a helping hand to, people who have done things that society considers wrong, whether they're abusive tax collectors or prostitutes. That, you know, we should not look upon any person as less human than we are. The book of James says faith without works is dead. . . . "Show me your works and I will know your faith." While there is no explicit reference to, let's say, homosexuality in the New Testament, no explicit reference to abortion, there are hundreds and hundreds of references to the imperative of acting to help people who are in genuine need, who are less fortunate than you, whom you can help, and you're supposed to do it without regard to your own economic or social standing.[37]

In fact, the religious sounding narrative carried through the entire speech he gave that day at the school.

In 1991, when I was young governor of my state and I had just started running for president, I said that if I were elected, I would try to enact a program in the United States to give young people all over our country a chance to serve in their communities for a year or two. Working with children, working with the elderly, working in national emergencies, whatever. Then, in December of 1991, I went to Boston early one morning, and I saw the oldest City Year project in Boston, Massachusetts. And I saw these young people in their City Year jackets. I saw them helping older people exercise in the morning, who had been trapped in more limited circumstances. I saw them working with little children.

A light came on in my head:

"This is what to do."

So in 1993, we passed the legislation. Now in America there are many organizations that participate in what we call AmeriCorps, our national service program. There are now over five hundred thousand young people, like the young people in these red jackets, who have been through that program. They have touched tens of millions of people.

If we inserted God into this text, Clinton could be the prophetic founder of a new religious movement. Searching intently for a national volunteer program, Clinton had a quasi-revelatory experience, but instead of seeing the light in a traditionally religious sense, a light went off in his head. As a result, Clinton felt an evangelical sense of moral urgency that drove him to found AmeriCorps, a movement he claims has transformed tens of millions of lives forever.

At this point in the speech Clinton leaned in, becoming even more intimate with this local crowd, and told a story of his personal relationship with *this* City Year group:

The last time I was here, almost two hundred of you, your predecessors, signed notes to me about City Year—what you were doing. And it was put into a big beautiful basket, which rests in a place of honor in my home.

When Clinton said this, my first thought was a cynical one. "Yah right," I thought. "With all the gifts and mail you get, this basket of letters is on your mantel—give me a break." But Clinton's next line had me visualizing that basket of letters, and yes, actually believing they exist somewhere in his home.

> *And sometimes when I'm discouraged* [pause], *I just walk over* [smile] *and reach in the basket* [he mimes picking up a letter], *and pick out one of the notes from a South African young person. And I think about what you can do to touch lives and give people new beginnings.*

After he picks up the imaginary letter the expression on Clinton's face is one of sublime peace, truly as if the burden of his cares had been magically lifted by this note. The story has come full circle. Now South Africa's City Year is encouraging Clinton, helping *him* to continue to move from the darkness to the light.

> *So you are about the future. And those of us, like me, who have more yesterdays than we have tomorrows, we owe it to you, and to your country, and to these students to give you that future. Keep up the good work, and I will try to help. Thank you.*

"Wow," I thought to myself. "He's really *that* good." It all happened so fast, like Michael Jordan soaring above the basket, making it look so easy, that no one could take in everything he was doing. I'm convinced that Clinton is operating on so many levels—his game is so complex—that all the pundits, scholars, and experts who claim a status as Clinton experts are just scratching the surface.

Clinton made George Saunders think of Michael Jordan, as well. "To observe Clinton up close is to get a miniseminar in the deficiencies of the media in conveying the real scale of our public figures. Comparing the man in person with the media-accreted version you have in your head, you feel the way you might if, having watched Michael Jordan on TV all those years, and having thus reduced him to *great quickness + fall away jumper + excellent clutch shooter*, you suddenly found yourself defending him one-on-one."[38]

And it wasn't just Saunders and I who reacted that way; all of the reporters were buzzing about Clinton. Admittedly, this was a handpicked group of journalists, invited to accompany Clinton to Africa. But they were also all senior correspondents for national publications who are supposedly used to meeting presidents and other celebrities. Yet, they talked about that speech the way men in a locker room talk about a great athletic play from the previous night's game.

· JULY 21, 2007 ·

Clinton Day Two: Lusaka, Zambia

A Message in a Bottle. This morning we were in Zambia. After breakfast I met with two grassroots AIDS activists, Felix Mwanza and Paul Ka-sonkomona, from the Zambian Treatment Advocacy and Literacy Cam-paign (TALC). We had arranged to meet in the lobby of the five-star hotel where I and the Clinton entourage were staying. Wearing HIV+ T-shirts and jeans, and looking a little scruffy (Paul literally wore a hood through the interview), they stood out and looked a little uncomfortable in these luxurious surroundings.

They both agreed that they were lucky to be alive. Paul and Felix were both now on ARV therapy that had been unavailable just a few years earlier. ARV treatment had cost one thousand dollars a month, making it unaffordable for virtually the entire population of Zambia. But in 2004, the president of Zambia declared AIDS a national emergency, and the government began offering ARV drugs at the vastly reduced price of ap-proximately ten dollars a month. But in a third-world country where 85 percent of the population earns less than two dollars a day, what would be a nominal copay in America was still unaffordable to most Zambians. With international aid, that price has been knocked down to zero. Since 2005, ARVs have been distributed by the government for free, and over ninety thousand patients are on the medication. A few years earlier there had been virtually no Zambians in treatment.

Recently, TALC began advocating for lower prices on the newer second-line drugs. For people like Paul, for whom conventional therapy has stopped working, these newer medicines offer a second line of defense. But these drugs are often the most expensive, because they are new and generic versions are not yet available. Paul was part of a delegation that met with the president of Abbott Laboratories, which makes the second-line medicine, Kaletra. Abbott's president claimed that the cheapest price for

Kaletra she could offer to Africa was $550 a month, complaining that Abbott was already taking a loss on ARVs in Africa as it was.

During the meeting, one of the men with Paul secretly e-mailed the Clinton Foundation, using his BlackBerry under the table. He received an immediate response: CF claimed that they could provide the drug for $350 a month, and they believed that in time they could bring the price down even further.

When Paul's colleague shared the contents of the CF e-mail in the meeting, the president of Abbott became incensed, and "unceremoniously" ended the meeting abruptly, claiming she had to fly to Washington, D.C., immediately because she had "promised to take her daughter to a movie."

"It was rude. She showed disrespect to all the people there," said Paul.

But as it turned out, they didn't need to deal with Abbott at all. "We thought it would take a long time for the second-line drugs to make it to Zambia, but they are already here. The CF people moved fast." Paul is now on the generic version of Kaletra. Generic prices for second-line drugs are heading toward the dollar-a-day mark in the contracts CF is currently negotiating.

Though the Clinton Foundation had negotiated the contracts, much of the money to pay for those drugs comes from U.S. president George W. Bush. In 2003, Bush announced the creation of the President's Emergency Plan for AIDS Relief (PEPFAR), a massive $15 billion commitment over five years for AIDS relief in Africa. Even the most partisan liberal AIDS activists credit Bush with having made a quantum leap in AIDS spending in Africa. Zambia alone received $149 million in 2006, and is scheduled to receive $200 million in 2007. Yet, given these facts, Bush has gotten surprisingly little credit in the hearts and minds of Africans, especially compared to Clinton. When I heard Paul and Felix make some veiled disparaging references to Bush, I asked what made them feel so critical toward the Bush administration.

They responded with a list of reasons.

Bush chose someone to head up PEPFAR with no experience regarding AIDS or public health. Indeed, Randall Tobias's main qualification was his background as the former CEO of the pharmaceutical giant Eli Lilly, which suggested that he was named, in part, to protect the interests of the pharmaceutical industry. Indeed, during its first two years of operation, PEPFAR spent money exclusively on American brand-name drugs. The ostensible reason was that the law allowed only FDA-approved drugs to be exported. "There was a string attached," said Paul. "The money had to be spent on American-branded drugs. So, the money was being brought here so you could take it back. The thing that hurt me is that these drugs were ten times more expensive, which meant that when I got my medicine there were ten other Zambians who were not getting theirs."

Then, in 2005, in response to protests, an accelerated FDA approval process was adopted that allowed quick approval of generics, and PEPFAR began purchasing them from India.

Another reason why Bush is not very popular in Africa—despite giving away $15 billion—is that his approach has been perceived by many as including an overzealous imposition of American Christian conservative values on the African people. For example, Bush has spent hundreds of millions of dollars across Africa for "abstinence training." While Bush is giving Zambia $200 million in 2007, half of that money is being funneled to religious nongovernmental organizations (NGOs). World Vision, an evangelical Christian organization, spent eight million federal dollars in Zambia last year on youth sports camps that train abstinence; peer counselor training programs that teach teenagers to educate their friends about the benefits of refraining from sex; and "coming of age ceremonies" in which pubescent boys and girls take vows of virginity. Groups like this have put over twenty-three thousand Zambian youngsters through abstinence training.

In 2002, when PEPFAR was created, Bush began promoting abstinence-only programs. All U.S.-funded AIDS prevention programs that did not center their approach on abstinence were subject to audits by the inspector general of the Department of Health and Human Services (HHS). The preference was for "faith-based" programs like World Vision. Randall Tobias described faith-based NGOs as "the backbone in many cases of the way in which we're implementing our work."[39]

Laura Bush visited Zambia just two weeks before Clinton. On June 26, 2007, she praised faith-based programs as "one of the greatest sources of hope" in Africa. She added, "There are several ways we can reach our young people. One of the effective ways is abstinence. . . . It brings back dignity and self-responsibility to young people, because they know their bodies are not supposed to be abused, and they should learn to say no."[40]

"Laura Bush has been touring Africa, glorifying virginity," said Felix, with a note of disdain. According to Felix, a number of young girls are seeking to protect their vaginal virginity by having anal sex, which is actually a more efficient way to transmit the disease. "If someone is coming to Zambia with a view to help Zambians, he ought to sit down with us to find out what we need. Maybe abstinence works in the U.S., but it doesn't here," said Paul.*

"We are not saying that abstinence is bad. But we are saying that if you cannot abstain, have protected sex."

Which brings us to the the third thing Paul and Felix don't like about Bush. PEPFAR's legal mandate is to promote prevention programs that emphasize three strategies, summarized by the acronym ABC:

Abstinence
Be faithful to your partner
Condoms

But PEPFAR has quietly tried to drop the C. The basic attitude, as expressed by Derek Gordon of Focus on the Family, a powerful evangelical group in Bush's conservative base, was: "Condoms promote promiscuity."[41]

In 2002, the Bush administration removed the "condom fact sheet"

---

* In fact, abstinence training doesn't work in the United States either. Though Bush spends $176 million a year domestically promoting abstinence education, it's not clear what benefit, if any, it has produced. A long-awaited, large national study found, according to *The Washington Post* (April 14, 2007), that, among American teenagers, those who underwent abstinence training were no different from other teens in the age at which they became sexually active; their level of sexual activity; or their adoption of safe sex practices. However, Bush officials, long known for their ability to ignore inconvenient science on topics like global warming, rejected the report. Harry Wilson, a top official in the Department of Health and Human Services, said that the administration has no intention of changing funding priorities in light of the data. "This study isn't rigorous enough to show whether or not [abstinence-only] education works," Wilson said. However, on August 14, 2007, an article in the science section of *The New York Times* entitled "Abstinence-Only Programs Not Found to Prevent HIV" reported on a review of the entire scientific literature conducted by two British researchers at Oxford University. Examining thirteen separate empirical studies, they, too, found that "abstinence-only programs had no significant effect in either decreasing or increasing sexual risk behavior."

from the "Programs that work" page on the HHS Web site. After protests by a number of groups, the fact sheet was restored, but the symbolic
act of removing the condom fact sheet was an early clue to PEPFAR's
agenda. Director Randall Tobias warned in his written guidelines that
groups receiving U.S. funding should not target youth with messages that
present abstinence and condoms as "equally viable."[42] Tobias has openly
denigrated the strategy of promoting condom use to stop the spread of
the disease. "Statistics show that condoms have not really been effective.
It's been the principal prevention device for the last twenty years, and I
think one needs only to look at what's happening with the infection rates
in the world to recognize that [it] has not been working."[43]

The problem is not that condoms are ineffective—it's a medical fact
that they prevent the spread of the infection (to be accurate, they are 97
percent effective). The problem is that we have been ineffective in getting
a sufficient percentage of the population to *use* them. Nonetheless, Tobias was signaling that PEPFAR would not exert much effort to promote
their use.

Forty to fifty percent of the direct health care services in Zambia are
delivered by faith-based groups. While they provide valuable, needed services, they are often "hesitant" to push condom use, according to the
International Herald Tribune.[44] Even the Zambian ministry of health
spokesman, Canisius Banda, who normally would be quite reluctant to
criticize Zambia's American benefactor, had to say that American faith-
based NGOs "are very strong on abstinence and being faithful," but they
"are weak on condom usage. They seem to have difficulty with that part
of the message."[45] Paul Zeitz, director of Global AIDS Advocacy, put it
more plainly: "People are dying as a result of this ideologically driven
policy."[46]

An even more ideologically charged issue is how to deal with sex
workers and condoms. Getting prostitutes to use condoms is an effective
way to slow the transmission of the disease. To conservatives, however,
the idea of educating sex workers and providing them with condoms
comes too close to endorsing prostitution. To mollify conservatives, the
PEPFAR law mandates that all individuals working for agencies who
receive PEPFAR money must sign a personal pledge condemning prostitution. As Randall Tobias explained it: "In order to receive money, organizations need to have a policy opposed to prostitution and sex
trafficking." As far as he knew, Tobias said, implementing the pledge had

produced "no problems on the ground."[47] Others, however, disagreed, pointing out that some programs targeting sex workers have been discontinued as a result of the pledge. Government-funded groups don't want to alienate their patron, PEPFAR, and lose their funding. Tobias did tout programs aimed at helping prostitutes find other means of gainful employment. While that is a laudatory goal, even if such programs were successful, new sex workers would take their place, and the population of active prostitutes would continue to spread the disease if they didn't use condoms.

The irony of all of this is that on April 27, 2007, Randall Tobias was forced to step down as head of PEPFAR because of a scandal: His cell phone number was found on the client list of a woman the papers dubbed the "D.C. Madam." Tobias claimed that the massages he received in his condo from the Pamela Martin and Associates Escort Service involved "no sex." (How's that for abstinence?) Nonetheless, Tobias resigned the next day, for "personal reasons."[48] Tobias was replaced by Mark Dybul, a physician with extensive experience in both public health and AIDS.

In the post-Tobias era, some things have changed for the better. In a press release dated September 19, 2007, the American embassy in Lusaka announced that the United States will donate forty million condoms to Zambia. "The donation represents a two-year supply for the entire country," according to the embassy.[49] It's a strange conversion ratio to consider: Because one Randall Tobias was caught allegedly having illicit sex, millions of Zambians will finally be able to have protected sex.

However, all that said, the Bush administration is far from the most pressing matter on Paul's and Felix's minds. There is still an AIDS crisis in Zambia that has nothing to do with either Bush or drug prices. While Lusaka, the capital city, has sixteen treatment centers, it is not unusual for rural Zambians to be hundreds of miles from the nearest clinic. Some patients, who are too poor to afford any other form of transportation, literally walk for days to get a month's supply of medicine. Even though Zambia has access to all the free ARV medicines it needs, the majority of people who need them don't get them, especially in the rural areas where most people live, because most of the country has no medical infrastructure. The cruel irony is that they have the life-saving medicine, but no way to deliver it.

Rural patients are also far away from access to required diagnostic tests. Most doctors will not prescribe ARV therapy without lab results from an expensive machine used to count CD4+ cells, a type of white blood cell important in fighting infections, also known as T-cells. HIV infects CD4+ cells, and the CD4+ count decreases as the HIV virus progressively eats away at the immune system. Once your CD4+ count falls below 200, you officially have AIDS, and are a candidate for ARV therapy. For a long time there were exactly two CD4+ machines in this entire nation of 12 million, and both were in Lusaka, the capital city.

This is not a new problem. Zambia, like most African nations, has had an urgent need for a rural health care infrastructure for some time. Stephen Lewis, the United Nations special envoy for HIV/AIDS in Africa from 2001 to 2006, personally raised the issue with the president of Zambia in 2005. "I had a very serious conversation with the president, quite an extensive one, discussing exactly these issues. The question of transportation costs in the rural areas, and the accessibility of district hospitals, and the provision of the drugs: These things were constantly being raised. But nothing really happened." It seemed incomprehensible to me that a government would feel no sense of urgency about saving their own people's lives—16 percent of the Zambian population is HIV+, and a very high percentage of the infected population live in rural areas.

Some of the trouble revolves around money. The chief bottlenecks to setting up treatment in rural areas are a shortage of qualified health care workers and a shortage of money to train and pay them. Yet, Zambia is either not able or not willing to pay the health care workers it already has. While I was there, the nurses were about to declare a strike because the government refused to pay a thirty-seven-dollar-a-month housing allowance, one they were legally obligated to pay because it was in the nurses' union contract.

The problem may not simply be a lack of dollars, but how and where the nation's money is spent. Zambia's government has been accused repeatedly of corruption, allegedly using the country's resources to line government leaders' pockets rather than to extend the public health system. For example, a number of health ministers were arrested in October 2006 for allegedly misappropriating the money allocated for the nurses' housing allowance.[50] Even Clinton acknowledged that "the country has had a lot of corruption problems."[51]

Perhaps equally important, the government does not like to be rushed or pressured, either by well-meaning foreigners offering aid, like Lewis, or by local advocacy groups, like TALC. In Zambia there is no tradition or precedent for the government dealing cooperatively with grassroots organizations and advocacy groups. "The government and the health ministry see us only as opponents," said Felix. Stephen Lewis, who has spent a lot of time in Zambia, had the same impression: "There's no question that the government was very hostile to TALC," though to Lewis it seemed that TALC was exactly what they claimed to be, a patient advocacy group with no other political agenda.

"We are not against the government," said Paul. "We just want to save our lives."

It's a very personal issue for Paul. He had recently lost his own sister to an untreated throat infection common among AIDS patients; their compromised immune systems make them targets for a host of opportunistic microorganisms. She lived in a rural area. Though Paul tried to persuade her to travel for help, she was too weak, and "she just gave up." For a moment, as his eyes began to tear, Paul had to turn away when he spoke about his sister.

Paul and Felix worked with TALC to produce a documentary movie about the problems of rural AIDS patients. It featured one man who had to walk seven days to the nearest clinic to get his monthly supply of medicine. "How can a weak sick person do that?" It was to be shown on television, but because Zambian TV is run by the state, the government was able to forbid the broadcast.

"We didn't know what to do," said Paul. "We mailed the DVD to the Clinton Foundation and about twenty other international AIDS organizations. It was a cry for help. It was like a message in a bottle."

I had to wonder, "Would it ever be read?"

· THE SOCCER FIELD ·

We came to a huge open space, covered with half a dozen soccer fields, to meet with youth from the Zambian Scout Association. The Scouts have adopted a program called Boostele, named after a uniquely Zambian form of break dancing that is now very popular among young people. Boostele's big draw is that it sponsors soccer leagues, and young African boys, like boys in most places, love soccer. Today's big occasion was a soccer tournament, and Clinton was there to bestow the trophies. The aim of Boostele is to teach leadership skills and health awareness. As part of that mission, they have begun teaching Zambia's twenty-three thousand Scouts about AIDS.

They do this, in large part, through chants and games. I witnessed one such exercise: Two rows of Scouts stood in parallel lines facing each other, wearing gray T-shirts and their official Scout kerchief, which is green with red, orange, and black stripes on the fringe. A charismatic adult leader walked up and down between the rows calling, and the Scouts responded. "I'm going to give you this yellow ball, and you put it behind your back. Then pass it around behind you." They passed the ball.

"Now." He pointed to a boy. "Do you know who has the yellow ball?"

"No."

"That's like HIV. You don't know who has it. Can you tell by looking who has HIV?"

"*No!*" they all chant.

"Michael, can you tell by looking who has HIV?"

"*No!*"

"Kunda, can you tell by looking who has HIV?"

"*No!*"

Clinton walked out from the clubhouse onto the lawn, working his way down a reception line.

Having surreptitiously defied the Secret Service, I managed to place myself only six feet behind the people whose hands he was shaking, and began videotaping. Clinton appeared to take his time with each person, even though he is actually with them for only a moment or two. Though it is brief, the visit feels intimate. As he approached each person, he broke into an infectious grin before shaking their hand. Actually, he wore one the whole time, but somehow every time his eyes lit on a new person, a brand-new smile dawned, just for them. I tried to figure out how he does that. One way is that he mixes up his expressions. Clinton often purses his lips, seeming to *suppress* a smile, as he makes eye contact. His eyes twinkle, and he shakes or cocks his head, with a knowing, ironic, almost conspiratorial expression. The combined effect is the sense that he and the person he is greeting share a deep, private bond of affection. "Psst," the look seems to say. "This is *entre nous.*" Most other politicians give the impression that they are working—exerting muscular and emotional energy—to smile. But Clinton appears to do the opposite: Pushing his lips together, sticking out his lower lip, crinkling the corners of his mouth, he is visibly exerting muscular energy to restrain a smile. So, when his smile finally bursts forth, it's because he has released it, holding himself back no longer.

Clinton walked toward the first man, stopped in front of him, looked him in the eyes, pursed his lips, tilted his head, and burst into his big, sunny, open-mouthed smile. Clinton grasped his hand, and then used his other hand to cup the man's forearm. "I'm so glad to see you again." He paused, stared even more intently into his eyes, and lowered his voice: "I was really touched that you came last night." Pause. "I hope we can talk more." Never breaking eye contact, Clinton shook the double-grasped hand one more time. The encounter lasted exactly fifteen seconds.

A Scout master handed Clinton a Zambian scouting scarf. "I was in scouting, you know, when I was a boy," Clinton explained, as he immediately removed his tie, handing it to a Secret Service agent, and began threading the kerchief around his neck. Clinton is an expert at joining with a crowd, and clothing can be one way to do that. At the City Year event, he told them how he loves to wear his City Year sweatshirt, placing that visual image in everyone's mind. For today's group, wearing this kerchief was an important way to connect.

Clinton moved on to the two rows of Scouts who had been hiding the yellow ball. He walked down one row, and then up the other, shaking every youngster's hand. And then made what appeared to be an impromptu ninety-second speech.

I've been doing this for years. I know young people in Haiti, in Cambodia, in Nigeria, every country, who were infected with HIV when they were children. And if no one had gotten them tested, and given them nutrition, and gotten them the medicine they needed, they wouldn't be around today. But they can all play football just like you. This is nothing to be ashamed of, nothing to be afraid of. Because people loved them and supported them, made sure they got the medicine when they needed it, they'll have normal lives. And they won't give the infection to others, 'cause they know they have it, they know how to live with it, and they know how to be good citizens and good members of the community. So you have to do this. Most people in Africa, most people in the world who have the virus, don't know it yet. So many people are still afraid. They're afraid to know. So when you do this, you are helping people get rid of their fears, get rid of their ignorance, and choose life. With all these cameras, your pictures are going to go all around the country, and all around the world, and you have no way of knowing what you may be doing for somebody just like you half a world away. Keep it up. And thank you.

The Scout leader who had been running the yellow ball exercise shouted, "Let's give President Clinton a big kilo!"

Together the Scouts clapped in time. Clap, clap, clap. Rest. Clap, clap, clap. *"Fight AIDS!!"* they shouted in unison.

Clinton ascended to a dais surrounded by several hundred Scouts, who sat on the ground at his feet and in the surrounding bleachers. To the left of the stage, five men in flowing, bright red batik pants banged congas strapped to their shoulders and chanted. A bare-chested muscular man danced wearing a grass skirt colored white, red, black, and green. He moved ecstatically, smiling, seemingly transported into another world. He jerked rhythmically, raising his hands up and down with his palms facing the sky, as if he were in the act of worship. I imagined him dancing around a fire deep in the jungle before a big battle against some tribal enemy. But it was Clinton he was dancing around, moving back and forth in front of the stage, and this battle was against a microscopic enemy, a virus, that has killed millions.

Clinton smiled with delight, clapping to the beat.

Once again he was preceded by a young person with an inspiring story to tell. Nineteen-year-old Memory Phiri contracted HIV when she was raped at fourteen years of age by a cabdriver. Memory had few resources to turn to for support. Both of her parents had died recently, and her family had been broken up, each sibling living with a different relative. She wanted to give up, to hide in shame. "I received a lot of stigma," she said. But something inside her refused to give up. She was tested, got medicine, and decided to go public with her story. She has since become an activist, lecturing to young people all over Zambia about the importance of testing, prevention, and treatment. "I asserted myself," she said. "I decided to live and not to die. The virus is just in my body; it is not the owner of my body. This is my body!" The crowd broke into thunderous applause. "I've lived now for five years with the virus. And here I am. I am not sick. I just turned nineteen last Friday. [Applause] I pay my brothers' school fees. [Applause] As youth, if we stand up and get involved in these issues, a lot of kids will come for testing because their fellow youth are standing up. If we stand up, nothing can stop us, because we have the power to fight this disease!"

During this entire speech Clinton gazed at Memory with glowing admiration. "Studying him, you begin to appreciate one of his political gifts: He is an expert *watcher*," *New Yorker* editor David Remnick has written. "He lets his lips slip slightly apart, an expression signalling pleasure and awe. . . . [H]e nodded, narrowing his eyes. He was projecting fixed engagement."[52] It's true. Whenever Clinton is onstage, waiting to be introduced, he looks at his host with palpable, affectionate appreciation that borders on wonder.

Memory introduced former Zambian president Kenneth Kaunda, a large, imposing man with a shaved head. He spoke about the fight against AIDS, and then ended with a rousing version of the Zambian national anthem, adding a chorus that included the words: "We shall fight and conquer AIDS." Kaunda introduced Clinton as "one of the most important statesmen in the world [who] cared more about the people of Africa than any other world leader."

After the introduction, Clinton began:

Everything that can be said was said just a minute ago, by Memory. I admire her. I thank her for her courage in talking about her experience.

He then shook his finger for emphasis.

And most important, refusing to live her life as a victim, and for claiming her life in all its fullness.

He paused and raised his finger high in the air, and then brought his finger down forcefully, saying as the pitch of his voice rose:

That is what every child in the world should do!

Thunderous applause. Clinton had spoken for twenty-eight seconds, and he had the crowd in the palm of his hand.

Clinton gave out trophies to the winners of the soccer tournament. Sitting down, he reached over with his left hand, grasped Kaunda's, and leaned in toward him, whispering something in Kaunda's ear with a conspiratorial smile—another five-second moment of intense intimacy.

More chanting and dancing, and we were hustled back onto the bus. The caravan, with Clinton in his vehicle and us in ours, rolled down the road accompanied by a police escort.

The Warehouse. After the soccer match Clinton toured a gigantic airplane hangar–shaped warehouse filled with rows and rows of boxes, stacked eight feet high, full of life-saving ARVs. This was a central storage facility, newly constructed by the Zambian government, where AIDS medicines could be kept ready for distribution.

We were met by an entourage of Zambian health ministers, who toured Clinton through the warehouse. Half a dozen times they stopped at a folding table with medical products displayed and poster board signs above illustrating the exhibit. A health ministry bureaucrat stationed at each table explained to Clinton what he was looking at. It reminded me of a high school science fair. At one table he viewed how one low-cost pill now replaces three expensive pills. At another he saw a stock of now affordable second-line drugs. A third displayed a line of new, cheap, portable HIV testing kits. At a fourth he reviewed a display of pediatric medicines.

At each stop Clinton appeared bowled over, awestruck by what he was seeing. But I knew there was something disingenuous about this reaction. These simple innovations would save hundreds of thousands of lives—certainly something to marvel at. But, in each case, the innovation that Clinton was so astonished by had not been introduced to Zambia by the health ministry official in front of him, but rather by the silent man two steps behind him. Ira Magaziner, best known for his leadership of Hillary Clinton's failed health care task force, is now Bill Clinton's head man in Africa. He works tirelessly, I was told, to solve Africa's health care crisis, and these products were one result. Magaziner "is always in the background," said Alan Solomont, former finance chairman of the Democratic National Committee, who knows both men well.[53] "Ira Magaziner could walk into a room and no one would notice."[54] Indeed, had I not been seated across the aisle from him on my flight to Zambia the day before, I would not have noticed him. And yet, he is the real workhorse managing CF's day-to-day operations. "Ira never stops working," said Melanne Verveer, First Lady Hillary Clinton's last chief of staff. All the CF staffers I spoke to in Africa told me how tirelessly he toils, flying a hundred thousand miles a year in coach to monitor all of

CF's work. The day I saw him (in coach) he was furiously scanning reports in big binders handed to him by his assistant. Sandy Berger calls Magaziner the "instrument" of Clinton's commitment to Africa.[55]

Thus, the Zambian health ministers standing in front of the card tables were showing Clinton *his own merchandise,* and yet he acted as if he was seeing it all for the first time, astonished by the miracle of Zambian know-how.

Clinton is a man who likes to get big things done in a hurry, even though most people would consider that well nigh impossible in Africa. Clinton understands that his interventions will only succeed if local politicians see them generating political capital for them. This little moment of political theater served everyone's purposes. Clinton and the Zambian ministers have a goal in common: They both want the Zambian government to get the credit for whatever is achieved, and take ownership of these programs both psychologically and literally.

When most nongovernmental organizations come to a poor country they set up a parallel health delivery system under their own banner. CF's core strategy is quite different. First, start a program, and then give it to the government. When CF sets up physical clinics or health programs, they are always built, by design, to be annexed into the national government's health system as quickly as possible. For example, working as a Fulbright research scholar, Patricia Siplon started a rural AIDS program in Tanzania with a grant from CF. Her program was quickly handed over to the government, and Siplon went back to teaching at her college in Vermont. "The Clinton Foundation jump-starts these programs," she said. "They get them running faster than the government would have, but they work in conjunction with the government, so that the government eventually can take them over." It's a win-win situation. Clinton certainly has no interest in administering a system of African clinics. He likes to jump-start things, and then go on to jump-start a bunch more. Curing AIDS in Africa is just one of half a dozen world-changing projects Clinton is involved in. He's working to cure childhood obesity, solve global warming—and, oh yes, he helped his wife run for president of the United States.

But Clinton has also found an approach that makes sense, not just for him, but generally. International aid experts have worried that setting up parallel systems is often not sustainable. For example, who would run Siplon's isolated jungle clinic after she went back to Vermont? In Kenya,

CF hired 250 nurses, paid them, and then gave them back to the government as government employees. Soon after, the Kenyan government announced a bold new outreach program with nurses going into rural areas where health care had been all but nonexistent. While this approach might seem like common sense, most NGOs don't operate that way. According to Stephen Lewis, the only other NGOs to embrace this local approach are Doctors Without Borders and Paul Farmer's Partners in Health. "It's an interesting strategy. They're doing it right from the outset, turning it over to the government." As a politician, Clinton knows what motivates politicians. It does nothing for a local politician to announce that a foreign NGO has come to town. But it does a lot for them to be able to boast, "Look at the progress *we* have made."

A large portion of the bill for the medicines in the warehouse was paid for by UNITAID, a multinational fund based in France that was formed in 2006 specifically for the purpose of buying cheap generic AIDS drugs for Africa. In 2007, it raised close to a hundred million dollars from a tax on airline tickets administered by forty-five countries. Clinton claims that the idea for UNITAID came from a conversation he had in his living room with former French foreign minister Philippe Douste-Blazy, who now heads UNITAID. Douste-Blazy and a French delegation, standing out in their slightly rumpled but fashionable suits, had also toured the soccer field and the warehouse.

When Douste-Blazy made his remarks, I was surprised that he spoke in French. Not very diplomatic, I thought, coming from France's former top diplomat, since this was not a French-speaking country. But wasn't that just so . . . French? A Zambian translator to the right of the stage was rendering Douste-Blazy's speech into English, though apparently not well enough for Douste-Blazy's taste. In the middle of his remarks he abruptly stopped speaking, mumbled something off microphone, and waved his hand dismissively. A member of the French delegation stood up quickly, came to the front, and took the microphone out of the hands of the Zambian translator. Douste-Blazy resumed speaking, and his colleague translated the rest of the speech. It was a shocking insult to our Zambian hosts, embarrassing them as too incompetent to find a good French translator. What a contrast. While Clinton was going to extraordinary lengths to compliment the Zambians, the French had casually insulted them.

When Clinton spoke, he praised the warehouse and its efficiency:

None of it would work if we didn't have an efficient distribution chain.
That's why we're here, and that's a great tribute to all these people. I've
not seen a better distribution chain in any other country in the world.
So, I hope by our coming here, all the rural people who have AIDS prob-
lems and other big health problems—tuberculosis, malaria—in terms of
general health, who have to stockpile and then distribute medicines in
a way that keeps them fresh and viable, will see this.

I thought Clinton was laying it on a bit thick here. I mean, let's be
real: This was, after all, *just* a warehouse (not even a refrigerated one at
that), but Clinton made it sound as if they had landed a Zambian on the
moon. Yet if Clinton was overdoing it, no one seemed to notice. CLIN-
TON VISITS ZAMBIA was the oversized headline in the *Sunday Times of*
Zambia the next day, above a featured picture of Clinton standing next
to Zambian president Levy Mwanawasa and shaking hands with a smiling minister. "Mr. Clinton commended the government for what he described as great achievements in the manner drugs were stored at MSL,"
read the article. Good press for Zambia's politicians who instantly used
it to their political advantage.[56] In the same article, Foreign Affairs Minister Mundia Sikatana is quoted as saying, "Mr. Clinton's visit was a
sign that, under President Mwanawasa's leadership, Zambia's profile has
risen tremendously in the global arena."[57]

One thing at the warehouse event confused me. When the health
minister, Dr. Brian Chituwo, introduced Clinton, he mentioned the need
for rural health care infrastructure, the very issue for which Paul and
Felix had been fighting. Both Paul and Felix had told me in our interview
that the government was in total denial about the problem, and was sup-
pressing any discussion of it. Stephen Lewis had also found the Zambians intractable on this issue.

When Clinton got to his next point, the mystery was solved.

What will keep people dying, what we will lack, is health care infrastruc-
ture and adequate distribution networks, one of which you have an-
swered in stunningly impressive fashion here. But this is something that
every donor country and every private person interested should be fo-
cusing on: how cruel it would be, now that we've made AIDS medica-
tion of high quality widely available at affordable prices, if people continue
to die because of inadequate health care facilities in rural areas. . . . Now

we have to honor the work that Zambia has done with this, to make this
a distribution center, by making sure that the money's always there for
the patients, and that people are trained in every community which
needs trained people to keep children and adults alive.

CF had solved the problem: They would pay to train medical personnel, creating enough manpower to fan out into the rural regions where most patients live; CF would pay their meager salaries; and then, once the program was up and running, CF would give it to the Zambian government, allowing Zambia's politicians to take ownership of it, which would both expand their sphere of personal power and allow them to claim credit for a major public health victory. Now, and only now, could the problem be acknowledged by the government without embarrassment. Now the issue became a mark of their success rather than a measure of their corruption and inadequacy.

In Clinton's knowing way with words, we see that the language he used to explain this new program is calculated to put the Zambian government in an entirely positive light. First he compliments the minister for bringing up the issue in his introductory remarks—as if the Zambians were the ones taking the initiative. He also says that this is a problem in virtually every country—it's not a uniquely Zambian failing. Indeed, since the Zambians have addressed issues of distribution in "stunningly impressive fashion," he frames this as just the next step for a government that has been on the cutting edge of AIDS relief. Only after protecting their self-esteem three different ways does Clinton drive home TALC's central point: It is cruel to let large numbers of rural people die just because no one can get it together to drive to the provinces and bring them medicine. But Clinton frames this tougher message not as a failing of the Zambians, but as a responsibility of the aid community. In fact, given the Zambians' pioneering work, it is the least CF could do "to honor the work Zambia has done with this magnificent distribution center." Reuters reported that Clinton had pledged "his foundation would provide skills training for more medical personnel to honor Zambia for its impressive fight against AIDS."[58]

Patricia Siplon has seen this dance before: "There is no implied criticism, no hint that these governments didn't move fast enough. Instead, he does it in a way that makes them look good. Ultimately, it looks like,

'Hey, the government is also interested in rolling out treatment in rural areas!' And it becomes integrated into their national plan." Clinton knows how to close a political deal, and hidden from the eyes of most people in that warehouse, he had just closed another one. The government TALC had found so immovable had just moved before my very eyes. It was now the official top priority of the Zambian health ministry to get AIDS drugs to rural populations. The smiling health ministers were proud and happy to do it.

"It just shows the power of Clinton," said Lewis, whose own efforts to move Zambia in this very same direction had produced little progress. "It takes Clinton to break through."

Clinton has been barnstorming through Africa (and much of the world) like it was the Third Congressional District of Arkansas, on a mission to bring universal access to AIDS treatment, and he is having an impact in a place that has proved refractory to all solutions: a real-life example of an irresistible force meeting an immovable object. Energized by Clinton, the previously intractable Zambian government was now racing toward progress.

In my mind, I saw Paul turning away to hide a tear as he told me of his sister's needless death. I visualized him mailing out his DVDs, like a castaway hurling a message in a bottle into the sea, desperately hoping someone would hear his cry.

Walking back to the bus, I thought of Paul, and I smiled.

My Dinner with Bill. A Clinton press staffer hopped onto the bus in one big bounce and asked with a big broad, devilish grin: "Who would like to have dinner with the president?"

You can imagine how many hands went up—mine among them.

When Clinton walked into the restaurant, everyone began buzzing. He made his way to the back where we were sitting, and began shaking hands as he walked around the table. When he shook mine it was clear he didn't know who I was. I dropped the name of one of his childhood friends, and I said that she had asked me to say hello.

"How do you know her?" he asked, brightening up. I explained that I was writing a book about him, and that I had spent time in Hot Springs and Little Rock with his friends. He put his arm around me, bent his head toward me, and leaned into me, so that his face and mine were only a few inches apart. He began to reminisce warmly about his friend in hushed, almost conspiratorial tones, as if he was revealing something very personal—just between us. While he spoke, his hand worked its way down to my upper arm, grasping my triceps.

It is difficult to describe that moment, since its very physicality overwhelmed me—as it does for all who come under this man's unique spell. For over a year, twelve hours a day, I'd done nothing but research and write about Clinton, all day long, without ever having met the man. Now he was hugging me! The whole thing probably lasted fifteen seconds, but I had now experienced for myself how he can create a memorable bond in a matter of moments.

To my delight, he did not sit at the head of the table, but in the middle, where he was close to everyone. He was right across the table, just two places up from me. Because the conversation was off-the-record, I can't quote what he said during our dinner, which is a shame, because he said quite a lot.

What struck me was the frankly hypomanic nature of this speech, which I have discussed earlier. Clinton spoke for what must have been close to a couple of hours, with eloquence, humor, and insight about an extraordinarily wide range of topics, all, it seemed, without taking a breath. The entire press corps was virtually speechless. Afterward, I asked several of them about that: Why hadn't they said anything? They were not silent out of deference but rather stunned by the power of his brain. "My mind was racing just trying to keep up with him" was a typical response.

George Saunders, who sat next to me, described our dinner in this way in his *GQ* profile of Clinton:

> One question and you're off to the races. . . . During these talks he's not the Bill Clinton you hear about—probing people for their stories, asking where they're from, listening intently as they talk about their dreams, their hometowns, their long epiphany-filled journeys through life. He's *talking*. He's talking, I think, because he (1) loves to talk, (2) does his thinking via talking, and (3) is easily the most interesting person at the table and knows this, and knows you know it. . . . [W]hen Bill Clinton is at your table, you don't really want anyone else talking, and that includes you. When you do talk you feel stupid. I mean you *are* stupid.

Saunders notes that he speaks in "thousand-word bursts" and recognizes the Clinton talkathon as a force of nature: "He talks the way an ice trawler breaks through ice, the way a mountain stream runs downhill. It happens because it must."

Personally, I was not content merely to observe Clinton. I was determined to personally engage him during what I knew might be my only chance at a conversation. But it was difficult to try and get a word in. The pause one normally waits for in polite conversation before speaking just never came. I had to down a few glasses of red wine before I had the courage to simply hurl myself into the cyclone of his monologue. The first time I spoke, he didn't stop speaking, but merely regarded me for a millisecond, out of the corner of his eye. I had thrown myself into the whirlwind and been blown back. Then I inserted a question, this time more forcefully. Clinton looked at me, smiled, and became even more energized. "Yes, that's right!" he said, with a light in his eyes, and he was "off to the races" with even greater animation, galloping through his oration at an even faster pace.

After dinner when Clinton got up from the table, the entire restaurant went berserk. People were waving, shouting, cheering, and thrusting themselves toward him; flashes were popping off like a strobe. I got one wonderful photo of Clinton in shirtsleeves, wearing a loosened red silk tie, looking ecstatic, as he appears to float serenely in a sea of excited, smiling young black women. It was a swirling moment of erotically tinged exuberance, their faces beaming, their arms surrounding him, and their hands caressing his shoulder and the fingers of his left hand (which displays his wedding ring).

"Now you see what the Clinton experience is *really* like," laughed a veteran photographer who had been shooting Clinton for years.

· JULY 22, 2007 ·

Clinton Day Three: Dar es Salaam, Tanzania

This day we were in Tanzania watching Bill Clinton fight malaria. Three million people die each year from malaria, one hundred thousand in Tanzania alone, mostly young children, who succumb the most quickly.

It is an unforgivable tragedy, because malaria is very treatable. "*Not one soul should ever die of malaria. Nobody,*" Clinton proclaimed from the stage.

Less than a year earlier, the Bill Gates Foundation had approached the Clinton Foundation to ask if it could do for malaria drugs what it had done for AIDS drugs. Today Clinton was there announcing a new initiative to reduce the price of the newest and most effective class of antimalarial drugs: artemisinin combination therapy (ACT).

Before his speech, Clinton had toured a local pharmacy across the road. Most people in Tanzania buy their antimalarial medicine over the counter at such shops, and they typically buy relatively ineffective drugs because the new ACTs, if they are even aware of them, are twenty times more expensive.

To get every malaria patient on ACT drugs, CF has done three things. First, it has helped bring down the cost of the ACTs to the exact same price point as the more popular, less effective drugs.

A typical dose of effective ACT drugs costs you the effect of about a month's salary. Even if we reduce the manufacturer's price, the drugs will remain unaffordable for many of you. But if we subsidize it and reduce the price, we can sell it to you for 5 percent of what it now costs, one twentieth. And everyone in Tanzania will be able to afford the malaria drugs in the areas where we can sell it, so that no one should die from this disease.

Second, he has arranged for the heavily discounted ACTs to be distributed over the counter at the medicine shops.

Only half the people in your country will visit clinics when they are ill. The rest of the people go to shops like those across the road, which I just visited. So, we have to change the strategy so all of you—if you need it—can go there and get the medicine that will work and you can afford.

And finally, Clinton had reached an agreement with the Tanzanian government to have the popular, ineffective medicines removed from the shelves. This last step is crucial, because if the old drugs were still for sale, many people would just use what they have always used. Most people here have probably never heard of ACT.

> *Lastly, as we put more of the right drugs on the shelves, we should take the wrong ones off. I want to thank the Tanzanian government for recently banning the so-called oral artemisinin therapies. These threatened to create drug resistance. They make you more difficult to cure if you take them. A lot of you know malaria comes back over and over again in a lifetime. So, I thank you, Minister, for getting rid of this drug and helping us to put the right drugs into the shops.*

Here is yet another example where a close working relationship with the government has paid off, because only the Tanzanian government has the authority to ban a pharmaceutical product. After Zambia I had come to appreciate the unique way Clinton merges his goals with those of the local politicians. The health minister who introduced Clinton only spoke twelve lines, and three of them were profuse thanks to Clinton for working so closely with his government.

> *Your Excellency, the government is very much pleased that the Clinton Foundation has agreed to work closely with us to improve access to high-quality, affordable antimalarials. . . . I would like to express our gratitude for your prodigious willingness to work closely with the governments to test subsidy delivery mechanisms into rural districts in our country. . . . In addition, Your Excellency, the government is looking forward to collaborating with the Clinton Foundation on streamlining and rolling out this facility module in additional regions.*

In turn, Clinton got his biggest applause of the day when he praised the health minister for his work.

> *Your minister of health has been amazing on this issue—you should be very proud of him. He has shown great leadership on this issue.*

When Clinton left the stage he began walking along the road, and pandemonium erupted. Suddenly everyone was running, shouting, rushing toward him. They hopped over ropes and barriers en masse. For a moment it was scary—a stampede seemed about to break out. This gigantic crowd was hungry for Clinton with an intensity that surprised and frightened me.

But Clinton was unfazed. Indeed, he looked blissful, reaching out his hand jovially to the jostling crowd of excited people, while the visibly nervous Secret Service quickly fell into formation around him, trying to wrest back control.

The setting African sun glistened like a golden halo against his silver hair. He reached deeply into the crowd, smiling beatifically, and a half dozen black hands reached back at once, grasping his fingers, his wrist, his elbow—they wanted, so badly, just to touch any part of him.

As I watched him there, the thought crossed my mind: "Character issue. *Character issue*. What character issue? The man is healing the sick in massive numbers. He is an altruistic personality—the height of expression of human character—writ large. These people who look down on Clinton, how many lives have they saved today?"

Character is not revealed by your worst mistake. Nor is it revealed by your best intentions. Intentions expressed in actions over time are what make up character. By that criterion, since little Billy Clinton began carrying his big Bible down the hill to church, he has been walking in the footsteps of moral giants. The crowd massing around him wanting to touch the hem of his garment was testimony that he has walked a long way.

· JULY 23, 2007 ·

Mamma Kathryn

Early this morning I left the Clinton entourage, having gotten little sleep the night before. To celebrate the last night of my Clinton adventure, I had stayed up drinking with the reporters at the hotel's outdoor bar, enjoying its stunning view of the bay. As we exchanged business cards I was reminded of the last day of summer camp, when everyone signs one another's yearbooks. Frankly, I felt sad saying good-bye to the press bus.

The twenty-minute flight to the island of Zanzibar brightened my mood. We flew very low over the city of Dar es Salaam—a crowded mosaic of rusted, corrugated roofs—and then we were cruising over a beautiful aquamarine ocean, where we could practically wave to the fishing boats below. Technically, Zanzibar is part of Tanzania, but culturally, historically, and geographically it is a world unto itself.

In order to see for myself the work CF is doing, I went to Zanzibar to meet a woman the locals call "Mamma Kathryn." Kathryn Sutton is a lively fifty-six-year-old divorced mother from Connecticut who came to Zanzibar on an impulse in the midst of a midlife crisis. Sutton, who comes from an educated family, had long regretted never having gone to college. She had married early, and after her divorce she had to raise her children as a single mother on her own, working as a bookkeeper. However, once her children were grown, she finally got her degree at Tufts University, in Boston. After finally achieving her dream, she didn't want to go back to another office job. She wanted to do something significant and different. Sutton's mother had died, leaving her a small inheritance—enough to live on for a year. She decided to go to Africa, armed only with her small bank account and a vague vision that she would help Africans with small-business development.

She found herself on the island of Zanzibar. Because of her interest in small-business development, someone working for a local NGO called her attention to a small AIDS support group. Kathryn's friend had been trying to encourage some entrepreneurial spirit among the women in the group, offering them the chance to weave handbags for a small profit. After a few months the entire group had collectively woven only two bags.

"Well, of course they weren't weaving bags," Sutton told me. "They were too sick to weave. And they knew that they were dying, so really, what incentive did they have?" Thus began the next chapter of Kathryn Sutton's life. She became deeply involved with the Zanzibar Association of People living with AIDS and HIV+ (ZAPHA+). The people of ZAPHA+ needed treatment, she concluded, not handbag-weaving opportunities.

Sutton is an energetic, exuberant, make-something-happen kind of person, with a touch of the hypomanic temperament, as she herself identified after viewing the Web site for my first book, *The Hypomanic Edge*.

Sutton went to Dr. Dahoma, the health minister in charge of AIDS for Zanzibar, and asked when ARVs were coming to the island. Maybe in a year or two, he said.

"But people are dying," Sutton protested.

The island also needed a CD4+ machine, but that wasn't in the budget either, Dahoma said. "What if I found a donor?" Sutton asked. "What if we got a good deal on a used machine?" Sutton simply would not accept no for an answer. One way or another, she was determined to intervene.

The head of ZAPHA+ is Farouk Abdullah, a tall, elegant fashion designer with a British accent (he lived in England for many years) and a flamboyant manner. Farouk mentioned to Sutton that he had received an e-mail from Stephen Lewis, then UN special envoy for AIDS relief in Africa, yet he had never bothered to answer it. "I was too lazy to bother writing back. I didn't even know who he was," Farouk admitted. Sutton bugged Farouk for weeks to respond. And finally, after a screaming fight, she demanded that he forward her the e-mail so she could respond, if he wouldn't.

Sutton appealed to Lewis. The situation in Zanzibar was utterly desperate. There were no ARVs on the island—none. And there was no way to get her people's CD4+ levels tested. Sutton was just hoping to raise enough money for ferry fare (thirty dollars per person) to transport them to the mainland at Dar es Salaam, where they at least could be tested. Lewis sympathized, and he suggested she contact the Clinton Foundation. This was February 2005.

"I e-mailed the people at the Clinton Foundation on a Thursday. The following Tuesday, I got a phone call: 'We're here at the Dar es Salaam airport; can you meet us in twenty minutes?'" This unbelievably rapid response, she would discover, was typical of the hypomanic light speed at which the Clinton Foundation operates.

CF's "speed and focus," said Lewis, is nothing less than "extraordinary." His first exposure to Clinton speed came at the International Annual AIDS conference, held in Bangkok in 2004. "I was feeling frantic about the little country of Lesotho. I was watching it die before my eyes," he said. This tiny African mountain kingdom has the world's third-highest infection rate; 29 percent of the population—320,000 people—are infected. There are 180,000 orphans who have lost their parents to AIDS. Lewis had never met Ira Magaziner before, but at the conference he introduced himself and asked: "Is there anything in the world you can do about Lesotho?"

"What do you mean?" asked Magaziner.

"They've got to have lower-cost drugs. They have no money, and they've got to have some help. They have absolutely no one."

Lewis was flabbergasted by the response. "Within one month," he said, "the Clinton Foundation had signed a memorandum of understanding with the Lesotho ministry of health to be the broker for low-cost drugs, and had actually put an in-country team in place. It took my breath away. If you did that with the UN, it would take two and a half years. I think the life of the country is going to be saved, and it would not have happened if they had not moved with that rapidity." What makes Clinton different is that he feels a "sense of urgency."

By the time Sutton sent her e-mail to CF, Lewis had already brought Zanzibar to their attention. He had turned to CF mostly out of desperation. Like Sutton, he had tried to get the ball moving by working with the local government, but had hit a wall. "I met with the president of Zanzibar, trying to get the island mobilized," he said. "No way. I knew if I went through the UN, it would take forever. I simply turned to Clinton. I just know if there is trouble, you just go to Clinton."

In her first meeting with the CF staff, Sutton laid the whole problem before them. Within days CF paid to have ZAPHA+ members' blood flown to Dar es Salaam for testing. Soon thereafter, they bought Zanzibar its only CD4+ machine. It then worked with the ministry of health to open an AIDS clinic and get the life-saving ARV medicine to the island. "If CF hadn't come in, it wouldn't have happened," said Sutton. Sutton e-mailed CF in February 2005. By March, the first ZAPHA+ members began treatment.

When I spoke to Lewis, I told him that when I thought of Clinton's progress in Africa, I had the image of Patton's army of tanks rolling through Europe at breakneck speed, barreling past all obstacles. Every time they hit a supposedly unbridgeable chasm, they threw up a pontoon bridge and kept rolling.

Lewis laughed. "That's a perfect analogy."

Pat Siplon, who worked with CF in Tanzania, agreed. "Whenever they set up a site, the first question they ask is, 'What are the bottlenecks that will keep this from happening?'" she said. "Then, they go in and take out those bottlenecks. Each time they go into an area, they say, 'So, what are the problems? Identify the problems for us, and then we'll work through how to make this happen.'" When Siplon was in Tanzania trying to get a rural treatment program going, "one of the huge things was transportation. So they paid for vehicles. Instead of people having to go to the hospital, the treatment professionals could go out to the villages."

"What else do you need?" Ed Wood, a senior CF staffer, asked Sutton.

A new center for ZAPHA+ was one obvious need. The group had been operating out of a small, dark storefront on the outskirts of Stone Town, the capital city. Lewis had visited the old ZAPHA+ center, and recalled that it was a dismal place. "We met in the most run-down hovel. It was so gloomy it made you weep," he said. "The eight people at the meeting were so defeated and broken; it was just the most mournful little gathering I think I've experienced. It was like a goddamn morgue."

Find any site for ZAPHA+ that you want, CF told Sutton, and we'll pay the rent. Sutton rented the nicest space she could find: a large, brightly lit ground-floor complex of offices surrounding a sunny courtyard. More important, it was located right in the center of town, across the street from the hospital and the AIDS clinic. AIDS groups have a lot of trouble getting anyone to rent to them, but Sutton threw President Clinton's name around, and resistance vanished. The price for this palatial office? A mere six hundred dollars a month. Usually, it's very hard to find aid organizations willing to pay for "overhead," like rent. Instead, they fund projects, and allow a small amount of overhead to be built into the budget. But that creates a catch-22: If someone doesn't pay the overhead, there is no space, equipment, or manpower to run the projects. ZAPHA+'s annual overhead is about thirty thousand dollars a year, which covers the rent, keeps the lights on, and pays the salaries of one full-time coordinator and a part-time staff. CF has covered most of that, and it has proven to be a good investment. Their full-time coordinator has become an able grant writer, and has been able to use his time to apply to other aid organizations for more funding. As a result, ZAPHA+ now receives money from a number of organizations, no longer depending exclusively on CF.

"Anything else you need?" Wood asked Sutton again.

"Well, a small salary and some health benefits would be nice," she said. Sutton was still living on her dwindling inheritance.

"Done," he said.

Sutton was hired by CF on the spot, without any need for an application, a meeting, an interview, or even so much as an e-mail.

Sutton had an audacious idea: She wanted ZAPHA+ volunteers to be part of the newly forming AIDS clinic staff. Thinking of groups like Alcoholics Anonymous, Sutton believed in the healing power found in groups of people afflicted with the same disease. The people coming to the AIDS clinic wouldn't just need access to medicine, she reasoned. They needed counseling, support, and community.

"No, of course not," replied the health ministry, in response to her idea, pointing out that ZAPHA+ members were not qualified to work in a medical clinic.

Undaunted, Sutton said, "Then we'll get them trained." She appealed to the CF, and was instantly granted funds to get five ZAPHA+ volunteers officially certified as AIDS counselors. It was an enormous honor for those first five, some of them leaving the island for the first time in their lives to receive their training. Now ZAPHA+ could offer educationally credentialed volunteers, and the ministry of health agreed to incorporate them into the program.

The program has been a huge success. They now have eighteen trained counselors working full- or part-time. All of these workers began as volunteers, but Sutton fought to get them paid. Again, CF footed the bill. While their full-time salary is a mere forty dollars a month, in an impoverished country, where the per capita income is under two dollars a day, this seemingly nominal stipend is actually almost a living wage. Now that the counselors have proven themselves, Sutton is trying to get them paid officially by the government when CF funding ends. In the meantime, the government has recently asked ZAPHA+ if they could provide more counselors. A visit to the AIDS clinic helped me understand why the government is eager for more counselors—they essentially run the place.

The morning we visited the clinic was one of the most moving moments of the trip. The clinic occupies the second floor of a medical building, a faded concrete structure with a large veranda that wraps around the rectangular space, with a stunning view of the ocean. In African style, most of the building is covered by a roof, but all hallways are open to the elements: Only the actual offices are fully indoors. When we climbed the steps we saw dozens of people lining the hallways. Some were waiting to have their blood drawn; others, many looking serious and tense, were waiting for their results; still others were waiting for checkups or medicines.

Every few steps Sutton was assailed by people who knew her. It seemed as if almost everyone in Stone Town knew her. She has a smidgen of the Clinton charisma—she seems to glow as she greets people, touching them, smiling at them, inquiring about their families. And they light up around her. I mentioned this to her, and she admitted to knowing that she has some charisma: "I affect people physically."

A government nurse, who seemed to be in charge, was on duty at the clinic when we arrived. She was happy to see Sutton.

"Busy today, yes?" asked Sutton.

"Just another Monday morning," she replied. "It's like this every day."

For Africa, where everything seems by Western standards to be more than a little dysfunctional, the whole operation seemed to be running surprisingly smoothly. Originally, the idea was for people to schedule appointments for testing. "But that doesn't work in Africa. People don't make appointments here. Few of them even have phones," said Sutton. Instead, the clinic works on a drop-in basis. You come, get blood drawn, and have a session with a counselor all in the space of a few hours.

In addition to the government nurse, there were several ZAPHA+ counselors on the premises, officially working alongside her. After people receive the results of their blood test, a ZAPHA+ counselor sits down to explain the results. "These people are terrified," said Sutton. "They think this might be a death sentence. It means a lot for someone to say: 'Look, I've got it, too. I'm alive. My life is going on. This is what your results mean. This is what you have to do. This is what you can expect.'"

There are practical things that need to be assessed: What kind of support does the patient have at home? Is there someone who can remind them to take their medicine? It's important to talk about side effects and other common problems. And, finally, it's important to ask about their feelings about the disease: the shame, the fear, the stigma. Stigma is an enormous problem everywhere, but particularly in Africa. The fact that the topic has been so utterly taboo among both the populace and the government has been a large part of the problem. A supportive community of fellow patients, who are also your neighbors (this is a very small town), is a powerful way to help someone feel that they are not alone. When you ask a question of a ZAPHA+ counselor, Sutton said, "they can answer from the heart." This kind of person-to-person education by patient experts has been shown by research to be effective.

In addition to the ZAPHA+ people who were working officially, we ran into three or four more in the halls. One man had brought a friend for testing; another had brought a young niece. Some people need this hand-holding to have the courage to get their blood tested, both because they are afraid to know the results and because they are nervous about being seen at the clinic. And then there were other ZAPHA+ people who seemed to be just hanging out. "This is sort of their clubhouse," Sutton said. An AIDS clinic might seem like an unlikely place for a social club, but it is a logical one for them. "If I'm ever feeling sorry for myself, I just need to come here," Sutton added, as we left the clinic, "and I always feel better."

From there we walked a half block to the ZAPHA+ center. I was entirely unprepared for what a joyous place it turned out to be. As we entered the courtyard, I nearly stepped into a large pan filled with gooey beige liquid—soap that was hardening in the sun. Seated around the courtyard in a circle, under a large blue tent, were over a dozen women in brightly colored traditional African dress. They were hand carving the big pans of dried soap into individual bars. The meager profit that comes from selling the soap helps to support them. So for them coming to the center is like going to work. "People need purpose," said Sutton, and the little businesses the center runs provide it, along with a very modest income that is sorely needed.

It was as if I had stumbled onto a large slumber party. The women were laughing and whispering to themselves. Clearly the presence of a male foreigner stimulated them: One woman made silly faces for my camera, causing the others to laugh at her clowning. The fact that these lighthearted, flirtatious women were Muslims, with covered heads, struck me.

We moved to the hallway, where some people were sorting out supply kits for volunteers to deliver to people who are sick at home. If you are too ill to come to ZAPHA+, ZAPHA+ will come to you. They will clean your house, make you food, help you wash, and make sure you are taking your medicine.

Sutton is constantly spinning out new ideas. For example, Stephen Lewis's charitable organization offered ZAPHA+, money to provide nutritional counseling, but no one was interested in attending a flip-chart lecture on the food pyramid. So Sutton decided to use the money to host a big monthly party at the center. Everyone gets together, cooks all day, and then has a feast at night. It was a big hit, and in the process, "hopefully some people learned to cook a little healthier."

To promote the use of condoms by sex workers, Sutton sent out ZAPHA+ volunteers (some of whom were former sex workers themselves) to the bars at night to give away condoms. CF now pays these patient experts twenty to forty dollars a month to give away condoms at bars. No doubt conservatives would rip out their hair at the idea of enabling prostitutes to practice their trade more safely, but sex with prostitutes is a very common form of transmission in Africa, as elsewhere, and it afflicts the innocent as well as the guilty. Faithfully married women are often infected by husbands who frequent prostitutes.

"People tell me all the time: 'I'm alive because of President Clinton,'" Sutton said. Indeed, the intervention of CF brought the ARVs to Zanzibar. Sutton showed me a photo of five ZAPHA+ members, dated March 24, 2005, the day the first five ZAPHA+ members took their first dose of medicine. Sutton introduced me to Khamis Mtumwa, one of the five people in the picture. Khamis had been so ill that he seemed to be "hours from death." He was so weak and confused that "he didn't even know where he was." A CD4+ count lower than two hundred means someone is in need of treatment. His count was nineteen. His immune system was essentially gone. "He really should have been dead."

Indeed, at first, the government doctor in charge of the ARV clinic refused to treat Khamis, arguing that he was beyond help. Khamis was so disoriented, the doctor said, the disease had gone to his brain, causing irreversible damage. In addition, the doctor argued that Khamis was too confused anyway to follow the treatment regimen. Sutton countered that his wife could give him the medicine at the appropriate intervals, but the doctor still refused. The doctor only finally relented when Sutton said: "I'm not going to leave this office until you give him the medicine."

Miraculously, in just a matter of weeks, Khamis began to recover. When I met him he appeared healthy and strong. Khamis now dedicates much of his time to serving as an officer of ZAPHA+.

In the hallway I also met a five-year-old girl, the daughter of one of the soap makers, who contracted HIV at birth. She was wearing a bright new purple dress. "What a beautiful dress!" Sutton said, appreciatively. The girl smiled and began twirling, showing off her newest treasure. Later Sutton showed me a picture of President Clinton holding the same girl in 2005, before ARV therapy. Though she was three in the picture, she looked more like an infant, with dark circles under her eyes and a listless blank stare—a shocking contrast to the prancing ballerina in the hallway.

We moved into the office, a modest room with a couple of desks, each with a computer. "If Clinton had not come, we never would have gotten help," said Farouk Abdullah, head of ZAPHA+. "One thing I like about the Clinton Foundation: There is a problem [he snapped his fingers in the air three times] they resolve it." By contrast, other aid agencies require lengthy grant applications, with budgets, goals, timelines, benchmarks, and endless reports. Often the process of getting a year's worth of funding takes that long.

Five months after Sutton's first meeting with the CF team, Bill Clinton came to Zanzibar, in July 2005, as part of his annual Africa tour, almost exactly two years to the day before my visit. One of the places Clinton visited was ZAPHA+. Farouk said, "In all the years we've been here, we never once got a visit from a single person at the ministry of health, though we'd invited them many times. But when Clinton came here, the meeting was exclusively for our members only, and a group of senior health ministers were waiting expectantly outside our door, *wishing* they could get in. When we came out, one of the ministers said: 'Farouk, you were with Clinton? You are more important than me!' Then they realized that this organization must be very important." Since Clinton's visit the health minister has visited ZAPHA+. What was good enough for Clinton, apparently, was good enough for him, Farouk said. "Now people remember ZAPHA+ as 'the place Clinton visited.' "

HIV and AIDS used to be things people didn't mention in polite company, and those who were afflicted often felt obliged to hide it to avoid being ostracized. Shopkeepers would often refuse to handle money touched by AIDS patients. One ZAPHA+ member gave a speech at a local festival. She got onstage and asked, "I have HIV. How many of you would shake my hand?"

Some people began to boo.

"Well, I just shook the hand of President Bill Clinton," she said proudly.

Farouk believes that "the whole country's attitude changed when Clinton came."

You would be hard-pressed to find an adult on the island of Zanzibar who does not remember Clinton's visit. Sutton took me down the winding narrow streets that Clinton walked, re-creating the day of his visit. Stone Town is a maze of alleys (it is impossible, they say, for anyone who is not a resident to avoid becoming lost in this labyrinth). The streets are bordered by faded, whitewashed buildings, many housing dusty storefronts selling crafts to tourists. We stopped in the shops where Clinton shopped. Everyone we met was only too happy to relive that moment, showing off framed pictures of themselves shaking his hand that were displayed proudly in the front of their stores.

Clinton impressed many in Zanzibar when he stopped at a street corner called "Jaws Corner," the local headquarters of the Tanzanian opposition party, Civic United Front (CUF), which happens to be dominated by African Arab Muslims. Unlike the larger nation of Tanzania, Zanzibar is over 90 percent Muslim. Five times a day one can hear the call to prayer echoing across the city. But Zanzibar is not like Afghanistan. Women walk alone freely. And while most women cover their heads, they tend to choose varied brightly colored scarves, as much for fashion as tradition. One shopkeeper, a woman covered entirely in black, appeared more seriously orthodox than the more brightly clad women I had seen. But when Sutton teased her about having a crush on Bill Clinton, calling Clinton her "boyfriend," the woman joined in the fun. "You tell Clinton to come back," she said, opening her mouth and wiggling her tongue provocatively and rapidly from side to side. "He'll be glad he came."

The geopolitical implications of a former American president reaching out to a Muslim population in Africa are no small matter. People differ in their assessment of the Islamist threat in Zanzibar. While I was there I was told repeatedly that Zanzibarians are a very tolerant people; Zanzibar's Muslims are not Islamists; and there is no history of anti-Western sentiment on the island. Zanzibar has a long tradition of being a cosmopolitan crossroads, mixing Africans, Arabs, Indians, and other cultures. However, not everyone shares that entirely benign view. Pat Siplon, who worked in Tanzania, said, "There's always been tension. Some Al Qaeda people that got sent to Guantánamo recently were from Zanzibar, and there are terrorists and all that stuff." There have been isolated Islamic terrorist attacks in Zanzibar and, of course, on the mainland: The American embassy in Tanzania was blown up by Al Qaeda in 1998. Aggravating the situation is the fact that Tanzania is not a full-fledged democracy. Though they have elections, the government sometimes rounds up and jails members of the CUF, including candidates on the ballot, right before the vote. Such oppressive tactics, naturally, tend to radicalize the opposition.

When Sutton and I got to Jaws Corner we saw men sitting at tables drinking coffee and talking, but I had the distinct impression that conversation stopped when I arrived. The men seemed to eye me carefully as I took pictures, in a way that gave me the creeps.

What we see in Zanzibar is a Muslim community that has not *yet* been pushed into the arms of extremists. But that could change. The fact that Clinton stopped at Jaws Corner scored needed diplomatic points for America. Siplon recalled that when he visited "these ultra-Islamic local politicians loved him." It's interesting to note that the story of Clinton's visit to Jaws Corner has become a local legend, and like many such legends, it has been embellished. Siplon said that "men were coming up to me and telling me about what a great man Clinton is, and how he's this American that they can relate to, because he had gone to Jaws Corner, and drank coffee, and just sat and talked politics with people. He was the only famous American they knew that cared about them." Sutton, who was standing next to Clinton the entire time, says that that is gross exaggeration. Clinton really just shook hands and walked through. But by now I was familiar with how a few seconds of intimacy with Clinton can feel like a lifetime relationship. In reality it may have been a simple meet and greet, but in the minds of Zanzibarians it has become magnified into a major event.

Laura Bush visited Zanzibar in 2005 as well, just days before Clinton, and received a very different reaction. Some say that it was not an accident that she toured Africa right before Clinton, and even stopped at the same countries. Allegedly, this was a strategy dreamed up by political consultant Karl Rove, as a way to preempt the Clinton visit, which would also explain why Laura Bush visited Africa again only a couple of weeks before Clinton during his 2007 trip. However, the effect of the inevitable contrast between them may have been the opposite of what the Bush administration intended. While Clinton walked the streets freely, Laura Bush "practically never left her bullet-proof limousine," said Sutton. For "security reasons," Laura Bush refused to meet with local politicians and journalists.

An editorial on July 19, 2005, in the Tanzanian daily newspaper, *The Guardian,* entitled "That American Exclusivity," thanked Laura Bush for sparing the time to visit, and thanked the Bush administration for increasing AIDS funding for Africa, but also stated that the trip was experienced by many Tanzanians as an insult.[59] Her brief contact with the populace only gave her a "glimpse of the situation on the ground." And her tight security "left the nation aghast." "The whole world watched

Tanzania being utterly humiliated by the American Secret Service and FBI personnel as they pushed away local security personnel." In the author's view, it might have been better for American-Tanzanian relations if Laura Bush had stayed home. "If Mrs. Bush were in so much danger while in Tanzania to deserve such shielding, was there any reason for her to even think of coming?"

Four days later the same paper reported on the Clinton visit under the headline "Clinton Magic Charms Dar."[60] While Laura Bush remained in a security bubble, emotion for Clinton, who refused to be contained by security constraints, bubbled over. "Both Tanzanian and US security officers seemed powerless as Clinton reached out and shook hands with journalists and dozens of people who wanted to catch a glimpse of the charismatic former American leader," was the article's lead. "An excited crowd that had gathered at the hotel lobby surged toward Clinton as he was leaving for the airport, giving his security a tough time trying to keep his frenzied fans back. The crowd eventually broke the security cordon and Clinton obliged by shaking the hands of his thrilled admirers." It sounded very much like the 2007 visit to Dar es Salaam that I witnessed.

Sutton had kindly invited me to spend the night at her home. She thinks that she may have one of the best apartments in Zanzibar. Her seven-story walk-up building is one of the tallest structures on the entire island, and she lives on a rooftop terrace with an extraordinary 360-degree view of Stone Town, including a beautiful view of the ocean, where we watched the sun set. From her terrace we looked down on the presidential palace, and its elaborate gardens, as well as on a cityscape of red-tiled roofs, balconies with laundry on the line. The spires of a dozen mosques shoot proudly into the air. The monthly cost for this fantasy penthouse apartment was five hundred dollars.

Five times a day the call to prayer echoes upward in an exotic other-worldly chorus. Sutton, who knows all the singers, called my attention to her favorites. It was a surprisingly beautiful, haunting, and soothing sound.

That night her driver brought us to a hotel whose dining room was an assortment of tables on the beach positioned around a bonfire, where we were serenaded by a man with a guitar singing in Swahili. We had a superb three-course dinner for two, featuring freshly grilled local fish, that cost me less than I'd been spending each morning for one breakfast at my luxury hotels.

· JULY 25, 2007 ·

Last Day

Normally, I'm am early riser, but I slept like a log. Kathryn had to knock twice to wake me. We didn't want to be late for our appointment at the health ministry. But when we arrived at 9:00 A.M., as planned the day before, no one seemed to be expecting us. The doctor we were supposed to meet with wasn't there. We were told that he was at a funeral. His assistant didn't seem at all apologetic that we had come for an appointment and been stood up.

"Maybe come back again tomorrow."

Unfortunately, that was not an option. I would be flying home in a few hours (or, rather, beginning the first of a series of flights that would bring me home thirty-six hours later). So we had the morning to walk around town, shop, and see the museum. I had to admit I wasn't too disappointed. It was nice to just be a tourist for a few hours.

Just like the previous day, as we walked through the streets, two or three people on every block greeted Sutton.

"*Jambo* [hello, in Swahili]," they called.

"*Jambo,*" she answered.

All seemed happy to see her. At each stop she introduced me.

"You are most welcome," they would say graciously, as they shook my hand.

"This is a lot of what I do every day," said Sutton. "I just walk around and talk to people."

CF had offered Sutton a promotion, the chance to become global director in charge of all AIDS self-help groups, but she turned it down. "I wouldn't be good at a bureaucratic job," she said. "I'm a hands-on person. Besides, Zanzibar is my home now." I said I could see why it would be difficult to think of ever moving away from this community, where she had formed so many relationships.

"It seems like everybody knows you," I said.

That reminded Sutton of a story. One day her gardener said: "Why did you not tell me that you are famous, Mamma Kathryn?"

"I'm not famous," she protested.

"Oh yes, you are very, very famous, Mamma Kathryn. You are the woman who brought us President Bill Clinton."

Epilogue

As I feared, despite my best efforts I was never able to get an interview with Bill Clinton. However, before I left for Africa, I thought it reasonable to assume that I might at least get a chance to ask him a question, since I would be with the press at several events where he might be taking questions. All the way to Africa, I asked myself: "If I can only ask Bill Clinton one question, what would it be?" On this safari, where I was hunting Bill Clinton, I anticipated that I might get only one clean shot at connecting with him on-the-record.

My chance came at the City Year event on July 19, my first day with him. After the event, he came out with his arm around a young girl—an orphan who had lost both of her parents to AIDS. At age seventeen, she was taking care of her two younger siblings. Having received aid from CF, she made it it a personal mission to make sure other girls got help as well. There were just a dozen of us from the press bus informally gathered around in the parking lot when Clinton and the girl came out. He beamed at her with affection, joked with her, praised her, and then hugged her—a big protective bear hug—resting his chin on her head. She leaned into him, wrapping her arms around him, and buried her head into his chest, smiling.

At the formal events, with hundreds in attendance, I had been too shy to ask my question, but now I just shouted it out: "Mister President, when you were eight years old, you walked to church alone. You wrote about that, and it's a memory etched in the minds of all your close friends from Hot Springs. Is the work you have done, and the work you are doing now, just a continuation of that journey?"

At first he looked taken aback, shaking his head and furrowing his brow. This oddly personal question about his experiences as an eight-year-old was totally out of context. It didn't just come from left field; it came from thousands of miles and half a century away.

But then, he paused, cocked his head, and thought for a moment, his eyes seeming to focus inward. He nodded, slowly, as a smile crept across his face. I had the feeling that he had never quite thought of it this way before, but now that he had pondered it, the idea felt not only right, but oddly familiar—as if he had known it all along. It is a look most therapists are familiar with, the look a patient gets when we offer them an accurate interpretation.

He burst into a luminous, knowing smile, looked at me, and locked his bright blue eyes onto mine. Strangely, it suddenly felt as if he were inside of me, as if there were now a direct neural connection between his eyes and my heart. Others had described Clinton's penetrating gaze to me, but I had never experienced it until now.

"Yes," he said, nodding. "It is."

LIST OF INTERVIEWS

Farouk Abdullah, July 23, 2007.
Zackie Achmat, July 19, 2007.
Gerry Adams, December 8, 2006.
Ron Addington, July 13, 2006.
Nancy Adkins, January 27, 2006.
Charles F. Allen, May 1, 2007.
Elizabeth Bagley, November 6, 2006.
Steve Barnes, April 27, 2007.
Paul Begala, December 19, 2006.
Alan Blinder, January 25, 2007.
Sidney Blumenthal, January 19, 2007.
Wilma Rowe Booker, January 18, 2006.
James Carville, March 2, 2007.
Joe Conason, October 11, 2006.
Paul Costa, August 29, 2006.
Larry Crane, July 17, 2006.
Rose Crane, January 26, 2006; July 13, 2006.
Marla Crider, January 25, 2006.
Patty Criner, July 18, 2006.
Jim Daugherty, July 17, 2006.
Ernest Dumas, July 15, 2006.
Nancy Eisenberg, February 6, 2007.
Reg Empey, December 7, 2006.
Mark Fabiani, November 10, 2006.
Richard Fenwick, January 26, 2006.
David Folsom, September 28, 2006.
Clover Gibson, January 27, 2006.
Paul Greenberg, July 17, 2006.
John Harris, February 10, 2007.
Virginia Heath, January 26, 2006.
Rachel Heffernan, January 27, 2006.
Ann Henry, April 27, 2007.
John Hume, December 5, 2006.
Eric Jackson, January 28, 2006.
Phil Jamison, September 8, 2006.
Paul Kasonkomona, July 21, 2007.

Dick Kelley, January 28, 2006.
Tony Lake, November 30, 2006.
Chris Lehane, November 13, 2006.
David Leopoulos, July 13, 2006;
    September 17, 2006.
Jerome Levin, February 9, 2007.
Stephen Lewis, August 3, 2007.
Jamie Love, August 16, 2007.
Jane Holl Lute, January 3, 2007.
Berenice Lyon, January 27, 2006.
Gene Lyons, October 4, 2006.
Richard McAuley, December 8, 2006.
Ann McCoy, July 18, 2006.
Robert McCrae, August 29, 2006.
Patrick McDermott, December 6, 2006.
Jenny Sue McKee, July 21, 2006.
David Maraniss, January 16, 2006.
George Mitchell, November 2, 2006.
Marge Mitchell, January 27, 2006.
Jewel Dean Moore, July 20, 2006.
Jim Morgan, January 11, 2006.
Bruce Morrison, November 7, 2006.
Khamis Mtumwa, July 23, 2007.
Michael Muldoon, September 2, 2006.
Felix Mwanza, July 21, 2007.
Meredith Oakley, July 17, 2006.
Conor O'Clery, October 31, 2006.
Niall O'Dowd, November 2, 2006.
Brian O'Dwyer, November 2, 2006.
Stella O'Leary, November 20, 2006.
Leon Panetta, February 9, 2007.
Martha Pope, November 10, 2006.
Joe Purvis, July 14, 2006.
Albert Reynolds, December 8, 2006.
Alice Rivlin, January 18, 2007.
Paul Root, May 6, 2007.

Mary Anne Salmon, July 18, 2006;
  April 30, 2007.
Jeffery Shafer, November 18, 2005.
Patricia Siplon, July 13, 2007.
Nancy Soderberg, December 18, 2006.
Dick Spring, December 6, 2006.
Kathryn Sutton, July 23, 2007.

David Trimble, December 3, 2006.
Mark Tuohey, February 27, 2007.
Trina Vargo, November 14, 2006.
Stephen Weatherford, October 31,
  2006.
Carol Willis, July 18, 2006.
George Wright, Jr., July 20, 2006.

NOTES

INTRODUCTION: THE PUZZLE

1. See David Maraniss, *The Clinton Enigma: A Four-and-a-Half-Minute Speech Reveals This President's Whole Life* (New York: Simon & Schuster, 1998), 10.
2. George Stephanopoulos, *All Too Human (A Political Education)* (Boston: Little, Brown, 1999), 4.
3. David Gergen, *Eyewitness to Power* (New York: Touchstone, 2000), 251.
4. Bill Clinton, *My Life* (New York: Alfred A. Knopf, 2004), 800.
5. Eugen Bleuler, *Textbook of Psychiatry* (New York: Macmillan, 1924), 485; Emil Kraepelin, *Lectures on Clinical Psychiatry* (Bristol, U.K.: Thoemmes Press, 2002; originally published 1908), 129–30; Emil Kraepelin, *Manic Depressive Insanity and Paranoia* (Edinburgh: E. and S. Livingstone, 1921), 125–31; Ernst Kretschmer, *Physique and Character* (New York: Harcourt and Brace, 1925), 127–32; Kurt Schneider, *Psychopathic Personalities* (Springfield, Ill.: C. C. Thomas, 1958), 69–78; H. S. Akiskal and G. Mallya, "Criteria for the 'Soft' Bipolar Spectrum: Treatment Implications," *Psychopharmacological Bulletin*, 23 (1987): 68–73; Kay Redfield Jamison, *Exuberance: The Passion for Life* (New York: Knopf, 2004), 4.
6. Ronald R. Fieve, *Moodswings* (New York: Bantam Books, 1997), 64.
7. Ronald R. Fieve, *Bipolar II* (New York: Rodale, 2007), 131.
8. Fieve, *Bipolar II*, 143–44.
9. William Coryell, Jean Endicott, Martin Keller, Nancy Andreasen, William Grove, Robert Hirschfield, and William Scheftner, "Bipolar Affective Disorder and High Achievement: A Familial Association," *Psychiatry*, 146:8 (1989): 983–88; M. Eisemann, "Social Class and Social Mobility in Depressed Patients," *Acta Psychiatrica Scandinavica*, 73 (1986): 399–402; Helene Verdoux and Marc Bourgeois, "Social Class in Unipolar and Bipolar Probands and Relatives," *Journal of Affective Disorders*, 33 (1995): 181–87.
10. American Psychiatric Association, *Diagnostic and Statistical Manual of Mental Disorders*, fourth edition, text revision (Washington, D.C.: American Psychiatric Association, 2000), 368.
11. Joe Klein, *The Natural: The Misunderstood Presidency of Bill Clinton* (New York: Doubleday, 2002), 40–41.
12. See Kay Redfield Jamison, *Touched with Fire: Manic-Depressive Illness and the Artistic Temperament* (New York: Free Press, 1996), 49–100; Ruth Richards, "Creativity and Bipolar Mood Swings: Why the Association?" in

Melvin Shaw and Marc Runco, editors, *Creativity and Affect* (Norwood, N.J.: Ablex, 1994), 44–72; Nancy Andreasen and Arthur Cantor, "The Creative Writer: Psychiatric Symptoms and Family History," *Comprehensive Psychiatry*, 15 (1974): 123–30; Nancy Andreasen, "Creativity and Mental Illness: Prevalence Rates in Writers and Their First Degree Relatives," *American Journal of Psychiatry*, 144: 10 (1987): 1288–892.

13. Author interview with Marla Crider, January 25, 2006.
14. Stephanopoulos, 35.
15. Author interview with Stella O'Leary, November 20, 2006.
16. Helen Fisher, *Why We Love: The Nature and Chemistry of Romantic Love* (New York: Henry Holt, 2004), 51–76.
17. Benedict Carey, "Living on Impulse," *New York Times,* April 4, 2005.
18. David Maraniss, *First in His Class* (New York: Simon & Schuster, 1995), 383.
19. Gergen, 273.
20. Quoted in John F. Harris, *The Survivor: Bill Clinton in the White House* (New York: Random House, 2005), xxi.
21. Harris, 433.
22. Author interview with Alan Blinder, January 25, 2007.
23. Quoted in Klein, 26.

1. LIKE MOTHER, LIKE SON

1. Virginia Kelley with James Morgan, *Leading with My Heart* (New York: Pocket Books, 1994), 26.
2. David Remnick, "The Wanderer: Bill Clinton's Quest to Save the World, Reclaim His Legacy—and Elect His Wife," *The New Yorker,* September 18, 2006, 54.
3. Kelley, 143.
4. Kelley, 107.
5. Kelley, 12.
6. Kelley, 12.
7. Kelley, 16.
8. Kelley, 15.
9. Author interview with Jim Morgan, January 11, 2006.
10. Kelley, 8.
11. Kelley, 6.
12. Kelley, 13.
13. Kelley, 15.
14. Kelley, 9.
15. Author interview with Virginia Heath, January 26, 2006.
16. William T. Coleman III, "Don't You Know Whose Table This Is?" In *The Clintons of Arkansas: An Introduction by Those Who Know Them Best,* Ernest Dumas, ed. (Fayetteville: University of Arkansas Press, 1993), 58.
17. Coleman, 58.
18. Jim Moore with Rick Ihde, *Clinton: Young Man in a Hurry* (Fort Worth, Tex.: Summit Group, 1992), 21.
19. Kelley, 285.
20. Quoted in David Maraniss, *First in His Class* (New York: Simon & Schuster, 1995), 423.

21. Kelley, 8.
22. Kelley, 9.
23. Kelley, 7.
24. Kelley, 9.
25. Kelley, 8.
26. Kelley, 9.
27. Kelley, 10.
28. Kelley, 89.
29. Bill Clinton, *My Life* (New York: Alfred A. Knopf, 2004), 117.
30. Author interview with Richard Fenwick, January 26, 2006.
31. Kelley, 17.
32. Kelley, 19.
33. Author interview with David Maraniss, January 16, 2006.
34. Kelley, 17.
35. Kelley, 18.
36. Kelley, 20–21.
37. Kelley, 29.
38. Kelley, 29.
39. Kelley, 31.
40. Kelley, 31.
41. Kelley, 34.
42. Kelley, 52.
43. Kelley, 61.
44. Kelley, 61.
45. Author interview with Rose Crane, January 26, 2006.
46. Maraniss, *First in His Class,* 21.
47. Lucinda Franks, "The Intimate Hillary," *Talk,* September 1999.
48. Quoted in Lynne Duke, "No Rest from the Query," *Washington Post,* August 5, 1999.
49. B. Clinton, 9–10.
50. B. Clinton, 10.
51. Kelley, 61.
52. Kelley, 78.
53. Kelley, 91, 151.
54. Kelley, 61–62.
55. B. Clinton, 8.
56. Kelley, 74.
57. Quoted in Gail Sheehy, *Hillary's Choice* (New York: Ballantine Books, 1999), 93.
58. B. Clinton, 48.
59. Jerry Oppenheimer, *State of a Union: Inside the Complex Marriage of Bill and Hillary Clinton* (New York: HarperCollins, 2000), 2.
60. Sheehy, 208.
61. Patrick Healy, "For Clintons, Delicate Dance of Public and Private Lives," *New York Times,* May 23, 2006, A1.
62. Quoted in Sheehy, 303.
63. Quoted in Sheehy, 308.
64. John Harris, *The Survivor* (New York: Random House, 2005), 379.
65. Oppenheimer, 130.
66. Quoted in Oppenheimer, 141.

67. Quoted in Oppenheimer, 141–42.
68. Quoted in Oppenheimer, 141.
69. Diane Blair, "Of Darkness and Light." In *The Clintons of Arkansas,* 63.
70. Author interview with Jim Daugherty, July 17, 2006.
71. Quoted in Sheehy, 69.
72. Quoted in Sheehy, 69.
73. B. Clinton, 10.
74. Quoted in Oppenheimer, 128.
75. Oppenheimer, 128.
76. Quoted in Maraniss, 326.
77. Kelley, 323.
78. Sheehy, 88.
79. Quoted in Sheehy, 88.
80. Quoted in Kelley, 204.
81. Kelley, 204.
82. Kelley, 204.
83. Kelley, 203.
84. Quoted in Sheehy, 88.
85. Kelley, 64–76.
86. Kelley, 67.
87. Kelley, 107.
88. Sheehy, 97.
89. Quoted in Sheehy, 97.
90. Kelley, 81.
91. Kelley, 81.
92. Kelley, 68.
93. Kelley, 74.
94. Kelley, 80–81.
95. Stanley Renshon, *High Hopes: The Clinton Presidency and the Politics of Ambition* (New York: Routledge, 1998), 177.
96. Kelley, 81.
97. Kelley, 79.
98. Kelley, 127–28.
99. Kelley, 128–29.
100. Kelley, 128.
101. Kelley, 66.
102. Kelley, 85–87.
103. Kelley, 76.
104. Kelley, 118.
105. Kelley, 110–11.
106. Kelley, 110.
107. Kelley, 258.
108. Kelley, 263.
109. Author interview with Eric Jackson, January 28, 2006.
110. Kelley, 284.
111. Kelley, 283.
112. Author interview with Berenice Lyon, January 27, 2006.
113. Joe Klein, *The Natural* (New York: Broadway Books, 2002), 3.
114. Author interview with Marge Mitchell, January 27, 2006.

2. SEARCHING FOR BILL CLINTON'S FATHER

1. Virginia Kelley, with James Morgan, *Leading with My Heart* (New York: Pocket Books, 1994), 44.
2. Kelley, 44.
3. Nigel Hamilton, *Bill Clinton: An American Journey* (New York: Random House, 2003), 33.
4. Author interview with Richard Fenwick, January 26, 2006.
5. Author interview with Wilma Rowe Booker, January 18, 2006.
6. Hamilton, 34.
7. Gene Weingarten, "The First Father," *Washington Post,* June 20, 1993; Bill Clinton, *My Life* (New York: Alfred A. Knopf, 2004), 5.
8. B. Clinton, 5.
9. Quoted in Carl Bernstein, *A Woman in Charge* (New York: Alfred A. Knopf, 2007), 480.
10. Quoted in Jim Moore, with Rick Ihde, *Clinton: Young Man in a Hurry* (Fort Worth, Tex.: Summit Group, 1992), 21.
11. Quoted in Moore, 22.
12. Hillary Rodham Clinton, interview by Charles F. Allen, February 15, 1991.

3. ONE IN A QUADRILLION

1. George Saunders, "Bill Clinton: Public Citizen," *GQ,* December 2007, 395.
2. Hillary Rodham Clinton, interview by Charles F. Allen, February 15, 1991.
3. Quoted in Nigel Hamilton, *Bill Clinton: An American Journey* (New York: Random House, 2003), 419.
4. William T. Coleman III, "Don't You Know Whose Table This Is?" In *The Clintons of Arkansas: An Introduction by Those who Know Them Best,* Ernest Dumas, ed. (Fayetteville: University of Arkansas Press, 1993), 57.
5. Quoted in Edmund Morris, *The Rise of Theodore Roosevelt* (New York: Ballantine Books, 1979), 23.
6. Phyllis Anderson, "Just Tell Your Story to Me." In *The Clintons of Arkansas,* 131–32.
7. Steve Lohr, "Slow Down, Brave Multitasker, and Don't Read This in Traffic," *New York Times,* March 25, 2007.
8. Hillary Rodham Clinton, interview by Charles F. Allen, May 1, 2007.
9. Quoted in E. Morris, 178; quoted in David McCullough, *Mornings on Horseback* (New York: Simon & Schuster, 1981), 257.
10. Bob Nash, interview by Jajuan Johnson, for Arkansas Oral History Project, September 18, 2006.
11. Quoted in Joe Klein, *The Natural* (New York: Broadway Books, 2002), 26.
12. John Brummett, *Highwire: From the Backroads to the Beltway—The Education of Bill Clinton* (New York: Hyperion, 1994), 27.
13. Quoted in David Gallen, *Bill Clinton as They Know Him: An Oral Biography* (New York: Marlowe, 1996), 157.
14. Falret quoted in Frederick K. Goodwin and Kay Redfield Jamison, *Manic Depressive Illness* (New York: Oxford University Press, 1990), 23.
15. George Stephanopoulos, *All Too Human (A Political Education)* (Boston: Little, Brown, 1999), 37–38.

16. Author interview with Ann McCoy, July 18, 2006.
17. David Remnick, "The Wanderer," *The New Yorker,* September 18, 2006, 45.
18. Virginia Kelley with James Morgan, *Leading with My Heart* (New York: Pocket Books, 1994), 196.
19. Bill Clinton, *My Life* (New York: Alfred A. Knopf, 2004), 23.
20. B. Clinton, 30.
21. Virginia Clinton Kelley, interview by Charles F. Allen, 1991.
22. Quoted in John Harris, *The Survivor: Bill Clinton in the White House* (New York: Random House, 2005), 156; Brummett, 37.
23. Lewis R. Goldberg and Tina K. Rosolack, "The Big Five Factor Structure as an Integrative Framework: An Empirical Comparison with Eysenk's P-E-N Model.'" In *The Developing Structure of Temperament in Personality from Infancy to Adulthood,* Charles E. Halverson Jr., Geldoph A. Kohnstamm, and Roy P. Martin, eds. (Hillsdale, N.J.: Lawrence Erlbaum, 1994), 32.
24. Paul T. Costa Jr. and Robert R. McCrae, *Revised NEO Personality Inventory (NEO PI-R) and NEO Five-Factor Inventory (NEO-FFI)* (Odessa, Fla.: Psychological Assessment Resources, 1992), 15.
25. Dick Morris and Eileen McGann, *Because He Could* (New York: Regan Books, 2004), 16.
26. Virginia Clinton Kelley, interview by Charles F. Allen, 1991.
27. Stephanopoulos, 77.
28. Morris and McGann, 16.
29. Robert Rubin, *In an Uncertain World* (New York: Random House, 2003), 134.
30. Morris and McGann, 17.
31. David Gergen, *Eyewitness to Power* (New York: Touchstone, 2000), 261.
32. Donald Baer, Matthew Cooper, and David Gergen, "Bill Clinton's Hidden Life: An Interview with Bill Clinton," *US News & World Report,* October 14, 1992, 29.
33. Woodward, *The Agenda: Inside the Clinton White House* (New York: Simon & Schuster, 1994), 55.
34. Costa and McCrae, 15.
35. Kay C. Goss, "Going to the Grassroots with the Governor," in *To the Grassroots with Bill Clinton,* Paul Root, ed. (Arkadelphia, Ark.: Peter Parks Center for Regional Studies, Ouachita Baptist University, 2002), 80–81.
36. Klein, 40–41.
37. Quoted in Jerome D. Levin, *The Clinton Syndrome* (Rocklin, Calif.: Forum, 1998), 112.
38. Klein, 42–43.

4. THE BOY WHO WALKED TO CHURCH ALONE

1. Quoted in Donald Baer, Matthew Cooper, and David Gergen, "Bill Clinton's Hidden Life: An Interview with Bill Clinton," *US News & World Report,* October 14, 1992, 30.
2. Quoted in David Maraniss, *First in His Class* (New York: Simon & Schuster, 1995), 35.
3. Quoted in Gail Sheehy, *Hillary's Choice* (New York: Ballantine Books, 1999), 101.

4. Virginia Clinton Kelley, interview by Charles F. Allen, March 10, 1991.
5. David S. Shribman, "Presidents and Prayer," *Boston Globe,* December 11, 1994.
6. Shribman, "Presidents and Prayer," December 11, 1994.
7. Stanley Renshon, *High Hopes: The Clinton Presidency and the Politics of Ambition* (New York: Routledge, 1998).
8. Virginia Clinton Kelley by James Morgan, *Leading with My Heart* (New York: Pocket Books, 1994), 142–43, 106.
9. Quoted in Sheehy, *Hillary's Choice*, 101.
10. Quoted in Baer, Cooper, and Gergen, 29.
11. Bill Clinton, *My Life* (New York: Alfred A. Knopf, 2004), 36
12. Carolyn Staley, interview by Charles F. Allen, February 5, 1991.
13. Quoted in Baer, Cooper, and Gergen, 30.
14. Quoted in Nigel Hamilton, *Bill Clinton: An American* Journey (New York: Random House, 2003), 123.
15. Kelley, 184; Maraniss, *First in His Class*, 227.
16. Quoted in Baer, Cooper, and Gergen, 40.
17. Quoted in Hamilton, 102.
18. Kelley, 84.
19. Quoted in Maraniss, 40.
20. Kelley, 142.
21. Roger Clinton, with Jim Moore, *Growing Up Clinton: The Lives, Times, and Tragedies of America's Presidential Family* (Arlington, Tex.: Summit Group, 1995), 3.
22. Carolyn Staley, interview by Charles F. Allen, February 5, 1991.
23. Kelley, 143.
24. R. Clinton, 8.
25. Quoted in Jim Moore, with Rick Ihde, *Clinton Young Man in a Hurry* (Fort Worth, Tex.: Summit Goup, 1992), 24.
26. Baer, Cooper, and Gergen, 29.
27. Jerome D. Levin, *The Clinton Syndrome* (Rocklin, Calif.: Prima Publishing, 1998), 12–13.
28. Kelley, 142.
29. Quoted in Ernest Jones, *Life and Work of Sigmund Freud* (New York: Basic Books, 1974), 12.
30. Quoted in Moore, 22.
31. Quoted in Sheehy, 99.
32. Sheehy, 99.
33. Quoted in Hamilton, 115.
34. Kelley, 134.
35. Moore, 25.
36. Patty Criner, interview by Charles F. Allen, February 5, 1991.
37. Kelley, 157.
38. Sheehy, 103.
39. Quoted in Sheehy, 103.
40. Kelley, 161, 91, 151.
41. Kelley, 158.
42. Kelley, 152.
43. Kelley, 62.
44. R. Clinton, 5.

45. Quoted in Sheehy, 322.
46. Quoted in Sheehy, 247.
47. John F. Harris, *The Survivor* (New York: Random House, 2005), xxiv.
48. Dick Morris and Eileen McGann, *Because He Could* (New York: Regan Books, 2004), 83.
49. Morris and McGann, 83.
50. David Gergen, *Eyewitness to Power* (New York: Random House, 2005), 273.
51. Morris, 87.
52. Quoted in Morris and McGann, 87.
53. Morris and McGann, 84.
54. Morris and McGann, 87.
55. George Stephanopoulos, *All Too Human (A Political Education)* (Boston: Little, Brown, 1999), 91.
56. Stephanopoulos, 96–97.
57. Gergen, 273.
58. Morris, 89.
59. Quoted in Harris, 334.
60. Quoted in Harris, 431.
61. Kelley, 138–39.
62. B. Clinton, 46.
63. B. Clinton, 51.
64. R. Clinton, 2–3.
65. Kelley, 169.
66. Kelley, 171.
67. B. Clinton, 46.
68. Harris, 214.
69. Harris, 154.
70. Terry McAuliffe, with Steve Kettmann, *What a Party!: My Life Among Democrats; Presidents, Candidates, Donors, Activists, Alligators, and Other Wild Animals* (New York: St. Martin's Press, 2007), 103.
71. Elizabeth Drew, *Showdown: The Struggle Between the Gingrich Congress and the Clinton White House* (New York: Touchstone, 1996), 303.
72. Drew, 348.
73. Harris, 217.
74. Quoted in Harris, 157.
75. Harris, 217.
76. Stephanopoulos, 404.
77. Quoted in Harris, 216.
78. Quoted in Harris, 216.
79. Harris, 216.
80. Quoted in Harris, 216.
81. Quoted in Drew, 333.
82. Quoted in Drew, 333.
83. Harris, 221.
84. Nancy Soderberg, *The Superpower Myth: The Use and Misuse of American Power* (New York: Wiley, 2005), 78.
85. Quoted in Soderberg, 81.
86. Quoted in Harris, 201.
87. Soderberg, 81.

88. Anthony Lake, *Six Nightmares: Real Threats in a Dangerous World and How America Can Meet Them* (New York: Little, Brown, 2000), 144.
89. Lake, 144.
90. Quoted in Harris, 198.
91. Lake, 144.
92. Quoted in Soderberg, 82.
93. Kelley, 176.
94. Kelley, 177; B. Clinton, 105.
95. Quoted in Kelley, 177.
96. Quoted in Kelley, 173.
97. Quoted in Kelley, 174.
98. John D. Gartner, "The Capacity to Forgive." In *Object Relations Theory and Religion: Clinical Applications,* Mark Finn and John D. Gartner, eds. (Westport, Conn.: Praeger, 1992).
99. Kelley, 181.
100. B. Clinton, 51.
101. R. Clinton, 3, 8.
102. Hillary Clinton, *Living History* (New York: Simon & Schuster, 2003), 96.
103. Diane Blair, "Of Darkness and Light," in *The Clintons of Arkansas,* Ernest Dumas, ed. (Fayetteville: University of Arkansas Press, 1993), 68.
104. Judy Gaddy, interview by Jujuan Johnson for Arkansas Oral History Project, April 13, 2006.
105. McAuliffe, 164–65.

5. THREE PAIRS OF SHOES

1. Bill Clinton, *My Life* (New York: Alfred A. Knopf, 2004), 35.
2. Diane Blair, "Of Darkness and Light," in *The Clintons of Arkansas,* Ernest Dumas, ed. (Fayetteville: University of Arkansas Press, 1993), 68.
3. David Maraniss, *First in His Class* (New York: Simon & Schuster, 1995), 14.
4. Maraniss, 14.
5. Maraniss, 12–13.
6. B. Clinton, 62.
7. Quoted in Jim Moore with Rick Ihde, *Clinton: Young Man in a Hurry* (Fort Worth, Tex.: Summit Group, 1992), 25
8. Patty Criner, interview by Charles F. Allen, February 5, 1991.
9. B. Clinton, 63.
10. B. Clinton, 62.
11. Quoted in Maraniss, 44.
12. Conor O'Clery, *Daring Diplomacy: Clinton's Search for Peace in Ireland* (Boulder, Colo.: Roberts Rinehart, 1997), 21.
13. Quoted in O'Clery, 22.
14. Carolyn Staley, interview by Charles F. Allen, February 5, 1991.
15. Quoted in Charles F. Allen and Jonathan Portis, *The Comeback Kid: The Life and Career of Bill Clinton* (New York: Birch Lane Press, 1992), 44.
16. David Pryor, interview by Charles F. Allen, February 15, 1991.
17. Quoted in Edmund Morris, *The Rise of Theodore Roosevelt* (New York: Ballantine Books, 1979), 178.

18. Edmund Morris, 730.
19. Quoted in Edmund Morris, 731.
20. David Gergen, *Eyewitness to Power* (New York: Touchstone, 2000), 254.
21. Quoted in Kay Redfield Jamison, *Exuberance* (New York: Knopf, 2004), 11.
22. Quoted in Edmund Morris, 505.
23. Jamison, 134.
24. David Pryor, interview by Charles F. Allen, February 15, 1991.
25. Quoted in Jamison, 11.
26. Jamison, 150.
27. Maraniss, *First in His Class*, 383.
28. Jamison, 138.
29. B. Clinton, 574.
30. Hillary Rodham Clinton, interview by Charles F. Allen, February 15, 1991.
31. Hillary Rodham Clinton, interview by Charles F. Allen, February 15, 1991.
32. Hillary Rodham Clinton, interview by Charles F. Allen, February 15, 1991.
33. Carol Williss, interview by Charles F. Allen, 1991.
34. Judy Gaddy, interview by Jujuan Johnson for Arkansas Oral History Project, April 13, 2006.
35. Quoted in Allen and Portis, 14.
36. William T. Coleman III, "Don't You Know Whose Table This Is?" In *The Clintons of Arkansas: An Introduction by Those Who Know Them Best*, Ernest Dumas, ed. (Fayetteville: University of Arkansas Press, 1993), 57.
37. Coleman, 57.
38. Maraniss, *First in His Class*, 292.
39. Quoted in Maraniss, 292.
40. Carol Rasco, interview by Jujuan Johnson, for Arkansas Oral History Project, April 28, 2006.
41. Maraniss, *First in His Class*, 354.

6. THE EDUCATION OF GOVERNOR CLINTON

1. Quoted in Meredith L. Oakley, *On the Make: The Rise of Bill Clinton* (Washington, D.C.: Regnery, 1994), 250.
2. Julie Baldridge, interview by Jujuan Johnson for Arkansas Oral History Project, April 5, 2006.
3. Quoted in Oakley, 204.
4. David Maraniss, *First in His Class* (New York: Simon & Schuster, 1995), 360.
5. Carol Willis, "History-Making Appointments." In *To the Grass Roots with Bill Clinton*, Paul Root, ed. (Arkadelphia, Ark.: Peter Parks Center for Regional Studies, Ouachita Baptist University, 2002), 40.
6. Julie Baldridge, interview by Jujuan Johnson for Arkansas Oral History Project, April 5, 2006.
7. Julie Baldridge, interview by Jujuan Johnson for Arkansas Oral History Project, April 5, 2006.
8. Quoted in Maraniss, 360.
9. Julie Baldridge, interview by Jujuan Johnson for Arkansas Oral History Project, April 5, 2006.

10. Julie Baldridge, interview by Jujuan Johnson for Arkansas Oral History Project, August 10, 2006.
11. Quoted in Oakley, 234.
12. Quoted in Oakley, 200.
13. Author interview with Patty Criner, July 18, 2006.
14. Quoted in Oakley, 200.
15. Julie Baldridge, interview by Jujuan Johnson for Arkansas Oral History Project, April 5, 2006.
16. John Brummett, *Highwire: From the Backroads to the Beltway; The Education of Bill Clinton* (New York: Hyperion, 1994), 6.
17. Julie Baldridge, interview by Jujuan Johnson for Arkansas Oral History Project, April 5, 2006.
18. Rudy Moore, interview, Arkansas Oral History Project, March 4, 2006.
19. Brummett, 6.
20. Bill Clinton, *My Life* (New York: Alfred A. Knopf, 2004), 295.
21. Maraniss, 387.
22. Dick Morris, *Behind the Oval Office: Getting Reelected Against All Odds* (Los Angeles: Renaissance Books, 1999), 51.
23. Jerry Oppenheimer, *State of a Union: Inside the Complex Marriage of Bill and Hillary Clinton* (New York: HarperCollins, 2000), 130.
24. Quoted in Nigel Hamilton, *Bill Clinton: An American Journey* (New York: Random House, 2003), 406.
25. Hamilton, 406.
26. Quoted in Gail Sheehy *Hillary's Choice* (New York: Ballantine Books, 1999), 143.
27. Hillary Clinton, *Living History* (New York: Simon & Schuster, 2003) 91–92.
28. Quoted in Maraniss, 399.
29. H. Clinton, 93.
30. Oakley, 271.
31. Sheehy, 148.
32. Quoted in Sheehy, 149.
33. Quoted in Sheehy, 147.
34. Quoted in Sheehy, 147.
35. Quoted in Hamilton, 402.
36. Quoted in Maraniss, 405.
37. Quoted in Jamison, 11.
38. Quoted in Sheehy, 143.
39. Maraniss, 391.
40. Quoted in Sheehy, 143.
41. Quoted in Hamilton, 438.
42. Maraniss, 403.
43. Dick Morris, 52.
44. Quoted in Hamilton, 441.
45. Quoted in Hamilton, 459.
46. Brummett, 262.
47. Quoted in Sheehy, 176.
48. Quoted in David Gallen, *Bill Clinton as They Know Him: An Oral Biography* (New York: Marlowe, 1996), 162.
49. Maraniss, 427.

50. Quoted in Oakley, 349.
51. Author interview with Ernest Dumas, July 15, 2006.
52. Sheehy, 178.
53. Brummett, 41.
54. Dick Morris, 52.
55. Author interview with Leon Panetta, February 9, 2007.
56. Author interview with Mary Anne Salmon, July 18, 2006.
57. Judy Gaddy, interview, Arkansas Oral History Project, April 13, 2006.
58. Quoted in Gallen, 163.
59. Quoted in Gallen, 163.
60. Virginia Clinton Kelley, interview by Charles F. Allen, March 10, 1991.
61. Hillary Rodham Clinton, interview by Charles F. Allen, February 15, 1991.
62. Quoted in Oakley, 274.
63. Quoted in Gallen, 157.
64. Author interview with Mary Anne Salmon, April 30, 2007.
65. Author interview with Charles F. Allen, May 1, 2007.
66. Author interview with Paul Root, May 6, 2007.
67. Quoted in Gallen, 142.
68. Quoted in Hamilton, 407.
69. Quoted in Hamilton, 408.
70. Quoted in Hamilton, 410.
71. Maraniss, 409.
72. Quoted in Sheehy, 152.
73. Quoted in Maraniss, 411.
74. Quoted in Jerome D. Levin, *The Clinton Syndrome* (Rocklin, Calif.: Prima Publishing, 1998), 154.
75. Quoted in Hamilton, 413.
76. Quoted in Hamilton, 413.
77. Quoted in Oakley, 285.
78. Quoted in Hamilton, 410.
79. Quoted in Oakley, 282.
80. Quoted in Gallen, 142.
81. Oakley, 282.
82. Quoted in Charles F. Allen and Jonathan Portis, *The Comeback Kid: The Life and Career of Bill Clinton* (New York: Birch Lane Press, 1992), 86.
83. Quoted in Allen and Portis, 99.
84. Quoted in Allen and Portis, 89.
85. Bobby Roberts, "Working the Legislative Session." In *To the Grass Roots with Bill Clinton,* Paul Root, ed. (Arkadelphia, Ark.: Peter Parks Center for Regional Studies, Ouachita Baptist University, 2002), 24.
86. Roberts, 24.
87. Roberts, 29.
88. Roberts, 30.
89. Roberts, 33.
90. Roberts, 33–34.
91. Kathy Van Laningham, "A Day in the Life." In *To the Grass Roots with Bill Clinton,* Paul Root, ed. (Arkadelphia, Ark.: Peter Parks Center for Regional Studies, Ouachita Baptist University, 2002), 108.
92. Oakley, 289.
93. Oakley, 289.

94. Oakley, 288.
95. Quoted in Oakley, 289.
96. Quoted in Maraniss, 414.
97. Quoted in Maraniss, 414.
98. Quoted in Gallen, 141.
99. Quoted in Gallen, 42.
100. Quoted in Donald Baer, Matthew Cooper, and David Gergen, "Bill Clinton's Hidden Life: An Interview with Bill Clinton," *US News & World Report,* October 14, 1992.

7. IT'S THE ECONOMY, GENIUS

1. Robert Rubin, *In an Uncertain World* (New York: Random House, 2003), 107.
2. George Stephanopoulos, *All Too Human (A Political Education)* (Boston: Little, Brown, 1994), 285.
3. Quoted in Stephanopoulos, 284.
4. Dick Morris and Eileen McGann, *Because He Could* (New York: Regan Books, 2004), 29.
5. Rubin, 144.
6. Hillary Clinton, *Living History* (New York: Simon & Schuster, 2003), 122.
7. Alan Greenspan, *The Age of Turbulence* (New York: Penguin, 2007), 143.
8. Greenspan, 143.
9. Greenspan, 144.
10. Bob Woodward, *Maestro: Greenspan's Fed and the American Boom* (New York: Simon & Schuster, 2000), 97.
11. Greenspan, 113, 162.
12. Greenspan, 161.
13. Quoted in Bob Woodward, *The Agenda: Inside the Clinton White House,* 84.
14. Bill Clinton, *My Life* (New York: Alfred A. Knopf, 2004), 461.
15. B. Clinton, 463.
16. Greenspan, 149.
17. B. Clinton, 463.
18. Quoted in Elizabeth Drew, *On the Edge: The Clinton Presidency* (New York: Simon & Schuster, 1994), 65.
19. Quoted in Drew, 98.
20. Drew, 67–68.
21. Quoted in Woodward, *The Agenda* 132.
22. Rubin, 114.
23. Quoted in Woodward, *The Agenda,* 127.
24. Nigel Hamilton, *Bill Clinton: Mastering the Presidency* (New York: Public Affairs, 2007), 105.
25. Quoted in Drew, 68.
26. Harris, 19.
27. Quoted in John F. Harris, *The Survivor,* 19.
28. Greenspan, 161.
29. Quoted in Woodward, *The Agenda:* (New York: Simon & Schuster, 1994), 329.
30. Woodward, *The Agenda,* 128.
31. Greenspan, 147.
32. Greenspan, 147.

33. Greenspan, 147.
34. Quoted in Woodward, *The Agenda*, 241.
35. Drew, 68.
36. Quoted in Woodward, *The Agenda*, 126.
37. Greenspan, 147.
38. Drew, 77.
39. Quoted in Woodward, *The Agenda*, 138.
40. Ruth Marcus and Anne Devroy, "Asking Americans to 'Face Facts,' Clinton Presents Plan to Raise Taxes, Cut Deficit," *Washington Post*, February 18, 1993.
41. Tom Shales, "The State of the Union: A Hard Pitch to Home," *Washington Post*, February 18, 2003.
42. Quoted in Shales, C1.
43. Woodward, *The Agenda*, 150.
44. Greenspan, 142.
45. Greenspan, 142.
46. Greenspan, 142.
47. Woodward, *The Agenda*, 139.
48. Woodward, *Maestro*, 100.
49. "To Rescue the Economy," editorial, *Washington Post*, February 18, 1993, A18.
50. Quoted in Drew, 80.
51. Gene Sperling, *The Pro-Growth Progressive: An Economic Strategy for Shared Prosperity* (New York: Simon & Schuster), 252.
52. Sperling, 252.
53. Sperling, 114.
54. Quoted in Sperling, 121.
55. Sperling, 113.
56. Hamilton, 100.
57. Harris, 86; Greenspan, 148.
58. Marcus and Devroy, February 18, 1993.
59. Quoted in Drew, 83–84.
60. Quoted in Marcus and Devroy, A1.
61. Quoted in Harris, 86.
62. Quoted in M. Stephen Weatherford and Lorraine M. McDonnell, "Clinton and the Economy: The Paradox of Policy Success and Political Mishap," *Political Science Quarterly* 111 (1996), 427.
63. Weatherford and McDonnell, 427.
64. Gwen Ifil, "Miscalculation, Then Embarrassment," *New York Times*, April 22, 1993.
65. John Aloysius Farrell, "Clinton's Stimulus Plan Dies in the Senate," *Boston Globe*, April 22, 1993.
66. Quoted in Weatherford and McDonnell, 432.
67. Quoted in Woodward, *The Agenda*, 78.
68. David Broder, "President in Trouble on the Hill," *Washington Post*, April 27, 1993.
69. John Brummett, *Highwire: From the Backroads to the Beltway—The Education of Bill Clinton* (New York: Hyperion, 1994), 20.
70. Woodward, *Maestro*, 108.
71. Gwen Ifil, "The Supreme Court: The News Media: After a Bid for Truce, the

White House and Press Corp Are at It Again," *New York Times,* June 15, 1993, A23.

72. Stephanopoulos, 175.
73. Brummett, 24.
74. Drew, 169; Woodward, *The Agenda,* 244.
75. Quoted in Woodward, *The Agenda,* 254.
76. Quoted in Woodward, *The Agenda,* 255.
77. Woodward, *The Agenda,* 244, 265.
78. Woodward, *The Agenda,* 298.
79. Woodward, *The Agenda,* 298.
80. Quoted in Woodward, *The Agenda,* 298.
81. Stephanopoulos, 177.
82. Quoted in Woodward, *The Agenda,* 299.
83. Stephanopolous, 179.
84. Quoted in Woodward, *The Agenda,* 300.
85. Stephanopoulos, 178.
86. Woodward, *The Agenda,* 302.
87. Stephanopoulos, 179.
88. Quoted in Woodward, *The Agenda,* 302, 310.
89. Quoted in Woodward, *The Agenda,* 310.
90. Quoted in Woodward, *The Agenda,* 311.
91. Bill Clinton, *Economic Report of the President, 2000* (Washington, D.C.: Government Printing Office, 2000).
92. Rubin, 125.
93. Woodward, *Maestro,* 195.
94. Rubin, 125, 122.
95. Greenspan, 170–71.
96. "Clinton Opens 'New Economy' Forum on High-Tech Business," *People's Daily,* April 27, 2000.
97. Greenspan, 186.
98. Greenspan, 186.
99. Greenspan, 149–50.
100. Carl Bernstein, *A Woman in Charge* (New York: Alfred A. Knopf, 2007), 254.

8. A THOUSAND WELCOMES

1. Nancy Soderberg, *The Superpower Myth: The Use and Misuse of American Power* (New York: Wiley, 2005), 54.
2. Quoted in Conor O'Clery, *Daring Diplomacy: Clinton's Secret Search for Peace in Ireland* (Boulder, Colo.: Roberts Rinehart, 1997), 15–16.
3. Anthony Lake, *Six Nightmares: Real Threats in a Dangerous World and How America Can Meet Them* (New York: Little, Brown 2000), 119.
4. Bill Clinton, *My Life* (New York: Alfred A. Knopf, 2004), 529.
5. Soderberg, 69.
6. Soderberg, 71.
7. Lake, 120.
8. B. Clinton, 529.
9. Soderberg, 72.
10. Quoted in O'Clery, 109.

11. Quoted in O'Clery, 109.
12. Quoted in O'Clery, 109.
13. Lake, 122.
14. B. Clinton, 581.
15. Gerry Adams, *A Farther Shore* (New York: Random House, 2003), 155.
16. Quoted in O'Clery, 114.
17. Adams, 155.
18. Quoted in O'Clery, 28.
19. Quoted in O'Clery, 116.
20. Quoted in O'Clery, 116.
21. Adams, 156.
22. Quoted in O'Clery, 144.
23. O'Clery, 145.
24. Quoted in Eamon Mallie and David McKittrick, *Endgame in Ireland* (London: Hodder and Stoughton, 2001), 326.
25. Quoted in O'Clery, 150–51.
26. Quoted in O'Clery, 161.
27. Quoted in O'Clery, 158.
28. Quoted in O'Clery, 160.
29. Quoted in O'Clery, 153.
30. Quoted in Adams, 179.
31. Salvador Minuchin, *Families and Family Therapy* (Cambridge, Mass.: Harvard University Press, 1974), 135.
32. Quoted in O'Clery, 209.
33. Quoted in O'Clery, 209.
34. Soderberg, 56.
35. Quoted in O'Clery, 221.
36. O'Clery, 217.
37. Adams, 202.
38. Quoted in O'Clery, 221.
39. George Mitchell, *Making Peace* (Berkeley: University of California Press, 1999), 25.
40. Quoted in Deaglàn De Bréadun, *The Far Side of Revenge: Making Peace in Northern Ireland* (West Link Park, Ireland: Collins Press, 2001), 15.
41. Quoted in O'Clery, 236.
42. Quoted in O'Clery, 236.
43. Quoted in O'Clery, 236–37.
44. B. Clinton, 686.
45. O'Clery, 242.
46. Quoted in Trevor Birney and Julian O'Neill, *When the President Calls* (Londonderry, Northern Ireland: Guildhall Press, 1997), 79.
47. B. Clinton, 686.
48. Quoted in O'Clery, 234.
49. Quoted in Birney and O'Neill, 75.
50. Quoted in Birney and O'Neill, 75.
51. Quoted in Birney and O'Neill, 121.
52. Quoted in Birney and O'Neill, 122.
53. Quoted in Birney and O'Neill, 127.
54. Quoted in Birney and O'Neill, 134.
55. Quoted in Birney and O'Neill, 135.

56. Quoted in Birney and O'Neill, 135.
57. Quoted in O'Clery, 239.
58. Quoted in Birney and O'Neill, 136.
59. Quoted in Birney and O'Neill, 137.
60. Quoted in Birney and O'Neill, 139.
61. Quoted in Birney and O'Neill, 139.
62. Quoted in Birney and O'Neill, 138.
63. Quoted in Birney and O'Neill, 141.
64. Quoted in Birney and O'Neill, 133.
65. Quoted in Birney and O'Neill, 162.
66. Quoted in Birney and O'Neill, 177.
67. Quoted in Birney and O'Neill, 133.
68. Quoted in Birney and O'Neill, 180.
69. Quoted in Birney and O'Neill, 180–81.
70. Quoted in Birney and O'Neill, 183.
71. Quoted in Birney and O'Neill, 184.
72. Quoted in Birney and O'Neill, 205.
73. Quoted in Birney and O'Neill, 180.
74. Birney and O'Neill, 202.
75. Quoted in Birney and O'Neill, 214.
76. Quoted in Birney and O'Neill, 218.
77. Quoted in Birney and O'Neill, 219.
78. Quoted in Birney and O'Neill, 220.
79. Quoted in Birney and O'Neill, 221.
80. David McKittrick, *The Nervous Peace* (Belfast: Blackstaff Press, 1996), 157.
81. Quoted in Birney and O'Neill, 221.
82. Quoted in O'Clery, 243.
83. Quoted in Birney and O'Neill, 223.
84. Quoted in Birney and O'Neill, 240.
85. Quoted in Birney and O'Neill, 250.
86. Quoted in Birney and O'Neill, 225.
87. Quoted in Birney and O'Neill, 251.
88. Quoted in O'Clery, 20.
89. Quoted in Birney and O'Neill, 253.
90. Quoted in Birney and O'Neill, 253.
91. Mitchell, 24.
92. Quoted in Birney and O'Neill, 237.
93. Mitchell, 49.
94. Quoted in Mitchell, 101.
95. Adams, 353.
96. Quoted in Mitchell, 177.
97. Quoted in Mitchell, 177.
98. B. Clinton, 784.
99. Adams, 347.
100. Adams, 350.
101. Mitchell, 179.
102. Quoted in Adams, 351.
103. De Bréadun, 135.
104. Soderberg, 74.
105. Lake, 128.

106. De Bréadun, 177.
107. "Remarks by the President at Irish American Community Event," Clinton Foundation.

9. THE HORSE-WHIPPING

1. Bob Woodward, *Shadow: Five Presidents and the Legacy of Watergate* (New York: Simon & Schuster, 1999), 272.
2. Jeffrey Toobin, *A Vast Conspiracy: The Real Story of the Sex Scandal That Nearly Brought Down a President* (New York: Simon & Schuster, 2000), 65.
3. Quoted in Geraldine Sealey, "The Hunted, or the Vast Right-Wing Conspiracy," *Salon,* June 17, 2004.
4. Hillary Rodham Clinton, *Living History* (New York: Simon & Schuster, 2003), 214.
5. Toobin, 67.
6. Bill Clinton, *My Life* (New York: Alfred A. Knopf, 2004), 183.
7. Gail Sheehy, *Hillary's Choice* (New York: Ballantine Books, 1999), 264.
8. H. Clinton, 214.
9. Quoted in George Stephanopoulos, *All Too Human (A Political Education)* (Boston: Little, Brown, 1999), 230.
10. Quoted in Stephanopoulos, 230–31.
11. Quoted in Stephanopoulos, 231.
12. Quoted in Stephanopoulos, 231–32.
13. Quoted in Stephanopoulos, 232.
14. Quoted in Stephanopoulos, 232.
15. Quoted in John F. Harris, *The Survivor: Bill Clinton in the White House* (New York: Random House, 2005), 108.
16. Quoted in Stephanopoulos, 238.
17. B. Clinton, 567.
18. H. Clinton, 211.
19. H. Clinton, 211.
20. H. Clinton, 211.
21. Woodward, *Shadow,* 237.
22. H. Clinton, 215.
23. Woodward, *Shadow,* 237–38.
24. H. Clinton, 215, 216.
25. Quoted in Woodward, *Shadow,* 239.
26. Quoted in Joe Conason and Gene Lyons, *The Hunting of the President: The Ten-Year Campaign to Destroy Bill and Hillary Clinton* (New York: St. Martin's Press, 2000), 135.
27. Quoted in Conason and Lyons, 118.
28. Quoted in Conason and Lyons, 185.
29. Robert G. Kaiser and Thomas B. Edsall, "The Two Theodore Olsons," *Washington Post,* May 17, 2001.
30. David Brock, *Blinded by the Right: The Conscience of an Ex-Conservative* (New York: Crown Publishers, 2002), 128.
31. Woodward, *Shadow,* 229.
32. Woodward, *Shadow,* 235.

33. Quoted in Conason and Lyons, 129.
34. Quoted in Sidney Blumenthal, *The Clinton Wars* (New York: Plume, 2004), 69.
35. Michael Kranish, "Note Left by Aide Reveals Distress, Makes Allegations," *Boston Globe*, August 11, 1993.
36. Quoted in Woodward, *Shadow,* 263.
37. Quoted in Conason and Lyons, 130.
38. Quoted in Woodward, *Shadow,* 268.
39. Quoted in Woodward, *Shadow,* 264.
40. Carl Bernstein, *A Woman in Charge* (New York: Alfred A. Knopf, 2007), 473.
41. Quoted in Conason and Lyons, 132.
42. Quoted in Conason and Lyons, 133.
43. Brock, 191.
44. Toobin, 77.
45. Quoted in Conason and Lyons, 608.
46. James Carville, . . . *And the Horse He Rode in On: The People v. Kenneth Starr* (New York: Simon & Schuster, 1998) 13.
47. Quoted in Woodward, *Shadow,* 266.
48. Quoted in Woodward, *Shadow,* 267.
49. Quoted in Woodward, *Shadow,* 268.
50. Woodward, *Shadow,* 337.
51. Sealey, "The Hunted" *Shadow,* June 17, 2004.
52. Toobin, 278.
53. *Shadow,* Woodward, 304.
54. William Safire, "Blizzard of Lies," *New York Times,* January 8, 1996.
55. Quoted in Carville, 80.
56. Quoted in *Shadow,* Woodward, 310.
57. Bernstein, 459.
58. Quoted in Blumenthal, 382.
59. Quoted in Carville, 46.
60. Quoted in Carville, 47.
61. Quoted in Blumenthal, 330.
62. James Carville, "America's Out-of-Control Scandal Machine," *Salon,* March 7, 1997; Jonathan Broder and Murray Waas, "Starr Strikes Back," *Salon,* April 16, 1998.
63. William Safire, "The Big Flinch," *New York Times,* January 20, 1997.
64. Susan Schmidt, "Starr Will Stay with Probe," *Washington Post,* February 22, 1997.
65. Broder and Waas, "Starr Strikes Back."
66. Quoted in Carville, 47.
67. Toobin, 482.
68. Bob Woodward and Susan Schmidt, "Starr Probes Clinton's Personal Life," *Washington Post,* June 25, 1997.

10. MONICA AND BILL: A ROMANTIC TRAGEDY

1. Lucinda Franks, commenting on her interview with Hillary Clinton, on *Larry King Live,* August 2, 1999.
2. "Clinton Cheated 'Because I Could,'" CBS News.com, June 17, 2004.

3. Monica Lewinsky, *Larry King Live,* February 28, 2002.
4. American Psychiatric Association, *Diagnostic and Statistical Manual of Mental Disorders,* 4th edition, text revision (Washington, D.C.: American Psychiatric Association, 2000), 701.
5. Quoted in Nigel Hamilton, *Bill Clinton: An American Journey* (New York: Random House, 2003), 114.
6. Quoted in Jim Moore, with Rick Ihde, *Clinton: Young Man in a Hurry* (Fort Worth, Tex.: Summit Group, 1992), 27.
7. Quoted in Jerome D. Levin, *The Clinton Syndrome* (Rocklin, Calif.: Prima Publishing, 1998), 20.
8. Quoted in Levin, 26.
9. Hamilton, 101.
10. Quoted in Hamilton, 101.
11. Tommy Caplan, interview by Charles F. Allen, 1991.
12. Gail Sheehy, *Hillary's Choice* (New York: Ballantine Books, 1999), 297.
13. Quoted in Sheehy, 325.
14. Kay Redfield Jamison, *Exuberance: The Passion for Life* (New York: Alfred A. Knopf, 2004), 150.
15. Sheehy, 149.
16. Quoted in Sheehy, 182.
17. Quoted in Sheehy, 190.
18. Quoted in Lucinda Franks, "The Intimate Hillary," *Talk,* September 1999.
19. Matt Ridley, *The Red Queen: Sex and the Evolution of Human Nature* (New York: Harper Perennial, 1993), 226.
20. Quoted in Charles F. Allen and Jonathan Portis, *The Comeback Kid: The Life and Career of Bill Clinton* (New York: Birch Lane Press, 1992), 12.
21. Quoted in Andrew Morton, *Monica's Story* (New York: St. Martin's Press, 1999), 98.
22. Quoted in Morton, 129.
23. Quoted in Meredith Oakley, *On the Make: The Rise of Bill Clinton* (Washington, D.C.: Regnery, 1994), 129.
24. Quoted in Hamilton, 289.
25. Bill Clinton, *My Life* (New York: Alfred A. Knopf, 2004), 566.
26. B. Clinton, 567.
27. Morton, 63.
28. Morton, 64.
29. Quoted in Morton, 65.
30. Quoted in Morton, 72.
31. Morton, 72.
32. Morton, 73.
33. Morton, 74.
34. Morton, 77.
35. Morton, 81.
36. Quoted in Morton, 84.
37. Morton, 82.
38. Quoted in Morton, 85.
39. Quoted in Morton, 86.
40. Morton, 86.
41. Quoted in Morton, 87.
42. Quoted in Morton, 90.

43. Quoted in Morton, 95.
44. Morton, 95.
45. Quoted in Morton, 96.
46. Morton, 99.
47. Morton, 100.
48. Morton, 103.
49. Quoted in Morton, 105.
50. Quoted in Morton, 108.
51. Quoted in Morton, 127.
52. Quoted in Morton, 129.
53. Quoted in Morton, 132.
54. Morton, 140.
55. Morton, 140.
56. Quoted in Morton, 140.
57. Morton, 140.
58. Morton, 140.
59. Morton, 141.
60. Morton, 141.
61. Quoted in Morton, 120.
62. Jeffrey Toobin, *A Vast Conspiracy: The Real Story of the Sex Scandal That Nearly Brought Down a President* (New York: Simon & Schuster, 2000), 104.
63. David Brock, *Blinded by the Right: The Conscience of an Ex-Conservative* (New York: Crown Publishers, 2002), 184–85.
64. Toobin, 194.
65. Toobin, 200.
66. Toobin, 200.
67. Quoted in Toobin, 201.
68. Quoted in Toobin, 201.
69. Quoted in Morton, 220.
70. Quoted in Morton, 220.
71. Quoted in Morton, 221.
72. Quoted in Morton, 221.
73. Morton, 224.
74. Bennet L. Gershman, "The Perjury Trap," *University of Pennsylvania Law Review,* 129 (1981): 626.
75. Woodward, 376.

11. HIGH NOON

1. Bill Clinton, *My Life* (New York: Alfred A. Knopf, 2004), 20.
2. B. Clinton, 21.
3. Susan Schmidt, Peter Baker, and Toni Lucy, "Clinton Accused of Urging Aide to Lie," *Washington Post,* January 21, 1998.
4. Andrew Morton, *Monica's Story* (New York: St. Martin's Press, 1999), 251.
5. Quoted in Morton, 251–52.
6. Jeffrey Toobin, *A Vast Conspiracy* (New York: Simon & Schuster, 2000), 114.
7. Toobin, 284–85.
8. Quoted in Sidney Blumenthal, *The Clinton Wars* (New York: Plume, 2004), 386.

9. Quoted in Steven Brill, "Pressgate," *Brill's Content,* p. 132.
10. Marvin Kalb, *One Scandalous Story: Clinton, Lewinsky, and Thirteen Days That Tarnished American Journalism* (New York: Free Press, 2001), 129.
11. Blumenthal, 347.
12. Kalb, 129.
13. Quoted in Kalb, 143.
14. Quoted in Blumenthal, 369.
15. Quoted in Kalb, 149.
16. Quoted in John F. Harris, *The Survivor: Bill Clinton in the White House* (New York: Random House, 2005), 314.
17. Harris, 315.
18. Blumenthal, 328.
19. Quoted in Harris, 307.
20. Quoted in Bob Woodward, *Shadow: Five Presidents and the Legacy of Watergate* (New York: Simon & Schuster, 1999), 389.
21. Blumenthal, 341–42.
22. Harris, 307.
23. Blumenthal, 341.
24. Blumenthal, 340–42.
25. Blumenthal, 342.
26. Quoted in Harris, 306.
27. Carl Bernstein, *A Woman in Charge: The Life of Hillary Rodham Clinton* (New York: Knopf, 2007), 490.
28. Blumenthal, 345.
29. Quoted in Woodward, *Shadow,* 394.
30. Quoted in Harris, 308.
31. Harris, 309.
32. Quoted in Harris, 308.
33. Bernstein, 485.
34. Quoted in Woodward, *Shadow,* 393.
35. Quoted in Harris, 309.
36. Harris, 309.
37. Quoted in Morton, 257.
38. Quoted in Harris, 309.
39. Blumenthal, 371.
40. Harris, 308.
41. Harris, 315–16.
42. David Maraniss, "In Clinton, a Past That's Ever Prologue," *Washington Post,* January 25, 1998.
43. Bernstein, 485.
44. Hillary Clinton, "This Is a Battle," CNN.com, January 28, 1998.
45. Quoted in Blumenthal, 374.
46. Harris, 312.
47. Woodward, *Shadow,* 396.
48. Quoted in Toobin, 258.
49. Woodward, *Shadow,* 396.
50. Quoted in James Carville, *. . . And the Horse He Rode in On: The People v. Kenneth Starr* (New York: Simon & Schuster, 1998), 83.
51. Quoted in Carville, 68.

52. Quoted in Carville, 69.
53. Helen Thomas, introduction to Susan McDougal with Pat Harris, *The Woman Who Wouldn't Talk* (New York: Carroll and Graf, 2003), xi.
54. Bernstein, 469.
55. Blumenthal, 361.
56. Quoted in Woodward, *Shadow,* 396.
57. Blumenthal, 367.
58. Blumenthal, 376.
59. Blumenthal, 378.
60. Harris, 314.
61. Hillary Rodham Clinton, *Living History* (New York: Simon & Schuster, 2003), 466.
62. Quoted in Gail Sheehy, *Hillary's Choice* (New York: Ballantine Books, 1999), 310.
63. H. Clinton, 466.
64. Quoted in Sheehy, 310.
65. Quoted in Toobin, 306.
66. Toobin, 307.
67. Toobin, 308.
68. H. Clinton, 472–73.
69. H. Clinton, 477.
70. H. Clinton, 477.
71. Sandy Grady, "Hillary Fights for Bill and for Herself," *Newark Star Ledger,* October 30, 1998.
72. H. Clinton, 481.
73. Quoted in Bernstein, 528.
74. Mary Leonard, "Energized First Lady Keeps Campaigning; Her Appeal Delights Party," *Boston Globe,* October 31, 1998.
75. Mary McGrory, "Big Winner Was—Will Be—Hillary," *Charleston Gazette,* November 11, 1998.
76. Tim Nickens and Adam Smith, "Campaigning to the Wire; First Lady Brings 'Fire and Brimstone' for MacKay," *St. Petersburg Times,* November 2, 1998.
77. McGrory, "Big Winner," November 11, 1998.
78. Katherine M. Skirba, "Hillary Clinton Praises Husband's Record, Bashes GOP," *Milwaukee Journal Sentinel,* October 18, 1998.
79. Steven Thomma, "The 'Woman Wronged' Trying to Save the Day for Democrats," *Charleston Gazette,* November 1, 1998.
80. William Goldschlag, "First Lady Hits Her Stride," New York *Daily News,* November 1, 1998.
81. Marsha Mercer, "Can Mrs. Clinton Keep Newest Image in Vogue?" *Richmond Times Dispatch,* November 29, 1998.
82. Mercer, "Can Mrs. Clinton?" November 29, 1998.
83. Bruno Tedeschi, "First Lady Comes to Aid of NJ Democrats; Gets Raves at Edison Stopover; Handling of Sex Scandal," *Bergen County Record,* October 28, 1998.
84. Leonard, "Energized First Lady," October 31, 1998.
85. "First Lady Stumps for Lehigh Valley Congressional Candidate," Associated Press, November 1, 1998.
86. Mike Glover, "Both Sides Focus on Turnout in Photo-Finish Race," Associated Press, November 1, 1998.

87. Scott Andrews, "Hillary Clinton Gets Standing Ovation as She Campaigns for Myrth York," Associated Press, October 21, 1998.
88. H. Clinton, 482.
89. B. Clinton, 823–24.
90. H. Clinton, 482.
91. McGrory, "Big Winner," November 11, 1998.
92. H. Clinton, 478–81.
93. Leonard, "Energized First Lady," October 31, 1998.
94. Thomma, "The 'Woman Wronged,'" November 1, 1998.
95. Glover, "Both Sides Focus," November 2, 1998.
96. Ceci Connolly and Terry M. Neal, "Get Out the Vote Heard Coast to Coast; Forecast Continues to Be for Low Turnout," *Washington Post,* November 3, 1998.
97. Connolly and Neal, "Get Out the Vote," November 3, 1998.
98. Quoted in "Clinton Raises Race Issue; GOP Sees Low Turnout as the Key to Victory," *White House Bulletin,* November 2, 1998.
99. Quoted in "Clinton Raises Race Issue," November 2, 1998.
100. Connolly and Neal, "Get Out the Vote," November 3, 1998.
101. Anne Scales, "Democratic Plan: Inspire Black Voters," *Boston Globe,* October 31, 1998.
102. Thomma, "The 'Woman Wronged,'" November 1, 1998.
103. Peter Lewis, "Telemarketing Calls Helped Democrats," *Seattle Times,* November 5, 1998.
104. Scales, "Democratic Plan," October 31, 1998.
105. Steven Holmes, "The 1998 Campaign: Racial Issues: Black Loyalty to Clinton Hinders GOP Outreach," *New York Times,* October 27, 1998.
106. Richard L. Berke, "The 1998 Elections," *New York Times,* November 4, 1998.
107. James Dao, "The 1998 Campaign: The Voters; In New York's Tight Race for Senate, Black Voters Could Be Decisive," *New York Times,* October 25, 1998.
108. Jere Downs, "Black Leaders Say Clinton Controversy Could Be Costly to Fox," *Philadelphia Inquirer,* October 13, 1998.
109. Sandy Grady, "Impeachment Train Grinds to a Halt," *Arkansas Democrat-Gazette,* November 7, 1998.
110. Grady, "Impeachment Train Grinds," November 7, 1998.
111. Quoted in Blumenthal, 493.
112. Dick Polman, "Impeachment Probe Is Next Big Issue," *Philadelphia Inquirer,* November 4, 1998.
113. Jane Fullerton and Susan Roth, "Clinton Relishes Democratic Wins; He Sees U.S. Repudiating Partisanship," *Arkansas Democrat-Gazette,* November 5, 1998.
114. Terry McAuliffe with Steve Kettmann, *What a Party!: My Life Among Democrats; Presidents, Candidates, Donors, Activists, Alligators, and Other Wild Animals* (New York: St. Martin's Press, 2007), 167.
115. Quoted in Woodward, 476.
116. McAuliffe, 167.
117. Tony Pugh, Elsa C. Arnett, Raja Mishra, and Frank Davies, "Black Turnout Proves to Be Key for Democrats," *Philadelphia Inquirer,* November 5, 1998.
118. Bill Sammon, "Democratic Strategy Pays Off as Black Votes Prove to be Pivotal," *Washington Times,* November 4, 1998.

119. Mary McGrory, "Voters Let It Be Known They Want GOP to Lay Off Clinton," *Seattle Post-Intelligencer,* November 6, 1998.
120. Pugh, Arnett, Mishra, and Davies, "Black Turnout," November 5, 1998, 25.
121. Tom Steadman, Robert Lamme, and Paul Muschick, "Edwards Upsets Faircloth; Turnout Helps Tip the Scales," *Greensboro News and Record,* November 4, 1998.
122. Kathy Kiely and Jessica Lee, "Core Democratic Voters Defy Predictions. Some '94 Defectors Return to Fold," *USA Today,* November 4, 1998.
123. B. Clinton, 824.
124. "Out of Shambles, Strength?" *The Economist,* November 7, 1998.
125. Polman, "Impeachment Probe," *Philadelphia Inquirer,* November 4, 1998.
126. Myriam Marquez, "The GOP Itself Killed the Impeachment Cause," *Orlando Sentinel,* November 15, 1998.
127. McGrory, "Voters Let It Be," November 6, 1998, 16.
128. "Impeachment '98: Hyde Pulling the Plug?" *The Hotline,* November 5, 1998.
129. Grady, "Impeachment Train Grinds," November 7, 1998.
130. Cokie and Steven V. Roberts, "The Election Fallout; Chuck in Pivotal Spot," New York *Daily News,* November 5, 1998.
131. Larry Swisher, "Stick a Fork in the GOP Revolution—It's Done," *Idaho Lewiston Morning Tribune,* November 8, 1998.
132. Richard L. Berke, "The 1998 Elections," *New York Times,* November 4, 1998.
133. Cokie and Steven V. Roberts, "The Election Fallout," November 5, 1998.
134. Grady, "Impeachment Train Grinds," November 7, 1998.
135. Quoted in Woodward, *Shadow,* 476; Jane Fullerton and Susan Roth, "Clinton Relishes," November 5, 1998.
136. McGrory, "Big Winner," November 11, 1998.
137. Mercer, "Can Mrs. Clinton?" November 29, 1998.
138. Ellen Warren, "Thanks to That Cad, Hillary the Victim Is Suddenly Hot," *The Oregonian,* November 26, 1998.
139. Francis X. Clines, "Once a Political Debit, Now a Political Force," *New York Times,* November 22, 1998.
140. Mercer, "Can Mrs. Clinton," November 29, 1998.
141. Mercer, "Can Mrs. Clinton," November 29, 1998.
142. Mimi Hall, "A Regal Renaissance for the First Lady; Year's End Finds Her in Vogue," *USA Today,* November 24, 1998, 12A.
143. Mercer, "Can Mrs. Clinton," November 29, 1998.
144. Quoted in Francis X. Clines, "Once a Political Debit, Now a Powerful Force," *New York Times,* November 22, 1998.
145. Quoted in McAuliffe, 168.

12. HEALING THE SICK

1. Quoted in Carol Felsenthal, *Clinton in Exile: A President Out of the White House* (New York: William Morrow, 2008).
2. Quoted in Felsenthal, 178.
3. Quoted in Felsenthal, 160.
4. Quoted in Felsenthal, 160.

5. Associated Press, "Aids Death Toll in Africa May Reach 100 Million by 2025," June 3, 2006.
6. Felsenthal, 162.
7. Quoted in Felsenthal, 162.
8. Samantha Powers, "The AIDS Rebel," *The New Yorker,* May 2003.
9. Alex Shoumatoff, "The Lazarus Effect," *Vanity Fair,* July 2007, 160; Nicoli Nattrass, *Mortal Combat: AIDS Denialism and the Struggle for Antiretrovirals in South Africa* (Scottsville, South Africa: University of KwaZulu-Natal Press, 2007), 79.
10. Quoted in Powers, "The AIDS Rebel," May 2003.
11. Celia W. Dugger, "Clinton Makes Up for Lost Time Battling AIDS," *New York Times,* August 29, 2006.
12. Michael Waldholz, "Makers of AIDS Drugs Agree to Slash Prices in the Third World," *Wall Street Journal,* May 11, 2000.
13. Waldholz, "Makers of AIDS Drugs," May 11, 2000.
14. Alex Shoumatoff, "The Lazarus Effect," *Vanity Fair,* July 2007, 160.
15. Dugger, "Clinton Makes Up."
16. Bill Clinton, "A Man Called Hope," *Vanity Fair,* July 2007, 169.
17. Clinton, "A Man Called Hope," July 2007.
18. Clinton, "A Man Called Hope," July 2007.
19. Remarks by President Clinton and President Nelson Mandela at African American Religious Leaders Reception, NARA.gov Web site.
20. Clinton, "A Man Called Hope," July 2007.
21. Remarks by President Clinton and President Nelson Mandela, NARA.gov Web site.
22. James Bennet, "The Testing of a President: The Visitor; Mandela, at White House, Says World Backs Clinton," *New York Times,* September 23, 1998.
23. Bill Clinton, *My Life* (New York: Alfred A. Knopf, 2004), 50.
24. Quoted in Gail Sheehy, *Hillary's Choice* (New York: Ballantine Books, 1999), 101.
25. B. Clinton, *My Life,* 42.
26. Felsenthal, 167.
27. Sarah Baxter, "I'm Hillary's Cheerleader in Chief," *Sunday Times,* September 9, 2007.
28. R. Emmett Tyrrell, Jr., *Boy Clinton: A Political Biography* (Washington, D.C.: Regnery, 1996), 26–27.
29. George Saunders, "Bill Clinton: Public Citizen," *GQ,* December 2007, 374.
30. John F. Harris, *The Survivor* (New York: Random House, 2005), 212.
31. Dugger, "Clinton Makes Up," August 29, 2006.
32. Author interview with Zackie Achmat, July 19, 2007.
33. Bill Clinton, *Giving* (New York: Alfred A. Knopf, 2007), 45.
34. Felsenthal, 166.
35. Quoted in Felsenthal, 157.
36. Quoted in Felsenthal, 157.
37. George Saunders, "Bill Clinton: Public Citizen," *GQ,* December 2007, 376–78.
38. Saunders, 376.
39. "The Age of AIDS; An Interview with Randall Tobias," U.S. State Department, May 30, 2006.
40. Associated Press, "Laura Bush Promotes Role of Faith-Based Organizations in Combating Disease in Africa," *International Herald Tribune,* June 28, 2007.

41. Geraldine Sealey, "An Epidemic Failure," *Rolling Stone,* June 12, 2005.
42. Sealey, "An Epidemic Failure," June 12, 2005.
43. "Bush's AIDS 'Coordinator' Denigrates Condoms," ACT UP, April 21, 2004.
44. Associated Press, "Laura Bush Promotes," June 28, 2007.
45. Associated Press, "Laura Bush Promotes," June 28, 2007.
46. Sealey, "An Epidemic Failure," June 12, 2005.
47. "An Interview with Randall Tobias," May 30, 2006.
48. Brian Ross and Justin Rood, "Senior Official Linked to Escort Service Resigns," ABC News.com, April 26, 2007.
49. Embassy of the United States, Lusaka, Zambia, "U.S. Government Donates 40 Million Condoms to Health Ministry," September 19, 2007.
50. "Zambia's Health Officials Arrested for Corruption," *People's Daily Online,* October 7, 2006.
51. Sylvester Monroe, "A Conversation with William Jefferson Clinton in Africa," EbonyJet.com.
52. David Remnick, "The Wanderer," *The New Yorker,* September 18, 2006, 49.
53. Quoted in Felsenthal, 164.
54. Felsenthal, 166.
55. Quoted in Felsenthal, 163.
56. "Clinton Visits Zambia," *Sunday Times of Zambia,* July 22, 2007.
57. "Clinton Visits Zambia," July 22, 2007.
58. Emmanuel Kwitemi, "Clinton Pilots Subsidized Malaria Drugs in Africa," Reuters, July 23, 2007.
59. "That American Exclusivity," *The Guardian* (Dar es Salaam), July 19, 2005.
60. "Clinton Magic Charms Dar," *The Guardian* (Dar es Salaam), July 23, 2005.

INDEX